Surrealism in Latin American Literature

Surrealism in Latin American Literature
Searching for Breton's Ghost

Melanie Nicholson

palgrave
macmillan

SURREALISM IN LATIN AMERICAN LITERATURE
Copyright © Melanie Nicholson, 2013.

All rights reserved.

First published in 2013 by PALGRAVE MACMILLAN® in the United States—a division of St. Martin's Press LLC, 175 Fifth Avenue, New York, NY 10010.

Where this book is distributed in the UK, Europe and the rest of the world, this is by Palgrave Macmillan, a division of Macmillan Publishers Limited, registered in England, company number 785998, of Houndmills, Basingstoke, Hampshire RG21 6XS.

Palgrave Macmillan is the global academic imprint of the above companies and has companies and representatives throughout the world.

Palgrave® and Macmillan® are registered trademarks in the United States, the United Kingdom, Europe and other countries.

ISBN: 978-1-137-28779-3

Xavier Villaurrutia, "Nocturne: The Statue," in *Nostalgia for Death: Poetry by Xavier Viallaurrutia & Hieroglyphs of Desire: A Critical Study of Villaurrutia by Octavio Paz.* Reprinted with permission of The Permissions Company, Inc., on behalf of Copper Canyon Press, www.coppercanyonpres.org.

Library of Congress Cataloging-in-Publication Data

Nicholson, Melanie, 1955–
  Surrealism in Latin American literature: searching for Breton's ghost / Melanie Nicholson.
    p. cm.
  Includes bibliographical references and index.
  ISBN 978-1-137-28779-3 (alk. paper)
  1. Literature, Experimental—Latin America. 2. Surrealism (Literature)—Latin America. 3. Spanish American literature—20th century—History and criticism. 4. Breton, André, 1896–1966—Influence. 5. Avant-garde (Aesthetics)—Latin America. I. Title.

PQ7082.E97N53 2013
860.9'980904—dc23   2012029347

A catalogue record of the book is available from the British Library.

Design by Scribe Inc.

First edition: January 2013

10 9 8 7 6 5 4 3 2 1

Transferred to Digital Printing in 2013

To Isaac and Daniel, for their patience and their laughter

Contents

Preface ix

Acknowledgments xi

Introduction 1

Part I: Contexts and Contours

1 Surrealism Is Dead, ¡Viva el Surrealismo! 15

2 The Latin American Connection 31

Part II: The Emergence of Surrealism in Latin American Literature, 1928–1950

3 Argentina's Pioneer Surrealists 47

4 Neruda and Anti-Neruda: Chile's Mandrágora Poets 59

5 Peru: The Surrealist Space between Mariátegui and Vallejo 77

6 The Two Faces of Early Surrealism in Mexico 103

Part III: A Surrealism of One's Own, 1950–1980

7 The Argentine Surrealist Journals 135

8 "Another Ship Must Be Launched": Surrealism in Argentine Poetry, 1950–1970 151

9 Chile: The Avatars and the Antagonists of *La Mandrágora* 175

10 Octavio Paz: Surrealism's Favorite Son 203

Conclusion: "Like a River" 227

Notes 235

Works Cited 245

Index 257

Preface

Surrealism as a historical movement was officially born with the publication of André Breton's first *Manifesto of Surrealism* in France in 1924. It swept quickly through Europe, gaining adherents both in literature and in the visual arts and rising to prominence in the cultural debates of the period. By the end of World War II, however, surrealism found itself embattled on several fronts. Many artists and intellectuals saw surrealism as unresponsive to the harsh realities of a war-torn continent; others felt compelled to question its spirit of optimism. By the late 1940s, surrealism—with its privileging of unconscious forces, eroticism, "black humor," and dream imagery—appeared to be much less relevant than existentialism with its emphasis on individual responsibility and artistic engagement. The historical surrealist movement effectively died with Breton's death in 1966. Yet surrealist thought has continued to exercise an enormous influence over many forms of cultural expression, both in Europe and abroad.

The premise of *Surrealism in Latin American Literature: Searching for Breton's Ghost* is that surrealism experienced a significant "afterlife" in Latin America in the wake of its demise in Europe. Surrealism first appeared in Argentina and Chile in the 1920s and 1930s, with groups that propounded the movement's values and practiced its techniques in a rather orthodox fashion. But it evolved over the course of the twentieth century into a heterodox and sometimes contestatory set of attitudes and approaches. Thus the "death" of surrealism in fact never occurred in Latin America as it had in Europe: in terms of the creative imagination, Breton's ghost continued to haunt Mexico and the southern continent for many decades.

This could not have occurred, certainly, if French surrealism had simply been transplanted *tel quel* to the other side of the Atlantic. Latin America's relationship to European surrealism is in fact a complex, perpetually evolving one. For example, key figures such as the Cuban novelist Alejo Carpentier or the Peruvian poet César Vallejo professed a disdain for surrealism, yet echoes of surrealism resound in their work. Conversely, Mexico's Octavio Paz spoke repeatedly of his admiration for Breton and championed surrealism's *actitud vital* or attitude toward life—and yet Paz was careful to distinguish his own poetic practices from traditional surrealist techniques. In sum, surrealism from Mexico to Chile has been alternately embraced and resisted, absorbed and transformed.

My method in this study combines literary history with the close analysis of key texts. Given that critical work to date on surrealist literature in Latin America has been fragmentary or limited in scope, my primary goal in *Breton's Ghost* is to present a coherent picture of the evolution of this aesthetic in the region. To this end, I have proceeded in a roughly chronological fashion, beginning in 1928 with the appearance of the first surrealist group in Argentina and ending in the 1980s, when surrealism as a literary approach becomes virtually indistinguishable from the broader literary context. Although tracking surrealist thought in a Latin American context necessarily begins by identifying a kind of orthodoxy, with French surrealism as the imported model, I am particularly interested in following certain authors as they struggled their way out of the Bretonian mold and into more original forms of expression.

Breton's Ghost is written for a broad academic audience. For students or scholars of Latin America with a limited knowledge of surrealism, this book provides an initial overview of the tenets of surrealist thought. For those familiar with surrealism but new to Latin American cultural history, each chapter provides a contextualization of the important historical, political, and aesthetic issues surrounding the emergence of surrealist-influenced groups or writers. Through this approach, *Breton's Ghost* contributes to our understanding of surrealism as a multidimensional international phenomenon. At the same time, it underscores the creative contributions of Latin American writers to an aesthetic once thought to be the patrimony of a handful of European men.

Acknowledgments

To all the following friends and colleagues, I express my immeasurable gratitude:

To all those at Bard College who gave me their unflagging support: Susan Aberth, Nicole Caso, Gabriela Carrión, Stephanie Kufner, Julia Rosenbaum, Marina van Zuylen, and others too numerous to name. To the students who share my excitement about surrealism.

To President Leon Botstein, Dean Michèle Dominy, and Bard College for helping to fund my research in Latin America and for granting the leave of absence that allowed me to complete the manuscript.

To my friends and colleagues elsewhere in the United States, for their thoughtful responses to my questions and for their careful reading of portions of the manuscript: Anke Birkenmaier, Susana Chávez-Silverman, Kent Dickson, Jill Kuhnheim, Naomi Lindstrom, Francine Masiello, Jacobo Sefamí, and Vicky Unruh. To Enrique Fierro, for being the first to introduce me to the marvelous world of surrealism.

To my friends and colleagues in Latin America, who were generous with their time and their ideas and who provided me with much-needed research materials: César Aira, Alberto Arias, Javier Cófreces, Dolores Etchecopar, Silvia Guiard, Cristina Piña, and Graciela de Sola in Argentina; Floriano Martins in Brazil; Andrés Ferrada, Federico Schopf, and Eduardo Thomas in Chile; Evodio Escalante and Iván Pérez Daniel in Mexico; and Rodrigo Quijano in Peru. A heartfelt thanks to Susana Wald and Ludwig Zeller in Oaxaca, who generously opened their home, their library, and their surrealist spirits to me.

For their invaluable editorial help: Daniel Berthold, Dorian Highland, and Emma Marschall. My deepest gratitude to Brigitte Shull and Maia Woolner of Palgrave Macmillan, who guided me cheerfully and professionally through the labyrinths leading from manuscript to printed book.

I am grateful to *Studies in 20th and 21st Century Literature* for permission to reprint an earlier version of the section in Chapter 8 on Alejandra Pizarnik and Hans Bellmer. I would also like to thank the following publishers and individuals for permission to reproduce copyrighted material:

Xavier Villaurrutia, for "Nocturne: The Statue," from *Nostalgia for Death: Poetry by Xavier Viallaurrutia & Hieroglyphs of Desire: A Critical Study of*

Villaurrutia by Octavio Paz. Reprinted with permission of The Permissions Company, Inc., on behalf of Copper Canyon Press, www.coppercanyonpres.org.

Gonzalo Rojas-May, Rodrigo Rojas-May, and Las Sílabas, Limitada for poems and excerpts from Gonzalo Rojas.

Luis G. de Mussy and Ediciones Finis Terrae, for the poem "El azar negro" by Jorge Cáceres.

Ludwig Zeller, for permission to reproduce his collages.

Every effort has been made to trace rights holders, but if any have been inadvertently overlooked, the publishers would be pleased to make the necessary arrangements at the first opportunity.

Introduction

In 1964, Roger Shattuck wrote in his introduction to Maurice Nadeau's now-classic history of surrealism, "I happen to believe that real importance attaches to the estimate we now make of surrealism. Like progressive education and pacifism, it lies close to the center of our immediate heritage; we ignore these matters at our own peril" (12). Yet in the years following this pronouncement, surrealism was variously ignored, regarded as a historical oddity, or at best celebrated for its contributions to culture. Recently, however, surrealism has reemerged as a nexus of tremendous scholarly interest, both in literature and in the visual arts. As one prominent art critic claims, "surrealism has returned with a vengeance" (Foster xi). This revival is evidenced in such publications as Sidra Stich's *Anxious Visions: Surrealist Art* (1990), Hal Foster's *Compulsive Beauty* (1993), Martica Sawin's *Surrealism in Exile and the Beginning of the New York School* (1997), Whitney Chadwick's edited volume *Mirror Images: Women, Surrealism, and Self-Representation* (1998), Mary Ann Caws's *Surrealist Painters and Poets* (2001), Gérard Durozoi's monumental tome *History of the Surrealist Movement* (reedited in 2002), and Johanna Malt's *Obscure Objects of Desire: Surrealism, Fetishism, and Politics* (2004), to name only a few. In 2001, London's Tate Gallery organized an extensive collection of surrealist works called "Surrealism: Desire Unbound," representing both the visual and the written arts; this exhibition was moved to New York's Metropolitan Museum of Art in 2001.[1] Although these studies and exhibitions take the Continental surrealist movement of the 1920s as their point of departure, they also document trends in later art and literature that demonstrate significant surrealist influence in many countries and across many artistic and literary genres. There has been a growing recognition, in other words, that the end of the historical surrealist movement by no means signified the end of surrealist-inspired expression. I felt compelled to write *Breton's Ghost* because, as Michael Benedikt suggests, "perhaps what Surrealism accomplished was to do more than merely persist, existing finally—as all literary movements must truly exist to survive—in terms of its impact on subsequent literature everywhere" (xxviii).

Fundamental to any contemporary appraisal of surrealism is the fact that the French movement of the 1920s bore seeds before it died, and that those seeds were carried aloft by many winds. Wallace Fowlie wrote in 1960 that "an historical study of surrealism makes it out to be anti-literary and anti-poetical. Yet today it seems to us the founder of a new literature and a new poetry. Born in Paris and nurtured by approximately ten men, it spread in all directions and has influenced men everywhere directly or indirectly" (202). There was something about surrealism's nondualistic conception of the world, about its radical rebellion against rigidities of many kinds, about its call to revive the collective as well as the individual imagination that could still excite artists and poets late into the twentieth century.

I suspect that this is not a simple question of the persistence of a body of aesthetic principles, but rather one of surrealism's adaptability to developments in contemporary Western thought and popular culture. The points of convergence are numerous. In attempting to map those points, we might begin with René de Costa's observation (a propos of Pablo Neruda's poetry) that "surrealism has left us with an appreciation for the suggestive power of discontinuous discourse" (*Poetry* 4). This mode of discontinuous discourse (approached in related but distinct ways by Anglo-American modernist writers) is now commonplace not only in literature but in photography, film, painting, and aspects of popular culture such as advertising.

From there, we could recall James Clifford's definition of surrealism as "an aesthetic that values fragments, curious collections, unexpected juxtapositions— that works to provoke the manifestation of extraordinary realities drawn from the domain of the erotic, the exotic, and the unconscious" (118). Clifford's essay on what he terms "ethnographic surrealism" stresses the surrealist principle of defamiliarization—that is, of making the familiar strange—as one of the foundational elements of twentieth-century anthropology. He goes as far as to suggest that surrealism, in its practice of "taking culture seriously, as a contested reality," in fact set the stage for what has become the modern French scholarly tradition (121). Finally, Clifford posits a connection between surrealism and Third World modernism, a theoretical thread that leads from 1920s France into the anticolonial or postcolonial discourse of figures such as Aimé Césaire (Martinique), Octavio Paz (Mexico), and Alejo Carpentier (Cuba) (127).

To follow this thread even further, arguments can be made for surrealism as a precursor to postmodernism. The postmodern fascination with hybridity, for example, is prefigured in the principle of the juxtaposition of unrelated elements, popularized by the surrealist practice of montage or collage. The art historian Robert Bolton observes that "surrealism, having not long ago been dismissed as a decadent, self-indulgent art, has recently been undergoing a reevaluation"; he goes on to claim that the movement's experimentation with defamiliarization "is now considered by some to be a forerunner of the postmodernist mentality, particularly as it addresses questions of linguistic shifts, figurative language, and the like" (51). Matei Calinescu argues that the Continental avant-garde, and particularly Dada and surrealism, prefigures several "postmodernist notes," including antielitism, antiauthoritarianism, gratuitousness, anarchy, nihilism, and the idea of chance (143). European theorists from Foucault to Kristeva to Derrida and Lacan have all drawn at some point from the deep well of surrealist thought: according to Margaret Cohen, "High surrealism must be included as an intellectual pressure to which the French theoretical avant-garde [of the 1960s and 1970s] responded" (12).[2] Taking all these "traces" into account, we can surmise that surrealism's survival in varied guises late into the twentieth century has much to do with its very adaptability—its ability to speak to contemporary cultural issues that its founders could perhaps never have imagined.

To be sure, much of what I have cited above about surrealism and its afterlife could be more broadly extrapolated from Western modernist aesthetics as a whole. The juxtaposition of unrelated entities, for example, was in common currency before the surrealists took it up as their *leitmotif*. It is not my purpose here to draw fine distinctions between surrealism and other manifestations of the avant-garde, such as futurism, German expressionism, or Dada. Rather, I follow the influential theorist Peter Bürger in taking surrealism—with all its contradictions, schisms, and outright failures—to be the chronological and ideological *ne plus ultra* of the avant-garde. Part of the status that surrealism gained as the most lasting and influential of the avant-garde movements is due to the presence of a single figure, André Breton, who was from its beginnings the recognizable (both revered and despised) face of surrealism. But apart from Breton's centripetal role, there was a "fullness of time" about the historical surrealist movement that allowed it to absorb crucial elements of the preceding movements, synthesize them, and re-present them, not only for a handful of adepts, but for a public that would stretch across great temporal and geographical distances.

* * *

There is true poetic justice in the fact that surrealism, as Fowlie suggests, began with a handful of European men yet has found many of its successors among women and non-Europeans. Following this migratory history, *Breton's Ghost* takes as its subject the journey of surrealism into one area of the world where the European paradigm was effectively and extensively "cannibalized" (to borrow a term from Brazil's avant-garde *Anthropophagist* movement). This is why the British critic Jason Wilson can claim that "surrealism had a massive influence on Latin American culture" ("Coda" 254) and Anna Balakian, one of the most respected literary historians of surrealism, argues that surrealism found in Latin America a fertile ground in which to thrive long after it had withered in Europe (7). Considering literary production in particular, the Hispanist scholar Merlin Forster declares that "the impact of surrealism in its various developmental stages on Latin American literature is widespread and of fundamental importance" (26). In spite of these well-founded claims, and in spite of a sizeable body of work dedicated to various aspects of Latin American surrealist literature, no previous study has attempted to organize this material chronologically or to present an overarching view of the topic. *Breton's Ghost* grew out of the need to address that lack.

Key texts that have traced the history of surrealism as a "universal" movement tend to minimize the importance of the Latin American contribution, particularly with regard to literature. Jean-Louis Bédouin's *Vingt ans de Surréalisme: 1939–1959* (1961) cites only four writers from Latin America, two of whom (Wolfgan Paalen and Roger Caillois) were actually Europeans. Similarly, J. H. Matthews's *An Introduction to Surrealism* (1965) mentions only the painters Wilfredo Lam from Cuba and Roberto Matta from Chile. Neither Mary Ann Caws's *The Poetry of Dada and Surrealism* (1970) nor Michael Benedikt's *The Poetry of Surrealism* (1974) includes any Latin Americans. More recently, Caws's extensive *Surrealist Painters and Poets: An Anthology* (2001) includes prose poems by the Martiniquan poet Aimé Césaire, a letter written by Frida Kahlo, and a brief essay by Roberto Matta, but nothing by Spanish American writers. In sum, although European and North American historians and critics have long considered the surrealist movement to be an international one, this view has generally not encompassed Latin American writers.

There is a plethora of work by Latin American critics on surrealist or surrealist-influenced literature, but full-length studies are rare and are typically circumscribed by national perspectives, period, or genre. Of special note in this category are Graciela de Sola's *Proyecciones del surrealismo en la Argentina* (1967), Luis Mario Schneider's *México y el surrealismo* (1978), and Gerald Langowski's *El surrealismo en la ficción hispanoamericana* (1982). Two important anthologies have gathered surrealist poetry from across Latin America: Stefan Baciu's *Antología de la poesía surrealista latinoamericana* (1974) and Floriano Martins's *Un nuevo continente: Antología del surrealismo en la poesía de Nuestra América* (2004). Baciu's introduction provides an extensive overview of surrealist movements and individual writers, and Martins's more recent anthology gives the reader a sense of the wide range of surrealist influence over Latin American poetry. In spite of these valuable contributions to scholarship in this field, no book-length study to date has provided a broad historical narrative examining the complex relationships between European and Latin American surrealism or the chronological development of surrealist-influenced literature within Latin America.[3]

In order to lend coherence to the study and to provide focused close readings whenever possible, I concentrate my analyses on brief, mainly poetic texts and on programmatic pieces such as manifestoes. This choice reflects the development of surrealist literature not only in Latin America but in other parts of the world as well, where lyric poetry has predominated. Much research remains to be done on the presence of surrealism in Latin American prose fiction. As noted above, Langowski's *El surrealismo en la ficción hispanoamericana* (1982) provides a lucid introduction to the subject. Important early novels often considered by critics to be surrealist in style were written by the Peruvians Martín Adán (*La casa de cartón*, 1928) and Gamaliel Churata (*El pez de oro*, 1957). Surrealist influences, combined with a profound indigenist strain, are also apparent in the work of the Guatemalan author Miguel Ángel Asturias, including *El Señor Presidente* (published in 1946, but originally written in 1923), *Leyendas de Guatemala* (1930), and *Hombres de maíz* (1949). Surrealism is a presence (both thematically and stylistically) in Julio Cortázar's novel *Rayuela* (1963) and in some of his short fiction. The presence of the unconscious as a primary driver of plot and character development is seen in Ernesto Sábato's *Sobre héroes y tumbas* (1961). This brief list could be greatly expanded; it is my hope that future research will follow these and other traces of surrealism in Latin America fiction, examining in particular the complex relationship between surrealism, the literature of the fantastic, and magical realism.

* * *

Breton's Ghost is divided into three parts. Part I provides an overview of surrealism both historically and conceptually, first in the context of its European origins and then in its Latin American context. Chapter 1, "Surrealism Is Dead: ¡*Viva el Surrealismo!*" departs from the oft-repeated motif of surrealism as a corpse, arguing within this metaphorical frame that the very contradictions inherent in surrealist thought and practice allowed it to develop a healthy "afterlife." This chapter presents the principal features of surrealist thought and its key literary techniques, taking particular note of the role of montage or juxtaposition in the creation of images and metaphors. It also provides a brief history of the surrealist movement, highlighting the crisis that faced the surrealists as they confronted the political realities of Europe in the period leading up to and including the Second World War. Chapter 2, "The Latin American Connection," presents a preview of surrealism's "leap across the pond," considering certain questions raised by this geographical, temporal, and cultural shift. Primary among these questions is that of Latin American identity, an inevitable issue for those writers whose postcolonial position created a complicated dynamic in the response to a movement born in Europe.

Part II, "The Emergence of Surrealism in Latin American Literature," examines the initial phase of surrealist group activity and literary production in Latin America, which occurred between 1928 and 1950. Chapter 3 follows the first surrealist group, headed by Aldo Pellegrini, as it makes its appearance in Buenos Aires shortly after the first surrealist manifesto was published in France. I examine certain texts from the journal *Que*, in which Pellegrini and his companions profess their unquestioning adherence to the ideals set forth by Breton. I consider the imbalance that arises between "total freedom of spirit" proclaimed by these fervent young men and their actual lives as medical students and conscientious citizens within a conservative society. In spite of its ephemeral existence (1928–30), *Que* brought to Buenos Aires a new spirit of excitement about language and the power of the unconscious, an innovative energy that would reemerge with much greater vitality two decades later.

Chapter 4 begins by examining the rather brief period in which Pablo Neruda, Latin America's most well-known and revered poet, experimented with surrealist imagery. The majority of this chapter, however, traces the philosophies and activities of the "Mandrágora" group that arose in direct opposition to Neruda's authoritative voice. Like Pellegrini's group, the Mandrágora writers remained rather orthodox in their espousal of surrealist ideals. But by creating a genre called "Poesía Negra," or "Black Poetry," they revealed their roots in English and German romanticism, an orientation that gives their work a distinctive flavor within the body of first-generation Latin American surrealist texts. Although the Mandrágora movement has been dismissed by certain critics as having little influence over subsequent generations of writers, I argue that, like Pellegrini's group, these writers carried out the foundational work whose impact became clear several decades later.

In Chapter 5, "Peru: The Surrealist Space between Mariátegui and Vallejo," I show how the Marxist thinker José Carlos Mariátegui opened a path for surrealist writing in Peru. Mariátegui's essays, published in the influential journal *Amauta* and elsewhere, introduced European surrealist texts into the Peruvian intellectual discourse of the 1920s and 1930s. Although no surrealist group arose there as others had in Argentina and Chile, three individual poets—Xavier Abril, César Moro, and Emilio Adolfo Westphalen—drew from their exposure to European surrealism in order to produce texts of imaginative intensity and lyrical beauty. In marked contrast, César Vallejo, Peru's most influential avant-garde writer, carried on an open polemic with surrealism, arguing that Latin American poets used this aesthetic to drift from their own cultural moorings. In the last part of this chapter, I examine the permutations of Vallejo's much-publicized declaration that by 1930 surrealism had become "un cadáver."

Chapter 6, "The Two Faces of Early Surrealism in Mexico," parts company from the previous chapters by focusing primarily on texts produced not by

Latin Americans but by European surrealists who visited or resided in Mexico. Surrealist literature and art had been coolly received in the nationalist fervor of 1930s post-Revolutionary Mexico, and until the return of Octavio Paz in the early 1950s, few Mexican writers showed anything but a passing interest in its ideas or its generative possibilities. On the other hand, Mexico represented for the Europeans, in the famous words of Breton, "the surrealist place *par excellence*." This chapter examines the complex dynamic that arises out of this sustained and often strained encounter.

Part III, "A Surrealism of One's Own, 1950–1980," moves forward into the moment when a more mature Latin American surrealism produced its finest and most varied works. After the slow percolation of surrealist discourse in the 1930s and 1940s, a new fervor arose from about 1950 onward. Aware of their belated status with respect both to the surrealist movement in Europe and the foundational groups in Argentina and Chile, this new generation of writers was careful not to identify too closely with its predecessors or to produce mere pale imitations of European surrealist texts. Their will to originality was informed by a whole new set of influences from both within and without Latin America: Vallejo in his posthumous works, the ever-evolving Neruda, Spain's Generation of 1927, Franz Kafka and the existentialists, Ezra Pound and T. S. Eliot, and the North American Beat generation—to name only the most evident. Several Latin American writers of this period made literary pilgrimages to Paris and participated in postwar surrealist activities there, experiencing both the renewed enthusiasm and the sense of critical self-consciousness that framed the movement in its later incarnations.

In Chapters 7 and 8, we turn our attention again to Argentina, where the indefatigable Aldo Pellegrini gathered around him a young group of writers and artists for whom surrealism was—in the words of one writer—a ship that must be launched again. In a moment that many critics consider to be the richest in Latin American surrealist production, four different journals with ties to surrealism were published in Buenos Aires. These little magazines and the polemics that grew up around them are the subject of Chapter 7. Although the journals were relatively short lived (1948–60), individual poets began to emerge in this same period with a marked "neo-surrealist" poetics. Chapter 8 follows the surrealist derivations and transformations in the work of Enrique Molina, Olga Orozco, and Alejandra Pizarnik.

The story of the Mandrágora group in Chile and its avatars is taken up again in Chapter 9, which highlights the work of Gonzalo Rojas (who had been associated with Mandrágora as a young man) and Nicanor Parra. The poetry of Rojas and Parra represents in many ways two distinct currents of Spanish American poetry that emerge in the second half of the twentieth century. The first, following in the tradition of high lyric poetry, is neoromantic or metaphysical in orientation and universalizing in theme; it is a current with evident ties to surrealism, and Gonzalo Rojas becomes its most original new voice. The second current is conversational and often ironic in tone, quotidian in subject matter, and sometimes politically or socially oriented. A particularly exciting form of this new poetry, called *antipoesía*, was popularized by Chile's Nicanor Parra. In the second part of this chapter, I show how, contrary to expectations, surrealism revealed itself to be one of the great tributaries flowing into the antipoetical river.

Chapter 10 brings the story of Latin American surrealism largely to a close with an exploration of the work of one man: Mexico's Octavio Paz. In a magnificent paradox, the country initially most resistant to the creative possibilities of surrealism would produce the writer who is, according to Balakian, "surrealism's sturdiest heir" (7). Of all the Latin American writers associated with surrealism, Paz is the most conscious of its aesthetic and historical significance. He is also aware of the evolution of surrealist thought and thus shifts the discourse away from the rebellion against bourgeois Western civilization and toward a search for transcendental or universal values. I follow this search through certain connections drawn by Breton and Paz between poetry and magic. Like the surrealists, Paz grounds his thought in the ancient belief in the *logos* as a power capable of transforming the world. Calling into question the Saussurian premise that language is an arbitrary convention linking signifier and signified, Paz revives the archaic concept of the direct correspondence between words and things, a correspondence that allowed words to effect real changes in the material world. By examining the dynamic interplay between Paz's poetry and his essays on poetry, I examine the viability of this seemingly archaic poetics in a postmodern world.

* * *

Breton's Ghost is one of many books that could be written on the vast and complex subject of surrealism in Latin American literature. The particular structure of this study highlights a handful of countries—Argentina, Chile, Mexico, and Peru—in which surrealism's presence was keenly (if controversially) felt. In every case but Peru, the history of surrealist expression in these countries also allows us to follow a chronological development that is crucial to our understanding of the subject. With regard to the countries not featured in *Breton's Ghost*, I offer here certain observations in the interest of presenting a broader picture of surrealism in twentieth-century Latin American literature.

First, it is important to note that surrealism arrived in numerous countries of this region not as the discrete movement that existed in Europe, but rather as part of a mélange of avant-garde ideas and practices. One key example of this admixture is the spirit of utter revolt against existing cultural structures that was initiated by Dada but absorbed by surrealism, a spirit reflected in movements such as Colombia's "Los Nuevos" in the mid-1920s and "Nadaísmo" in the 1950s and 1960s. The revolutionary spirit was likewise reborn in the "Tzántzicos" movement in Ecuador and in the collective of Venezuelan artists and writers known as "El Techo de la Ballena," both active throughout the 1960s. The main objective of these groups was to scandalize the bourgeoisie and thus to open the way for fresh forms of expression. Each of these movements drew from the early avant-garde model of violent rejection of the society they inhabited, but they cannot be identified as strictly surrealist.

Even more common in writers from across the continent is an exaltation of the unconscious as the site of aesthetic inspiration. This mode of thought in twentieth-century poetics, which was rooted in nineteenth-century romanticism and given its modern idiom by Freudian psychoanalysis, can be attributed to ideas promulgated by the surrealists. In Latin American literature, such ideas took shape in a thematics of the irrational and an insistence on the "magical" forces of language. This is an orientation apparent for example in the writers of the "Grupo Viernes" in Venezuela, particularly in its most prominent member, Vicente Gerbasi. In a related development, the work of Gerbasi's younger compatriot José Sánchez Peláez is emblematic of a kind of mystical eroticism—the belief in erotic love as an irrational power giving meaning to the universe—that grew out of surrealist thought and characterizes the work of many Latin American writers.

In even broader and more diffuse ways, the exaltation of the unconscious took shape in the use of oneiric, visionary, or hallucinatory imagery, which would become hallmarks of much twentieth-century Latin American poetry. Writers such as Raul Bopp, Jorge de Lima, and Murilo Mendes in Brazil; Luis Vidales and Álvaro Mutis in Colombia; Ida Vitale and Marosa de Giorgio in Uruguay; Hérib Campos-Cervera in Paraguay; and José Lezama Lima in Cuba—to name only a few—show surrealist affinities through the free-associative or irrational structure of their images and metaphors. In all of the above cases, surrealism exercised a decisive influence over the development of Latin American literature. But it did so as part of a tapestry of foreign influences and native cultural developments from which it is difficult to extract a singular surrealist thread.

In considering the purported "failure" of surrealism to materialize as a well-defined movement in many parts of Latin America, we must acknowledge the legitimate desire for cultural autonomy that held sway over the region in the first half of the twentieth century. Perhaps the most instructive example of this dynamic is Brazil, where, in the context of an early enthusiasm for avant-garde experimentalism, "the tree of Brazilian modernism could have produced an openly and explicitly surrealist branch. But this branch did not grow" (Ponge 57).

Brazil's primary movement of this period, whose principles were aphoristically laid out in Oswald de Andrade's *Manifesto de Antropofagia* (1928), sought a way to simultaneously embrace the discoveries of the European avant-garde and to celebrate Brazil's autochthonous culture. The anthropophagists argued that Brazilians had the ability to consume and digest the products of other cultures, assimilating them into new and original forms. Surrealism was for them only one of those digestible products, barely distinguishable from Dada, futurism, or any other European cultural import. This attitude, generally dismissive of surrealism as a viable model in its own right, exists in contradistinction to the more open embrace of the movement in other countries. But throughout Latin America, the tension between the autochthonous and the foreign continued to inform the processes of adaptation and reappropriation that characterized surrealism's reception in the region.

Finally, it is worth noting that a belated but energetic form of surrealist activity emerged from the combined efforts of writers and visual artists in several Latin American countries. An early case occurred in the Dominican Republic, where a group that gathered around the exiled Spanish painter Eugenio Grannell and the Chilean poet and diplomat Alberto Baeza Flores organized a number of surrealist activities in the decade of the 1940s. The following two decades saw a strong resurgence of interest in surrealism in Brazil. The salient figure of this period is Sérgio Lima, who resided in Paris between 1961 and 1963, where he came into contact with Breton and the postwar surrealist groups. Lima's own work, which includes poetry, painting, collage, and film, has been profoundly marked by surrealism, and he has been instrumental in keeping the surrealist spirit alive in collectives such as the Grupo Surrealista São Paulo and the "Decollage" group, which continues to be active to this day. In these and numerous other instances, Latin American artists and writers have succeeded in erasing the rigid boundaries between modes of aesthetic expression, an erasure that the original surrealists held as an ideal but were largely unable to achieve.

* * *

The Argentine writer Julio Cortázar wrote an essay in 1949 that cautioned its readers not to consider surrealism as defunct. Cortázar's testimonial at mid-century stands as evidence of surrealism's ongoing vitality in the Latin American setting: "But it pays to remember that from the first surrealist game with little pieces of paper this verse was born: *The exquisite cadaver will drink the new wine*. Be careful with this dead man who is very much alive, who wears the most dangerous of suits, that of false absence, and who—present as never before, there where no one suspects it—rests his enormous hands on time in order to keep it from moving on without him, the one who gives it meaning"[4] ("Un cadáver viviente" 350). As I noted earlier in this introduction, the metaphor of the corpse appears with remarkable insistence in the discourse surrounding surrealism. Since Breton's former surrealist companions first declared him to be *un cadavre* in the internal conflicts of the late 1920s, the image has reinserted itself wherever discussions of surrealism's viability or influence arise. I have used the phrase ¡*Viva el surrealismo!* as the subtitle to Chapter 1 precisely because the ongoing presence of surrealism in Latin American literature attests to one important way in which the "exquisite cadaver" of European surrealism found a new and rejuvenated existence.

PART I

Contexts and Contours

CHAPTER 1

Surrealism Is Dead, ¡Viva el Surrealismo!

> Le surréalisme—qui fait long feu—en tant que doctrine autonome, en tant que méthode spécifique, n'existe pas. Mais, fait historique, ce feu illumine encore le paysage intellectuel jusqu'à l'horizon.
> —Paul Nougé, *Histoire de ne pas rire*

Introduction

What is surrealism? Surrealism is a tangled web of contradictions. This is, paradoxically, both its raison d'être and the limitation that it strives perpetually to overcome. It is also, I would argue, the condition that has granted it a long afterlife beyond the borders of World War II–era France. André Breton claims in one of his most famous pronouncements, "Everything tends to make us believe that there exists a certain point of the mind at which life and death, the real and the imagined, past and future, the communicable and the incommunicable, high and low, cease to be perceived as contradictions. Now, search as one may one will never find any other motivating force in the activities of the Surrealists than the hope of finding and fixing this point" (*Manifestoes* 123–24). The surrealists sought through a dialectical process to resolve the antinomies they saw as alienating modern man from himself, from what they imagined to be authentic existence.[1] There is no stasis in this process. The *point sublime* could only be reached momentarily and provisionally, before it in turn became the starting point of a new dialectic. It comes as no surprise, given the dialectical structure of surrealist thought, that surrealism when viewed historically should present itself as a series of contradictory elements or stances, a thesis and antithesis at times momentarily resolved. First and foremost in this series, of course, is the opposition of reality to the dream, or of rational to irrational thought. By cultivating the irrational, surrealists sought the absolute but insisted that it was reachable only through the here-and-now. The aim was not to reach a spiritual beyond but to access a heightened form of existence in this world, what Ferdinand Alquié calls "everyday life transfigured" (13). This means that in terms of creative production, the values of imagination and antirationalism were offset by an almost scientific attention to the details of the material world.

Further contradictions appear as we try to make sense of the original French surrealist movement and the ideas that energized it. Surrealism is simultaneously traditional and ultramodern, pessimistic and optimistic, destructive and constructive.[2] These contradictions lead the Argentine writer Ernesto Sábato to characterize surrealism (with tongue in cheek) as "that odd admixture of dialectical materialism and Lautréamont, of fourth dimension and clairvoyance, of madhouse and proletariat" (79). The key point I wish to make here is that the dichotomous and unresolved nature of surrealist thought was precisely what allowed it to survive over time and to reinvent itself in cultural contexts vastly different from that of its origins. The "outright contradiction" at the heart of the first *Manifesto of Surrealism*, says Michael Benedikt, was "as productive to the growth of Surrealism beyond its early years as any deliberate allowance for variation" (xvii). Roger Shattuck emphasizes the important role of these unresolved antinomies when he suggests that "the excitement of the surrealist object or work is its attempt, not to obliterate or climb higher than the big contradictions, but to stand firmly upon them as the surest ground" ("Introduction" 22). This excitement—embracing both devoted enthusiasm and bitter vituperation—established surrealism's place as the latecomer but also the latestayer among avant-garde movements.

Defining Features of Surrealist Thought

By the late twentieth century, the adjective "surreal" had settled itself in English parlance as a general name for the odd, the unexpected, or the absurd. Surrealism's founders, however, had in mind something much more specific, and any study of the movement and its sequelae must address itself to these original intentions. The following pages present the key tenets of surrealist thought as it developed in France in the 1920s and 1930s, which will serve as a foundation for a more extended look at Latin American surrealist literature.

Surrealism was originally conceived not as a literary or artistic school, much less a set of techniques or a mere style. It was rather a mode of thought that was meant to subvert all conventional modes of thought and even to change the nature of thought itself. The most sustained effort at explaining surrealism conceptually is Ferdinand Alquié's *The Philosophy of Surrealism*, first published in French in 1955. Alquié observes that surrealism "involves an authentic theory of love, of life, of the imagination, of the relations between man and the world" (2). For him, "all this supposes a philosophy," an assumption that allows Alquié to reconcile his admiration for Breton—the movement's "intellectual and reflective consciousness"—with his admiration for Plato, Descartes, and Kant (2, 4). *The Philosophy of Surrealism* provides coherent analyses of the surrealist concepts of love, liberty, poetry, revolt, beauty, and the interplay of the imaginary and the real, among others; it also analyzes surrealism's relationship to literature, to the Western metaphysical tradition (particularly to Descartes, Hegel, and Kant), and to Marxist thought. Interwoven into these concerns are certain consistent notions that make it possible to examine surrealism on a conceptual level. These notions allow us to see in surrealist thought a set of meaningful contradictions or productive tensions.

Alquié openly acknowledges the problem at the heart of his own project (and of any attempt to understand surrealism), which is the very desire to conceptualize surrealism in rational and coherent terms. He presents the problem as a series of questions that set the "surrealist state" against any attempt to explain it: "Will one who has participated in the surrealist state be able to find a different expression for what he has already been given? How will he escape, in order to talk about it, this interpenetration of dream, waking, poetry, madness, whose fusing announces, promises, troubles, *but does not allow knowing*? Will every step toward clarity not be abstraction and betrayal?" (109; emphasis added). On a certain level, Alquié is pointing here to the problem facing any attempt to make sense of a work of literature or art, to express its "meaning" in terms other than those of the work itself. There is in surrealism—which is a set of principles but also a *praxis*—an immediacy of experience that resists codification, something that does not "allow knowing." And yet, as Alquié insists, there is also in surrealism an aspiration to reason, which is, significantly, "a new reason in which man as a whole may find his image again" (110). This very aspiration to reason justifies an examination of surrealism as a philosophy, provided that we keep in mind its character as both a mode of thought and a practice of life.

In the first surrealist manifesto, Breton formulates a dictionary definition that reads, "SURREALISM, *n*. Psychic automatism in its pure state, by which one proposes to express—verbally, by means of the written word, or in any other manner—the actual functioning of thought. Dictated by thought, in the absence of any control exercised by reason, exempt from any aesthetic or moral concern" (*Manifestoes* 26). Surrealism's ideal of revealing the inner workings of the psyche characterizes it as a state of mind, an attitude toward existence: this is why Walter Benjamin speaks of the early surrealists as "a closely knit circle of people pushing the 'poetic life' to the utmost limits of possibility" (178). Historically, the emphasis on seeking a poetic existence—as opposed to simply writing poetry—was no doubt rooted in the crisis in European thought represented by the First World War, a crisis that led to a radical expansion of the role of the writer or artist in interpreting and transforming the world. In fact, surrealism conceived as an attitude toward life or *actitud vital* would become one of the strongest features of its creative appropriation by Latin American writers.

In response to the debacle of the Great War, the surrealists proposed a total revolt against reason and rational discourse, which they saw as largely responsible for the bankrupt state of the Western world. Speaking at Yale University in 1942, with Europe sunk deeply into the Second World War, Breton asks, "What is the narrow 'reason' that is being taught if this reason must, from life to life, give way to the unreason of wars?" (*Free Rein* 55). In a similar vein, logic is characterized disdainfully by the surrealist writer Pierre Mabille as "that obliging servant [who] proposes false certainties and false solutions" (6). Especially in its later developments, this deliberate unfastening from reason led in some cases to what Balakian calls "a high dose of mysticism" (48), a feature that differentiates surrealist thought from psychoanalysis and that draws it closer to certain other modes of the irrational such as occultism or spiritism still in vogue in the early twentieth century.

Liberated mental activity and the revolt against the strictures of rational thought put the attentive mind in touch with *le merveilleux*. "The marvelous," a crucial concept that is defined only obliquely by Breton, refers to dream imagery, to various forms of revelation, or to unusual ways of perceiving quotidian reality. (In the latter sense, it is related to James Joyce's notion of *epiphany*.) The ongoing discovery of the marvelous was the only aesthetic principal to which the surrealists unfailingly adhered. Mabille stresses the notion that the marvelous is accessible to all with the pithy phrase "*the marvelous is everywhere*" (14), and Breton defines the surrealist aesthetic by asserting that "the marvelous is always beautiful, anything marvelous is beautiful, in fact only the marvelous is beautiful" (*Manifestoes* 14). If the smooth surface of normally perceived reality can be broken by the eruption of the marvelous, the surrealist's task is either to instigate that rupture or simply to witness and perhaps record it. In keeping with this task, Breton frames the descriptions of his travels in the West Indies and Mexico in terms of *le merveilleux*. It is important to note here that the surrealist perception of the marvelous as an inherent quality of Latin American reality will inform and complicate the relationship of local writers to their own geographies and cultures.

Beyond the dream poetics that draws the unexpected out of the unconscious mind, the marvelous is intimately related to *le hasard objectif* or "objective chance": the notion that the objective world can produce unexpected revelations as it interacts with the human psyche. Projected desire, in other words, can "create" an object in the material world. This line of thinking produced both the characteristic surrealist image in poetry and the surrealist object in painting, photography, and sculpture. The surrealists walked the streets of Paris prepared for random encounters, or they carried out daily routines in a receptive state of mind, always poised to identify that moment in which an exterior event corresponded exactly to an interior illumination. This expectation is the basis of Aragon's *Le Paysan de Paris* (1926) and of Breton's most famous work, *Nadja*. Both texts are semiautobiographical narratives that explore the psychic ramifications of events that in themselves may appear unremarkable. Almost from the moment it appeared in 1928, *Nadja* became required reading for several generations of Latin Americans.

Breton's brand of surrealism gradually shifted away from the "scientific" pursuit of psychic knowledge toward more esoteric strains of thought that identified the marvelous with the magical or the sacred. Studies of comparative religion such as those carried out by Mircea Eliade contributed to a revaluation of non-Western approaches to spirituality. The sacred, in this context, was conceptualized not in orthodox religious terms (most of the original surrealists were agnostics or atheists), but in terms of the *numinous*, a notion popularized by Rudolf Otto's seminal work *The Idea of the Holy: An Inquiry into the Non-rational Factor in the Idea of the Divine and Its Relation to the Rational* (1917). Like *le merveilleux*, the concept of the sacred is intimately tied to the principal of objective chance: the transcendent reveals itself to the alert mind at unexpected moments, always from within the here-and-now. The surrealists insisted on this grounding of the numinous in the ordinary, banal, or even morbid details of everyday existence.

The association of the marvelous with the sacred was further bolstered by the broad dissemination of works by early twentieth-century anthropologists such as James Frazer, Marcel Mauss, Claude Lévi-Strauss, and Lucien Lévy-Bruhl, as well as by Karl Jung's studies of myth and the collective unconscious. Breton is clearly speaking in Jungian terms when he claims that with surrealism, art becomes a question of "*the creation of a collective myth*" (*Manifestoes* 232). From the studies of the early anthropologists, the surrealists and other avant-garde practitioners drew the conclusion that other cultures, particularly those deemed "primitive," provided an access to the marvelous that was more direct and somehow more authentic than that available within their own European cultures. The "renegade surrealist" Georges Bataille makes the remarkable claim that "the quest for primitive culture represents the principal, most decisive and vital, aspect of the meaning of surrealism, if not its precise definition" (71). For their inspiration on this front, the surrealists researched (often firsthand) the contemporary societies of Oceania, Africa, and the Pacific Northwest. The pre-Columbian cultures of Mesoamerica and South America—and to a lesser degree, the contemporary cultures of this region—also provided them with valuable material.³

From a historical perspective, the avant-garde's fascination with the primitive has proved to be one of its most problematic features, as it often reflects an attitude of disparagement toward the very peoples whose thought it emulated. In *Surrealism and the Exotic*, Louise Tythacott sums up the situation: "In their radical critique of the dominant world-view of their time, then, the Surrealists deliberately extolled the virtues of peoples whom Western culture had traditionally debased. Yet this uncritical mingling of the primitive, the mad, and the child had dangerous implications, for it was precisely the idea that non-Western peoples resembled children or the insane, and were thereby incapable of self-determination, that had ideologically justified colonialism" (55). As we will see at various points in this study, the discourse of the primitive, the marvelous, the magical, and the mythical will frame to a great degree the approach of the European surrealists to Latin America, and it will in turn prove to be one of the most complicated features of Latin American writers' appropriation of surrealist thought and practice.

The Surrealist Text and the Primacy of the Image

The principal surrealist technique for delving into the unconscious in order to access the reign of the marvelous was automatic writing, which involved recording with pen or typewriter the uninterrupted flow of what Breton calls "undirected thought" (*Free Rein* 59). In these exercises there was to be no preconceived subject, and the writer was to proceed as quickly as possible, without the intervention of any critical consciousness. Octavio Paz makes an important distinction when he states that automatic writing was not a recipe for writing poems but "a psychic exercise, a convocation and an invocation meant to open the floodgates of the verbal stream" ("André Breton" 49). In the early stages of the surrealist movement, much of this activity was carried out in groups: one member would record the "spoken dream" of another, or two members would carry on a dialogue in which one would pose a question and the other would answer in a logically unconnected or absurd way. The *cadavre exquis* or "exquisite cadaver" was another favorite activity, in which participants drew segments of a body (or wrote lines of a poem) on a sheet folded over so that the previous participant could not know what was there: the result was a collective drawing or poem in which unlikely juxtapositions created sparks of humor or new ways of seeing. In short, any method that loosened the rational structures of thought was explored; thus word games, puns, anagrams, aphorisms with double meanings, and other forms of linguistic play were appreciated not for their mere entertainment value—as critics often charged—but as a means of opening doors onto other realms of consciousness. The emphasis on group activity provocatively called into question "the nature of the work of art as it has developed since the Renaissance—the individual creation of unique works" (Bürger 56).

In keeping with the surrealist ideal of reaching and reproducing "pure thought," in which genre distinctions have no relevance, the surrealist literary text can take the form of poetry, prose, or some combination of the two. Genre boundaries are further blurred in collaborative compositions such as artists' books or in paintings or collages that include the written word.[4] Almost without exception, surrealist texts are brief, acting as documentation of momentary psychic illuminations. This is why, for orthodox surrealism at least, narrative fiction is problematic. Breton wrote disparagingly (and humorously) of the realist novel in his first manifesto: "The circumstantial, needlessly specific nature of each of [the novelists'] notations leads me to believe that they are perpetrating a joke at my expense. I am spared not even one of the character's slightest vacillations: will he be fairhaired? what will his name be? will we first meet him during the summer? So many questions resolved once and for all, as chance directs; the only discretionary power left me is to close the book, which I am careful to do somewhere in the vicinity of the first page" (*Manifestoes* 7). Although pure psychic automatism can certainly follow a narrative line (as it often does in dreams), the extended linear structure of the traditional novel does not lend itself well to surrealist techniques. The structural demands of realist fiction, furthermore, tend to detract from the full exercise of the imagination that was the goal of surrealist practices.

Unlike some other manifestations of the literary avant-garde, surrealism did not promote experimentation with the shape of the text on the page or with metrical form, sonorous effects, or grammatical structures. The recording of thought itself was the surrealists' primary purpose, as opposed to experimentation per se. For this reason, says Breton, "very few neologisms show up, and . . . this continual flow brought about neither syntactic dismemberment nor disintegration of vocabulary" (*Manifestoes* 299). The surprising effects produced by many automatic texts arise not from broken syntax but from free association, in which words or phrases are strung together without obvious logical connection. Alternatively, segments of otherwise intelligible description or narrative are interrupted by images or phrases that seem out of place, disrupting the reader's expectation of meaning. In the words of Michael Riffaterre, "Automatism opens wide the associative lock: whereas controlled writing aims for the one appropriate word, subordinates inappropriate words to a context in which they can be assimilated, and favors semantic and stylistic harmony and a unity of tone going from word to word, automatic writing by contrast replaces a word with its satellites and tonal unity with continuous transcoding" (232).

Eschewing morphological or syntactical experiments, the surrealists cultivated the image as the primary vehicle for expressing the marvelous. When Breton observes, referencing Baudelaire, that "it is true of Surrealist images as it is of opium images that man does not evoke them: rather they 'come to him spontaneously, despotically,'" he is speaking of objective chance in a verbal or visual mode (*Manifestoes* 36). Furthermore, by granting the image the power to bring about a change in the consciousness of both writer and reader, the surrealists connected poetic language with ancient notions of the sacred nature of the logos. That is, they appealed to concepts of language in which the presumably natural link between word and thing implied the word's power to effect change in the material world. This is why the surrealist exaltation of the image, observes Mary Ann Caws, reveals "an almost superstitious faith in language as a magic incantation, effective *out of all proportion* to its intelligible content" (*Poetry* 20). The notion of the word-image as magical incantation became central to the poetics of several Latin American writers, particularly Olga Orozco and Octavio Paz.

The surrealist image is primarily *oneiric*; that is, it mimics the imagery of dreams in which a synthesis occurs between objective reality and the subjective imagination. This type of imagery is strikingly illustrated in a fragment from a poem by Alejandra Pizarnik: "una niña de seda / sonámbula ahora en la cornisa de niebla" [a silk girl / sleepwalking now on the cornice of mist] (*Obras completas* 100). The image created here is not necessarily obscure—the reader is able to visualize a girl sleepwalking on a cornice. But the mimetic potential of the image is derealized through the adjective "silk" (applied to the girl) and by the semantically related noun "mist" (applied to the cornice): both qualifiers soften the hard edges of reality, contributing to the dreamlike atmosphere. More important, the girl's state as "sonámbula" (while walking on a cornice) evokes in the reader a sense of vulnerability, of fear. As with many surrealist images, an affective impression is communicated in spite of—or perhaps because of—the lack of a clear representation of the material world.

Similar to the image but more complex in its functions, the surrealist metaphor also works to disrupt habitual attitudes toward language and representation. It was important to the surrealist project that disconcerting or illogical metaphors be considered as evidence of the eruption of the unconscious into everyday mental processes. Taking as their mantra the well-known formulation of the nineteenth-century writer Lautréamont (Isidore Ducasse)—in which he describes his young male protagonist as being "as beautiful as the fortuitous encounter upon a dissecting table of a sewing machine and an umbrella"—the surrealists sought to establish verbal and visual links between incongruous elements (263). The technique of juxtaposition was not invented by the surrealists; as Roger Shattuck observes, it was the preeminent device of the avant-garde broadly speaking (*Banquet* 257). Dada and surrealism, however, took juxtaposition beyond its status as mere device and "developed it equally as a 'major' logic and a 'minor', subversive antilogic" (Freeman 63). In short, the surrealist metaphor created through arbitrary juxtaposition was believed to produce a spark of illumination, an unexpected way of seeing the world.

What are the thematic concerns of surrealist writing? Although it can be difficult to identify particular themes in often hermetic surrealist texts, those that most often emerge revolve around the triad of love-liberty-poetry, first articulated by Breton in his book *Arcane 17* (1947) and later named by Octavio Paz the "triple axis" (*Obras* 2: 213). Surrealist writers are concerned with desire of all sorts, but particularly with erotic desire freed from social convention—that is, *l'amour fou*, or mad love. By concentrating on male heterosexual desire in particular, and by linking it to a spiritual or sacred notion of love, the early surrealists arrived at an essentializing view of "woman" that is the basis for a longstanding feminist critique of the movement. The idealization of the female *other*, coupled with the surrealists' fascination with the irrational nature of children and the mentally ill, led to a veritable obsession with the figure of the child-woman or *femme enfant*, of which Breton's fictionalized Nadja is the emblem. This figure represents the meeting place of seductive womanhood and innocent-but-wise childhood. The male surrealists invariably saw the *femme enfant* as a source of poetic inspiration for them and generally did not trouble themselves with the question of creative inspiration for women artists: there was, and is, no male equivalent of the *femme enfant*.

The desire for freedom of thought, expression, and action in all realms of life forms the second major thematic hub of surrealist poetry. The rejection of all imposed limitations, the desire to transcend or to expand known reality, the aspiration to reach the *point sublime* of earthly existence: these reiterations can give the surrealist text a sense of optimism and dynamism that sets it apart from other texts. On another level, the theme of liberty carries obvious social and political implications. In the context of the historical surrealist movement, initiated soon after the Bolshevik Revolution, neither the revolt against bourgeois social constraints nor the emancipation of the proletariat was ever far from the surrealist project. As Peter Bürger argues with regard to the avant-garde art of this period in general, "A new type of engaged art becomes possible. One may even go a step further and say that the avant-gardiste work does away with the old dichotomy between 'pure' and 'political' art" (90–91). For surrealism, however, the mandate to seek total freedom of the spirit came into immediate conflict with the desire to participate in political emancipation movements, which invariably carried their own set of constraints.

I note finally that the dialectical consciousness itself—that is, the desire for a synthesis of opposites and the awareness of synthesis as a perpetually unstable condition—is a concern of much surrealist poetry, one that is interwoven into the themes of love, liberty, and poetry. As Caws notes, "Surrealism is based on a permanent movement of unification, in which the distance between the perceiver and the perceived, reality and the imagined, the abstract and the concrete, thought and the illogical image is drastically reduced and even, under ideal conditions, suppressed altogether" (*Poetry* 205). In surrealist texts, common motifs representing antinomies striving toward synthesis include darkness/light, presence/absence, unity/plurality, language/silence, movement/stasis, and of course life/death. The dynamic tension between movement and stasis is embodied, for example, in the image of "a tree firmly rooted, yet dancing," from the first and last stanzas of Octavio Paz's circular poem "Sunstone" (whose debts to surrealism have been widely acknowledged) (*Obras* 11: 217, 233).

The Historical Surrealist Movement: A Very Brief History

European surrealism was born from the ashes of the short-lived Dada movement near the end of the decade of the 1920s. From Dada it inherited its emphasis on spontaneity and its radical antibourgeois stance. Thus Breton's words still echo Dada when he proclaims in the *Second Surrealist Manifesto*, "Everything remains to be done, every means must be worth trying, in order to lay waste to the ideas of *family, country, religion*" (*Manifestoes* 128). Surrealism also appropriated from Dada (in principal, at least) its refusal of "art for art's sake"; that is, it sought to eliminate "the aesthetic" as a category separate from lived experience. But as Dada's flagrantly destructive impulses burned themselves out, surrealism emerged as a largely constructive set of attitudes and ideals.

When Breton published the first *Manifeste du surréalisme* in 1924, he was borrowing a term already coined by another French poet in 1917: Guillaume Apollinaire had called *surréaliste* his own comic drama *Les mamelles de Terésias*. The term was well suited to Breton's desire for worldly transcendence, stated in the first manifesto in dialectical terms: "I believe in the future resolution of these two states, dream and reality, which are seemingly so contradictory, into a kind of absolute reality, a *surreality*, if one may so speak" (*Manifestoes* 14). In the early period, the surrealists as a sort of creatively intoxicated group (including Louis Aragon, Pierre Naville, Paul Éluard, Philippe Soupault, Edmond Desnos, and Benjamin Péret) could be seen in Parisian bars and cafés, in private homes, and in the "Bureau of Surrealist Research" experimenting with various techniques associated with automatism.

Much of surrealism's fascination with the strange, the unexpected, the bizarre, dream worlds, and hallucinatory states—in short, with the untrammeled human imagination—can be traced to its cultural roots in English, French, and especially German romanticism. But surrealism's particularly modern nature could not have evolved without the discoveries of late nineteenth- and early twentieth-century psychiatry and psychoanalysis. As Paz remarks, "With a magnificent violence that mingles exasperation and despair, Surrealism brings together the Romantic vision and the discoveries of psychoanalysis. There is a very real and, for that reason, fertile contradiction here: Surrealist oneirism merges prophecy and obsession, clairvoyance and psychic disturbance, Novalis and Freud" ("Hieroglyphs" 128). Breton, in his early association with Dada, had rejected any links to psychoanalysis, but by the mid-1920s he had come to embrace certain aspects of it.[5] Simply stated, the psychoanalytic practice of verbalizing the unconscious was appropriated by the surrealists for the work of poetic or artistic production. They saw psychoanalysis as a vehicle for unlocking the repressed self and its creative powers. Thus when Breton declares that the goal of surrealism is "the total recovery of our psychic force by a means which is nothing other than the dizzying descent into ourselves, the systematic illumination of hidden places and the progressive darkening of other places, the perpetual excursion into the midst of forbidden territory," he is applying implicitly Freudian terms (*Manifestoes* 136–37). In Breton's writings from the late 1920s forward, there is evidence that he also sought a justification in psychoanalytic theory for what would become the surrealist notions of love (as a release from sexual inhibitions) and humor or the sense of the "ludic."

In the period between the two world wars, surrealism dominated the avant-garde scene in France, claimed enthusiastic followers in most European countries, and began its migration to other continents. Some of Europe's most prominent intellectuals and artists called themselves surrealist at some point during the interwar period, including (in addition to those already mentioned) Eileen Agar, Luis Buñuel, Leonora Carrington, René Char, Salvador Dalí, Max Ernst, Leonor Fini, Alberto Giacometti, Julien Gracq, Michel Leiris, Dora Maar, André Masson, Meret Oppenheim, Francis Picabia, Jacques Prévert, Man Ray, Kay Sage, Yves Tanguy, Dorothea Tanning, and Remedios Varo—and this list is by no means exhaustive. Even such broadly influential figures as Pablo Picasso and Federico García Lorca, while not identifying directly with surrealism as a movement, produced works that reveal close affinities with its aesthetics: they are part of an expansive group that James Clifford calls the movement's "fellow travelers" (118).

In the *Second Manifesto of Surrealism* of 1929, Breton left theorizing largely aside in order to denounce various members (including Aragon, Antonin Artaud, Desnos, Naville, and Soupault) for their presumed disloyalty, effectively "excommunicating" them from the movement. (Years later, Breton would admit the excessive nature of this action and lament its consequences.) The fundamental breach within the ranks to which Breton was responding concerned the role of the intellectual within the socialist revolution, a question no serious intellectual of the day could elude.[6] In Europe in the 1920s, Marxism presented itself as the revolutionary path that all progressive and humanist thinkers were invited to travel. However, as Nadeau points out, "Breton and his friends were too jealous of their autonomy and of the value of their own ideas to identify them with a revolutionary doctrine chiefly based on economics and the history of social relations" (117–18). Furthermore, the Communist Party demanded such strict adherence to its dogma that it eventually required its surrealist members to renounce their affiliation with that movement. Needless to say, this produced a deep ambivalence within the group. The Spanish critic Guillermo de Torre recalls the situation with a certain poignancy: "One faced an unavoidable dilemma: relinquish the free interpretation and translation of the world, or relinquish participation, in the sphere of practical action, in the transformation of the world" (394).

Breton joined the Communist Party in 1929. His solution to the dilemma, for as long as it proved workable, was to continue his surrealist activity in an autonomous sphere, all the while proclaiming the movement's support for the Revolution. But Breton's solution did not work for the surrealists as a whole. Over the next several years the surrealists maintained a strained relationship with the Communist party, which was moving in an increasingly Stalinist direction. In 1935, after being denied permission to speak before the Congress of Writers for the Defense of Culture, Breton renounced his party membership, establishing himself from that point forward as an outspoken critic of Stalinism. This stance signaled his definitive split from Aragon and Éluard, whose allegiance remained with the Stalinist Soviet Union. In the text of the speech that Breton had prepared to present before the Congress of Writers, he raises a staunch defense of the surrealist revolt as primarily an act of the spirit: "It is not by stereotyped declarations against fascism and war that we will manage to liberate either the mind or man from the ancient chains that bind him and the new chains that threaten him. It is by the affirmation of our unshakeable fidelity to the powers of emancipation of the mind and of man that we have recognized one by one and that we will fight to cause to be recognized as such. 'Transform the world,' Marx said; 'change life,' Rimbaud said. These two watchwords are one" (*Manifestoes* 241). Characteristically in this text—and for some, maddeningly—Breton remained constant to the ideal of reconciling the antipodal points of thought and action, freedom of the spirit and betterment of the material conditions of life. In *Communicating Vessels*, he would proclaim that the poet of the future "will surmount the depressing idea of an irreparable divorce between action and dream" (147). But in spite of Breton's fervent hope, this "depressing idea" would continue to haunt the surrealists, both in Europe and abroad.

The gap between those who favored active political engagement and those who favored autonomous surrealist activity only widened in the decade of the 1930s, as both the surrealists and the ex-surrealists grappled with their response to the Spanish Civil War (1936–39) and to the lengthening shadow of Nazism. Visiting Mexico in 1938, Breton allied himself openly with Leon Trotsky, who had settled there in exile from Stalinist Russia. The encounter proved fruitful, as Trotsky and Breton coauthored "For an Independent Revolutionary Art," a tract that champions the freedom of artistic thought and practice, even as it insists on the role of art in bringing about social and political revolution. In true surrealist spirit, its criticism of the cooption of art for state purposes was scathing: "Now that it has rid itself of all the artists whose work showed the slightest evidence of a love for freedom, even on the level of form, Hitlerian fascism has forced those who could still consent to holding a pen or a brush to become lackeys of the regime and to celebrate it by command, within the limits of the worst kind of convention" (*Free Rein* 30). The manifesto goes on to criticize the Soviet Union for the same assault against artistic freedom. Although his coauthorship of this document offered Breton a momentary solution, the fundamental problem of the divide between intellectual-artistic freedom and revolutionary participation would haunt the surrealist movement until long after the Second World War. In Mexico, Breton's alliance with Trotsky and Diego Rivera and his criticism of Stalinist socialism drew heavy fire from many of that country's prominent intellectuals, creating a hostile environment for the reception of surrealism that persisted long after his departure.

In spite of the debilitating nature of the conflicts surrounding questions of political allegiance and artistic freedom, surrealism as an artistic movement gained momentum in the late 1920s and early 1930s, especially with the addition of Salvador Dalí to its ranks. Dalí's "paranoiac-critical method" provided painters with a new means to plumb the depths of the psyche and to register their discoveries in profoundly disturbing—and sometimes comic—images. In many ways, the enormous and successfully scandalous surrealist exhibition at the Galerie des Beaux-Arts in Paris in 1938, representing 70 artists from 14 different countries, marked the apex of the movement. In artistic terms at least, surrealism seemed poised at that moment to leap even higher.

But with the outbreak of World War II, many surrealists were scattered into exile, and the group lost whatever coherence it had managed to maintain until that point. Fleeing the German occupation of France and traveling by way of Martinique (where he "discovered" the Francophone surrealist poet Aimé Césaire), Breton settled in New York in 1941. There he joined a community of émigré artists that included André Masson, Marcel Duchamp, Yves Tanguy, Max Ernst, Marc Chagall, Roberto Matta Echaurren, Piet Mondrian, and Kurt Seligmann. The fact that many other members of the surrealist group—notably

Éluard—stayed in France and actively participated in the Resistance movement only exacerbated the tensions among them. Breton experienced his five-year sojourn in the United States as an uneasy exile (significantly, he never attempted to learn English), but his presence there proved critical to the spread of surrealist thought to the Americas. One important activity in this period was the founding of the review *VVV* (1942–44), a journal of art and literature directed by Breton, Duchamp, and Ernst. Among the contributors to *VVV* were the Peruvian poet and critic Xavier Abril; the Chilean poets Braulio Arenas, Jorge Cáceres, and Enrique Gómez-Correa; their compatriot the painter Roberto Matta; and finally the Cuban painter Wilfredo Lam—some with direct ties to the Parisian movement and all identifying with the surrealist impetus in their respective countries.

When Breton returned to France in 1946, the changed face of Europe made the resumption of prewar surrealist activities virtually impossible. Within the intellectual community, existentialism had by and large replaced surrealism as an ideology more suited to the physical and spiritual devastation brought about by the war and the Holocaust. In his essay "Situation of the Writer in 1947," Jean-Paul Sartre, the most widely recognized spokesperson for this changed sensibility, carried out a sustained attack on the ideals and the methods of the surrealists. Sartre rejects the abstracting and universalizing view of the human condition espoused by the surrealists, arguing instead that the writer must acknowledge *and write from* his particular historical vantage point. He therefore ridicules Breton and his group for believing that "any means were good for escaping consciousness of self and consequently of one's situation in the world" (152).[7] Sartre is uncompromising in his condemnation of the surrealists, mainly on the grounds of their lack of meaningful political engagement: "They were all victims of the disaster of 1940: the reason is that the moment for action had come and that none of them were armed for it. Some killed themselves, others are in exile; those who have returned are exiled among us. They were the proclaimers of catastrophe in the time of the fat cows; in the time of the lean cows they have nothing more to say" (164).

It is difficult to imagine a more damning indictment of the surrealist project, and for that reason it is difficult to imagine—if Sartre was right—that surrealism might have "anything more to say." But in point of fact the French movement did reconstitute itself to a certain degree in the postwar period. In the words of the French critic Henri Peyre, "Breton returned from his American exile, shook his lion's mane in Montmartre, rallied new disciples, excommunicated others as he explained how only the mythical and magical ambitions of the Surrealists could bring any hope of salvation to a decrepit world" (23). The younger adherents that breathed new life into the French movement included Jean Louis Bédouin, Joyce Mansour, José Pierre, and Jean Schuster, who would assume leadership of the movement on Breton's death. A surrealist exposition held at the Maeght Gallery in 1947, though largely a retrospective, served to remind the French public of the broad reach of the movement. The exposition brought home to Parisians, says Peyre, "the tragic gravity which underlay most of the Surrealists' eccentricities and the bitter confirmation which their blasphemies had received from the war" (23).

Surrealism as an organized movement lost energy in the 1950s and 1960s, ending definitively in 1969 via a pronouncement by Schuster. Although neosurrealist groups of the last decades of the twentieth century have repudiated Schuster's declaration, historians tend to agree that the surrealist movement as such had ended by 1969. Yet there is also general agreement that, as David Hopkins claims, surrealism's influence has become "pervasive in the world at large" (25). *Breton's Ghost* aims at demonstrating that surrealist influence remained strong for many decades in parts of Latin America, not merely in the diffuse cultural sense to which Hopkins alludes, but precisely in the field of literary production. Long before Breton's death in 1966, certain writers had taken up and carried forward the surrealist banner in places far from France—though the banner's design had been blurred and its hues had shifted.

CHAPTER 2

The Latin American Connection

Introduction

The Romanian critic Stefan Baciu has argued that outside of France, one can speak of a surrealism with defined characteristics only in Latin America ("Introduction" 16). While I would question the exclusive nature of Baciu's claim, I share his insight that there is a genuinely distinctive quality about Latin American surrealism. Moreover, I will argue that surrealism played a significant role in the development of Latin American literature—particularly poetry—throughout much of the twentieth century. As the chapter structure of *Breton's Ghost* indicates, surrealism was experienced not as a singular force across the continent at a specific point in time, but rather as an ebb and flow of literary energies that varied from country to country and writer to writer and that occurred within two rather distinct periods. Out of this ebb and flow arise the defined characteristics to which Baciu referred, which I will sketch out broadly in the current chapter before examining their more concrete manifestations.

Several of the most renowned critics of Latin American literature, including Julio Ortega, Roberto González Echevarría, Jean Franco, Jason Wilson, José Miguel Oviedo, and Octavio Paz, have acknowledged the importance of surrealism to the region or to particular writers. Other voices have arisen in full or partial opposition to this claim: Enrique Lihn, Klaus Meyer-Minnemann, and Sergio Vergara, among others, have minimized the importance of French surrealist thought or even decried its sway over Latin American writers. The most sustained argument to date against a positive valuation of surrealism in the literature of the region was made in 2002 by Valentín Ferdinán in his article "El fracaso del surrealismo en América Latina" [The Failure of Surrealism in Latin America]. Given that Ferdinán's essay raises several important issues that emerge in the following chapters, I consider his primary points of contention here.

Ferdinán's argument is twofold: first, he critiques the historical surrealist movement, and second, he examines the presence of surrealist thought in Latin America and its effect on artistic and literary production there. In the first segment, Ferdinán asserts that surrealism failed to achieve its aims as a movement in Europe and elsewhere, and that this failure is rooted in the fact that it "neutralized" the revolutionary character of Dada (87). Whereas Dada had effected a true break with bourgeois art, surrealism, he claims, reinserts its activity into the aesthetic sphere and in doing so reinforces the distinction between art and life that previous avant-garde movements had attempted to dissolve. Ferdinán's observations at this level correspond to a broad historical debate about the place of surrealism in twentieth-century ideologies and artistic practices, a debate that has engaged thinkers from Benjamin to Adorno to Lacan, and one that is not likely to be definitively resolved. Although there is a consensus that André Breton's goal of promulgating a total revolution of the spirit was not achieved, there is also widespread agreement that surrealism, often through underground or circuitous routes, exercised a profound impact on the development of philosophy, aesthetics, and popular culture. Ferdinán's primary contention in this first phase of his argument—that surrealism failed in its mission of reinserting art into life—has already been conceded on various fronts. The evidence of my own research reveals that the surrealist revolution that was initially embraced with enthusiasm in Latin America as a way of "changing the world" eventually came down to a way of writing poetry, taking photographs, or painting pictures. But even if we consider this eventuality to be a *fracaso*, it does not follow that we should dismiss the enormity of the enterprise. Insofar as there is an element of the Icarus myth in the story of surrealism's overreach and its subsequent "failure," the story still bears telling.

Ferdinán's argument with regard to the role of surrealism in Latin America articulates legitimate neocolonial concerns about the implantation of cultural models from abroad; in raising these questions, he shares the views of other critics whose commentary will be considered at various points in *Breton's Ghost*. The key question is whether or not a movement generated in Europe can truly speak to the cultural concerns of a region like Latin America. Ferdinán answers fully in the negative, basing his conclusions on what he calls the fundamental inadaptability of surrealism to the Latin American context (73). Within the specifically literary sphere, he contests the assertions of Graciela de Sola and Stefan Baciu, both of whom argue (in 1967 and 1974, respectively) for a significant presence of surrealism in this body of literature. Following Baciu's distinction between the truly surrealist writers and those who are merely *surrealizantes* ("surrealizing" or surrealist-influenced), Ferdinán points out that Octavio Paz is the only figure of merit within the first group—and Paz, as he accurately notes, "is not a fully surrealist writer" (75).

In order to respond to these contentions, I must first call into question Baciu's categorization of writers into those who are truly surrealist and those who are merely *surrealizantes*, a distinction that leads to problematic assumptions. While substantiating the importance of surrealism in Latin America, Baciu undermines his project by following a rather strict Bretonian schema for determining who belongs to the surrealist club and who does not. Baciu's purpose is to avoid an overinclusiveness that ultimately dilutes the category of "surrealist writing," and his approach can be useful in clarifying the limited surrealist reach in writers like Oliverio Girondo or Pablo Neruda. But the very rigidity of Baciu's distinction between *surrealista* and *surrealizante* ultimately privileges those writers who had some direct contact with the historical French movement over those who did not, many of whom are "belated" writers who practiced a creative appropriation of surrealist principles. In my estimation it is this latter group, which includes important figures such as Enrique Molina, Gonzalo Rojas, and Alejandra Pizarnik, whose work in fact develops the "distinctive characteristics" of which Baciu speaks and for whom the adjective *surrealizante* is unnecessarily reductive.

Applying Baciu's criteria, Ferdinán ascertains correctly that many writers generally acknowledged as surrealists in Latin America—such as Aldo Pellegrini, Julio Llinás, or Braulio Arenas—failed to rise above the level of minor poets (75). When considered from a historical perspective, however, it becomes clear that the contribution of these figures rests less on the quality of their individual creative work (although many of their texts are worthy of sustained attention) than on their role as instigators of change, as cross-cultural diplomats, and as translators and editors of international literature.

More important, Ferdinán's contention that (with the exception of Octavio Paz) the only bona fide Latin American *surrealistas* were "poetas menores" fails to take into account the full spectrum of surrealist activity in Latin America (75). That is, he tends to focus on those figures that emerged in the earliest surrealist promotions, such as Aldo Pellegrini's group in Buenos Aires and the Mandrágora poets in Chile. These poets and movements, which I explore in Part II of this study, must be considered as foundational, and their largely orthodox adoption of European surrealism must be seen as a necessary first step toward a more fully nuanced form of surrealist expression. I will argue, furthermore, that Emilio Adolfo Westphalen, César Moro, and Enrique Molina, slightly later poets whose work Ferdinán also largely dismisses, are writers with significant debts to surrealism who rise above the status of "minor poets." In sum, I hope to dismantle, with evidence from a wide array of texts, the argument that the influence of surrealism in twentieth-century Latin American literature "is only tangential," and that surrealism fails to open a path for works of far-reaching significance (76).

Latin American Surrealism: A Convoluted Tale

Chapter 1 followed the trajectory of European surrealism from its official inception in 1924 through its period of greatest strength (1924–39) to its formal demise in 1969. For several reasons, this rise-and-fall narrative is not applicable to the development of surrealism in Latin America. The lack of a relatively unified movement with a defined trajectory, headed by a single charismatic leader, makes Latin American surrealist literature a difficult topic to approach, one that is further complicated by the period of time involved—five decades—and the vast geographical expanse of the region. Like any other broad cultural phenomenon, especially one that has been inherited and then reconfigured, Latin American surrealism refuses to fit into a neat package, and its manifestations from one country or writer to another may reveal themselves to be, on examination, quite distinct. For example, it is possible to explain Argentina's relatively stronger embrace of French surrealism by taking into account the long history of that country's cultural ties with France. Mexico, on the other hand, encountered European surrealism exactly at the moment when it was striving to establish a strong national—that is, autochthonous—character in the immediate wake of the 1910 Revolution, a fact that helps to explain the largely negative reception of surrealism in that country. The nativist impulse, including an embrace of the indigenous elements of national cultures, also affected the reception of surrealism in other countries such as Brazil, Ecuador, and Paraguay. In countries such as Colombia, Peru, and Uruguay, the avant-garde in general and surrealism in particular confronted a stubbornly conservative intelligentsia. But in Peru, surrealism was actively promoted—with some success—by the country's most progressive and influential thinker of the twentieth century, José Carlos Mariátegui. In short, surrealism in each of these countries must be considered both separately and within a larger regional framework.

Taking these variances into account and limiting the focus to certain key countries, I have divided the narrative of Latin American surrealism into an early period of assimilation of French surrealism (1928–50) and a later period of creative adaptation (1950–80). These chronological divisions are not arbitrary, but neither are they fixed: they are meant to articulate a strategy for organizing an otherwise rather tangled narrative. Within these time frames, we will follow certain organized movements and certain individual figures for whom surrealism—in its various transformed guises—becomes a significant *actitud vital* and literary aesthetic.

What did these transformed guises look like? Most important, the chronological gap between the historical French movement and its development in Latin American literature led to a certain disparagement of early surrealist techniques—in particular automatism and the various methods of creative production that sprang from it—in favor of a more conscious and controlled cultivation of the oneiric image. In a departure from one of French surrealism's most fundamental tenets, Latin American writers questioned the notion of the unconscious as a depository of individual or collective truths. But they retained a reverence for the *product* of the early surrealist experiments with automatism. It is for this reason that Balakian notes that Latin American surrealist literature "is crystallized in poetic imagery rather than in technical devices of simple wordplay and collage" (7). This should not surprise us, given that even in the context of the French surrealist movement, Breton's "pure psychic automatism" and the texts it produced did not take long to reveal their problematic nature. The various methods of delving into the unconscious, including the *cadavre exquis* and other group activities, had opened the surrealists to criticism by detractors who saw these activities as mere "parlor games."

By the late 1920s, when surrealism was just appearing on the Latin American horizon, European surrealist writers and artists had already begun to modify the methods of automatism, admitting greater conscious control. Breton's own stance remained ambivalent. As late as 1953, Breton speaks of psychic automatism as "a flow whose course one cannot try to direct" but simultaneously admits that, once the surrealists had found the source of their *materia prima*, "we had no interest in reproducing it to the point of satiety" (*Manifestoes* 298, 299). This latter comment points to a shift away from total adherence to automatism, a direction that the majority of surrealist-affiliated writers in Latin America would follow. The overall result, as many texts examined in this study will show, was a deft management of the surrealist image that lent a sensual and imaginative richness to a language that valued lucidity over obscurity.

The second major development in Latin American surrealist literature consists of the incorporation of surrealist materials—irrational and startling images or metaphors, modes such as "black humor" or objective chance, or the thematic triad of love-liberty-poetry—into compositions that would not otherwise be identified as surrealist. This approach has its most vivid exemplar in Chile's Nicanor Parra, who professed an attraction to many surrealist principles but who developed an *antipoesía* that generally subverted these same principles. In Chapter 9, I examine Parra's antipoetry as a kind of "photographic negative" of surrealist expression. Like several of his contemporaries, Parra incorporated everyday language into the lexicon of poetic expression, often employing an ironic and overtly demythologizing tone. The coexistence of these elements with the heightened lyricism of surrealist texts created a hybrid mode of expression that came to characterize much Spanish American poetry in the latter half of the twentieth century.

Each of the writers whose work will be considered in the following chapters puts his or her personal stamp on the poetics of surrealism, in ways too numerous to mention here. But the two broad developments described above—the controlled use of the surrealist image or metaphor and the incorporation of surrealist materials into otherwise nonsurrealist texts—will serve as a framework within which to explore individual authors and texts. What emerges from the picture as a whole is the abundant evidence of a richly productive interface between Latin American writers and a surrealist poetics in subtle but constant metamorphosis.

The Communicating Vessels

One metaphor I find useful in representing Latin American surrealism is that of the "communicating vessels." Following Breton's metaphor of dream and reality as *vases communicants*, we can conceptualize surrealism in this region as two separate but interconnected presences. In the first case, as I will argue at length in the following chapters, surrealism's manifestations in Latin American literature represent a multifaceted case of cultural assimilation, contestation, and adaptation. Writers from Mexico to Argentina, as they became exposed to European surrealism, found that it resonated in meaningful ways with their own experiences and desires, and they subsequently produced their own surrealist-inspired texts. An exploration of the wealth, variety, and often paradoxical nature of these texts is the primary concern of *Breton's Ghost*.

The second of the two communicating vessels involves the projection of an imagined surrealist space onto Latin America. In this case, Mexico, the Caribbean, and South America were framed first as sites of the surrealist *merveilleux* and then, more broadly, as sites of the magical and the "marvelous real." This is a view that points to surrealism as a precursor to the magical realism of the internationally recognized Boom writers in the 1960s and 1970s. In most cases, this projected imaginary originated in the European mind. But a full consideration of Latin American surrealism must take into account the mythologizing and exoticizing impulses of both Europeans and Latin Americans. The metaphor of communicating vessels helps to describe the exchanges that took place precisely because, like liquids passing from one vessel to another, the distinction between the autochthonous and the foreign is not always clear and that very "communion" of artistic energies is thought-provoking in itself. Octavio Paz points out, for instance, that "to be able to speak of Peruvians with their language of bone and lunar stone, César Vallejo had first to adopt the innovations of the European avant-garde" (*Convergences* 222). The Guatemalan novelist Miguel Ángel Asturias, likewise, discovered the indigenous traditions of his native country while studying in Paris, and his literary reconstructions of Mayan legends owe much to surrealist and expressionist techniques. In the last portion of this chapter, I will discuss Cuba's Alejo Carpentier as a third example of mutual exchange: one that is particularly rich in its complexities and that will help frame the subsequent discussion of Latin American surrealist literature.

In the interwar period and in the years immediately following World War II, Europe found itself profoundly questioning the very structure of its political, social, and cultural institutions. In this context, the "primitive" or "exotic" cultures of the African or South American continents provided the members of the European avant-garde with a concrete site for intellectual investigation. In many cases, their travels to these countries also provided a source of creative inspiration. The inevitable question that arises from this situation is, to what degree do such practices on the part of the European avant-gardists lead to an aesthetic and ideological colonizing of the "other?" The question is particularly apt in the case of the surrealists, for whom absolute freedom was the goal of all thought and activity. We might ask, then, to what degree the surrealist objectivizing view of Latin America paradoxically undermined the goal of human liberty by restricting the terms of self-identity for Latin American artists and intellectuals.

To attempt to answer this question, let us first consider some of the texts in which certain aspects of Latin American realty are presented as surrealist "found objects," with their implications of the marvelous or the exotic other. As it turns out, the notion of Latin America as a site of "natural" or organic surrealism is surprisingly widespread on both sides of the Atlantic and surprisingly persistent over time. Using a phrase that has since become a cipher for the exoticizing impulse of the avant-garde, Breton famously commented that he found Mexico to be the surrealist place *par excellence* (qtd. in Schneider 137). Echoing Breton, the Romanian surrealist painter Jacques Hérold expressed as late as 1978 a view still held by some of Europe's intellectuals: "It is obvious that the Continent where voodoo is still practiced in certain regions is closer to Surrealism than the battlefields of Europe or the guns of Indochina, and thus it was much closer to the dream. I am sure that in Asia there are also places that are particularly apt for surrealist behavior, as there used to be in Europe, but I want to underscore a certain primacy of Surrealism in Latin America. I agree with Breton that in that period, the best place for Surrealism was Latin America" (qtd. in Baciu, *Surrealismo latinoamericano* 73). By employing the phrase "primacy of Surrealism," Hérold conflates what I have presented as the two faces of Latin American surrealism: he indicates that Latin America is a proper place for "surrealist behavior" in general, without making any distinction between the native-born and foreigners to the region. At first glance, this might appear to be an inclusive gesture that brings surrealist behavior within the purview of all. And yet when he identifies voodoo as being closer to "the dream" than the battlefields of Europe, he signals a perspective that excludes those for whom voodoo may be an accepted belief or everyday practice.

Key to the European avant-garde fascination with Latin America was its mix of ancient and modern cultures and in particular the survival of tribal cultures into the twentieth century. The French writer and dramatist Antonin Artaud, who belonged briefly to the Parisian group and whose thought was heavily influenced by surrealism, traveled to Mexico City in 1937 and from there into the land of the Tarahumara in Mexico's northern desert. Alluding to Mexico's pre-Columbian cultures, he proposes that "this world of obligatory servitude in which a stone comes alive when it has been properly carved, the world of organically civilized men whose vital organs too awaken from their slumber, this human world enters into us, participating in the dance of the gods without turning round or looking back, on pain of becoming, like ourselves, crumbled pillars of salt" (*Theater* 11). Speaking as a European who finds his own culture in a "crumbled," exhausted, or dead state, Artaud glimpses the possibility of renewing art—and through art, all of life—via contact with indigenous cultures. "To our disinterested and inert idea of art," he claims, "an authentic culture opposes a violently egoistic and magical, i.e., *interested* idea" (*Theater* 11). The notion that authenticity can be found in greater measure outside the confines of Europe is one that will reverberate through much of the cultural commentary of the period, as will the conflation of authenticity with the magical or the nonrational.

Artaud's observations in this text appear to cast a positive valence on the Tarahumara. First, they inhabit a world of "organically civilized men," terms that frankly contradict the identification of the indigenous with the primitive. Second, he finds this to be a potent *human* world in which the carving hand can not only create art but also confer life on the inanimate. In contrast to the dead God of Europe, Artaud imagines "the gods" of this place as dancing and inviting humans to participate. In sum, there is no doubt that in this passage at least, Artaud presents the Mexican indigenous "others" as spiritually superior to their European counterparts. But one can argue that this positive attitude toward the object of his scrutiny is yet another form of colonization, which might be called "mythification." Artaud presents an ideal picture of the Tarahumara and their spiritual connection to the material world, but on what basis does he arrive at this conclusion? We know from other texts—two of which I will investigate in Chapter 6—that Artaud did not communicate verbally with his Tarahumara hosts (or did so in a very limited way), and that he was repelled by indigenous customs as much as he was attracted to their mythical content.

I cite one final and chronologically later example of the European surrealist appraisal of the Latin American as surrealist "other." Breton's journey to New York in 1941 took him first to Martinique and then to Haiti, where he would join Pierre Mabille. In Martinique he met and developed a friendship with the surrealist poets Suzanne and Aimé Césaire, coming into contact with the "Négritud" movement that was taking shape in French colonies and former colonies.¹ This contact spurred an important development in the surrealist relationship to the "other," as the avant-garde fascination with the primitive absorbed an anticolonial consciousness. As David Hopkins claims, with the Martiniquan contact "surrealism truly became a language of the culturally marginalized" (24).

In his introduction to *Refusal of the Shadow: Surrealism and the Caribbean* (1996), Michael Richardson makes a strong case for what he sees as "a determined anti-colonialist attitude within surrealism," one that becomes more pointed and self-conscious after the lived experiences of Breton and others in the Americas (3). Tracing the history of the surrealists' protests against European colonialism, beginning with the Riff rebellion in Morocco in 1926, Richardson argues that the surrealists transcended in many ways the patronizing or distancing attitudes of earlier ethnographers and vangardists. Perhaps because they arrived late on the avant-garde scene, armed with a critical consciousness of the ethnographic practice, the surrealists were more alert than their predecessors (and many of their contemporaries) to the ideological dangers of attraction to the exotic other. This was particularly true in the matter of racial differences. In an interview given during his stay in Haiti, Breton even acknowledges discomfort with the term *primitive* (which he uses only with the qualifier *so-called*) and seeks to clarify that that *la pensée primitif* refers not to an inferior stage of civilization but to a mode of thinking—closely related to the poetic mode—that has in fact been denigrated in the West (Richardson 23). In sum, says Richardson, "the exile of so many surrealists in the Americas during the second World War undoubtedly led them to question their relation to their own culture in a fresh way and underlined in their minds sensitivity to otherness, displacement and inter-cultural relations" (22). Richardson's analysis allows us to view in more nuanced terms the role that Latin America played in the development of surrealist thought in Europe, as well as the effect that surrealist thought may have had on Latin Americans' perceptions of their own cultures.

In our consideration of this latter effect, an important point of departure is the Spanish poet and essayist Juan Larrea, who gave voice to the most extensive development of the concept of Latin America as a surrealist locale. Larrea was born in Spain but traveled to Paris as a young man, where he engaged with the avant-garde community and with the surrealists in particular. In 1926, he edited with César Vallejo the avant-garde journal *Favorables París Poema*, whose first issue opens with a manifesto of decidedly surrealist flavor. After the Spanish Civil War, Larrea moved to Mexico and eventually to Argentina, where he spent the latter portion of his life.

Larrea's extensive writings on surrealism cannot be characterized as literary history or criticism: they are largely philosophical and even mythical in tone and content. Heavily influenced by Oswald Spengler's *The Decline of the West* (1918), Larrea posited the "New World" as the site of the renewal of Western civilization.[2] Larrea's 1944 tome *El surrealismo entre Viejo y Nuevo Mundo* argues that surrealism is a way station in the evolutionary process through which Western civilization is passing toward what he calls "universal Reality" (90). In Hegelian fashion, and drawing on a Spenglerian view of the rise and fall of civilizations, Larrea claims that the South American continent represents the "creative note" in the unfolding of the Universal Spirit (91). He credits surrealism with being a method of foretelling "the imminence of a superior consciousness . . . identified with America" (93).[3]

Larrea's work provides crucial links between Spain, France, and Latin America within the context of surrealism. His work as editor (he cofounded the important journal *Cuadernos Americanos* in Mexico), literary critic, and biographer of César Vallejo earned him the respect of the Latin American intelligentsia. Though European in origin and well-versed in the ideologies of the Parisian avant-gardes, he had spent significant time in Latin America by the time he wrote *Surrealismo entre Viejo y Nuevo Mundo* and thus could be considered an "insider" with respect to both worlds. This book, both in its original version and in its re-edition in 1967 under the title *Del surrealismo a Machu Picchu*, has been widely read and debated throughout the Spanish-speaking world. His vision of the New World as the site of a rejuvenated universal reality, the place where a "superior consciousness" was unfolding under the aegis of surrealism, resonated profoundly for some Latin American writers.

Given the fascination with the marvelous and the primitive that the European surrealists inherited from previous avant-garde thought and then developed through various ethnographical practices, it is not surprising that European writers from Artaud to Breton to Larrea would adopt a view of Latin America as kind of reified "other." What is more surprising, perhaps, is the number of Latin American writers who also subscribe to the notion that surrealism particularly befits that region. Valentín Ferdinán posits that surrealism, which gave writers and artists the necessary vocabulary for naming the marvelous, the grotesque, or the improbable, "created the conceptual frame that allowed for a self-referential description that Latin Americans so needed" (95). In Ferdinán's view, this framework has had a deleterious effect on Latin American writers from the early surrealists through the magical realists, in that it substantiates a distorted view of reality that has become "almost an involuntary celebration of poverty and corruption" (95). I share Ferdinán's concern with the dangers inherent in any abstract or idealizing views of a culture, as well as his observation that such views can be located both outside and inside that culture. Yet I believe that other less negative appraisals must be considered if we are to achieve a balanced picture of Latin American surrealism. In the remainder of this chapter, I will present the case of the renowned Cuban writer Alejo Carpentier (1904–80) as a touchstone for such a balanced approach.

The Ambivalent Surrealist Gaze of Alejo Carpentier

Carpentier's literary career offers a prime illustration of the *vases communicants* in which European and Latin American aesthetic values flow in both directions. His formative years had been largely spent in a Cuban avant-garde milieu inspired by the European movements, a background that allowed him to arrive in Paris in 1928 "impersonating a French surrealist poet" (González Echevarría 57). And yet paradoxically, Carpentier found himself in a European capital whose zeal for Cuban voodoo art, Afro-Caribbean music, and *santería* rituals was palpable. Given this circumstance, it is no surprise that Carpentier's own literary production should seek, like the liquid in the vessels, a point at which the native and the foreign level each other out. This is true in terms of language, choice of materials, point of view, and even audience: Carpentier finds himself in the position of "translating for two" as he attempts to make sense of Cuban culture for both a French audience, for whom he wrote in French, and a white Creole audience in Cuba, for whom he wrote in Spanish (Birkenmaier 22).

Carpentier's years in Paris during surrealism's "heroic" period and his association with surrealist poets and artists there left a permanent imprint on him. In an article called "En la extrema avanzada: Algunas actitudes del 'surrealismo'" published in 1928, he presents surrealism in positive terms: "If you read the admirable *Manifesto of Surrealism* by André Breton, you will learn the secrets of a magical art, one whose discovery constitutes the most important poetic event since the literary eruption of Arthur Rimbaud" (454). Over the long span of his career, Carpentier would continue to share with the surrealists a belief in the values of ethnography (in this case, with an eye toward Cuba's African-American and indigenous peoples) as well as an interest in comparative religion or mythology. In his novels, the unconscious looms large as a motivating force, often in the form of collective beliefs that escape rational explanation, providing further evidence of an early surrealist orientation.

However, once he had resettled in Cuba in 1939, Carpentier began to explore ideas that would propel him away from the French movement. By this point, he had embarked on the intellectual project of delineating Cuba's historical and cultural specificity, and he saw that many European values no longer served this cause. As Carpentier himself states, "The Latin American returns to his own world and begins to understand many things" ("Marvelous" 83). The document in which he most fully develops his refashioned aesthetic principles is an extensive essay called "On the Marvelous Real in America," which serves as a prologue to his 1949 novel *El reino de este mundo*. Here Carpentier reveals that it was on a trip to Haiti in 1943 that he first discovered the principle of unexpected juxtaposition (the *sine qua non* of surrealist technique) at work in an American setting. In that place, he explains, "I saw the possibility of establishing certain synchronisms, American, recurrent, timeless, relating this to that, yesterday to today. I saw the possibility of bringing to our own latitudes certain European truths" ("Marvelous" 84).[4] Carpentier calls the phenomenon he witnessed first in Haiti and later in his native Cuba *lo real maravilloso*—the marvelous real—and explicates the concept as an aesthetic category related to but distinct from surrealism in certain crucial ways.

Having once called surrealism the most important literary event since Rimbaud, Carpentier now attacks it pointedly. The surrealists, he states, do not experience the marvelous but rather *manufacture* it "by tricks of prestidigitation, by juxtaposing objects unlikely ever to be found together: that old deceitful story of the fortuitous encounter of the umbrella and the sewing machine on the dissecting table that led to ermine spoons, the snail in a rainy taxi, the lion's head on the pelvis of a widow, the Surrealist exhibitions" ("Marvelous" 85). Carpentier cites the Cuban painter Wilfredo Lam (who had also been schooled in Parisian surrealism) as the artist who finally taught Latin Americans to see the magic of their own tropical vegetation. It is impossible to truly believe in the marvelous, he insists, without *faith*—and the European surrealists lack faith. As a result, "the marvelous invoked in disbelief . . . was never anything more than a literary ruse" ("Marvelous" 86). To all of this falsity and pretension, Carpentier opposes the reality of Latin America, where one comes into contact with the marvelous real "at every turn" (86). After developing this notion at length, he ends the essay by reaffirming those factors that justify his claims: "Because of the virginity of the land, our upbringing, our ontology, the Faustian presence of the Indian and the black man, the revelation constituted by its recent discovery, its fecund racial mixing [*mestizaje*], America is far from using up its wealth of mythologies. After all, what is the entire history of America if not a chronicle of the marvelous real?" (88).

From its initial publication in Caracas in 1948, this essay has been widely read throughout Latin America.[5] Its harsh critiques of French surrealism, especially when taken out of the context of Carpentier's own relationship to the movement, almost certainly contributed to ambivalent or negative attitudes toward surrealism on the part of many artists and intellectuals. Yet I would posit that while his rejection of surrealism in favor of *lo real maravilloso* appears to signal a decisive rupture, one can read in it instead a kind of synthesis that allowed for a productive adaptation of surrealist thought.

González Echevarría asserts that on Carpentier's return to Havana, the Cuban writer was able to see the city's previously hidden charms "not only because of the perspective afforded by time and memory, but also because Surrealism has taught him how to look at things in a different way" (95). Developing this argument further, Birkenmaier contends that for Carpentier, as well as for other Latin American writers of the era, the surrealist gaze "permitted them to accept their own society as a modern, heterogeneous one, full of tensions, but within the same discursive field as the Europeans" (15). It was surrealism's dynamic way of *looking*, in other words, that prepared Carpentier to see Haiti and Cuba for the multivalent entities that they were. This led him to the conviction that a comprehensive view of Latin America must take into account not only its concrete history of characters and events but also its saints, its superstitions, its music, its popular traditions, and the fundamental hybridity of its landscape and its people.

In the final analysis, Carpentier's ongoing dialogue with surrealism (of which I have sketched only the bare outlines here) permits us to revisit certain critical issues of Latin America's postcolonial status with regard to European intellectual culture. Using this frame of reference, Amaryll Chanady analyzes the role of Carpentier's *lo real maravilloso* within the complex relationships that make up what she calls the "New World imaginary." Chanady reminds the reader that although Carpentier posits the marvelous as *ontologically* rooted in the region (for him, this locale is "marvelous" in its very essence), this assumption must be considered within a discourse of both American and European views of the colonized space. In brief, Chanady asserts that Carpentier appropriated the surrealist critique of rationality in order to subvert the colonizers' assumption of the inferior reasoning capacities of the colonized: "Whereas the Surrealists criticized a hegemonic intellectual and literary canon in their own society and looked toward the European Other for inspiration in a movement largely inspired by exoticism, Carpentier also used the concept of the marvelous real as a marker of difference in a Latin American discourse of identity rejecting European influence" (137). Stated differently, Carpentier claims a territory in which the literary marvelous has a more legitimate reason for existing than in France, where "the marvelous" had first emerged as a category of thought. In doing so, he turns the Europeans' discovery into a *de facto* argument for the cultural difference—and presumed superiority—of the colonized.

Chanady's reading offers important insights into Carpentier's argument and into the role of surrealist thought in Latin America. One of her crucial assertions is that it is simplistic to criticize Carpentier for initially identifying with a European perspective or for imitating European conventions (137). This type of criticism, implicit or explicit, often constitutes the subtext of any discussion of the Latin American avant-garde; it is a criticism that can come from without or within and is one that must be duly examined in the specific context of each writer. By taking an alternative stance, we can interpret Carpentier's strategy as a constructive appropriation of French surrealism, in which he used imported ideas to advance his own distinctly American purposes.

I would argue, in conclusion, that it is important for readers not to disavow Carpentier's surrealist underpinnings—as he himself seemed so eager to do—in the effort to locate his thought in an "original" Latin American sphere. The Parisian surrealists, after all, had first discovered the marvelous within their own urban reality, a fact that makes Carpentier's claim that the marvelous is found "at every turn" in Latin America an iteration and not a rejection of surrealist principles. The very phrase *marvelous real* could be parsed as a perfect example of surrealist juxtaposition of unlike terms. In the end, Carpentier's reduction of French surrealism to a caricatured image of fur-covered teacups and rainy taxis—that is, his own overt rejection of European influences—should not prevent us from acknowledging those influences when they appear. As will be the case with many of the writers in this study, Carpentier developed his ideas (and his literary practices) in part as a reflective reconfiguration of European ideas. With this synthesis in mind, we return to the metaphor of the communicating vessels and to the notion of surrealism as a fluid movement between continents and cultures. To begin following that movement in its concrete developments, Chapter 3 takes us to the Southern Cone, where the first declared surrealist movement appeared in Latin America.

PART II

The Emergence of Surrealism in Latin American Literature, 1928–1950

CHAPTER 3

Argentina's Pioneer Surrealists

Introduction[1]

The first Latin American surrealist journal appeared in Buenos Aires in 1928, merely four years after the publication of André Breton's first manifesto in Paris. But surrealism's trajectory from that point forward was not a swift or a smooth one. Rarely taking the form of an identifiable movement, it developed in a series of fits and starts, imitations and rejections, proclamations and denials, and ultimately in a broad and multifaceted diffusion. As I pointed out in Chapter 2, this trajectory follows different paths from those of European surrealism, reaching its greatest effervescence in the 1950s. Part II of this book follows two of those paths, both located in the Southern Cone region and both appearing as the group activity of young writers impassioned by French surrealism. The present chapter will highlight a small magazine called *Que* and the group that formed around it in Buenos Aires at the close of the second decade. Chapter 4 will explore the Mandrágora movement, a somewhat later and more sustained engagement with surrealism in Chile. Both these movements, I argue, constitute important foundational moments in the trajectory of Latin American surrealist literature.

The intercontinental travels of certain avant-garde writers such as Jorge Luis Borges and Oliverio Girondo in the teens and early twenties, as well as the exchange of literary ideas, works, and journals that resulted from these travels, made Argentina one of the early focal points of Latin American vanguardist activity. The short-lived but important movement known as *ultraísmo*, with Borges at its head, dominated the scene in Buenos Aires between 1921 and 1927.[2] Within this period, news of surrealism began to reach the southern shores, with notes about "el super-realismo" (the early Spanish term for *le surréalisme*) and translations of texts by French surrealists in Argentine avant-garde journals such as *Proa*. Hugo Verani attributes the rapid demise of *ultraísmo* principally to the appearance of surrealism, which signaled, above all, "an opening toward new forms of irreverence, as well as the initial melding of the renovating and nonconformist vanguards into a movement of greater depth and diversity of interests" (47). The relatively broader scope of surrealism (as opposed to *ultraísmo* or other avant-garde movements) prompts Graciela de Sola to argue that surrealism can be viewed as the most important artistic and ideological movement of the twentieth century in Argentina (7).

Part of the early interest in surrealism came from within the *ultraísta* movement in the person of Oliverio Girondo (1891–1967). Whereas Borges rather quickly renounced his *ultraísta* experiments and returned to formally traditional lyric poetry, Girondo continued to develop an avant-garde poetics throughout his long career. Girondo, however, was an iconoclastic figure whose perpetually inventive work does not fit easily under the rubric of surrealism or any other movement. The full story of surrealism's early origins in Buenos Aires begins with Girondo's friend and fellow poet Aldo Pellegrini. First-wave Argentine surrealism is embodied in the figure of Pellegrini (1903–73), who worked untiringly in his capacity as poet, translator, and editor to maintain an active dialogue between Argentine and European literature. Furthermore, in his capacity as mentor, Pellegrini inspired numerous younger writers. As we will see in Chapter 7, he not only introduced surrealism to Argentina but was instrumental in initiating its second and more fertile period in the 1950s.

Aldo Pellegrini and the Argentine "Fraternidad Surrealista"

A medical student in Buenos Aires when Breton published his first manifesto, Pellegrini was an avid follower of the European avant-garde. His son Mario Pellegrini recalls that one of his father's mottos was "Hay que ser europeizantes"— that is, we must study and absorb European culture (personal interview). Although this commentary could be taken as a sign of a "colonized" mentality, Pellegrini is in fact voicing a reality of Argentine literary-artistic culture, which traditionally has looked to Paris rather than to Lima, Santiago, or New York for its inspiration. In 1926, in response to an inquiry he sent to the French publisher Gallimard, Pellegrini received copies of the journal *La Révolution Surréaliste* and the first of Breton's manifestoes. Inspired by what he found there, he gathered several friends around him, shared the new materials, and the first Latin American surrealist group was born. (Pellegrini also began at that point a personal correspondence with Breton that would last for decades, though they did not meet until Pellegrini traveled to Paris in 1959.) The young men who formed the ranks of this group, including Elías and Ismael Piterbarg, Mariano Cassano, and David Sussman, were all medical students as Breton himself had been, and like Breton they shunned any identification with what they considered to be the literary establishment. Pellegrini recalls, "Together we formed a kind of surrealist fraternity, one that experimented with automatic writing" (qtd. in De Sola 111). They published only two issues of the journal *Que* [What], in 1928 and 1930.

Practically speaking, *Que* was a publication of scarce resources that reached a very limited readership, and its immediate impact was negligible. But despite these limitations, the two issues of *Que* serve as important initial documents in the history of Latin American surrealism. An examination of some of the texts included in this journal will allow us to glimpse the curiosity and fervor that surrealist thought awakened in Argentina in the decade of the 1920s. It will also allow us to pose initial questions about the dynamic interplay between orthodoxy and reinvention that characterized Latin American surrealism, questions that form the basis of this study as a whole.

The Little Magazine *Que*

Serving as the introductory text to the first issue of *Que*, an unsigned proclamation appears under the title "Pequeño esfuerzo de justificación colectiva" [Brief Attempt at a Collective Justification].[3]

> Justificación de esta revista: Buscar en la expresión la evidencia de nuestra propia y oculta estructura (palabra, espejo del hombre) y quizás también algo como una necesidad irresistible de pensar en voz alta.
> Justificación de nosotros: Seres atraídos hacia sí mismos por una extraordinaria fuerza centrípeta. (Pellegrini, *Valija* 19)
>
> [Justification for this journal: To seek in the act of expression the evidence of our own hidden structure (word, mirror of man), and perhaps also something like an irresistible necessity to think out loud. / Justification for ourselves: Beings drawn to each other by an extraordinary centripetal force.]

The collective "we" of the speaking voice refers to the handful of young men who founded *Que*. But in the process of identifying "the word" as their principle tool, they also project their circumstance onto a more generalized "man." With the phrase "palabra: espejo del hombre," they assert the value of language not as a tool for communication but as the very mirror of the self, employing a fundamentally psychoanalytic metaphor. Further evidence of the psychoanalytic orientation of this text occurs in the allusion to "our own hidden structure," which is presumably the structure of the unconscious. By "thinking out loud," the authors of this declaration follow the surrealist practice of searching for meaning in unpremeditated "spoken thought."

In contrast to the vociferous public proclamations of many avant-garde collective texts, the "Justificación" in *Que*'s first issue continues to emphasize a search for interior or subjective truth. In this spirit, the speakers claim that "hemos acudido a la única manera de existir en densidad (es decir sin disolvernos) que es la introspección" [we have turned to the only way of existing with density (that is, without dissolving), which is introspection] (*Valija* 19). The concern here is not (as in other avant-garde manifestoes) with the artist's place in society but with the integrity of the solitary being. The introspective attitude is further explored in the subsequent passage:

> En esta actitud se distinguen dos partes:
> 1 placer de una ilimitada libertad expansiva.
> 2 posibilidad de conocernos (especie de método psicoanalítico, pero en el cual no partimos de ningún prejuicio sobre nuestra propia estructura)
>
> [In this attitude, there are two distinct parts: / 1st: The pleasure of an unlimited, expansive freedom. / 2nd: The possibility of knowing ourselves (a kind of psychoanalytic method, but one that does not emerge from any pre-formed notions of our own structure)].

By placing the discussion of the introspective process in the context of a group manifesto spoken by a plural subject, Pellegrini and his companions imply that such a process, though necessarily grounded in the individual, draws the group together in collective action. Although such action is defined by the surrealist watchword "freedom," it seems clear from the language of the manifesto that the Argentine surrealist fraternity was not concerned at this point with political or social freedom, but rather with a freedom located in the self, a liberty to explore the "unlimited" possibilities of knowing the self.

The subsequent portion of the "Justificación" reads as a page taken directly from a French surrealist text, reiterating in a different context the overarching theme of liberty:

> Si desvaloramos la vida es por la evidencia de un destino. Vomitamos incontenibleinente sobre todas las formas de resignación a este destino (cualidad máxima del espíritu burgués) y miramos con simpatía todos los aspectos de una liberación voluntaria o involuntaria: enfermedad, locura, suicidio, crimen, revolución. (*Valija* 19)
>
> [If we devalue life, it is because of the evidence of a destiny. We vomit uncontrollably on all the ways of being resigned to that destiny (the most notable quality of the bourgeois spirit), and we look sympathetically upon all those aspects of voluntary or involuntary liberation: illness, madness, suicide, crime, revolution.]

Describing the avant-garde manifestoes that proliferated across Latin America in the decade of the twenties, Vicky Unruh observes that the bourgeois adversary "was constructed with images of fossilization, decay, decrepitude, inauthenticity, and physical and emotional malaise," while the collective voice of the manifestoes characterized itself as youthful, vital, powerful, and authentic (40). This is a description applicable to the above-cited passage in its contestatorial we-they rhetoric. The writers of *Que* devalue the life they see as constrained by bourgeois rigidity, fatefully predetermined, a "destiny" as opposed to the choice of a free being. At this point the language turns deliberately distasteful—the speakers "vomit uncontrollably" on anything that resigns itself to that destiny—in a textual performance of their rejection of good taste. They embrace, instead, the abject in all its forms, since those forms symbolize freedom. By placing a positive valence on madness, suicide, crime, and so forth, the *Que* group is signaling not only a literary revolt meant to modernize the expression common to their milieu but also a return to the romantic paradigm of values that privileges the lone, rebellious poet.

The final section of this manifesto concerns itself primarily with language, which is conceived in archetypal terms:

> Justificación de nuestra expresión: Toda palabra está en el corazón mismo de los problemas del ser. Es decir, que para un hombre determinado, su misterio toma la forma de sus palabras (en un sentido más amplio: toma la forma de sus signos). Justificación del nombre de la revista: interrogación primera y máxima, desnuda de todos los ornamentos ortográficos, reducida a su pura esencia verbal. (*Valija* 19)
>
> [Justification for our expression: Every word is found in the very heart of the problem of being. That is, any given man's mystery takes the shape of his words (in the broadest sense: it takes the shape of his signs). Justification for the name of this journal: first and maximum interrogation, stripped of all orthographic elements, reduced to its pure verbal essence.]

Late in life, Breton stated that "surrealism, as an organized movement, was born of a far-reaching operation having to do with language" (*Manifestoes* 297). In line with this thinking, Pellegrini and his group reinforce their belief that the problems of being cannot be conceived apart from the problems—or the powers—of language. The "mystery" of existence is not only expressed by language; it is equivalent to language (which they also construe broadly as "signs"). Finally, the writers justify their choice of the title *Que*, written without the orthographic accent that would clearly mark it as an interrogative in Spanish. Paradoxically, they wish the title to be read as an interrogative, pointing to the questioning spirit that marks the group and its activities, but they also wish to strip it of the one sign that would give the word an unequivocal character.[4]

Both issues of *Que* included lyric poetry and prose poems, proof that the Argentine surrealists, like the French, gravitated toward poetic language as the primary mode of exploration and expression. Mario Pellegrini notes that the members of this group chose to publish under pseudonyms as a sign of their disdain for literary vanity (5). In the first issue, Aldo Pellegrini published a series of "philosophical poems" under the pseudonym "Adolfo Este." The fifth of this series, a prose poem entitled "Ver" [Seeing], is an exquisite example of automatic writing whose title evokes the surrealist motif of sight that arose in the previous discussion of Alejo Carpentier:

> El pie cubría una voz estrangulada por el rectángulo apacible de la aventura. Dos paralelas o dos niños, salían de sí mismos para encontrar aspectos inéditos que ellos bautizaban: automóvil, casa, sol, suelo. Si uno perdiera el pequeño libro que lleva en la mano desaparecería inmediatamente por la razón de que toda existencia depende en un sentido absoluto de... Reconciliaos con la vida; total, un hombre ha perdido sus dos manos y ha hablado con una simplicidad que partía el alma de la posible utilización de dos manos de cera que substituirían las caricias de la mujer por un ruido sordo. El día abadonó su forma de candela para adquirir la de una mesa servida. Meditad sobre los accidentes en pleno día. Catástrofes obscenas y ojos desanimados, he ahí el balance de nuestra vida. (*Valija* 23)
>
> [The foot was covering a voice strangled by the gentle rectangle of adventure. Two parallel lines or two children came out of themselves to find unheard-of aspects that they baptized: automobile, house, sun, ground. If one were to lose the little book he carries in his hand, he would disappear immediately, since all existence depends on an absolute sense of... Become reconciled with life; at any rate, a man has lost his two hands and has spoken with a directness that broke the heart of the possible use of two wax hands that would replace the caresses of a woman with a muffled sound. The day gave up its candle shape to take the shape of a table already set. Contemplate accidents that occur in the light of day. Obscene catastrophes and dejected eyes: here is the sum of our life.]

The first line of "Ver" is built on an extended surrealist metaphor: a metaphor in which none of the terms serves to clarify the others. The initial image of a "foot covering a voice" is in itself impossible to visualize, although a foot over a throat or a mouth is conceivable. This first image is further complicated by the voice's strangulation by a "gentle rectangle." In spite of the illogical combinations here, the images taken together evoke a sense of repression or silencing, with the rectangle acting as a symbol of constricted rational thought. In the following line, the two children act out the surrealist desire to "come out of oneself" and in doing so to discover the unexpected, the surrealist *hasard objectif*. They then proceed to name these "discoveries," which are in fact quotidian realities (automobile, house, etc.) but which take on an aspect of novelty or re-creation by the children's Adamic act of baptizing them. The following sentence tricks the reader in the way the dreaming mind tricks the dreamer: just when an understanding is about to occur (the answer to the question of what all existence depends on), the sentence breaks off ("un sentido absoluto de…") leaving an unnamed revelation to occupy the space of the ellipses.

The dictum that follows the ellipses—"Become reconciled with life"—reads as an ironic counterpoint to the previously cited manifesto "Pequeño esfuerzo de justificación colectiva," which spoke of the need to "vomit" on the bourgeois resignation to life. Several of the phrases that follow the dictum allude to truncated modes of human existence that surrealism decries—the loss of hands or the transformation of the hands into wax limbs and the replacement of erotic or affectionate contact (the woman's caresses) with "muffled noise." The final sentences of the passage express another imperative ("Contemplate accidents"), which implores the reader to meditate on the chance happenings of daily existence, suggesting that the substance of life may be contained in its dejected (literally "soulless") eyes and its "obscene catastrophes." This last phrase may be an allusion to the surrealist valuation of the abject, which was emblematized in the above-cited "Justification" by illness, madness, suicide, crime, and revolution.

In addition to the manifestos and brief prose pieces, numerous lyric poems published in *Que* reflect the desire to fuse unconscious with conscious thought. Pellegrini's short poem "Paisaje sobre una mano" [Landscape on a Hand] is one of the richest of these pieces in its use of surrealist imagery:

> Caballos gigantes que llevan los despojos de los hombres
> Y aplastan entre una y otra risa los hijos inmóviles de las
>   aventuras.
> La risa
> Es la perdición de esa mujer roja
> izada hasta perderse de vista sobre el mástil del control de la razón
> Tan alto que todas las manos extendidas no la alcanzan
> Flamea arriba como una bandera.
> Su sangre
> es un pájaro. (*Valija* 26)

[Giant horses that carry off the remains of men / And crush between peals of laughter the immobile sons of adventure. / Laughter / Is the perdition of that red woman / hoisted so high she's out of sight on the mast of control of reason / So high that no outstretched hand can reach her / She flutters up there like a flag. / Her blood / is a bird.]

The title of this poem—"Landscape on a Hand"—suggests a sort of prophetic reading of an individual's destiny. The giant horses of the first lines bear no direct relation to the other images in the poem; they simply signal a tremendous physical force that exceeds human control. Black humor, one of the touchstones of surrealist revolt against the seriousness of bourgeois existence, appears in the absurd image of laughing horses that crush immobile beings. The final, extended image of the poem, a red woman riding the "mast of control of reason," is the victim of laughter (it is her "perdition"). But she also represents visually the surrealist *point sublime* or transcendence of limitations, as she is hoisted so high on the mast that grasping hands cannot reach her. The poem ends with a relatively straightforward metaphor for freedom: the woman's blood is a bird. In this brief and superficially illogical poem, Pellegrini manages to interweave into his images several primary surrealist motifs, including laughter, the feminine, the dynamic tension between mobility and immobility, and most important, the desire for freedom, particularly freedom from reason. If we return to the title, "Ver," we can appreciate this series of images as Pellegrini's attempt to suggest a new—liberated—way of seeing (and of writing poetry).

The second and final issue of *Que* (December 1930) contains a long automatic text called "Libertinaje de los solenoglifos" [Licentiousness of the Solenoglyphs],[5] signed with the name "Filidor Lagos," another of Pellegrini's pseudonyms. Toward the end of this piece, "Lagos" states that at a gathering of the members of the surrealist fraternity, he proposed a "collective declaration" (*Valija* 37). Here Pellegrini employs what Unruh cites as a common strategy "to legitimize a single speaker through the support of a concrete collectivity" (37). The declaration, employing the magazine title *QUE* as the enunciating subject, reads as follows:

1. QUE desconoce el Conocimiento humano y se declara anti-Moral.
2. QUE protesta contra toda Ley o Norma (escrita o no) que modifique o coarte cualquier acto espontáneo del hombre.
3. Manifiesta su repudio por las instituciones como Nación o Familia, por la Civilización y por el Progreso.
4. Reconoce la suprema importancia de las afinidades de muerte: Amor, suicidio, cadáveres, fragmentos de cuerpo humano, excrementos.
5. Frente a todo lo repudiable rehabilita los símbolos del asco: mano extendida rechazando, vómitos, gargajos, puah. (*Valija* 37)

[1. QUE refuses to recognize human Knowledge and declares itself Anti-Moral. / 2. QUE protests against every Law or Norm (written or otherwise) that modifies or restricts any of man's spontaneous acts. / 3. It declares its repudiation of institutions such as Nation and Family, of Civilization and Progress. / 4. It recognizes the supreme importance of the relationship of death to: Love, suicide, cadavers, fragments of the human body, feces. / 5. In the face of all it renounces, it rehabilitates the symbols of disgust: the hand held out in a gesture of rejection, vomit, spit, yuck!]

This text follows the model of the avant-garde manifestos much more closely than the "Justificación" that introduced the first issue of *Que*. According to Francine Masiello, the authors of such manifestoes typically assume the metaphor of militant combativeness in order to assure the loyalty of the fellow "combatants" and to discourage the opposing forces (71). Rhetorically, these manifestoes often follow a two-part structure, first denouncing certain people, ideas, or practices with angry rhetoric and then proposing a new vision and plan of action. While the militant terms adopted by the drafters of this document correspond to the first part of this structure, the second, more constructive or affirmative counterpart is notably lacking.

Furthermore, the speakers' identification with the particularly negative or violent forces of revolt gives this text a tone not common to Latin American manifestoes but surprisingly similar to that of Breton's second manifesto, published earlier that same year (1930).[6] Breton states, for example, that "surrealism was not afraid to make for itself a tenet of total revolt, complete insubordination, of sabotage according to the rule" (*Manifestoes* 125), rhetoric that is echoed by the Argentine group's "protest against every Law or Norm." In both cases, the desired revolt has as its goal the total liberation of the human spirit. Similarly, the *Que* manifesto's rejection of nation and family resonates with Breton's proclamation that "everything remains to be done, every means must be worth trying, in order to lay waste to the ideas of *family, country, religion*" (*Manifestoes* 128). For both the European and the Argentine surrealists, these social institutions represented negative forces that stifled the free exercise of the imagination.

Apart from its relatively dark and violent tone, this last *Que* declaration (like the previously cited "Justificación") echoes in many ways the Latin American manifestoes that proliferated in Argentina, Brazil, Mexico, and other Latin American countries in the period ending approximately in 1930. This text reflects the fundamental problematics of the Latin American *vanguardia*— that is, the often contradictory tensions between constructive and destructive impulses, between the old and the new, and between the autochthonous and the foreign. Paradoxically, while the European avant-garde dismissed its own inherited culture as exhausted or decrepit, the "new" for the Latin American *vanguardistas* was often perceived as emanating from Europe. In a similar paradox, the emergent body of middle-class intellectuals in Latin America in the 1920s and 1930s was in the process of gaining self-consciousness, a process that often involved the vindication of cultural traditions, even as the intelligentsia in Europe was engaged in ongoing literary and artistic parricide. The relative youth of national cultures in America is an important factor here: with scarcely a century of independence from colonial status behind them, these nations tended not to project an exhausted or cynical self-image, but rather a relatively idealistic and forward-looking one. This meant that the Latin American *vanguardistas* were divided between the impulse to create imaginatively, which often meant following ill-fitting European models, and the contrary impulse to consecrate their still-forming national literatures, which meant following traditional but autochthonous models.

The dilemma is a broadly cultural one, but on another level, it is a profoundly existential and personal one. In the case of Aldo Pellegrini's fledgling surrealist group, there is an inescapable irony in the fact that a coterie of medical students declares itself to be antiknowledge, antimoral, anticivilization, and antiprogress. One imagines an uncomfortably bifurcated existence for these educated and idealistic young men who longed to incarnate a spirit of revolt but whose social milieu and chosen profession demanded allegiance to conventional mores. Indeed, their very future as doctors and leaders of the intelligentsia depended on progress in the very spheres of human knowledge they repudiated. Pellegrini and his friends, impassioned by the rhetoric and the ideals of surrealism that reached them in the form of imported texts, are emblematic in many ways of the Latin American *vanguardia*, and their situation is one that would repeat itself in varying modes for each of the surrealist-affiliated writers I will follow in this study.

As numerous commentators have pointed out, the historical avant-garde movements were typically made up of educated white males—the quintessential bourgeoisie of early twentieth-century Europe. The relationship of these men to their class of origin was highly ambivalent: the members of Dada and other avant-garde groups were "economically privileged poets on the warpath" (Strong 29). The historical situation of the Latin American *vanguardia* is further complicated by the lack of a significant and long-standing bourgeoisie that could serve as the object of attack and derision. In the first two decades of the twentieth century, the landed *criollo* oligarchies that had dominated Latin America's economic, social, and political structures since the wars of independence were being steadily displaced by an ascendant middle class. The weakening of the ruling families brought about a demographic shift away from the *latifundias* and toward burgeoning urban centers; it also brought about a new political awareness and concern with social inequalities in the educated class. Each of these factors contributes to the ideological formation of the Latin American *vanguardistas*, who shared their sense of youthful rebellion with their European counterparts but whose lived situations, needs, and strategies for revolt therefore differed in sometimes fundamental ways. In Enrique Pezzoni's terms, they were caught between *decoro* (decency, good taste, stylistic perfection) and *ruptura* (breaking with the past), an ambivalence that he sees as eventually causing the implosion of the movement (13–14). In sum, it is evident that the Latin American *vanguardia* (including Pellegrini's pioneer surrealist group) was generally more conservative than the European avant-garde, enacting a desire for aesthetic novelty and freshness rather than a total rebellion against a bankrupt society.[7]

It was perhaps this schism between the desire for revolt and the very real need to conduct themselves in conscientious and socially responsible ways that led to the demise of the Argentine "surrealist fraternity" a mere four years after its formation. Although the rise and fall of Pellegrini's group was particularly swift, this trajectory points to a characteristic of avant-garde groups on both continents—namely, "the disparity between their radical hopes and their actual achievements" (Strong 2). As we have seen, there is evidence in the texts of *Que* that the members of this group intuited from an early moment the difficulty of bringing about radical change in the society they inhabited. They declare outright in the "Justificación" that "en realidad estamos decididos a no intentar nada fundamental fuera de nosotros" [in reality we are determined not to attempt anything fundamental outside of ourselves] (*Valija* 19). It is for this reason, I believe, that they were drawn to the particularly psychoanalytical and introspective aspects of surrealism. Theirs was from the start a subjective, personalized rebellion, exactly the type of rebellion that would increasingly characterize Bretonian surrealism from the late 1930s onward, as the ideal of political and social progress in Europe slipped farther out of reach.

The third issue of *Que*, which was to have focused on the theme of death, never materialized. The respected and broadly circulated Argentine journal *Sur*, directed by Victoria Ocampo, continued to publish translations of texts by European surrealists such as Breton, Éluard, and de Chirico. But broadly speaking, the decade of the 1930s was one in which political and cultural rigidity in Argentina had a profoundly dampening effect on avant-garde activity. The short-lived experiment carried out by Pellegrini, Piterbarg, and their companions came to an end in 1930. The true "surrealist adventure" in Argentina, reinitiated by Aldo Pellegrini but carried forward by a younger generation, would not begin until the 1950s, a topic to which I will return in Chapters 7 and 8.

CHAPTER 4

Neruda and Anti-Neruda
Chile's Mandrágora Poets

Introduction

Chile was the site of early and influential avant-garde experimentation. In 1916, Vicente Huidobro (1892–1948) published an *ars poetica* that announced his *creacionista* movement, and his long poem "Altazor" (published in 1931, although written much earlier) came to be widely regarded as the culmination of presurrealist avant-garde poetics. Apart from his own highly innovative work, Huidobro opened Chile to the international movements of the day by transporting from Paris and Madrid numerous journals, manifestos, and books. This exposure, together with Huidobro's general militancy in favor of the avant-garde, would stimulate a marked shift in the poetic sensibilities of his contemporaries.

Huidobro's relationship to surrealism as an approach to literary creation was fundamentally a critical one, and his resistance sheds light on the mixed reception of surrealism in Latin America as a whole. As René de Costa points out in his incisive essay "Huidobro y el surrealismo" (1977), the Chilean poet joined many of his European contemporaries in protesting primarily against the practice of automatic writing and the approach to creativity that it implied. Huidobro was present at the birth of surrealism in Paris, and his response was immediate. In 1925, he published a collection of essays in French titled *Manifestes*, in which he states his position regarding the practice of automatism, which turns writers into mere *improvisateurs*: "They are not the masters, but the slaves of their mental imagery" (qtd. in de Costa, "Huidobro" 78). This is the crux of the issue for Huidobro. The idea of entering into a trancelike state and waiting for unconscious images to dictate themselves to the conscious mind was anathema to his aesthetic stance, which championed the creative will of the poet. As de Costa concludes, Huidobro was concerned about the secondary role that surrealism attributed to the creative act (78). At issue was not the *type* of image produced—in fact, surprising, nonrepresentational images had been a commonplace of avant-garde poetics from the start—but rather the state of mind from which such images emerged. Huidobro sounds a call in 1925 that would be often echoed by later Latin American writers. Whether through his direct influence or through other means, the practice of automatic writing across the region would be discarded rather quickly, even as the surrealist image would become firmly established.

In the same year as Huidobro's *Manifestes*, the Chilean poet's younger contemporary Pablo Neruda (1904–73) published *Tentativa del hombre infinito*, a hermetic and little-read collection of poems that is often considered to be the first surrealist-influenced book in Spanish-American literature (Verani 41; Alazraki, "El surrealismo de *Tentativa*" 31–32). For many years, critics perhaps incautiously assumed the importance of surrealism to Neruda's poetics; later critics, however, have been careful not to designate Neruda as a surrealist per se, although most acknowledge the presence of surrealist imagery in much of his early work.[1] Jaime Alazraki explores the surrealist techniques apparent in *Tentativa del hombre infinito*, concluding that Neruda's surrealism is the product of late avant-garde affinities, rather than the direct influence of Breton's group. Alazraki also points out that Neruda's preferred reading list in the early 1920s overlaps that of the surrealists, a factor that he believes accounts for much of what appears as surrealist influence. Nineteenth-century romanticism in general, and in particular Lautréamont, Rimbaud, and Mallarmé, provided Neruda with models for the obscure, visionary poetry that characterizes not only *Tentativa* but also the first two volumes of *Residencia en la tierra* (1935 and 1937), the later works that cemented Neruda's reputation as a major poet.

As Hugo Verani observes, the early Neruda finds in surrealism "a form suitable for representing his chaotic perception of reality, a world view identified with the formless, the indeterminate, the oneiric, the irrational and the sensual, with a boundless and spontaneous vitality" (41). What distinguishes Neruda's early work from orthodox surrealism is the refusal to practice automatism as such: the insistence on revision is paramount to his poetics.[2] The resulting texts often succeed in evoking unconscious or irrational mental processes, to powerful emotional ends. "Breton wanted to capture the voice of the subconscious," says de Costa; "Neruda wanted only to create the style of that voice" (44). We can safely speculate that the emulation of Neruda's poetics by succeeding generations of writers—the phenomenon that came to be known as "Nerudismo"—contributed significantly to a broadly disseminated surrealist *style* in Spanish American poetry, alongside a certain skepticism toward surrealist techniques.

The Mandrágora Group and "Poesía Negra"

Although Neruda dominated the literary scene in Chile from the mid-1920s onward, a Chilean avant-garde movement arose in the 1930s and flourished independently of him—indeed, in keen opposition to him. Neruda's ambivalent or negative response to surrealism was countered by the wholehearted embrace of the French movement on the part of a small but vocal group of Santiago writers anchored in the literary journal *Mandrágora*.

In 1935, almost a decade after Pellegrini had formed his group in Buenos Aires, an important anthology of contemporary poetry brought several *vanguardista* writers to the attention of an eager Chilean readership. The first prologue to the *Antología de poesía chilena nueva*, edited by Volodia Teitelboim and Eduardo Anguita, points to 1925 as the year in which "the new poetry acquires a definitive shape," citing the Argentine journal *Martín Fierro* as a stimulus for the aesthetic of innovation in Chile (Teitelboim 393). In the second prologue to this anthology, the poet Eduardo Anguita identifies *creacionismo* and surrealism as the two "convergent directions" of this vital new literature (395). Although Anguita credits surrealist techniques with the potential to plumb the depths of human consciousness, he cites Breton's own doubts about the practice of automatism by way of asserting that surrealism has not yet found a way to "copy unconscious materials" (396). This prologue signals an important feature of Latin American surrealism: with the exception of Pellegrini's early group, Latin American writers inherited a European surrealism that had already begun to reflect on itself. Thus a self-conscious awareness of its own limitations, an inherent "belatedness," characterizes this aesthetic almost from its inception.

The *Antología de la poesía nueva* featured Huidobro and Neruda as its standard bearers. Certain other poets included in the collection, most notably Pablo de Rokha (1894–1968), Rosamel del Valle (1901–65), and Humberto Díaz Casanueva (1906–92), were loosely associated with the surrealist movement, as they experimented with oneiric imagery and free-associative techniques without fully embracing the Bretonian doctrine. But out of the somewhat amorphous gathering representing the "new poetry" in Chile emerged a group of writers who openly identified themselves as surrealists. This first self-confessed surrealist group gathered around the journal *Mandrágora: Poesía, filosofía, pintura, ciencia, documentos*, whose seven issues saw the light in Santiago between 1938 and 1943.

In the political and economic spheres, the late 1930s and the early 1940s constituted a period of populist and socialist sentiment in Chile, coupled with a widespread sense of solidarity with antifascist movements in Europe. *Mandrágora*'s inaugural year, 1938, was a crucial one. Orlando Jimeno-Grendi draws an explicit connection between the historical context of that moment and the poetic sensibility of the Mandrágora poets:

> Imminent ascent to the government of the Popular Front in Chile; the Spanish Civil War shakes the world; fascism and Nazism undermine the values narcissistically established by the Western bourgeoisie in the forms of traditional democracy. Spengler's prophetic nightmare appears to be fulfilling itself: the West is witnessing the twilight of its culture. The young writers of Mandrágora, who in that climate are reading Ortega y Gasset and forging their thought in the heat of the "isms" of the inter-war period, will be brutally confronted by those intense contradictions . . . It was natural, in the judgment of the Mandrágora group, to feel convulsed by what Jaspers has called limit-situations, and to seek a convulsive form of expression. (110–11)

The evidence of this historically grounded "convulsive" poetics is apparent in the first issue of *Mandrágora*, which ends with a brief section called *No pasarán*—"They shall not pass"—a phrase widely recognized as the Spanish Republican call to arms. In this section the collective voice declares, "Una vez más reafirmamos—ahora desde estas páginas de *Mandrágora*—nuestra fe en la emancipación del glorioso proletariado español y confirmamos nuestra verdadera posición de combate contra el fascismo y sus aliados naturales, el capitalismo y la religión" [We reaffirm—now, from these pages of *Mandrágora*—our faith in the emancipation of the glorious Spanish proletariat, and we confirm our true position of struggle against fascism and its natural allies, capitalism and religion] (qtd. in de Mussy 138).[3] The Chilean historian Luis de Mussy, who has written extensively on the Mandrágora movement, notes the profoundly questioning sensibility that defined this period. He says of the Mandrágora group in particular, "The testimony of these Chilean surrealists was one of total criticism and absolute irony in the face of the socio-cultural structures evident in the society of that time" (13). The combined factors of modernization (particularly in the capital), increasing prosperity and political participation among the Chilean middle class, and the election of the populist and left-leaning president Pedro Aguirre Cerda in 1938 provide the precise context in which the Mandrágora group championed the surrealist principle of human liberty. De Mussy describes the character of this generation of intellectuals in terms of "the spirit of rupture [*el rupturismo*], the drive for transformation, for inquiry, for the consolidation of the new" (24).

Mandrágora's prime mover was Braulio Arenas (1913–88), a prolific poet, novelist, and essayist. Accompanying Arenas in the original group were Teófilo Cid (1914–54) and Enrique Gómez-Correa (1915–95). Among the three, it was Gómez-Correa who—like Aldo Pellegrini—remained faithful to surrealist ideals until his death. A fourth member was Jorge Cáceres (1923–49), who joined the group when he was barely 15 years old and died under mysterious circumstances at the age of 26. Other important collaborators in the journal included Huidobro—with whom the group maintained a dynamic, mostly friendly relationship despite their ideological differences—Fernando Onfray, and Gonzalo Rojas. (The work of Rojas will be considered at length in Chapter 9.)

The Mandrágora group's activities were carried out in relative isolation within Chile until 1942, when Arenas began corresponding with both Benjamín Péret and André Breton. Arenas's "Letter from Chile," published in March of 1943 in the New York surrealist magazine *VVV*, marks the group's conscious shift from the national to the international stage. In this letter, Arenas acts as spokesperson for the Mandrágora group, declaring their solidarity with the international surrealist movement:

> A la hora presente, superados todos los propósitos que dieron vida al grupo Mandrágora, nosotros superamos también nuestra posición nacional y adherimos con entusiasmo a la posición internacional del surrealismo. Al efecto, terminada la trayectoria gloriosa de la Mandrágora, comienza para nosotros otra no menos importante: la trayectoria surrealista. (qtd. in Langowski 214)

> [At the present time, having reached all the goals that gave birth to the Mandrágora group, we move beyond our national position and enthusiastically affiliate ourselves with the international position of surrealism. To this end, with the glorious trajectory of *Mandrágora* having reached its conclusion, another no less important trajectory begins: that of surrealism itself.]

Embracing this international perspective, *Mandrágora* published in translation several European avant-garde writers such as Alfred Jarry, Péret, Éluard, and Breton, as well as reviews of works such as Breton's *L'amour fou* and Éluard's *Cours naturel*. By introducing these texts to an intellectual Southern Cone readership, *Mandrágora* accomplished a feat of literary diffusion that the Argentine journal *Que* had not even attempted. Through their travels and written correspondence, members of the group also established personal contacts and maintained a dialogue with many members of the international surrealist community. In 1948, Jorge Cáceres traveled to Paris, where he collaborated with Breton and other postwar surrealists. Gómez-Correa also spent time in the French capital in 1949–50, as a result of which his books of poetry were illustrated by René Magritte and Jacques Hérold. Within Latin America, the Mandrágora poets maintained literary friendships with Aldo Pellegrini, César Moro, Enrique Molina, and Octavio Paz. All these contacts, coupled with the publication of contemporary French texts in translation, served as important modes of dissemination and cross-fertilization of ideas relating to surrealism.

In addition to the publication of the journal, the Mandrágora group staged readings, lectures, and acts of public protest that Luis de Mussy calls "poetic terrorism" (76). They also published books, including collaborative texts with European surrealists, under the Ediciones Mandrágora imprint. Not content to limit themselves to the literary sphere, they organized surrealist exhibitions in 1941, 1943, and 1948 that included written texts, paintings, collages, and "ready-mades." The last of these exhibitions reflected the increasingly international character of Chilean surrealism, presenting works by Breton, Magritte, Victor Brauner, Hans Arp, André Masson, and Edmund Gorki, alongside Wilfredo Lam from Cuba and Chile's own Roberto Matta.

To this list of activities must be added the occasional public demonstrations by the Mandrágora group, the most infamous of which was the disruption of an homage to Pablo Neruda at the University of Chile in July of 1940. According to *Mandrágora*'s own version of the incident (recounted in the fourth issue, which was published in the same month), Arenas walked on stage and interrupted Neruda's reading, tearing the text from his hands and thereby causing an uproar that effectively brought the event to a close. This was the act that cemented Neruda's disdain for the group and for the organized surrealist movement as such. The tension between the two parties is patent throughout the seven issues of *Mandrágora*.

For Arenas and his cohort, Neruda represented the worst form of literary egotism and self-interested pandering to bourgeois tastes. Since the publication of *Veinte poemas de amor y una canción desesperada* in 1924, Neruda had become a force to be reckoned with in Chile, an imposing figure seen "strutting about Santiago with a long black cape, presiding over literary banquets, and surrounded by bohemian friends" (de Costa, *Poetry* 41). The Mandrágora group, coming of age in the shadow of this black cape, reacted vociferously. In the journal's first issue, they declare it their moral obligation to sketch a portrait of "[el] intrigante número uno, de cierto pez opaco que vive sembrando el odio y la columna" [the number one schemer, a certain opaque fish who lives disseminating hatred and slander] (136). Their vituperative sketch (a prime example of black humor) continues as an uncompromising *ad hominem* attack on Neruda: "Es un hombrecito biscoso [sic] que ha vuelto a América, después de una corta ausencia, sólo a hacerse propaganda y a sembrar la discordia con un grupo policial y un pequeño rebaño de súcubos organizados para desprestigiar a todos los que le hacen sombra al hombrecito, que tiene alma y cuerpo de Bacalao" [He is a slimy little man who has returned to America after a short absence, only to promote himself and to sow discord, with his bodyguards and his little flock of succubi organized to disparage all those who cast a shadow over the little man, who has the soul and the body of a Codfish] (136). The author of this unsigned column casts aspersions not only on Neruda as a person but also on his poetry and his role as poetic spokesman: "Con estos antecedentes y una poesía de tía grasienta se quiere dar humos de poeta de trascendencia Americana, de gran español y hasta de comunista" [With this background and with the poetry of a greasy aunt, he tries to put on airs of a transcendent American poet, of a great Spaniard, and even of a Communist] (136).

The hyperbolic nature of this anti-Neruda rhetoric may be difficult to comprehend for those not immersed in the cultural milieu of Santiago in 1938. Mandrágora's negative assessment of Neruda's poetry appears particularly questionable, given his now-consecrated place as Spanish America's best-known and most-revered poet. From a historical perspective, however, we must take into account the strong public presence and political influence of Neruda and his allies in the Alianza de Intelectuales de Chile, a phenomenon that may have forced the Mandrágora group into a more extreme and polemical stance than they would otherwise have adopted. We might also venture that the group's intransigent opposition to their famous compatriot reflects an uncompromising position vis-à-vis the vanguardist's ethical stance in the world. Called to protest against anything that smacked of hypocrisy, personal myth-making, or the use of art for political ends, the Mandrágora group came to view Neruda as the Goliath against whom they were ethically compelled to fling their rhetorical stones.

Apart from their attacks on Neruda and the literary establishment he had come to embody, the Mandrágora poets express their revolutionary position not through calumny but through a poetics of psychic and linguistic exploration. The journal's recurrent themes, deriving from the romantic arch-themes of imagination and freedom, include madness, love and sexuality, desire in all its manifestations, dreams, the unconscious (and automatism as a means to reveal it), transgression, violence, the occult, non-Christian religions, and poetry itself. The first issue of the journal opens with an extensive essay by Arenas called "Mandrágora, poesía negra" [Mandrake: Black Poetry] that serves as the group's manifesto. The parallels here to the Bretonian manifestos are patent; even more than the proclamations in Pellegrini's *Que*, they underscore the relative orthodoxy that marked surrealism's early appearance in Latin America. Although surrealism per se is not mentioned until the end of the essay, its tenets are evident throughout. Arenas recalls the familiar surrealist triumvirate of love, liberty, and poetry within an indictment of history up to the present moment and a new hope for the future: "Hasta ahora fracasaron ruidosamente las conciliaciones. Se volverá, pues a elegir los nombres vanamente queridos y aborrecibles de poesía, libertad, unidad y placer, dándoseles otros significados; es decir, una clasificación verdadera" [Until now, conciliations have failed sensationally. We will once again choose the vainly loved and detested names of poetry, liberty, unity, and pleasure, giving them other meanings—that is, giving them their true classification] (125).

Like Breton and the Argentine surrealists, Arenas sees the unconscious as the path to authentic existence: "Que el impulso de la submersión en el hondo sueño sea la voz de partida, la voz de alarma" [May the impulse to submerge ourselves in the deep dream be a call to action, a cry of alarm] (125). He speaks of delving into the unconscious as a matter of "optical exercises," reflecting that "si fuera posible cerrar los ojos, con la misma resolución con que se toma un útil de labranza o un cuaderno, se pisaría la tierra firme por primera vez o se escribiría directamente del natural" [if it were possible to close the eyes with the same resolve as when picking up a planting tool or a notebook, we would step for the first time on solid ground or would write directly from our natural disposition] (124). Implicit here is the idea that the inner world, the world that one sees when *closing* the eyes, is the true world, the world of "verdadero ser": true being, unadulterated by rational thought. Arenas does not question this characterization of the unconscious. Nor does he question automatism as a method for reaching the unconscious or for producing poetry, as Huidobro had done in 1925 and as many later Latin American writers would do.

The mandrake plant that gives the journal its title serves as a powerful symbol for Arenas and his cohort. Belonging to the poisonous nightshade family, the mandrake has traditionally been used in magic rituals, due perhaps to its hallucinogenic properties and to the fact that the roots often bifurcate in ways that cause it to resemble a human figure. Arenas explains the group's chosen symbol in hermetic prose that employs the surrealist techniques of free association and unexpected juxtapositions. He depicts the mandrake as

> esa ave marina, esa planta nupcial que da la muerte al que se apodere de ella, la fascinante hada de los suburbios, la que canta canciones de infancia a la puerta de los prostíbulos y al pie de las horcas, y que sin embargo sabe, con un gesto, apartar esa mediocre realidad que la rodea, para dar la vida, la poesía, y el amor a los que cojan con verdadera desesperación frenética un útil de labranza o un cuaderno para arrancarla o describirla, y es con ustedes que puedo exhibir y hacer girar— riesgo y fascinación aparte—esa planta nupcial, símbolo eterno de la poesía negra, la planta de la MANDRÁGORA. (124)

> [that marine bird, that nuptial plant that brings death to the one who takes possession of it, the fascinating fairy of the suburbs, the one who sings children's songs at the door of brothels and at the foot of gallows, and who nevertheless knows how, with a single gesture, to push aside the mediocre reality that surrounds her, in order to give life, poetry, and love to those who seize with true frenetic desperation a planting tool or a notebook in order to tear it out or to describe it, and it is with all of you that I can exhibit and rotate—risk and

fascination aside—that nuptial plant, eternal symbol of black poetry, the plant called the MANDRAGORA.]

Arenas's characterization of the mandrake (a noun marked as marked as feminine in Spanish) is structured around oppositions and irrational connections: it is both a sea bird and a plant, and as a plant it is dually associated with marriage and death. It is, moreover, a fairy—not of mythical forests but of suburbs—who sings for prostitutes and executioners. This heterogeneous characterization prepares the reader for the mandrake's symbolic role in separating "mediocre reality" from that true life sought by the surrealists—life associated, not surprisingly, with love and poetry.

It is important to distinguish the term *poesía negra* in the Mandrágora context from the historical *Négritud* movement, in which poets from France to the Antilles attempted to incorporate the Afro-European or Afro-American experience into avant-garde poetry. Rather than a racial connotation, blackness here points to an esoteric worldview in which the occult forces of language are the primary instrument for revealing hidden truths (or in psychoanalytic terms, the unconscious). This orientation constitutes one of the most salient features of the Chilean group, and it may well have developed in the earliest days of the group's formation in 1932 and 1933, when in their native city of Talca, Arenas, Cid, and Gómez-Correa translated romantic writers such as Goethe, Blake, and Achim von Arnim. Throughout the essay "Mandrágora, poesía negra," we find a semantic field pointing to the "dark side" of romanticism: *negro, noche, terror, nictálope* (pertaining to night vision), *demonio tóxico, visiones sobrenaturales y afrodisíacas*—and finally the mandrake itself, with its legendary aphrodisiac and poisonous properties.

Directly contradicting Huidobro's call for lucid control of the creative process, Arenas considers poetic inspiration "a prophetic dictation," claiming that when it comes to poetry, "es necesario que se apodere de nosotros el furor sagrado inaprehensible por la memoria" [it is necessary for a sacred fury, inapprehensible by memory, to overcome us] (125). This sentence highlights the essay's romantic view of the imagination as a dark and terror-filled place from which poetry springs. The romantic notion of what Arenas calls "the cosmic terror of the imagination" is overlaid here with a surrealist sense of objective chance: "Y si yo defiendo la validez del terror como sentido poético, es porque él nos permite vivir en pánico, es decir, vivir alertas, vivir despiertos, vivir acechando lo desconocido a cada segundo" [And if I defend the validity of terror as a poetic sensibility, it is because it allows us to live in panic—that is, to live alert, to live wide-awake, to live ready to ambush the unknown at every moment] (125). This passage clearly evokes Breton's claim that the mind can productively call on "fear, the attraction of the unusual, chance, [and] the taste for things extravagant" (*Manifestoes* 16). It also underscores the profound enthusiasm with which the Mandrágora poets embraced not only the creative but also the existential promise of surrealism, the desire to "live alert" even when that state implied discomfort, fear, or even "panic."

Ultimately, nineteenth-century romanticism and twentieth-century surrealism are fused in Arenas's free-associative lyrical summary of "poesía negra":

> He aquí el terror, la muerte por asfixia, la mujer amarrada a los cuatro horizontes y desgarrada físicamente. He aquí el nombre repentino de POESÍA con su fugacidad desgarrante. Ella es NEGRA como la noche, como la memoria, como el placer, como el terror, como la libertad, como la imaginación, como el instinto, como la belleza, como el conocimiento, como el automatismo, como la videncia, como la nostalgia, como la nieve, como la capital, como la unidad, como el árbol, como la vida, como el relámpago. (126)

> [Here is terror, death by asphyxiation, the woman tied to the four horizons and physically ripped apart. Here is the sudden name of POETRY with its brazen fleetingness. She is BLACK like the night, like memory, like pleasure, like terror, like freedom, like the imagination, like instinct, like beauty, like knowledge, like automatism, like clairvoyance, like nostalgia, like snow, like the capital, like unity, like the tree, like life, like lightning.]

As these passages and others in "Mandrágora, poesía negra" suggest, the Chilean group's overall orientation was darker and less effervescent than that of other manifestations of surrealism, both in Europe and in other Latin American countries. The *Mandrágora* texts draw from nineteenth-century romanticism not only in the appeal to psychic darkness but also in their call for extreme, even violent, responses to bourgeois rigidity. In an essay titled "Yo hablo desde Mandrágora" [I speak from Mandrágora] in the journal's second issue, Gómez-Correa goes as far as to posit the call to revolt in terms of a cosmic battle between the human subject and the objective world. In this moment of intense conflict, he claims, man either submits to his own annihilation or he enters into battle with the forces of evil, risking everything (144).

We have seen that for those participating in the European avant-garde, the rigid forms of bourgeois life evoked sometimes violent responses, although this violence was typically one of attitude and language more than of action. As Osorio, Unruh, Strong, and others have convincingly demonstrated, in the relatively younger nations of Latin America the situation was further complicated by the fact that the object of protest was less well defined or more ambivalently related to the protesters than was the case in Europe. The third issue of *Mandrágora* (June 1940) opens with an extensive essay by Gómez-Correa titled "Notas sobre la poesía negra en Chile" [Notes on Black Poetry in Chile], in which he identifies the very lack of an American poetic tradition as one of the fundamental problems facing his generation. Young writers in Europe, he claims, have had something to hurl their cries of protest against, something to spit upon, something to destroy; in contrast, the young generations of the Americas have little or no native culture [*cultura autóctona*] to which they can respond (155). Gómez-Correa cites Edgar Allan Poe as the only true poet in the American tradition, and then (with certain reservations) he adds Walt Whitman and the Nicaraguan *modernista* Rubén Darío to this sparse list. The rest, he says despairingly, is false classicism, false romanticism, and hopeless academism (155). If the past is a vacuum, so is the present: those who participate in the contemporary literary scene find themselves drowning in "un mar de calumnias y de pequeñas discusiones de café" [a sea of slander and petty arguments in cafés] (155). Into this vacuum, says Gómez-Correa, surrealism swept as a refreshing new aesthetic vision: "Para nosotros, el surrealismo es lo que para Baudelaire fue el romanticismo: la expresión más reciente de la belleza" [Surrealism is to us what romanticism was to Baudelaire: the newest expression of beauty] (156, n. 1).

The remainder of "Notas sobre la poesía negra" examines certain principles of orthodox surrealism: the struggle against anything that curtails human liberty; the promise of psychoanalysis; and love, madness, and dreams as "la médula misma de la vida" [the very marrow of life] (157). Evoking Rimbaud and the entire platform of the nineteenth-century *poètes maudits*, he declares that "puesto que la crueldad, el vicio, el crimen, el mal congénito, la violencia, sirven para poner en evidencia la vida, es señal que ellos no son sus contrarios. Por la inversa, la práctica de estos actos implica una intensificación de vitalidad" [since cruelty, vice, crime, congenital evil, and violence serve to place life in relief, this is a sign that they are not its opposites. Quite the contrary, the practice of these acts implies an intensification of vitality] (157). This passage confirms once again the Chilean group's location on a line of dark romanticism that passes from Sade, Baudelaire, and Lautréamont through Gilles de Rais and Georges Bataille. The principle of affirming life by denigrating anything that leads to its stagnation implies that only total revolt will serve to reinstate life in its authentic forms: "Por eso estamos contra la burguesía, contra el fascismo—mientras éste sirva de protección a las instituciones eternizadas por el régimen capitalista—contra la familia, contra las leyes, contra la religion, contra la moral y contra los revolucionarios de pacotilla" [This is why we are against the bourgeoisie, against fascism—to the extent that it serves to protect those institutions eternalized by the capitalist regime—against family, against laws, against religion, against morality, and against petty revolutionaries] (159). Implicit in this extreme rhetoric of protest is the same dilemma that had faced Pellegrini's group in Argentina a decade earlier: for young men of education and means, it was easier to draw up manifestoes of total rebellion than to actually practice lawlessness, rejection of family, or amoral behavior in general.[4] Political alignments with anticapitalist and antifascist causes were more practicable, and *Mandrágora* makes several frank pronouncements to this effect. Beyond this, their revolutionary energy was largely channeled into poetry itself.

Lyric poems are an important component of *Mandrágora*'s texts, most of which were written by the members of the Chilean group or by European surrealists. Given the faith in automatic writing articulated in the theoretical texts, it comes as no surprise that most of the poems are highly imagistic, stripped of narrative or discursive elements, and hermetic in nature. I cite two brief examples here, beginning with Jorge Cáceres's "El azar negro" [Black Chance] from *Mandrágora* No. 3 (June 1940):

> En mis pies luchaban el bien y el mal
> Pequeña lámpara del gran día negro
> Que humedece su espejo de alondras
> Yo llenaba mis cabellos de plumajes invisibles
> Cuando la mujer del tercer día cruzó la calle 62
> Fue repentinamente
> Los cabellos de sus senos se hacían invisibles
> Para que la boca vele el sabor de los labios
> El sol que me habla ya no la conocía después
> Ese sol de sales cenicientas ya no hila
> El sol que tú llevas es lo que yo ignoro
> Mendiga de sonrisas
> Esas manos de granito
> Que acarician demasiado tarde
> Que yo dejé al pasar. (161)

[Good and evil battled in my feet / Little lamp of the great black day / That dampens its mirror of larks / I was filling my hair with invisible plumage / When the woman of the third day crossed 62nd Street / It happened suddenly / The hair of her breasts turned invisible / So that her mouth might veil the taste of her lips // The sun that speaks to me now did not know her after that / That sun of ashen salts no longer spins its cloth / The sun you carry is what I ignore / Beggar woman of smiles / Those granite hands / Caressing too late / That I left behind as I passed.]

The poem's title, "El azar negro," links the French surrealist *hasard objectif* with the adjective *black*, Mandrágora's preeminent qualifier. The poem alludes to a female figure reminiscent of Breton's Nadja, whose actions and conditions seem arbitrary or inexplicable: she crosses a city street and her breast hair turns invisible. She appears to exist in conflictive or tragic relation to the lyric speaker, since the hands' caress comes "too late." The poem places this enigmatic collection of images in a framework marked as the battle between good and evil, but it does not clarify which players in this mythic battle are represented by the speaker and the mysterious woman. The reader is left with an affective impression of loss, bewilderment, or disillusionment, but with no clear narrative to bind these negative sensibilities.

A poem by Gonzalo Rojas in the sixth issue (September 1941) evokes erotic desire in a much more transparent way, recalling the Bretonian *amour fou* by placing erotic love in a context that undermines traditional values. I cite here only the first two of the four stanzas that comprise "La novia infame" [The Vile Bride]:

> Amada vende tu cuerpo al azar
> Al fastidio y al frenesí
> Tus ojos hijos de mi corrupción
> La vejez de mis lágrimas malditas
> Perlas para tu práctica elegancia
> Tu elegancia de perra perseguida
> Por un cadáver de amor corporal
> Y por el otro que soy
>
> El infierno es tu cuerpo para mí
> La podredumbre en traje de sortija
> La novia espiritual
> Quién va a librarte de mi esclavitud
> Perversa de carácter fratricida
> Negra hermosura inútil
> Tu sangre corre por mi voluntad
> Puedes reír
> Puedes bailar
> Te permito hacer y renacer
> Reina mía desnuda encadenada (190)

[Beloved, sell your body to chance / To disgust and to frenzy / Your eyes children of my corruption / The old age of my accursed tears / Pearls for your practical elegance / Your elegance of a bitch hunted / By a cadaver of corporal love / And by the other that I am // Hell is your body for me / Decay in a bejeweled dress / Spiritual bride / Who will free you from my slavery / Perverse and fratricidal / Black and useless beauty / Your blood runs through my will / You can laugh / You can dance / I let you create and be reborn / Queen of mine, naked and enchained]

In contrast to the previously cited poem by Cáceres, this poem reads much less like an automatic text; indeed, the poet maintains control over the poem in the way his speaker maintains control over the woman he addresses. "La novia infame" is surrealist in theme—featuring love or eroticism beyond the bounds of "good taste" or orthodox Judeo-Christian ethics—and its insistence on certain terms such as *corrupción*, *malditas*, *infierno*, and *perversa* tie it to the Baudelairian tradition of decadent poetry.

Rojas's use of poetic devices (which in many cases are lost in translation) tighten the poem's rhetoric. In the first line, for instance, the phrase *al azar* means "at random," but Rojas ties this prepositional phrase to the two that follow—"Al fastidio y al frenesí"—creating a string of objects to which the *novia* is asked to sell her body (the first being "to chance"). The alliteration of the *p* creates a hammering effect in the lines "Perlas para tu práctica elegancia / Tu elegancia de perra perseguida," and the repetition of the final *a* in the line "Reina mía desnuda encadenada" suggests an obsessive, melancholy rhythm. In short, "La novia infame" stands as evidence that the Mandrágora poets were capable of tremendous craft and precision in fashioning poetry that was surrealist in theme and in free-associative techniques. This is the brand of surrealism that would outlast the relatively brief life of organized surrealist groups in Latin America.

Mandrágora's fifth and sixth issues contain only poetry and brief editorial notes and announcements: by 1940, the era of proclamations, attacks, and defensive postures had passed. Both internal divisions and the new and terrifying reality of the Second World War brought shifts in the journal's direction. The seventh and final issue of *Mandrágora*, published in 1943, became the mouthpiece for one lone writer and editor, Enrique Gómez-Correa. This issue comprises a single 16-page essay, into which Gómez-Correa inserts his own poems as well as texts by Arenas, Rosamel del Valle, Jorge Cáceres, and Teófilo Cid. Bearing the title "Testimonio de un poeta negro" [Testimony of a Black Poet], the essay reiterates the now-familiar call to throw down the old order: "Las doctrinas, el mundo total de las ideas hasta ahora conocidas, debe ser arrastrado al más absoluto descrédito" [Every doctrine, the entire world of ideas known until now, should be dragged into total discredit] (196). And poetry is to be the instrument of this cultural upheaval.

Echoing the surrealist conflation of poetry and life, Gómez-Correa proclaims that "la poesía negra debe invadir toda nuestra vida, dominar todos nuestros actos cotidianos" [black poetry should invade all of life, dominate all our daily acts] (197). Apparently compelled to justify his solo act in this publication, he explains the group's internal rifts in terms of the enormity of Mandrágora's endeavor: "Pensad tan solo en todos esos ejemplares de una auténtica juventud que no han tenido las suficientes fuerzas para resistir la enorme tensión espiritual y de sacrificio que ha significado permanecer fiel a la actividad proclamada por la Mandrágora, y han quedado perdidos al lado del camino" [Think only of all those exemplars of an authentic youth who have not had enough strength to resist the enormous spiritual tension and sense of sacrifice inherent in staying faithful to the activity proclaimed by Mandrágora, and who have fallen by the wayside] (207). The essay ends with a final succinct affirmation, quasi-religious in tone: "Yo me siento poseído por el entusiasmo" [I feel possessed by enthusiasm] (209).

It is tempting to see this testimony as the swan song of the Mandrágora group, and several critics have adopted this largely negative view. In his 1994 book *Vanguardia literaria: Ruptura y restauración en los años treinta*, Sergio Vergara notes that issues 5 and 6 contain no theoretical texts and no foreign collaborators; he concludes from this evidence that "a double movement toward the interior of the group is brought about, which leads to a solipsism" (223). Vergara and Klaus Meyer-Minnemann end their review of the seventh issue with a categorical judgment: "The final isolation of *Mandrágora* could not have been more perfect" (63).

Taking a contrary stance, Susan Foote's article "El surrealismo en Chile y la revista *Leitmotiv*" argues convincingly that the demise of *Mandrágora* as a publication does not point to the group's dissolution but rather to its reorientation. The evidence of this shift in focus is the appearance of *Leitmotiv: Boletín de hechos & ideas*, which was published in December of 1942 (no. 1) and again in December of 1943 (nos. 2 and 3). Notably, the majority of *Leitmotiv*'s Chilean contributors are the former members of the Mandrágora group. Directed by Braulio Arenas, this journal represents in many ways a *Mandrágora* come of age. Though still clearly dedicated to surrealist principles, it had broadened its scope and dropped almost entirely its association with *la poesía negra*—a decision that undoubtedly prompted Gómez-Correa's solo act for the final issue of *Mandrágora*. Contrary to Vergara's argument that the Mandrágora group solipsistically folded in on itself, Foote asserts that in *Leitmotiv* these writers seek "almost desperately a tactical change in response to the new historical juncture represented by the Second World War" (44).

Toward a Reassessment of the Mandrágora Movement

The last organized act of the Chilean surrealist group was an international art exhibition at the Dédalo gallery in Santiago in 1948. In the realm of Chilean visual arts, the star of Roberto Matta was rising, and this exhibition helped to solidify his reputation. (Matta was one of the few plastic artists from Latin America to participate fully in the international surrealist movement and to exercise a considerable influence over painters worldwide.) But in the literary sphere, the enthusiasm evinced by Gómez-Correa was on the decline. Although Arenas introduced a new surrealist-affiliated journal called *Gradiva* in 1952, it soon became clear that the cultural impetus necessary to sustain any collective surrealist activity in Chile had waned.

What mark, if any, did the Mandrágora group leave on the literary culture of its time? Responses to this question by critics both inside and outside of Chile differ widely. In Meyer-Minnemann and Vergara's largely negative assessment, "the political, social and literary context of Chile in this period obviously could not sanction a poetic project with proposals so radical that in the end they proved to be incompatible with any other venture" (69). These critics go on to argue that in light of this cultural incompatibility, the literary and sociopolitical effects of Mandrágora's presence appear relatively insignificant (69). The poet and novelist Enrique Lihn, one of the outstanding figures of the subsequent generation of writers, largely shares this negative view, lamenting that Mandrágora merely duplicated the hermetic nature of European surrealism. As a poet fundamentally concerned with communicating with the reader, Lihn faults the Mandrágora writers for employing "a language of little or no cultural resonance in our country, not even in the literary environment" ("El surrealismo en Chile" 95).

It seems reasonable to surmise, along with these critics, that one of the problems facing the Mandrágora group was that of diffusion: like the pioneer group in Argentina, their publications and activities reached a limited audience and therefore their message had minimal impact. But if we distinguish between the question of immediate impact and that of longer-term effects, Mandrágora's presence in Chile emerges as a more complex phenomenon. Though little attention may have been paid to their demonstrations or their publications in the 1930s and 1940s, the group can be credited with initiating a significant, albeit slow and subtle, shift in Chilean literary culture. This is the stance taken by the respected critic Cedomil Goic, who asserts that in retrospect we can view the Mandrágora group as "a guiding force for its generation" (22). Gonzalo Rojas credits Mandrágora with introducing a certain rigor of diction into Chilean poetry and for "that opening toward a world beyond the village, far beyond what we saw as the trap represented by the homegrown [*criollo*] style of the period" (J. Piña 104). In similar terms, Ludwig Zeller, a poet and collage artist who joined the group toward the end of its official existence but who maintained longstanding literary friendships with its members, credits the movement with bringing foreign literatures to the attention of the Chilean reading public and for "allowing a freedom of vision and poetic expression, the possibility of an autonomy from the political sphere" (personal interview). Perhaps Mandrágora's greatest vindicator is Octavio Paz, who charges that in Latin America as a whole, the critical response to the group and its work has been clouded by indifference and "hostile silence." In Paz's own view, "the attitude of the Chilean surrealists was exemplary: not only did they have to confront conservative groups and the 'black guard' of the Catholic Church, but also the Stalinists and Neruda" ("Sobre el surrealismo hispanoamericano" 12). Paz thus praises the radical nature of the group's acts and their written work, dismissing the question of any immediate social effect.

To these testimonials I would add the fact that the Mandrágora group initiated or reinstated a dialogue with contemporary Latin American and European intellectuals, a dialogue that would become crucial to writers of the 1950s and 1960s. This internationalist orientation meant that in spite of their chosen romantic genealogy, which can be perceived as anachronistic, the Mandrágora writers participated in the forward-looking *esprit nouveau* that characterized the avant-garde movements. By promoting cosmopolitan and antiprovincial views, and by fervently opposing the official literary culture of the period, these writers introduced a note of modernity into the Chilean cultural milieu of the day.

CHAPTER 5

Peru
The Surrealist Space between Mariátegui and Vallejo

Introduction

In Argentina and Chile, as we have seen, a fairly orthodox surrealism was promoted in the 1920s and 1930s by small groups of fervent believers. These groups, headed by Aldo Pellegrini in Buenos Aires and by Braulio Arenas and Enrique Gómez-Correa in Santiago, published journals and promoted literary activity based on the principles of automatism and the subversion of social and cultural norms. The Argentine and Chilean groups each existed for only a brief span of years, and their impact on contemporary literature in their respective countries was limited. Yet the reach of their influence over younger generations of writers was arguably quite significant—a subject I will explore more thoroughly in later chapters. Although cohesive surrealist groups did not materialize during this early period in other Spanish American countries, certain individual thinkers and writers with ties to the French movement served as important conduits for surrealist thought.

Peru in the early twentieth century was a largely rural and oligarchical country where late-romantic and *modernista* literary modes still persisted. In the uneven evolution from *modernismo* to *la vanguardia* in Peru, the poet José María Eguren (1874–1942) stands as an important intermediary. Américo Ferrari in fact sees Eguren as a clear precursor to the surrealists, given the oneiric quality of his images and the thematic concern with *lo maravilloso* apparent in many poems. Widely considered to be Peru's premier symbolist poet, though most accurately placed among the late *modernistas*, Eguren himself was aware of "a new breath and a new light in the artistic current" (qtd. in Ferrari 212), and he actively supported the poetic development of younger poets such as César Vallejo, César Moro, and Emilio Adolfo Westphalen. His texts are populated with phantasmagoric forms and landscapes, nocturnal scenes, marine plants and animals, and figures that appear and disappear as in dreams. The highly imaginative, nonmimetic, and even ludic quality of his work set him apart from his contemporaries, most notably the popular poet José Santos Chocano, most of whom practiced declamatory styles within narrowly nationalistic themes.

Broadly speaking, the conservative intellectual and social atmosphere in Lima was hostile to avant-garde thinking and expression. According to Mirko Lauer, "In Peru the poetic avant-garde was an embattled attempt to modernize in a place where practically everything denied modernity" (77). As in other Latin American countries, the antiaristocratic forces rooted in the emergent middle class were ill prepared or insufficiently motivated to carry out a full-blown cultural revolution. Thus the spirit of revolt associated with the avant-garde touched a select few and enjoyed a certain success for a number of years but failed to produce native-born movements of consequence. Most Peruvian writers in the decades of the 1920s and 1930s were intrigued by experimental techniques, but only a few developed full identities as *vanguardistas*, and vanguardism as a whole failed to bring about significant changes in the cultural life of the nation.

The small Peruvian avant-garde that did exist was a largely politicized group. Reacting against the urban-oriented plutocracy that characterized the long presidency of Augusto B. Leguía (1908–12 and 1919–30), they sought an alignment with leftist politics. This alignment provided fervor and energy, but it may also have limited the scope of aesthetic experimentation, reducing literature in some cases to pamphleteering. Moreover, in these decades the Marxist orientation was not yet deeply felt as a national phenomenon: prior to 1930, there was in Peru no Communism per se, and the Bolshevik revolution was "a piece of news, but not a lived experience" (Lauer 80). Finally, it is worth noting that as a nation with a large but historically marginalized indigenous population, Peru in the early twentieth century struggled to reconcile this native social and ethnic reality with cosmopolitan currents of thought. In certain writers, an *indigenista* orientation (an attempt to examine and ascribe value to native cultures) existed alongside an enthusiasm for experimental techniques largely imported from Europe. Lauer argues in fact that it was among the *indigenista* writers, especially Gamaliel Churata (Arturo Peralta) and his brother Alejandro Peralta, that Peruvian *vanguardismo* had the most powerful and long-lasting effect (77). Churata, as I noted in the Introduction, was the author of *El pez de oro*, a fully vanguardist novel that displays a mixture of indigenist and surrealist modes. Among other important vanguardist texts produced in Peru in the decade of the 1920s, a short list would include César Vallejo's groundbreaking collection *Trilce* (1922), Alberto Hidalgo's *Simplismo* (1925), Alejandro Peralta's *Ande* (1926), Carlos Oquendo de Amat's *5 metros de poesía* (1927), and Martín Adán's novel *La casa de cartón*, also heavily influenced by surrealism. Vanguardist literary journals of note included *Boletín Titikaka* (1926–31), *Trampolín-Timonel-Rascacielos-Hangar* (1926–27), and most important, *Amauta* (1926–30). In the following pages I will take up the important question of surrealism's relationship to *Amauta* and to its influential founder.

José Carlos Mariátegui and the Journal *Amauta*

The story of surrealist literature in Peru begins with Latin America's greatest twentieth-century political philosopher, José Carlos Mariátegui. Mariátegui was born into poverty in 1894; he suffered from chronic ill health and died in 1930 at the age of 35. In this short span, however, he managed to revolutionize Peruvian political and social thought and to exercise enormous influence over the intellectual life of his nation and of Latin America as a whole. An avowed Marxist, Mariátegui endeavored to open Peru's conservative, provincial society to revolutionary currents of thought and artistic expression. Trained early as a journalist (with an avocation for poetry), he entered into active political life in 1918. The turmoil following the reelection of Leguía to the presidency in 1919 forced Mariátegui into exile in Europe, where he traveled widely and witnessed the cultural ferment taking place in the years just after World War I. Upon his return to Peru in 1923, Mariátegui assumed the editorial direction of the important journal *Claridad* and began teaching, lecturing widely, and publishing political essays. In addition to the establishment of the Socialist Party of Peru in 1928, his most important contribution to Peruvian intellectual life was the journal *Amauta*, which was published under his direction between 1926 and 1930.

Amauta, which Jorge Schwartz calls the most important organ of Peruvian culture in the 1920s, promoted both *lo nuevo* and the reevaluation of Peru's indigenous culture in terms of national cohesion and progress (329). *Amauta*'s double-edged program thus embodies a common Latin American vanguardist approach: it was liberal in its search for new modes of cultural expression, but conservative in its embrace of pre-Hispanic values within an ideology of nation-building. Its eclectic concerns ran from politics to history to art, and it supported various manifestations of the international and Latin American literary avant-garde, in particular surrealism. Américo Ferrari claims in fact that *Amauta* constitutes an outstanding guide to the history of Peruvian poetry at that moment in the early twentieth century (218). In its scarce four years of existence, *Amauta* published approximately two hundred texts by more than fifty poets—most of whom were Peruvian, but who represented other countries as well—in an eclectic mix that reflected several new trends in Latin American expression.

In the opening sentences of his essay "Presentación de *Amauta*," published in the first issue in September of 1926, Mariátegui set forth the intellectually independent character of the journal and its adherence to the *zeitgeist* of the times: "Esta revista, en el campo intelectual, no representa un grupo. Representa, más bien, un movimiento, un espíritu. En el Perú, se siente desde hace algún tiempo una corriente, cada día más vigorosa y definida, de renovación" [This journal represents no single group within the intellectual field. Rather, it represents a movement, a spirit. In Peru we have felt for some time now a certain current of renovation, which is every day more vigorous and well-defined] (333). In spite of Marátegui's Marxist-Leninist convictions, the journal (whose title means in Quechua "wise man" or "counselor") was not narrowly ideological; on the contrary, it opened a space for genuine debate on numerous national and international issues. It was broadly disseminated beyond the borders of Peru, especially in Mexico and Argentina.

Mariátegui holds an important place in the history of Latin American surrealism because of the admiration he frankly expressed for the movement's ideals in his writings and for his inclusion in *Amauta* of the work of young writers such as Xavier Abril, Martín Adán, and César Moro. Estuardo Núñez makes the claim that "the early reception of surrealism in Peru is due to the manifest sympathy that this movement awakened in the restless mind of José Carlos Mariátegui and to his actions, which stimulated the concerns of the young poets of that period" ("Recepción" 40). In July of 1926, less than two years after the publication of Breton's first *Manifesto* and in the same year that the first surrealist group gathered in Buenos Aires, Mariátegui published a vindication of surrealism as a broad cultural, spiritual, and political movement:

> La insurrección suprarrealista entra en una fase que prueba que este movimiento no es un simple fenómeno literario, sino un complejo fenómeno espiritual. No una moda artística sino una protesta del espíritu. Los suprarrealistas pasan del campo artístico al campo político. Denuncian y condenan no sólo las transacciones del arte con el decadente pensamiento burgués. Denuncian y condenan, en bloque, la civilización capitalista. (*El artista y la épocaa* 42)

> [The surrealist insurrection is entering a phase that proves that this movement is not a simple literary phenomenon, but a complex spiritual phenomenon. Not an artistic fashion but a protest of the spirit. The surrealists are moving from the artistic camp into the political camp. They denounce and condemn not only the intercourse of art with decadent bourgeois thought; they denounce and condemn capitalist civilization as a whole.]

Having been exposed to the literary and artistic avant-garde in Europe between 1919 and 1923, Mariátegui followed these movements closely on his return to Lima. Like Pellegrini, he saw in surrealism a set of principles that he believed could produce a necessary "protest of the spirit" on South American soil, and like Pellegrini he worked assiduously to bring that protest to fruition. He seems to have been aware, however, of certain misperceptions that accompanied surrealism's introduction into Latin America. In 1930, Mariátegui affirmed the arduous discipline that characterizes surrealist practice:

> A los que en esta América tropical se imaginan el suprarrealismo como un libertinaje, les costará mucho trabajo, les será quizás imposible admitir esta afirmación: que es una penosa disciplina . . . Pero insisto absolutamente, en la calidad rara—inasequible y vedada al snobismo, a la simulación—de la experiencia y del trabajo de los suprarrealistas. (*El artista y la época* 43)
>
> [For those who in this tropical America imagine surrealism to be pure licentiousness, it will take a great effort, and perhaps it will be impossible, to admit this affirmation: that it is a laborious discipline . . . But I absolutely insist on the rare quality—unattainable and off-limits to snobbery, to pretense—of the experience and the work of the surrealists.]

It is clear from this passage that Mariátegui felt compelled to adopt a defensive posture against those in "tropical America" who saw surrealism as frivolous or "licentious."

Between 1926 and 1930, notes published in *Amauta* followed all the principle developments in the evolution of French surrealism. Notably, although the resources of *Amauta* guaranteed a much broader readership than Pellegrini could achieve with the journal *Que*, the Peruvian intelligentsia of the 1920s proved as resistant as their Argentine counterparts to the absorption of avant-garde ideas that were foreign in origin. An attitude of insularity and a desire to promote autochthonous literature and art in Peru may explain why a surrealist movement never materialized there as it did in other countries. Yet despite the lack of an organized movement, surrealism became part of the intellectual and aesthetic dialogue of the day. Several of the poets whose work saw the light in the pages of *Amauta* would align themselves with surrealism, and one of them—César Vallejo—would raise a resounding cry against it. In the next section, I trace certain developments in the work of Xavier Abril, César Moro, and Emilio Adolfo Westphalen, all poets whose work carries the mark of surrealist attitudes and techniques, before considering Vallejo's radical rejection of surrealism.

The Peruvian Surrealists

Xavier Abril

Xavier Abril (1905–90) was the first writer of the Andean region to have direct contact with European surrealism and to disseminate its values both as a poet and as a literary critic. His older brother, Pablo Abril, an enthusiastic promoter of art and literature, introduced Xavier to the world of avant-garde letters, and in particular to César Vallejo, whose work Abril would be the first to study extensively. Abril traveled to Europe in 1925, where he threw himself into the contemporary literary scene. In 1927 he presented his poetry (accompanied by a prologue written by Vallejo) in an exposition at the Casa de América Latina in Paris, in conjunction with the paintings of the Peruvian surrealist artist Juan Devéscovi. Having seen Abril's poetry in this exposition, Breton wrote a commentary that was later reprinted in *Amauta*, in which he compares Abril's adolescent rapture with that of the "iluminados" Rimbaud, Lautréamont, and Jarry. Taking note of Abril's Peruvian origins, Breton praises "that country that astonished us in high school, with its singing birds, its jungles, and the mountain ranges of its history" (Mariátegui, *Amauta* 18: 84). Ricardo Silva-Santisteban notes wryly that Breton, who did not read Spanish, could hardly have given an accurate appraisal of Abril's work (81). It is also apparent from his commentary that Breton took Abril's work as an excuse to comment in vague and exoticizing terms about Perú, much as he would later do in Mexico.

Reestablished in Lima in 1928, Abril began a fertile period of collaboration in widely read literary journals such as *Variedades* and *Mundial*, but especially in *Amauta*. In the years between 1924 and 1930, Abril identifies himself as an admirer of surrealism, and his poetry shows direct surrealist influence. In a poetic prose text, Abril boasts of his own role in bringing avant-garde trends to Peru, simultaneously acknowledging the profound influence that Mariátegui's revolutionary politics had exercised over him:

> Yo he traído a la poesía sudamericana el *surmenage*, la taquicardia (1926), el temblor, el pathos, "el terror al espacio" (1927). Después de mis primeros ensayos y experimentos literarios (1923–1925), hice un viaje a Europa. Asistí al debate del *Surréalisme*; pero a mi vuelta al Perú (1928), me ganó la revolución, el marxismo, en la prédica de Mariátegui. (*Poesía soñada* 49)[1]

> [I have brought to South American poetry nervous breakdowns, tachycardia (1926), tremors, pathos, "the fear of space" (1927). After my first literary attempts and experiments (1923–1925), I made a trip to Europe. I witnessed the debate over *Surréalisme*, but on my return to Peru (1928), I was won over by the revolution, by Marxism, in the teachings of Mariátegui.]

From Abril's language here ("me ganó la revolución") we can infer that in contrast to Mariátegui, he questioned whether experimental poetics and revolutionary politics could coexist peacefully. One seemed destined, in his view, to win out over the other. His own creative work shows evidence of this questioning as early as 1928 and gradually shifts away from a surrealist poetics and toward a more direct Marxist engagement.

Abril's early essay "Estética del sentido en la crítica nueva" [The Aesthetic of Sense in the New Criticism], which was published in *Amauta* in 1929, serves as a kind of Peruvian surrealist manifesto. In it Abril adopts the first-person plural perspective common to avant-garde manifestoes, in this case invoking a collective "we the surrealists":

> Los más nuevos, los surréalistes, queremos un cinema del sueño. Para ello hace falta una vida del sueño. Una cultura del sueño. No pasarán muchos años para que este deseo se realice coincidiendo exactamente con la madurez—¿Clasicismo?—del arte nuevo, y entonces sean las obras de Freud, los diccionarios de esta sensibilidad hoy incomprendida por los gordos suicidas del mundo. (Mariátegui, *Amauta* 24: 52)
>
> [We the newcomers, the *surrealists*, desire a cinema of dream. For this, one needs a life of dream. A culture of dream. Not many years will pass before this desire is realized, coinciding exactly with the coming of age—the Classicism?—of the new art, and then the works of Freud will become the dictionaries of this sensibility which is today misunderstood by the uncouth suicides of the world.]

In an obvious surrealist gesture, Abril directly connects creativity to dream-life and individual dream-life to a broader "culture of dream." Like Breton he manifests a prophetic optimism about the future of recent developments in art, and he connects the new sensibility to the revelatory potential of the unconscious. One striking element here is the link between dream states and the cinema. It is interesting to note that Abril's piece was published in 1929, the very year that Luis Buñuel and Salvador Dalí produced their quintessentially surrealist film *Un chien andalou*. Whether or not Abril was aware of this or other surrealist films, it is clear that he is voicing an increased awareness among surrealists internationally in the power of the visual oneiric image.

The title of Abril's first major publication, *Hollywood* (1931), reiterates his interest in films as an emblem of creative consciousness. The book is subtitled *Relatos contemporáneos* and contains five sections of imaginative prose. In the first, "Autobiografía o invención," Abril calls attention to his place of origin: "Nací en 1906, en Sudamérica" [I was born in 1906, in South America] (15). He develops his poeticized autobiography in terms that explain both the book's title and his early adherence to surrealism:

84 • Surrealism in Latin American Literature

> La enfermedad del sueño completó mi técnica poética . . . ¡Qué bien se está en el sueño, bajo los sótanos marinos, entre las algas, como en aquarium [sic]! Se es completamente pez. Una verdadera felicidad . . . Para mí la vida sigue siendo un continuado *film* de sueño. El Hollywood del sueño. Esto no deja de ser una felicidad y un dolor. (17)
>
> [The dream illness completed my poetic craft . . . How wonderful to be in the dream, beneath the vaults of the sea, among the algae, as in an aquarium! One is completely a fish. True happiness . . . For me, life has not ceased being a continuous dream-film. A dream Hollywood. This is in fact both a joy and an affliction.]

Apart from the patently surrealist insistence on the dream state, this passage evinces the surrealist technique of unexpected juxtapositions with its fluid semantic shifts between illness, marine life, and the trope of Hollywood films. Abril's claim that to inhabit the dream state is to be "completely a fish"—and happily so—recalls Breton's comment that "the mind of the man who dreams is fully satisfied by what happens to him" (*Manifestoes* 13).

Hollywood was followed by two volumes of poetry: *Difícil trabajo*, published in 1935 but incorporating poems dating back to 1927, and *Descubrimiento del alba* in 1937. Both volumes contain poems of a surrealist character as well as other more politically motivated and technically simplified compositions. From a historical perspective, Xavier Abril can be credited with an early effort to achieve "an American version of surrealism" in his creative texts (Núñez, *Literatura peruana* 45) and with increasing the visibility of surrealism in Peru through his critical essays. Abril's approach to literary surrealism is unique in its explicit ties to the cinema of his era, which takes shape in his work as a metaphorical view of life as a "dream-film."

César Moro

Like Xavier Abril, César Moro served as a direct conduit between European and Peruvian writers in the 1920s, 1930s, and 1940s. But of the two, only Moro earned a reputation as an important—albeit little-studied—poet. Moro was in fact the only Latin American writer to have participated directly in the original Parisian surrealist movement (prior to World War II), and is the figure dubbed by Jason Wilson as "Spanish America's most orthodox surrealist" ("Coda" 264). Born Alfredo Quíspez Asín in Lima in 1903, Moro seemed always to have lived his life as an outsider, "un extranjero nato" [a born stranger/foreigner] in the words of Américo Ferrari (238). Several critics have pointed out the double exile to which Moro subjected himself, first as a Peruvian who wrote most of his work in French, and second as a surrealist. To this must be added the social exile that Moro as a homosexual experienced in the conservative *Limeñan* society in which he was raised, as well as later in France and Mexico.

Uncomfortable with the provincial sensibility of the Peruvian capital (one late poem dubs it "Lima la horrible"),[2] Moro left for Paris at the age of 23. He lived in the French capital between 1925 and 1933, during the very heyday of the surrealist movement. There he met Breton, Éluard, and the other members of the early Parisian group, with whom he aligned himself aesthetically while maintaining a certain intellectual distance. Upon his return to Peru, Moro collaborated with Emilio Adolfo Westphalen to promote surrealism, publishing texts and organizing in 1935 a small surrealist exhibition, the first of its kind in Latin America. Moro's introductory essay for the single issue of the journal *El Uso de la Palabra*, which he and Westphalen edited in 1939, reveals a disparaging attitude toward the current state of Spanish American letters. Given that state, Moro presented the new journal as an agent of change, one that "hunde deliciosamente los pies en la limonada aguada que es el arte y la literatura de América" [deliciously sinks its feet into the diluted lemonade that is the art and the literature of America] (*Los anteojos de azufre* 15).

A decade spent in Mexico between 1938 and 1948 allowed Moro to develop close personal ties with the exiled surrealists residing there, including Benjamin Péret, Wolfgang Paalen, Alice Rahon, Leonora Carrington, and Remedios Varo, as well as with important Mexican writers such as Xavier Villaurrutia. In 1940, Moro collaborated with Paalen (and with Breton, who remained in France) on the "Cuarta Exposición Internacional del Surrealismo" in Mexico City. Moro himself was a painter of considerable talent, holding one-man shows in Paris (1926), Brussels (1927), and Lima (1938). Finally, Moro made an invaluable contribution to the internationalization of surrealism by translating and publishing in Mexico the work of Éluard, Péret, de Chirico, Breton, Carrington, and others.

As in the case of Xavier Abril and many others, Mariátegui played an indispensable role in launching Moro's poetic career, publishing his early poems in *Amauta* (no. 14) in 1928. But from this moment on, Moro's ties to Peruvian literature would loosen. Moro's case is a complicated one because he wrote and published the vast majority of his work in French, even after returning to Latin America after his eight years in France.[3] From a historical perspective, one could argue that Moro's decision to write in a foreign tongue was unfortunate, first and foremost because he severely limited his Spanish-speaking readership. Indeed, his reputation in Spain and Latin America today rests largely on the one small volume written entirely in Spanish, *La tortuga ecuestre* [The Equestrian Turtle], which was published posthumously in 1959. Second, as a foreigner and a nonnative speaker, he failed to gain an audience among French readers.

It is possible to argue conversely, however, that the decision to write in French was a felicitous one. Such a choice had at least one important Spanish

American precedent: Chile's foremost avant-garde poet, Vicente Huidobro, had traveled and lived widely in Europe and wrote much of his poetry in French (or published in French what he had originally written in Spanish). Moro's choice, similarly, allowed him to participate more fully in literary activity in Paris: in particular, he collaborated in 1931 in *Le surréalisme au service de la Révolution*, the principle organ of the surrealist movement in France in that period. José Miguel Oviedo defends Moro's "radical and meaningful decision" as a deliberate self-positioning within an international sphere ("Sobre la poesía" 102–3). Whether writing in French or Spanish, Moro as an exiled poet seems to have found a creative home in surrealism's rebellious and self-marginalizing stance. In the words of Julio Ortega, "He is a surrealist and more than a surrealist: he assumes surrealism's rebellion, its profound sense of change as a moral response, and he explores it on his own account and within his own personal adventure" (147). In the following pages I will examine several texts of poetry and poetic prose by Moro in order to probe his highly subjective appropriation of surrealist techniques.

A short prose piece called "La poesía surrealista," which first appeared as Moro's introduction to the *Antología del surrealismo*, an international collection that he translated and published in Mexico in 1938, affirms his shared affinities with the movement in stylistically surrealist prose:

El surrealismo es el cordón que une la bomba de dinamita con el fuego para hacer volar la montaña. La cita de las tormentas portadoras del rayo y de la lluvia de fuego. El bosque virgen y la miríada de aves de plumaje eléctrico cubriendo el cielo tempestuoso. La esmeralda de Nerón. Una llanura inmensa poblada de sarcófagos de hielo encerrando lianas y lámparas de acetileno, globos de azogue, mujeres desnudas coronadas de cardos y de fresas. El tigre real que asola las tierras de tesoros. La estatura de la noche de plumas de paraíso salpicada con sangre de jirafas degolladas bajo la luna. El día inmenso de cristal de roca y los jardines de cristal de roca. Los nombres de Sade, Lautréamont, Rimbaud, Jarry, en formas diversas y delirantes de aerolito sobre una sábana de sangre transparente que agita el viento nocturno sobre el basalto ardiente de insomnio. (*Versiones del surrealismo* 13)[4]

[Surrealism is the cord that ties the fire to the dynamite that will blow up the mountain. The meeting place of lightning-bearing storms and the rain of fire. The virgin forest and the myriad of birds with electric feathers covering the stormy sky. Nero's emerald. A vast plain inhabited by sarcophagi of ice enclosing lianas and acetylene lamps, globules of mercury, naked women crowned with thistles and strawberries. The royal tiger that razes the territories of treasure. The stature of the night with its feathers of paradise spattered with the blood of giraffes decapitated in the moonlight. The immense day of rock crystal and the rock crystal gardens. The names of Sade, Lautréamont, Rimbaud, Jarry, in the diverse and delirious shapes of meteorites over a bedsheet of clear blood that rattles the night wind over the burning basalt of insomnia.]

Though in its role as an introductory essay this piece is meant to serve as an explanation of surrealism, the passage reads like an automatic text whose images seek an internal logic. In representing surrealism metaphorically as a conductor, a path for potentially destructive forces, Moro recalls Breton's own trope of the *fils conducteurs*—the mental or linguistic "conducting wires" that channel creative energy. The conducting wire is an appropriate metaphor for Moro's text itself, which reads as a rapid firing of separate images that have suggestive power but apparently lack coherence. Moro's painterly imagination is more than evident in this piece, particularly in the oneiric image of a plain dotted with icy sarcophagi, which brings to mind Yves Tanguy's flat and seemingly infinite landscapes punctuated by starkly silhouetted objects.

Although this piece resists precise textual explication, by applying Michael Riffaterre's argument that the extended metaphors of automatic texts do in fact convey meaning, we can trace certain lines of semantic association. The first of these has to do with explosive energy, suggested in terms such as *bomba, dinamita, fuego, eléctrico,* and *tempestuoso*. Another series of associations points to hidden or enclosed energies (the virgin forest, the mountain, sarcophagi of ice with living vines and lamps inside). A third semantic field (overlapping in some cases with the first two) involves images of concentrated light: storm clouds containing lighting, "Nero's emerald,"[5] globules of mercury, "territories of treasure," rock crystal, and "burning basalt." Linking these three interconnected fields to the original term of the extended metaphor—surrealism—the reader can comprehend on an imagistic if not a rational level that surrealism brings an explosive energy to the rigid cultures it encounters, that it represents a tremendous potential force waiting to be released, and that the surrealist state of mind is a source of dense lucidity.

One image from "La poesía surrealista" that fails to fit into the schema outlined above is that of the "naked women crowned with thistles and strawberries," a rather direct allusion to the double character of erotic desire. As this image suggests, Moro's poetry is on the whole quintessentially erotic (although the object of desire is rarely marked as feminine). It is the reiterative textualization of surrealism's *amour fou*, the sublimation of erotic desire in images whose character is obsessive and hallucinatory. A handful of passages allude to the loved one's presence, but in the vast majority of Moro's work the loved one is absent. Thus the erotic encounter is not celebrated as much as it is vividly imagined, as illustrated by the succinct verse "Cierro los ojos y tu imagen y semejanza son el mundo" [I close my eyes and your image and likeness are the world] (*Obra poética* 56). When Guillermo Sucre states that "love is as much desire as the imagination of desire," his assertion goes to the heart of Moro's poetics (344).

Moro's erotic imagination is often transgressive, relentlessly exploring the limits of the madness, delirium, and revolt against social convention that give *amour fou* its peculiar character. (It is no accident that he mentions Sade and Lautréamont in the above-cited piece.) For Moro, madness offered a dynamic trope for heightened states of desire and the unconventional language needed to represent them. Insanity as both theme and method is invoked directly in the poem "A vista perdida" [Lost to Sight], whose first lines read

> No renunciaré jamás al lujo insolente al desenfreno suntuoso de pelos como fasces finísimas colgadas de cuerdas y de sables
> Los paisajes de la saliva inmensos y con pequeños cañones de plumafuentes
> El tornasol violento de la saliva
> La palabra designando el objeto propuesto por su contrario
> El árbol como una lamparilla mínima
> La pérdida de las facultades y la adquisición de la demencia
> El lenguaje afásico y sus perspectivas embriagadoras
> La logoclonia el tic la rabia el bostezo interminable
> La estereotipia el pensamiento prolijo
> El estupor . . . (*Obra poética* 53)

[Never will I renounce unblushing luxury the sumptuous rampage of hairs like delicate fasces hanging from ropes and sables / The immense landscapes of saliva with their little fountain pen quills / The violent sunflower of saliva / The word designating the object proposed by its opposite / The tree like a minimal night lamp / The loss of the faculties and the acquisition of dementia / Aphasic language and its intoxicating perspectives / Logoclonia, tics, ravings, the interminable yawn / Stereotypy, prolix thought / Stupor . . .]

The poem continues at length in this vein, enumerating all those elements the speaker vows "never to renounce." As Sucre points out, this enumeration strays farther and farther from the initial verb phrase "No renunciaré jamás" toward noun phrases that seem to have little connection to the verb *renuniar* or to each other (348). But I would argue that taken together, these phrases provide a litany of rebellion by pledging an allegiance to *otherness*, particularly the otherness associated with carnal desire and with irrationality, both touchstones of surrealist thought. The speaker's wish to "acquire dementia" invokes Rimbaud's call for the poet-as-seer to enact "the long, gigantic and rational derangement of all the senses," a state of consciousness only achievable through the loss of the rational faculties (307).

Moro links this irrational state directly to language, indeed, to a surrealist dialectical view of language, by including in his list "The word designating the object proposed by its opposite." With such a word the poet turns language inside out, blocking its communicative function and opening infinite possibilities of unexpected meaning. The desire to divest language of its quotidian roles is reiterated in the allusion to "aphasic language and its intoxicating perspectives." If aphasia is the loss of ability to use or understand words, then "aphasic language" is language that operates outside ordinary discourse, allowing an "intoxicated" relationship to verbal expression. The next two verses enumerate various other symptoms of mental illness, some related directly to language: *logoclonia* is the ability to read only the last syllable of words; *stereotype* in this context is the involuntary repetition of gestures, movements, or verbal utterances; *prolix thought* refers to the inability to separate main ideas from tangential details in speech. The lyric voice of "A vista perdida" embraces all these conditions, presumably for their promise of exceptional mental states and means of expression.

After another long litany of anaphoric verses beginning with the noun "Stupor" (alluding once again to an abnormal mental state), the poem ends with these lines:

> El grandioso crepúsculo boreal del pensamiento esquizofrénico
> La sublime interpretación delirante de la realidad
> No renunciaré jamás el lujo primordial de tus caídas vertiginosas
>   oh locura de diamante (*Obra poética* 54)

[The grandiose northern twilight of schizophrenic thought / The sublime delirious interpretation of reality / Never will I renounce the primordial luxury of your giddy tumblings oh diamond madness]

This ending seals the poem's identity as a surrealist *ars poetica*, one that focuses primarily on the celebration of nonrational states of mind. Apart from the framing structure afforded by the oath "Never will I renounce," the poem's method is unstable; that is, it consists of an accumulation of images with no apparent connection. The final phrase "oh locura de diamante" creates a paradox by associating madness with the qualities of diamonds: brilliance, solidity, and supreme value. This phrase might be read as an imagistic re-presentation of the "the word designating the object proposed by its opposite," since madness and diamonds operate in fundamental opposition. But in surrealist terms, "diamond madness" can be understood as the *point sublime* where the two opposites converge, suggesting a hard-edged lucidity in states of dementia. This image in fact recalls the similar set of images of compacted light woven throughout the previously cited prose piece "La poesía surrealista."

The poem just examined is taken from Moro's only collection written in Spanish, a slim volume of poems called *La tortuga ecuestre* that is widely considered to be his most realized work. Written in the space of a few months in 1938–39, these poems were Moro's response to an intense affair with "Antonio," a young Mexican army lieutenant. According to Moro's friend and editor André Coyné, the volume's title recalls an actual incident from earlier in Moro's life, when he witnessed two turtles copulating in a park in Lima. This antediluvian image of sexual desire made such an impression on him that he immediately acquired a turtle, named it "Cretina," and began conceiving of the scene he had witnessed as an allegorical frame for a cycle of poems ("El poeta y su bestiario" 88). In *La tortuga*, two animal figures appear with some regularity: the turtle, representing the poet-lover, and the tiger, representing the beloved. The players in this fantastical erotic drama are named directly and conjointly at one point as "Antonio Cretina César" (*Obra poética* 65)—but apart from this brief mention, overt autobiographical or erotic detail is eschewed in favor of allusion and allegory.

Oviedo identifies three motifs or landscapes that provide a certain semantic unity for the otherwise hermetic poems of *La tortuga*: (1) a marine or submarine world, consisting of strange fish, holothurians (sea cucumbers), and entranced turtles; (2) frozen landscapes, complete with fir trees, lichen, kingdoms, and castles, which Moro draws from German romanticism, fairy tales, and possibly from the scenography of Max Ernst's paintings and collages; and (3) nocturnal wanderings—another romantic element—under the moonlit spell of erotic ecstasy ("Sobre la poesía" 103). Given the proliferation of fauna—both real and imagined—that populate his work, it is also possible to read Moro's poetry as a kind of surreal bestiary.

As a final illustration of Moro's unique poetic imagination, I cite in its entirety the poem "Un camino de tierra en medio de la tierra" [A Dirt Road in the Middle of the Earth]:

> Las ramas de luz atónita poblando innumerables veces el área de
>   tu frente asaltada por olas
> Asfaltada de lumbre tejida de pelo tierno y de huellas leves de
>   fósiles de plantas delicadas
> Ignorada del mundo bañando tus ojos y el rostro de lava verde
> ¡Quién vive! Apenas dormido vuelvo de más lejos a tu encuentro
>   de tinieblas a paso de chacal mostrándote caracolas de espuma de
>   cerveza y probables edificaciones de nácar enfangado
> Vivir bajo las algas
> El sueño en la tormenta sirenas como relámpagos el alba incierta
>   un camino de tierra en medio de la tierra y nubes de tierra y tu

> frente como un castillo de nieve y apaga el alba y el día se enciende
> y vuelve la noche y fasces de tu pelo se interponen y azotan el
> rostro helado de la noche
> Para sembrar el mar de luces moribundas
> Y que las plantas carnívoras no falten el alimento
> Y crezcan ojos en las playas
> Y las selvas despeinadas giman como gaviotas (*Obra poética* 52–53)

[Branches of astonished light infinitely populating the breadth of your forehead assailed by waves / Paved by fire woven with soft hair and with the slight traces of fossils of delicate plants / Ignored by the world bathing your eyes and face with green lava / Who goes there? Barely asleep, I return from a distance to your dark encounter at a jackal's pace, showing you snail shells of beer foam and probable constructions of muddied mother-of-pearl / To live beneath the seaweed / The dream in the storm sirens like lightning bolts the uncertain dawn a dirt road in the middle of the earth and clouds of earth and your forehead rises up like a castle of snow and snuffs out the dawn and the day ignites and the night returns and fasces of your hair intervene and whip the frozen face of night / To sow the sea with dying lights / So the flesh-eating plants don't go hungry / So eyes can grow on the beaches / So the disheveled jungles can groan like gulls]

It would be difficult to recognize this as a love poem were it not for certain images that evoke the beloved's physical being ("your forehead," "your eyes and your face," "fasces of your hair"), which exert a gravitational pull on the otherwise incongruous proliferation of images. Like many of Moro's poems, "Un camino de tierra" privileges the power of the lover's imagination over the loved one's actual presence.

The speaker of this poem is primarily one who dreams. Having fallen asleep, he finds himself far away, and from that place he returns not to an embrace but to a dark encounter (or to an encounter with darkness: the phrase "encuentro de tinieblas" is ambiguous). Reality in this environment is "uncertain," little more than the "probable constructions" of a beautiful but fragile material like mother of pearl. The final portion of the poem dangles precariously from the infinitive phrase "To live beneath the seaweed," a desire that employs the trope of the ocean as a probable metaphor for the unconscious. In the long automatic sequence that follows this phrase, images are connected paratactically ("the dream in the storm sirens like lightning bolts the uncertain dawn a dirt road"), a technique that heightens the unreal, oneiric quality of the poem. By giving the lover the mythic power of "extinguishing the dawn," Moro is perhaps employing a classic trope of love poetry, suggesting that daylight or waking reality is the lovers' enemy. Finally, in the tradition of Sade, Baudelaire, and Lautréamont, eroticism appears in images of primitive violence or bestiality, including hair that "whips the frozen face of night," carnivorous plants that must be fed, and jungles that groan or howl.

Like the previously cited piece "La poesía surrealista," this poem operates by means of the accumulation of images that cause strong sensory impressions but that resist logical explanation. There is a sensuous recreation of the lover ("fire woven with soft hair"), there are images of delicacy and vulnerability ("slight traces of fossils," "castle of snow"), and there is everywhere the threat of violence ("assailed by waves," "sirens like lightning bolts," "flesh-eating plants"). If there is a sense of amorous plenitude in this poem, it does not derive from a love-object external to the poem, nor does it celebrate the erotic encounter or even the fantasy of encounter. Rather, as Elena Altuna observes, the enjoyment resides in the construction of a linguistic object, placing language in the center of the absence (120).

Moro's contact with French surrealism was both intense and relatively prolonged, and it shaped his poetics profoundly. Like his compatriot Xavier Abril and like so many who formed the original Parisian group, Moro eventually distanced himself from surrealism as an organized movement. Nevertheless, until his death in 1953 he continued to nurture the friendships he had cultivated with the surrealists he had known in Mexico and Peru. In spite of his dissent from Breton and Éluard over surrealism's exaltation of heterosexual and monogamous love, Moro continued to profess admiration for the founders of surrealism and to defend the validity of its promise to "open wide the doors of dreams" ("Presentación" 476). In terms of Spanish American surrealism, César Moro holds an important place first as a poet and painter, and second, as an international ambassador for surrealist ideals through his work as translator, editor, and organizer of exhibitions. As late as 1947–48, Moro coedited with Emilio Adolfo Westphalen *Las Moradas*, an eclectic journal with evident surrealist underpinnings. In the light of the recent resurgence of interest in Moro's work, his words in the year before his death seem prophetic: "Uno da todo para no tener nada. Siempre para comenzar de nuevo. Es el costo de la vida maravillosa" [One gives everything to have nothing. Always in order to begin again. This is the cost of the marvelous life] (*Obra poética* 253).

Emilio Adolfo Westphalen

In 1931, Westphalen published a "Letter from Peru" in the Dutch journal *Front*, in which he spoke of his fellow *vanguardistas* as "fieros cazadores, con el arco tendido y la flecha segura hacia la selva peruana de incultura y estupidez y la monstruosa fauna poética, quienes afirman plenos de fe, la nueva poesía verdadera, salvaje y sin nombre" [fierce hunters, with their bows outstretched and their arrows pointed straight toward the Peruvian jungle of uncouthness and stupidity and the monstrous poetic fauna, those who affirm with great faith the new, true poetry, wild and nameless] (Núñez, *Literatura peruana* 46). This zealous declaration reiterates the familiar avant-garde disgust with bourgeois culture. By locating "incultura y estupidez" in the Peruvian jungle, however, Westphalen sounds a particularly American note, albeit one that perhaps inadvertently equates ignorance and lack of culture with the geographically remote, economically underdeveloped character of his country's interior. When he speaks of the "monstrous fauna" of Peruvian poetry, he is undoubtedly referring to the moribund *modernismo* still in vogue among many Peruvian readers in the 1920s. But the trope of the jungle as the site of ignorance points to one of the contradictory tendencies of Latin American *vanguardismo*, a rejection of the autochthonous (past and present) in order to embrace the modern, which was conventionally associated with Europe. Adding yet another twist, Westphalen also applies the adjective *salvaje* to the new poetry whose praises he sings, underscoring the ambivalence with which Latin American writers approached the notions of modernity and artistic revolt within their own cultural sphere.

Westphalen (1911–2001) is a poet of sparse production who is considered, along with his friend and literary ally César Moro, to be Peru's most accomplished surrealist-influenced writer. In adolescence he discovered the work of William Blake and of José María Eguren, discoveries that prepared the way for his gravitation toward surrealism. A frequent visitor to the literary gatherings in the home of Eguren, Westphalen published his first poems in *Amauta* in 1929 (no. 24) and his first volume of poetry, *Las ínsulas extrañas*, in 1933. This book, whose title is taken from a phrase by the Spanish mystic poet San Juan de la Cruz, was followed almost immediately by *Abolición de la muerte* in 1935, which opens with a quote from Breton. Westphalen's reputation as a poet rests squarely on these two collections. *Las ínsulas extrañas*, as Camilo Fernández Cozman observes, was a work with true innovative potential within a local literary scene still characterized by late *modernista* and nativist rhetoric in the line of José Santos Chocano (20). In 1970, an anthology called *Vuelta a la otra margen*, edited by Mirko Lauer and Abelardo Oquendo, challenged the obscurity into which many avant-garde poets—including Westphalen and Moro—had fallen. Soon thereafter (in 1977), a series of essays by prominent critics in the journal *Creación y Crítica* presented Westphalen as one of the founders of contemporary Peruvian poetry. Both publications initiated a new critical appreciation of the Peruvian avant-garde in general and of Westphalen in particular.

Westphalen's connection to the French surrealist movement was much more tenuous than Moro's; in fact, it was his friendship with Moro, rather than any direct contact with the Parisian movement, that stimulated Westphalen's fascination with surrealism. In 1935 the two poets collaborated on a surrealist exposition of paintings and poetry in Lima, and in 1939 they published a pamphlet called *El Uso de la Palabra* (the first issue of a journal that was not continued) whose surrealist orientation is patent. Westphalen's own early work has been labeled by critics as everything from orthodox surrealist to heterodox surrealist to largely independent of surrealist influence. Fernández Cozman's term "de estirpe surrealista" [of surrealist lineage] (42) seems to fit Westphalen best when we take into account the proliferation of oneiric imagery and semantic fragmentation that is balanced by a lucid consciousness on the part of the speaker. On the whole, critics agree that Westphalen's early work enters a territory in which irrationality is featured as a means to self-knowledge. Roberto Paoli argues that Westphalen creates a poetics of rupture, "given that he was interested in founding with his poetry a new form of knowledge that would abolish a world built and organized according to the ordinary laws of thought" (95). The techniques of surrealism, particularly the juxtaposition of unrelated elements, opened for Westphalen a route to this unconventional *gnosis*.

One of the poetic texts that most clearly illustrates Westphalen's surrealist lineage is the 1935 poem "César Moro" from the collection *Belleza de una espada clavada en la lengua* [Beauty of a Sword Thrust into the Tongue]. I cite the poem in its entirety:

> Por un campo de miga de pan se alarga desmesuradamente una manecilla de reloj
> Alternativamente se iluminan o se apagan en ella unos ojos de cangrejo o serpiente
> Al contraluz emerge una humareda de pestañas caladas
> Y dispuestas como una torre que simulara una mujer al desvestirse
> Otros animales más familiares como el hipopótamo o el elefante
> Hallan su camino entre el hueso y la carne
> Una red de ojos de medusa impide el tránsito
> Por el arenal que se extiende como una mano abandonada
> A cada paso una bola de marfil dice si el aire es verde o negro
> Si los ojos pesan iguales en una balanza cruzada de cabellos
> Y encerrada en un acuario instalado en lo alto de una montaña
> Rebalsando a veces y arrojando a veces como una catapulta
> Cadáveres rosados o negros o verdes de niños a los ocho extremos
> Cadáveres pintados según las cebras o los leopardos
> Y que al caer se abren tan hermosamente como una caja de basura
> Extendida en medio de un patio de mármol rosado
> Atrae a los alacranes y a las serpientes de aire
> Que zumban como un molino dedicado al amor
>
> Aparte un hombre de metal llora de cara a una pared
> Visible únicamente al estallar cada lágrima (*Otra imagen deleznable* 77–78)

[The hand of a clock extends immeasurably across a field of bread crumbs / In it the eyes of a crab or a snake alternately flash or die out / Against the light, a smoke cloud of drenched eyelashes emerges / While, positioned like a tower that might simulate a woman undressing, / Other more familiar animals like the hippopotamus or the elephant / Find their way between bone and flesh / A net of jellyfish eyes blocks the passage / Across the sandpit that stretches out like an abandoned hand / With every step an ivory ball tells whether the air is green or black / Whether eyes weigh the same on scales crossed by locks of hair / And enclosed in an aquarium placed on a mountaintop / Sometimes overflowing and sometimes catapulting out / The rose-colored or black or green corpses of children at the eight extremes / Corpses painted like zebras or leopards / That open out splendidly as they fall like a box of garbage / Spread out in the middle of a patio of pink marble / It attracts the scorpions and snakes of the air / That buzz like a mill consecrated to love // Elsewhere a man made of metal cries with his face to the wall / Visible only with the bursting of each tear]

"César Moro" bears many of the marks of surrealist poetry, particularly in its accumulation of striking but irrational images and in its overall inscrutability. The poem resembles Moro's own work in its distinct visual quality, rendered here as a desolate mental geography that recalls certain paintings by Dalí. Less accessible to the reader than much of Westphalen's work, this poem reads as an automatic text that revisits certain of his predilect themes, namely time ("una manecilla de reloj") and paradox or uncertainty. The proliferation of animal images here—particularly those that are archetypally unappealing or threatening such as the hippopotamus or the snake—pays homage to the bestiary quality of Moro's poetry. Notably, the animals in Westphalen's poem exercise a certain agency—they find their way, they block passage, they feed on carrion—while the humans lack all agency, being represented here by the corpses of children that are either held in an enclosed space or hurled out of it. Leslie Bary notes that in this and other poems of Westphalen's early period, surrealist elements are evidenced in isolated anatomical elements (hands, eyes, eyelashes, bone, and flesh) and in the "macabre aesthetic" derived from Lautréamont (68). The final two lines of the poem, in which a man cries with his face to a wall, introduce a sentimental tone that comes as a surprise in this context. By suggesting that the weeping man (perhaps the eponymous César Moro) is visible to others only in the flashes of light that are his tears, the poem speaks to the theme of alienation so central to twentieth-century Western poetry.

Westphalen's own poetic career suffered a long hiatus between 1940 and 1971, but during this period he edited important journals such as the surrealist-leaning *Las Moradas* (in collaboration with Moro), *Revista Peruana de la Cultura*, and *Amaru*, all of which strove to modernize Peruvian culture. During this period he served as a cultural attaché, translator, and essayist while living in Italy and Portugal. Emerging from his self-imposed silence, between 1980 and his death in 2001 Westphalen wrote and published several more volumes of poetry and collections of essays on poetry and art. Even as late as 1990, Westphalen spoke of the importance of recognizing surrealism as a broad movement of the spirit and of César Moro's crucial place in it. In an address delivered at an international colloquium on Latin American surrealism in Lima, Westphalen gives an ardent testimony of his belief in surrealist ideals. He insists on the need to avoid reducing surrealism to a literary school or a set of rhetorical devices, though he acknowledges the significance of these manifestations. "Mas lo que importó ante todo a sus componentes," he claims, "era una puesta en juego muy diversa y audaz, una ambición que habrá que calificar de desmesurada: intentar nada menos que la más grande y pavorosa aventura" [But what mattered most to its participants was something very different and daring that was set in motion, an ambition that can only be described as outsized: to attempt nothing less than the greatest and most terrifying adventure] ("Digresión sobre surrealismo" 203). Significantly, it was this spirit of adventure that Peru's most important avant-garde poet, César Vallejo, refused to acknowledge or validate in his famous polemic against surrealism.

Vallejo's "Autopsy" of 1930: Was Surrealism Really Dead?

César Vallejo (1892–1938) is generally recognized, along with Pablo Neruda, as the most important Spanish American poet of the twentieth century. As a solitary figure and an unrelenting iconoclast, Vallejo found it impossible to participate in the surrealist movement even for a period of time, as Moro and Westphalen had done. His outspoken rejection of surrealist techniques intensified the dialogue around surrealism that took place in Latin America in the 1930s and 1940s, giving it a particularly negative turn.

One of Vallejo's most famous poems, written only months before his death, unfolds as a series of scenes or situations to which the poet-speaker responds with anguished rhetorical questions:

> Un hombre pasa con un pan al hombro
> ¿Voy a escribir, después, de mi doble?
> Otro se sienta, ráscase, extrae un piojo de su axila, mátalo
> ¿Con qué valor hablar del psicoanálisis?
> Otro ha entrado a mi pecho con un palo en la mano
> ¿Hablar luego de Sócrates al médico?
> Un cojo pasa dando el brazo a un niño
> ¿Voy, después, a leer a André Breton? (*Obra poética* 266)

[A man walks by with a stick of bread on his shoulder. / Am I going to write then about my double? // Another sits, scratches, extracts a louse from his armpit, kills it. / What good is there in talking about psychoanalysis? // Another has entered my chest with a club in his hand. / How to converse with the doctor about Socrates? // A lame man passes by holding a child's hand. / After that, am I going to read André Breton?]

The poem continues for nine additional stanzas, each delineating scenes of everyday suffering or mundane corruption witnessed by the speaker, who finds himself at a loss to respond in any meaningful way. At the core of the poem is the profound scrutiny to which the speaker subjects his own poetic vocation, his own immersion in an intellectual culture that values the life of the mind over that of material existence and its misery. Vallejo's inclusion of André Breton in the enumeration of vacuous emblems of intellectual life is no accident: Breton had come to represent for him the very antithesis of a valid response to the human suffering he had witnessed in his native Peru and in his travels throughout Europe and the Soviet Union. As Vallejo commented in a letter to Pablo Abril in 1928, "Voy sintiéndome revolucionario y revolucionario por *experiencia vivida*, más que por *ideas aprendidas*" [I feel myself becoming a revolutionary, and a revolutionary through *lived experience* more than through *learned ideas*] (qtd. in Castañón 29). This lived experience included not only his observation of extreme poverty and exploitation among the miners of Peru or the peasants of Russia but his own penury—the struggles against poverty and illness that he faced since arriving as an exile in Paris in 1923.

Vallejo's firsthand experiences of suffering prepared him for his studies of Marxism, which provided a theoretical justification for the deeply held conviction that he must work in his capacity as an artist and intellectual to counteract the oppressive forces of capitalism. He joined the Communist Party in 1928 and made three separate trips to the Soviet Union in 1928, 1929, and 1931. The poetry written in the last decade of his life reflects an unwavering solidarity with the proletariat, although it avoids presenting this stance in doctrinaire or transparently ideological language. I spoke earlier in this chapter of Mariátegui's enthusiastic support of avant-garde literary expression, which he saw as an integral part of a broad social revolution that would subvert cultural norms. Vallejo's response was more ambivalent and more complex. On the one hand, his embrace of socialist ideals made him utterly impatient with much avant-garde experimentation. Considering the historical context of the last decades of Vallejo's life, Víctor de Lama notes that the avant-garde literature being produced in Paris at that moment, especially surrealist literature, "seemed cold and irresponsible to him because it was dehumanized" (43). On the other hand, Vallejo steadfastly defended the independence of aesthetic practice within the political sphere; that is, he defended the right of artists and writers to create as they saw fit, and he did not hold them responsible for the political uses to which their work might be put ("Literatura proletaria" 518).[6]

When Vallejo wrote his essay "Autopsia del superrealismo" in February of 1930, he made known his unequivocal opposition to the surrealist movement, flatly declaring it "a corpse" (468). Published almost simultaneously in Lima (in *Amauta*), Buenos Aires, and Santiago de Chile in the spring of 1930, this virulent essay had far-reaching consequences for the reception of surrealism in Latin America.[7] Surrealism for Vallejo, far from constituting the powerful movement of the spirit that Breton and others had proclaimed, was merely one in a series of "makeshift" and "ephemeral" literary schools (466). Intended as a broad indictment of Western capitalist society and the spiritual decadence it represented, Vallejo's essay directly associates surrealism with the splintering of social and artistic consciousness that characterizes his era: "A partir de la declaración surrealista, irrumpe casi mensualmente una nueva escuela literaria. Nunca el pensamiento social se fraccionó en tantas y tan fugaces fórmulas" [Since the surrealist declaration, nearly every month a new literary school bursts onto the scene. Never has social thought been so broken up into so many fleeting formulas] (466). After declaring the death of surrealism, Vallejo pronounces a bitter discourse over the corpse, claiming that the surrealist manifestos were nothing but "inteligentes juegos de salón" [clever parlor games] related to automatic writing, morality, religion, and politics (466).

At a crucial juncture of the essay, Vallejo sustains that it was only when Breton proposed synthesizing surrealism and Marxism that the movement acquired any social significance and became, albeit momentarily, a constructive force (467). What he sees as the inherent pessimism and "desperation" of surrealism, however, soon led to an impasse over Marxist thought: "La crisis moral e intellectual que el superrealismo se propuso promover . . . se anquilosó en psicopatía de bufete y en clisé literario, pese a las inyecciones dialécticas de Marx y a la adhesion formal y oficiosa de los inquietos jóvenes al comunisimo" [The moral and intellectual crisis that surrealism intended to stir up . . . became fossilized in writing-table psychopathy and literary cliché, despite all the injections of Marx's dialectics and the formal, diligent adherence of those restive youth to Communism] (467).

Vallejo's vilification of surrealism occurs within an important historical context—namely, the ever-increasing influence of Marxist thought (both in Europe and in Latin America) and the growing sense of anxiety preceding the Second World War. Within that context, the surrealists' own struggle to clarify the movement's political and aesthetic parameters had reached a flash point. At issue, as we saw in Chapter 1, was whether surrealism should commit itself directly to the socialist revolution by subordinating its own ideals to those of the Communist Party, or whether the fundamental surrealist doctrine of absolute individual freedom obviated the adherence to any political doctrine or party. Vallejo's "Autopsia" appeared in March of 1930, only one year after the meltdown that had occurred within the French surrealist group in 1929 and four months after the publication of Breton's calumnious *Second manifeste*. Vallejo in fact takes his central trope, the corpse, from the pamphlet called "Un cadavre" in which several of the disaffected surrealists virulently assailed both the movement and its leader. Vallejo thus aligns himself unequivocally with those who saw Breton as "a false revolutionary and a false communist" (Nadeau 168).

Breton had argued repeatedly that no social revolution could occur prior to a revolution of the mind or spirit—and thus, after a certain vacillation, he renounced the Communist Party. Vallejo counters Breton's position directly by asking, "¿Puede hablarse de liberación espiritual mientras no se haya hecho la revolución social y material, y mientras se vive dentro de la atmósfera material y moral de la producción y de las relaciones burgueses de la economía?" [Is it possible to speak of spiritual liberation while the social and material revolution has not yet occurred, and while we live within the material and moral atmosphere of bourgeois production and economic relationships?] (*Ensayos* 465). Within this philosophy of material revolution, the "Autopsia" reduces surrealism to "[un] cenáculo meramente literario . . . una impostura de la vida, un vulgar espantapájaros" [a mere literary coterie . . . an imposter of life, a common scarecrow] (468).

In sum, the "Autopsia" reveals Vallejo's fierce resistance to the separation between sociopolitical and aesthetic revolutions. The true poet, in his view, must rebel simultaneously against unjust material conditions and atrophied literary conventions. Gustav Siebenmann points out that since the conflation of the artistic and the political spheres was a trait common to Spanish American *vanguardistas*, for Vallejo "politics and literature formed a unity and were the same thing; or said differently, he considered his literary vanguardism as another form of political vanguardism, more elevated and complete than the latter" (36). This view corroborates Mariátegui's attempts to celebrate literary *vanguardismo* as an integral part of his program of social liberation.

With the advantage of historical perspective, we can evaluate Vallejo's indictments of surrealism on certain key points. We know now that the proliferation of avant-garde movements and schools, the "fleeting formulas" that he implicitly attributes to early surrealist proclamations, had been set in motion long before Breton arrived on the scene. Retrospectively, most critics and historians agree that surrealism was the culmination of the avant-garde impulse and not the cause of its fragmentation. Similarly, the spiritual decadence that Vallejo lays at the feet of surrealism is now generally accepted to be the result of an early twentieth-century cultural exhaustion, infinitely exacerbated by the effects of the Great War. Far from being the cause of this decadence or sense of exhaustion, surrealism in fact strove to replace it with a new creative energy. Most significantly, we can certify that Vallejo's characterization of surrealism as a dead movement by the early 1930s was, as history has amply proved, patently mistaken.

In contrast, his claim that surrealism was ineffectual as a vehicle for political revolution was not far off the mark: both Breton's second manifesto and the response to it by disaffected surrealists attest to the fracturing of the original group, due in large part to the irresolvable question of surrealism's relationship to the socialist revolution. More important, Vallejo's impatience with pure creative freedom divorced from concern for human suffering reflects an attitude that would become widespread in Latin America. As Goic observes, "In concert with the traits of a negative reception of surrealism in our literature, Vallejo rejects everything cerebral, everything that doesn't have its roots in life" (19). In retrospect, we can view Vallejo's "Autopsia" as not only "in concert with" but as one of the reasons behind the negative (or at least ambivalent) view of surrealism held by many Latin American writers and intellectuals. Following Vallejo, the majority of writers would question orthodox surrealism's ideal of total revolution and would likewise eschew its group activities, particularly those related to automatic writing. What Vallejo failed to observe or foresee, nevertheless, was the profound sense of spiritual and aesthetic adventure that surrealism would offer his own countrymen César Moro and Emilio Adolfo Westphalen, as well as numerous other writers across the continent.

With Moro's death in 1956, the initial era of surrealism in Peru came to a close. The late 1950s and 1960s saw a new generation of writers—principally Jorge Eduardo Eielson, Javier Sologuren, and Blanca Varela—whose contact with surrealism proved fruitful. The multitalented Eielson (1924–2006)—a poet, novelist, painter, and sculptor—formed part of the group of young Latin Americans that gathered in Paris in this period, and like Moro, he would remain in self-exile from Peru for the majority of his life. Critics tend to agree that Eielson's early volume of poetry *Reinos* (1945) is enriched by the surrealist image and that later collections such as *Mutatis mutandis* (1967) evince a surrealist sense of the ludic. Blanca Varela (1926–2009), who became a major voice in twentieth-century Latin American poetry, collaborated with Westphalen and Moro on the journal *Las Moradas* in the late 1940s. In 1949 she traveled to Paris, where she established a friendship with Octavio Paz that would become crucial to her development as a poet. Critics have pointed in particular to Varela's 1959 volume *Ese puerto existe* as a prime example of second-wave Peruvian surrealism. In a review of her collection *Destiempos*

(1959), Paz says of Varela, "She is a surrealist poet, if by this we mean not a movement, a 'style' or a school, but a spiritual lineage" (*Obras* 3: 352). Paz's term "estirpe spiritual" speaks to the diffuse but persistent affinities with surrealism that were shared by many writers of Varela's generation, in Peru and across Latin America.

CHAPTER 6

The Two Faces of Early Surrealism in Mexico

Introduction: A Chilly Reception

To speak of surrealism in Mexico prior to 1950 is to tell two separate but interlaced stories. One story is that of international surrealists who visited or even took up long-term residence in Mexico. The list is long and includes such luminaries as André Breton, Antonin Artaud, and Luis Buñuel. This story posits Mexico as a surrealist object, a site of potential surrealist encounters. It is a narrative of non-Mexicans who find surrealism in that country's history, its geography, its colors, and its indigenous or *mestizo* people.[1] The other story is that of Mexico's own response to surrealism, including both the surrealist-influenced works produced by certain Mexican writers and the debates that emerged from the presence of the international group of émigrés. In terms of literary history, it is evident—though perhaps unfortunate—that the first of the two tales is more compelling; in fact, while the impact of surrealism on Mexican writers in the first half of the century was minimal, the impact of Mexico on European surrealists was enormous. In the following pages, I examine the paradox that defines Mexico in this period as simultaneously the least and the most surrealist of countries.[2]

The early *vanguardista* movement that gained the greatest momentum in Mexico was *el estridentismo* or "stridentism," which operated (like Argentina's *ultraísmo*) in a very limited sphere between 1921 and 1927. An early manifesto published by Manuel Maples Arce, the de facto head of the *estridentista* group, declared, "Es necesario exaltar en todos los tonos estridentes de nuestro diapasón propagandista, la belleza actualista de las máquinas, de los puentes gímnicos reciamente extendidos sobre las vertientes por músculos de acero, el humo de las fábricas" [We must exalt in the most strident tones of our propagandistic pitch the present beauty of machines, of athletic bridges robustly extended across the slopes by steel muscles, of the smoke of factories] (Verani 89). With the Mexican Revolution recently ended, and the exhausted and impoverished populace struggling to recreate itself as a nation under new rules that touched practically every aspect of civic and political life, it is no wonder that these echoes of Italian futurism did not resound loudly. Nevertheless, the *estridentistas* did succeed in shaking off the remaining vestiges of *modernismo* in Mexican literature, both by experimenting with new forms such as the *caligramme* (popularized by Apollinaire in France and introduced into Mexico by the poet José Juan Tablada) and in embracing both painting and photography as forms of expression analogous to poetry.

The fleeting *estridentista* movement was followed in the 1930s and 1940s by the "Contemporáneos," a more substantive and influential group that gathered around a journal of the same name. Like the *estridentistas*, the Contemporáneos group sought to integrate the written word and the visual arts, and in this spirit it published reproductions of works by Picasso, de Chirico, Joan Miró, and Dalí, among others. The Contemporáneos poets, including Jorge Cuesta, José Gorostiza, Salvador Novo, Bernardo Ortiz de Montellano, Gilberto Owen, Jaime Torres Bodet, and Xavier Villaurrutia, attempted to bring Mexican poetry into the modern Western tradition by adopting a cosmopolitan attitude. The Contemporáneos writers engaged both in translation and in serious literary criticism, a tradition that reaches its twentieth-century apex in the essays of Octavio Paz. But ultimately, their characterization as "contemporary" (i.e., avant-garde) writers is debatable. In general, these poets followed neoromantic and neosymbolist lines as they produced lyric poetry of serious intent and grave tone. Although avant-garde in their utilization of surprising images and, in some cases, of word play or experimental poetic structures, the Contemporáneos were for the most part conceptual and metaphysical poets whose themes were timeless and universal. Paz remarks that while the previous generation could deceive itself that the democratic ideals of the Mexican Revolution would be realized over time, the Contemporáneos, who had witnessed both the violence of the revolution and the corruption that followed it, "could no longer believe in the revolutionaries or in their programs, so they isolated themselves in a private world, populated by the phantoms of eroticism, dreaming, and death" ("Hieroglyphs" 104). Thus, although they shared surrealism's preoccupation with the unconscious, particularly with the tension between Eros and Thanatos, the fundamentally introspective, pessimistic, and conservative nature of the Contemporáneos prevented them from welcoming the surrealist play of possibilities.

Bernardo Ortiz de Montellano (1899–1949), the director of the Contemporáneos group from 1928 to 1931, was one of the first Mexican writers to give serious consideration to surrealism in his own work. Though not an orthodox surrealist poet, Ortiz de Montellano creates a body of poetry centered on the motif of the dream, as evidenced by the title of his posthumous collected work, *Sueño y poesía* [Dream and Poetry] (1952). His best-known poem, "Segundo sueño," presents a long dream sequence modeled after Sor Juana Inés de la Cruz's famous philosophical poem *Primero sueño*. In addition to his poetry, Ortiz de Montellano's critical essays (one of which I examine later in this chapter) demonstrate a relatively receptive attitude toward surrealism's possible contributions to Mexican culture—an attitude rare among his contemporaries.

Xavier Villaurrutia (1903–50) was a prolific poet, dramatist, and art critic who became one of Mexico's most important intellectual figures. A brief look at a poem by Villaurrutia will illustrate both the Contemporáneos' attraction to and their distance from surrealist techniques. Villaurrutia is best known for his collection of poems *Nostalgia de la muerte*, first published in 1938 but developed and reedited over the course of two decades (1928–46). In the series of "Nocturnes" and "Nostalgias" that constitute this volume, the poetic voice returns obsessively to themes of desire, absence, solitude, self-reflexivity, and of course, death—all of which he renders through the imagery of walls, shadows, mirrors, statues, stairways, and parts of the body.

I cite in its entirety one well-known poem from this collection, "Nocturno de la estatua," which was dedicated to the painter and poet Agustín Lazo:

> Dream, dream of night, the street, the stairway
> and the scream of the statue unrounding the corner.
> Run to the statue, and find only the scream,
> long to touch the scream, and find only its echo,
> long to grasp the echo, and find only the wall,
> run to the wall and touch a mirror.
> Find in the mirror the assassinated statue,
> pull it out from the blood of its shadow,
> dress it in a flutter of eyes,
> caress it like a sister who suddenly appears,
> shuffle the chips of its fingers
> And repeat in its ear a hundred times a hundred hundred times
> until you hear it say: "I'm dying of sleep." (12)[3]

Paz observes that the "Nocturnos" series from which this poem is taken "represent[s] the moment when Villaurrutia most decisively embraces the aesthetics of the avant-garde, and even ventures into the outskirts of Surrealism" ("Hieroglyphs" 127). The nightmarish atmosphere that permeates this poem certainly evinces the dream-state, that great commonplace of surrealism, but the tight construction of the poem reveals a lucid consciousness that artistically controls the oneiric vision.

This is no mere coincidence: Villaurrutia himself, speaking of the work of Gorostiza and Ortiz de Montellano, observes that "the irrationalism, the automatism of the new poetic schools has not entered with the invading energy that has entered other things, given that the Mexican is a limited being whose greatest intoxication consists precisely of keeping himself lucid and who, even at the moment of sleep, prefers to stay awake" ("Introducción" 772). Here Villaurrutia is commenting on the poetry of his generation and even extending his judgment to include a kind of essentialist observation on the "wakeful" character of Mexicans. This commentary, in which Villaurrutia makes clear that he values the lucid consciousness that directs the dreaming imagination, provides us with a window into the Contemporáneos' ambivalent attitude toward surrealism.

In Spanish, "Nocturne: The Statue" works off an obsessive repetition of the /s/ sound (*soñar, escalera, estatua, esquina, sólo, asir, hacia*, etc.), which adds to the shadowy, soporific nature of the dream narrative. With the exception of the penultimate line, every line in the poem ends in an /a/ or an /o/ vowel sound, which adds to the effect of tight control. The infinitive verb forms that initiate most of the verses (*soñar, correr, hallar*, etc.) give the poem an eerie sense of a missing subject: although there is desperate activity occurring at every moment, we cannot identify any actor. In fact, the statue being chased and subsequently—as a murdered cadaver—dressed, caressed, and played with has greater physical presence in the poem than the perpetrator of these actions. In an image that participates in surrealist black humor, the unnamed subject amuses himself with the dead statue's fingers as if playing with poker chips. In sum, Villaurrutia's poem shares with surrealism a fascination with the shadowy territory between dream and waking states, and its images recall the irrationality and absurdity of the surrealist imagination. But the poem's carefully controlled structure—down to the last eerie phrase, "I'm dying of sleep"—gives the impression of a nightmare recalled in daylight, rather than the "pure psychic automatism" championed by Breton.

We could consider many more examples of poetry from the Contemporáneos group, but the conclusion would be the same: apart from the timid experimentation with disconnected imagery and the motifs of dreams and unexpected encounters, surrealism occupied only a circumscribed space in Mexican poetry in the first half of the twentieth century. Within the broader cultural milieu of the period, it fared no better. News of the French movement began appearing in brief newspaper reviews and translations of articles written in France as early as March of 1925, just months after the publication of the first surrealist manifesto.[4] Almost from the start, the early reviewers were skeptical or openly rejecting of surrealism. Although sometimes praising its ability to free the poetic image from logical constraints, most slung accusations at the surrealist movement, calling it derivative and unoriginal, a mere escapist fantasy, a passing fashion, another -*ism* without consequence.

In August of 1928, the *Contemporáneos* journal published a translation by Jaime Torres Bodet of a story by Apollinaire, including an introduction called "La cirugía, género suprarrealista" [Surgery, a Surrealist Genre]. This is the moment in which the Contemporáneos group was beginning to take shape as the new face of Mexican poetry, and Torres Bodet's focus on surrealism is symptomatic of a growing discourse around the movement. In October of that same year, Torres Bodet published in *Contemporáneos* a review of Breton's *Nadja*, which he faults for lacking a clear plot and for failing to "organize" the liberty that is its primary focus (qtd. in Bradu 15). In Torres Bodet's view, when compared to the stories by Edgar Allan Poe with regard to the sense of mystery evoked, *Nadja* comes up short.

The poet and essayist Jorge Cuesta (1903–42), another young writer making his name in *Contemporáneos*, was the only member of this group who had traveled to Europe and met Breton and others of the French group. But this experience was not enough to convince the highly rational Cuesta of the validity of the surrealist project. His reviews of the poetry of Éluard and Desnos, published in *Contemporáneos* in May and November of 1929 respectively, criticize the irrational surrealist image and present Desnos and Breton as participants in a cult of mysteries and alchemical communications. The literary historian Luis Mario Schneider remarks about this period in Mexico, "With Jorge Cuesta, we have poetic surrealism in Éluard and living surrealism embodied in Breton and Desnos. Though brief, this experience of Jorge Cuesta with the surrealist group in Paris will allow Mexican writers to begin to take more seriously the movement's meaning, its transformative significance, even though this in no way implies an assimilation of its postulates" (28). From 1929 forward, many Mexican writers and critics would treat surrealism with cautious respect, approaching it as an intriguing movement that deserves careful explanation to the reading public. But none (before Paz) would express enthusiasm for its creative possibilities as did Pellegrini's group in Argentina or the Mandrágora poets in Chile. Surrealism as a catalyst for creative work in Mexico would be embraced, paradoxically and problematically, by a series of outsiders.

The Hallucinatory Voyages of Antonin Artaud

The languid early reception of surrealism in Mexico was suddenly energized by the arrival in 1936 of the French playwright, poet, actor, and essayist Antonin Artaud (1896–1948), whom Anna Balakian calls the "dark angel of surrealism" (243). The ultimate iconoclast and a man who suffered from bouts of mental illness from adolescence forward, Artaud is one of the European figures of the period that has generated the most sustained interest among Latin American readers. Artaud initially rejected the idea of joining the surrealists: in a letter dated October 1924 he states with an ironic twist, "I have met all the Dadaists who wanted to entice me on to their latest Surrealist boat, but nothing doing. I'm much too much of a surrealist for that" (qtd. in Hayman 54). Artaud's tongue-in-cheek comment is in fact prophetic, for though he was in many ways the ideal surrealist, his fierce individualism complicated his relationship with the group from the first moment of contact. He did join the group in the fall of 1924, and early in 1925 took over the direction of the Surrealist Bureau of Research. Over the next two years, Artaud published poems and prose pieces regularly in *La Révolution surréaliste* and was the sole editor for the third issue of that journal.

This official connection was short-lived, however. Artaud's loyalty to certain disaffected members of the group and his refusal to join the Communist Party resulted in his official withdrawal from the movement in December of 1926. Nevertheless, surrealism left a permanent mark on his thought. In the words of Susan Sontag, "Despite Artaud's passionate rejection of surrealism, his taste was Surrealist—and remained so" (xxvii). No doubt the most significant aspect of Artaud's contact with surrealism was its influence on his theories about the theater—theories that profoundly altered the character of dramatic writing, direction, and performance in the twentieth century.[5] For the purposes of the present study, it is crucial to observe that Artaud's early involvement with surrealism had a marked effect on his interpretation of the realities he confronted in his travels in Mexico.

Mexico had been the object of Artaud's theatrical fantasy long before his plans to visit the country materialized in 1936. His second manifesto on the theater, written between 1930 and 1933, describes a play to be called "The Conquest of Mexico," which he had conceived as "the first spectacle of the Theater of Cruelty" and which would concretize his ideas for the physical and psychical space of the theater. The play as Artaud envisions it in this manifesto is not performable: it reads more like a surrealist poem than a play script. The stage directions for the fourth and final act, for instance, describe the scene surrounding Montezuma's abdication of the Aztec throne: "Lights and sounds produce an impression of dissolving, unraveling, spreading, and squashing—like watery fruits splashing on the ground. Strange couples appear, Spaniard with Indian, horribly enlarged, swollen and black, swaying back and forth like carts about to overturn. Several Hernando Cortez's enter at the same time, signifying that there is no longer any leader. In some places, Indians massacre Spaniards; while in front of a statue whose head is revolving in time to the music, Cortez, arms dangling, seems to dream. Treasons go unpunished, shapes swarm about, never exceeding a certain height in the air" (*Theater* 131).

This is a patently surrealist text in its use of oneiric imagery and unexpected juxtapositions and in the oneiric forms seen as "dissolving" and "unraveling." It is also arguably surrealist in its portrayal of Hernán Cortés, a historic figure conventionally characterized as active and rational, in a dreaming and inactive state with "arms dangling." The chaos unleashed by the abdication of Moctezuma is just one example of how *The Conquest of Mexico* served to present Artaud's unshakeable notion that certain "primitive" cultures—like those of pre-Columbian Mexico—embodied a cosmic unity and a vitality that Western civilization could no longer claim.

Increasingly disillusioned with the stagnation of European culture, Artaud determined to experience Mexican reality for himself. In a letter to the French Minister of Foreign Relations dated August 1935, he lays out his philosophy and the purpose of his journey. We have a great deal to learn, he tells the minister, from the secrets of ancient Mexican culture, especially at a time when every country in the world is struggling to find a "collective dynamism." Here Artaud speaks of his journey as a *mission*: "My mission, if there is a mission, would consist in extricating and fixing that dynamism" (*Oeuvres complètes* 8: 342). Though his journey to Mexico was eventually sanctioned by the French government, Artaud's later writings reveal that this was, more than an official or ethnographic mission, a personal pilgrimage to find a lost cosmology and to heal his own diseased psyche.

When Artaud finally arrived in February of 1936, the Mexican intelligentsia was prepared to welcome him, largely due to the efforts of the Contemporáneos poet Jaime Torres Bodet, who was then serving as a cultural attaché in Paris. Under the auspices of the Universidad Nacional Autónoma de México, Artaud gave three public lectures in February of 1936. The texts of each of these three lectures,[6] which focus on surrealism and its place in the socialist revolution as well as on the origins of the theater, are rather free-associative and prophetic in their rhetoric, far from the structured discourse that the public might have expected. One of the primary messages Artaud wants to convey to his Mexican audience—and particularly to the youth—is that the indigenous cultures of that land held the secrets to its future: "Mexico's Indian blood holds an ancient secret of the race"; his concern is that whereas "present-day Mexico copies Europe, in my view it is European civilization that should ask of Mexico its secret" (*Oeuvres* 8: 183). This was a message that neither the postrevolutionary government under Lázaro Cárdenas, nor the intelligentsia under the leadership of figures like José Vasconcelos and Alfonso Caso, nor the largely *mestizo* population were likely to welcome, especially coming as it did from a European with no direct experience of autochthonous Mexican culture. Here the tables are turned and turned again: the French writer preaches to his Mexican listeners that they should reject the European model—not in favor of their own current cultural projects, but in favor of a return to their own mythic past. Yet in Mexico in 1936, *mestizaje*—the mix of European and indigenous races—had been elevated practically to the status of a national religion, and the indigenous minorities were either ignored or swept up in schemes of assimilation. Mexico's pre-Columbian past, while appreciated on some levels, was subordinated to ideologies of progress. This political and social reality, which Artaud either misunderstood or chose to ignore, left a wide breach between his lectures and their reception. His first glimpses of this situation are captured in a telling comment he made in a letter to the French editor Jean Paulhan: "This population of Whites (Creoles) and half-breeds would be very happy to hear no more about the Indians" (*Selected* 365).

The lack of true communication and integration that Artaud experienced in his six months in Mexico City (a city that Artaud saw as a halfway-point between corrupt European civilization and authentic existence) led him to carry out his dream of traveling to the interior to witness indigenous culture firsthand. Once again he secured the support of officials in both the government and the national university, who contracted him to write a series of articles on his findings. In August of 1936, practically penniless and in the throes of withdrawal from heroine, Artaud managed to employ a guide and travel 750 miles north by train and then on horseback into a remote corner of the Sierra Madre, land of the Tarahumara. The impact of this journey on Artaud was enormous. According to Schneider, "The actual road that Artaud traveled through the mountain ranges of Chihuahua encompasses a chronological time that is concise in days, but that is reconfigured and suffered over many years"—during the 12 years, to be precise, that were left to him before his death (91).

The essay "A Voyage to the Land of the Tarahumaras" was first published in Spanish translation in *El Nacional Revolucionario* in Mexico City in October of 1936, shortly after Artaud's return to the capital. The first section of this essay, called "The Mountain of Signs," describes in quasi-mystical terms the landscape he encountered: "The land of the Tarahumara is full of signs, forms, and natural effigies which in no way seem the result of chance, as if the gods, whom one feels everywhere here, had chosen to express their powers by means of these strange signatures in which the figure of man is hunted down from every side" (*Selected* 379). Artaud is determined to glimpse a kind of human intelligence behind the geography of these harsh mountainscapes. He describes the play of light on the rock walls, which caused him to see—repeatedly—certain nightmarish figures such as that of an "animal's head carrying in its jaws its effigy which it devoured" (*Selected* 380). This entire passage has a hermeneutic quality, as the litany of hallucinatory images marches forward toward what he is sure will be a revelation of hidden meaning: "I saw . . . I saw . . . I saw . . . I seemed to read everywhere" (*Selected* 379–80). In several instances, Artaud's European paradigms (often esoteric in origin) impose themselves on the American landscape, resulting in curious explanations:

> There is in the Cabala a music of Numbers, and this music, which reduces the chaos of the material world to its principles, explains by a kind of awesome mathematics how Nature is ordered and how she directs the birth of the forms that she pulls out of chaos. And everything I saw seemed to correspond to a number. The statures, the forms, the shadows always presented the recurring numbers 3, 4, 7, 8. The broken-off busts of women numbered 8; the phallic tooth, as I said, had three stones and four holes; the forms that became volatile numbered 12, etc. I repeat, if someone says that these forms are natural, I shall not argue; it is their repetition which is not natural. And what is even less natural is that the forms of the landscape are repeated by the Tarahumara in their rites and their dances. And these dances are not the result of chance but obey the same secret mathematics, the same concern for the subtle relations of Numbers which governs the entire Sierra region. (*Selected* 381)

In this passage Artaud turns to the Cabala and to Pythagorean notions of the mathematical ordering of the universe in order to explain what must otherwise have appeared to him to be a bewilderingly chaotic *terra incognita*.

In echoes of his third Mexico City lecture, Artaud insists, without any empirical support for his argument, that this tribe represents a more ancient and therefore more authentic culture than any of those known in Europe: "And I find it strange that the primitive people of the Tarahumara tribe, whose rites and culture are older than the Flood, actually possessed this science well before the appearance of the Legend of the Grail, or the founding of the Sect of the Rosicrucians" (*Selected* 382). Similarly, in a letter to the governors of Mexican states, Artaud claims that Mexico and Tibet were "nodal points of world culture" and that the Mexican Indian rituals were living evidence of that fact (qtd. in Hayman 106). It seems to him that in the Sierra Madre he has stumbled on the very origins of human existence, and in a quintessentially surrealist manner he is determined to make sense of it for himself without relying on rational thought.

That very impulse will lead Artaud to seek out a particular remote village where the ritual of the peyote is performed and to persuade the "sorcerers" who lead this ritual to allow him to participate. The story of this experience is told in the second section of "A Voyage to the Land of the Tarahumaras," which is called simply "The Peyote Dance." An even more markedly surrealist text than "The Mountain of Signs," this piece is part narrative recounting of the event, part reflection on its meaning from a temporal distance, and part impressionistic and often hermetic poetic prose. Throughout, the presence of the self as *body* is paramount, as it is in so much of Artaud's writing. "This cataclysm which was my body," this "ill-assembled heap of organs," hinders at every turn the explorer's attempts to participate fully in the experience of living among the Tarahumaras (*Selected* 382, 383). He begins "The Peyote Dance" by expressing frustration that even after his arduous journey, followed by 28 days of waiting, "I had not yet come back into myself, or I should say *gone out* into myself, into this dislocated assemblage, this piece of damaged geology" (*Selected* 382). Artaud's use of the word *geology* to mark his own infirm body within the imposing geology of the Sierra Madre provides an initial clue about the subjective subtext of this piece. In fact, his own emotions overwhelm him even before the actual ritual begins. "For to have come this far, to find myself at last on the threshold of an encounter and of this place from which I expected so many revelations, and to feel so lost, so abandoned, so deposed," he muses, as a way of explaining "that interstitial pain which every night pursued me" (*Selected* 383). The words *threshold*, *encounter*, and *revelations* all point to the ponderous sense of subjective meaning that Artaud brought to this experience, which contrasts sharply with the image of his own broken self.

As he waits, able to communicate only partially through his Spanish-speaking guide, Artaud questions the very assumptions that had led him to this place: "And all of this, for what? For a dance, for a rite of lost Indians who no longer even know who they are or where they came from and who, when you question them, answer with tales whose connection and secret they have lost" (*Selected* 383). The preconceived notions Artaud brings to bear on the lived experience are patent here. In Europe he had read widely about indigenous cultures, and in Mexico City he had consulted anthropologists about the Tarahumara in particular. Given the language barrier, we can presume that the judgment he exercises on the individuals in the village of Norogachic—claiming that they have lost their sense of origins and identity and even the secret of their own tales—reveals preconceptions Artaud brought with him. If he is aware of these preconceptions, he does not say so.

As it happened, Artaud was permitted not only to observe but also to participate in the peyote ritual, which he describes with a fair amount of detail. Again, his perception of American reality is overlaid by a European schema. As he watches the ritual dance, he is visited by a complex vision of a Nativity painting by Hieronymus Bosch. The long period of his "horrible waiting," followed by the preparatory rituals he had just witnessed, finally culminated "in a circle peopled with Beings, here represented by ten crosses." This scene surprises him with its syncretic and gender-bending iconography: the ten Beings represent the Invisible Lords of the Peyote, and among them, "the Male Principle of Nature, which the Indians call *San Ignacio*, and its female, *San Nicolás!*" (386). At this point, Artaud's fascination with numbers and numerology causes him to shift from a relatively objective chronicle to a purely subjective conclusion: "*Ten* crosses in the circle and *ten* mirrors. *One* beam with three sorcerers on it. *Four* priests (*two* Males and *two* Females). The epileptic dancer, and *myself*, for whom the rite was being performed" (387). This last phrase leads us to question whether Artaud was aware of himself as an ethnographic participant-observer, a kind of cultural tourist for whom the Tarahumara were staging a performance, or if he narcissistically presumes a greater role in the ritual than what his hosts had intended.

In writing of this experience later, Artaud affirms that the peyote dance is after all a human ritual, a set of conventional forms without any a priori meaning. If he had expected his journey to reveal some profound truth to him, he acknowledges the failure. After describing in detail the peyote "rasp," a wooden wand inscribed with various symbols that the master sorcerers use to perform "those acts of exorcism which pull the Elements apart," he confesses, "And this is precisely the aspect of the mysterious tradition which I did not succeed in penetrating" (390). He admits that the Peyote sorcerers had managed to guard their deepest secrets. During his own part in the ritual, he recalls, they had laid him down so that the ritual would descend on him: "There was this rolling vault, this physical arrangement of cries, tones, steps, chants. But above everything, beyond everything, this impression that kept recurring that behind all this, greater than all this and beyond it, there was concealed something else: *the principle*" (391).

What strikes the reader here is that Artaud's participation in the peyote ritual gave him very little in the way of new knowledge; furthermore, if he had sought for himself a psychic or physical cure, nothing of the sort occurred. And yet the experience serves to intensify his conviction that true meaning exists behind or beyond what the senses or the rational mind can perceive—within something he calls *the principle*. Here Artaud approximates Pierre Mabille's studies of universal myths and Breton's gradual turn toward occult ideologies. In this way Artaud's texts show yet another facet of the surrealist concern with the revelation of hidden—though fundamentally human rather than divine—realities.

In retrospect, it is clear that Artaud did not accomplish his stated mission of convincing the Mexicans to reevaluate the indigenous cultures in their midst. His "ethnographic surrealism" did, however, serve to heighten the European perception of Mexico as a site of the strange, the primitive, and the mythical. His experience among the Tarahumaras was the subject of numerous articles that Artaud published in France in such widely circulated venues as *La Nouvelle Revue Française*, beginning with "The Mountain of Signs" in 1937 and ending with a strange poetic piece called "Tutuguri," written in the Ivry-sur-Seine clinic scarcely two weeks before his death.

The reception of this same material in Mexico itself is difficult to gauge, but it was certainly more limited and more tentative than in Europe. More than twenty of Artaud's articles on the Tarahumaras and other subjects relating to Mexico's mythic past were translated into Spanish and published in Mexico City periodicals, most notably in *El Nacional*, between April and November of 1936. One of the most intriguing early responses was written by the Contemporáneos poet Bernardo Ortiz de Montellano and published in *El Nacional* in July of 1936. "Artaud y el sentido de la cultura en México" first identifies Artaud as a surrealist and emphasizes the goal of renovating European culture. He maintains that Artaud's particular form of surrealism tends toward "un espiritualismo total de orden místico . . . de orden mágico panteísta de unidad con la naturaleza, genuino de las culturas indígenas de América" [a total spiritualism of a mystic kind . . . of a kind of magical, pantheistic unity with nature, which is genuine among the indigenous cultures of America] (qtd. in Schneider 80, n. 53).

In the most reflective and, for our purposes, the most revealing part of this essay, Ortiz de Montellano states, "Nosotros hemos discutido mucho y con más o menos fortuna estos temas, pero necesitamos que otros ojos venidos de otros pueblos nos descubran la realidad de nuestra propia vida como lo hace Artaud, con apasionado lirismo" [We have discussed these themes often, with varying degrees of success, but we need other eyes from other places to reveal to us the reality of our own life as Artaud does, with passionate lyricism] (Schneider 80, n. 53). Strikingly, Ortiz de Montellano's attitude echoes Artaud's by assuming the inadequacy of the Mexican people to interpret their own reality. Discussing the "profound" difference in values between Europe and America, he claims that what Mexicans lack in greed and thrift, they gain in a sense of life as "pasión, tumulto, goce, aun cuando sea breve" [passion, fervor, enjoyment, though it be brief]. Echoing a socialist exaltation of the proletariat, Ortiz de Montellano then commends the Mexican *campesino* for being "el que conserva la cultura heredada" [the one who conserves his inherited culture].

After citing one of his own previous articles, in which he had praised the "voluptuous" indigenous appreciation of death (coupled with the Spanish ability to *think* about death), Ortiz de Montellano concludes the article with this observation:

> Creo como Artaud que el mundo prepara un tipo humano que no sea el simple fantasma que la civilización del chofer . . . y la burguesía han fabricado en otros pueblos, sino el hombre vinculado a las fuerzas de la vida y de la naturaleza para mandar en ellas; pero también creo que en México aún nos falta asimilar ciertos aspectos de la cultura europea y de la civilización que, como la ciencia, son ya conquista definitiva del hombre futuro y el elemento base de su universalidad. (Schneider 80, n. 53)

[Like Artaud I believe that the world is preparing a kind of human being who will not be the mere ghost created by the civilization of the chauffeur . . . and the bourgeoisie in other countries, but rather man linked to the forces of life and nature in order to take charge over them; but I also believe that in Mexico we still need to assimilate certain aspects of European culture and civilization which, like science, are the definitive conquest of future man and the fundamental basis of his universality.]

The most notable aspect of Ortiz de Montellano's essay is its very ambivalence, which suggests that Artaud provoked at least one prominent Mexican intellectual to thoughtfully reassess his own culture. On the one hand, Ortiz de Montellano reasserts his estimation of particular aspects of the culture that Mexicans have long valued (the passion for life, the reverence for death, the *campesino*'s closeness to both nature and tradition); on the other hand, he welcomes an outsider's view of Mexico and even asserts a societal need for that external perspective. Artaud's writings prompt Ortiz de Montellano to insist—in an era of fervent Mexican nationalism—that Europe can still provide a stimulus for advancement in certain areas like science and "civilization." The ultimate irony here, of course, is that Artaud had gone to Mexico to teach its inhabitants precisely the opposite—that Mexicans should reject corrupt European culture and that Mexico's future lay hidden in its own most ancient and marginalized peoples.

Breton in the Land of Waking Dreams

Less than two years after Artaud's enigmatic journey, André Breton arrived for a four-month stay in Mexico, and with him Mexico's fate as a surrealist object was sealed. Although he was officially sponsored by the French government as a cultural attaché to Mexico, he was given no specific mission. In fact, one of Breton's own reasons for this visit had little to do, at least directly, with Spanish America or with Franco-Mexican relations: Breton planned to meet with Leon Trotsky, whose split with the Stalinist-run Communist Party had occasioned his exile to Mexico in January of 1937. (As is well known, Trotsky was assassinated by an agent of the Stalinist regime in Mexico City in 1940.) A decade after the internal crisis that began in 1927, the surrealists were continuing to wrangle over the appropriate relationship to maintain with the socialist revolution. For Breton and several (though not all) of his associates, the desire to reject everything associated with the increasingly dictatorial Stalin was paramount by the late 1930s, and thus the figure of Trotsky was an appealing one for many surrealists.

One of the important outcomes of the meeting with Trotsky was the publication of the *Manifesto for an Independent Revolutionary Art* (July 25, 1938), drafted by Breton and Trotsky, but signed, for tactical reasons, by Breton and Diego Rivera. The already-famous Mexican muralist and the painter Frida Kahlo served as Breton's hosts, facilitating his encounter with Trotsky and traveling with him to Mexico's interior. Another reason behind Breton's visit to Mexico was Antonin Artaud: reconciled with Breton a decade after his expulsion from the movement, Artaud shared his Mexican experience with Breton. This exposure appears to have awakened an old dream for Breton, who recalls in a 1952 interview with André Parinaud that "no matter how little I tend by nature to like travel, Mexico—perhaps because of some childhood memories—was the one country that attracted me. I hasten to add that I was not disappointed" (*Conversations* 145). His response to Mexico was generally positive in spite of the fact that throughout his four-month stay there, Breton was dogged by the negative fallout from his association with Trotsky, one of several factors that led to a very mixed reception among Mexican intellectuals.

The surrealist-affiliated poet and painter Agustín Lazo had prepared the way for Breton's arrival with his "Reseña sobre las actividades sobrerrealistas," an extensive and lucid essay published by the national university in March of 1938, just weeks before Breton's arrival. This 18-page pamphlet explains surrealism in straightforward terms and is accompanied by reproductions of work by Dalí, de Chirico, Miró, and others. A similarly informative and supportive publication was the May 1938 issue of the respected *Letras de México*, dedicated entirely to surrealism and to Breton, whom the editor Octavio G. Barreda dubs "the great French poet" (qtd. in Bradu 87). One of the major collaborators in this journal was the Peruvian César Moro, who had arrived in Mexico only a month before Breton; included are several of Moro's translations of surrealist writers and his own poem titled "André Breton." Breton's famous essay "Surrealism and Painting" is also translated and printed in this issue, accompanied by reproductions of work by Hans Arp, Hans Bellmer, Salvador Dalí, Óscar Domínguez, Wolfgang Paalen, Ives Tanguy, and others. Fabienne Bradu concludes that this issue of *Letras de México* represents "the greatest and best effort by Mexican writers to divulge the principles of surrealism during Breton's stay in Mexico" (89).

In spite of these early affirmations of surrealism, notes of discord began to sound not long after Breton's arrival. On several occasions throughout his stay, Breton complained—with apparent justification—that preparations for his activities had not been well organized. In terms of public appearances, he succeeded in giving only the first of three scheduled lectures at the Universidad Nacional de México. The subsequent two lectures were poorly announced in the press and then cancelled at the last minute: Breton arrived to find the conference room doors closed (Bradu 148).[7] Yet apart from the apparent failure of the lecture series, Breton was able to disseminate his ideas through certain periodicals, including the popular magazine *Hoy*, which published a questionnaire the day after his first lecture. Breton's extensive responses to this questionnaire cover an array of topics from contemporary French literature and painting to the French response to fascism (Bradu 92–98).

Another public venue of note was Breton's presentation at the premiere of Buñuel and Dalí's film *Un Chien andalou*. The text of this presentation was not published in Mexico and was only discovered among his papers after his death. Reviews of the opening as an event, however, were numerous, including a positive assessment by Xavier Villaurrutia. "This film's sensuality," remarks the Contemporáneos writer, "is something simultaneously vivid and mournful; the eye sliced by a razor and the ants in the hand are, among many others, truly realized metaphors" (qtd. in Schneider 132). A less generous assessment is offered by Efraín Huerta, a younger poet who would make his name as a part of the group that formed around the journal *Taller*. Huerta's review of the event pokes fun at Breton and mentions his relationship with Trotsky, whom he also implausibly labels a surrealist (3).

The derisive tone of Huerta's review is characteristic of much of the response of Mexico's intelligentsia to Breton's presence and to surrealism overall. In contrast to the often Eurocentric perspective of a country like Argentina, Mexico's overtly nationalistic discourse in the years following the Revolution of 1910 precluded any open embrace of an artistic movement rooted in France. In other words, the struggle to come to terms with *la mexicanidad* kept the country's cultural focus squarely within its own borders and resisted any influences viewed as (post)colonialist or imperialist. Moreover, Breton's alliance with Trotsky made him the natural enemy of the Communist Party in Mexico at a moment of general fealty to Stalin. The anti-Trotsky forces (many of whom had connections with the administration of Mexico's National University) organized boycotts of Breton's lectures and propagated a view of Breton as the dictatorial "Pope" of surrealism (L. Andrade 181). A letter drafted by the cultural arm of the French Communist party (the International Association of Writers for the Defense of Culture) in fact suggested that its Mexican counterparts should shun Breton as a false revolutionary: "Fearing some misunderstanding, we wanted to inform you of the true situation of André Breton, which does not represent in any way the revolutionary spirit of French literature" (qtd. in Bradu 143). The negative response to Breton is pointedly summarized in an editorial in the newspaper *El Universal*, published when the columnist mistakenly thought that Breton had left the country: "Now that Breton has left and cannot accuse us of being inhospitable . . . we must speak of his failure . . . Let him gather up his export materials and content himself with having learned something from us during his journey, since he was unable to teach us anything" (qtd. in Bradu 191, 192–93). These comments would prove prophetic: for numerous reasons, the first years of the surrealist revolution had little effect on Mexican letters, and Breton's visit did little to change that situation. With scarce exceptions (such as Ortiz de Montellano), the powerful head of the French surrealist movement was unable to "teach them anything." What Mexico did for Breton and for European surrealism, however, is an altogether different story.

No doubt the most extensive and incisive interview conducted during Breton's stay in Mexico we owe to the Honduran poet Rafael Heliodoro Valle, who was living at the time in Mexico City. The interview was printed under the title "Diálogo con André Breton" in the periodical *Universidad de México* in June of 1938. In response to Heliodoro Valle's questions about his attraction to Mexico, Breton mentions the "black humor" that he had found in popular artists such as José Guadalupe Posada, one of many factors that made Mexico a truly vibrant country for him. When asked if there is "a surrealist Mexico," Breton provides an answer that has since become iconic: "Apart from everything I have said, Mexico tends to be the surrealist place *par excellence.*" He goes on to say, "I find Mexico to be surrealist in its contours, in its flora, in the dynamism gained from its mixture of races, and even in its highest aspirations" (qtd. in Bradu 128).

Whatever complaints Breton might have had about his official reception there, and however cool his welcome might have been among certain writers and intellectuals, on his return to France he carried with him not only a set of treasured artifacts but also a set of impressions that largely corroborated his original fantasies. These impressions, presented in an essay called "Souvenir du Mexique" [Memory of Mexico] that Breton wrote shortly after his return home in 1938, fed the European surrealist imagination from that moment forward. This extensive essay was first published as a special section of *Minotaure* in May 1939, with a cover illustration by Diego Rivera and photographs by Manuel Álvarez Bravo. From the essay emerges a portrait of a complex country, one that Breton wishes to herald as a model to be followed. The organizing metaphor he employs is the *agave* or century plant, a kind of botanical phoenix that pulls enough moisture from the desert to periodically send up a single flowering shoot. The essay's first sentence links the agave to the ability of human life to renew itself perpetually in Mexico: "Red, virgin land impregnated with the most generous blood, a land where man's life has no price, always ready like the omnipresent agave expressing it to burst into a single final bloom of desire and danger!" (*Free Rein* 23). The rhetorically conventional term "virgin" ties Mexico in the European imagination to those supposedly pure places not yet touched by civilization. But in the remainder of this essay Breton seems to underscore the opposite of virginity: that is, he presents modern Mexico as a place created by layer upon layer of civilization.

Unlike Artaud, who has little use for the historical realities of Mexico, Breton calls to mind both the 1810 War of Independence and the Revolution of 1910–20 as evidence that "there is still one country in the world where the wind of liberation has not abated" (23). He sees everywhere in the countryside not only the agave and the magnificent organ cactus but also the phantasm of "a gun-bearing man with fiery eyes . . . standing there in his magnificent rags: he may, at any time, rise unaided from the depths of unawareness and adversity" (23). Breton thus ascribes value to the illiterate soldier (mestizo or *indio*)—the very figure immortalized in Mariano Azuela's *Los de abajo* [The Underdogs, 1916] and other novels of the revolution—as the type of person who embodies the surrealist ideal of liberation at all costs. The political, even military aspect of liberation is highlighted as Breton praises *campesino* generals like Emiliano Zapata who formed part of the "admirable upthrust" that led "the most shamefully exploited section of the population" to victory (24). In this initial portion of the essay, Breton seems content to echo the postrevolutionary narrative that presented Mexico as a young, socially conscious democracy built from below. He acknowledges the corruption of the state apparatus but passes over this quickly to assert that "it is nevertheless true that Mexico is bursting with the hopes that have been successively placed on other countries—the USSR, Germany, China, Spain—and that, during the last historical period, have been dramatically thwarted" (24). Returning to his central metaphor of the agave-phoenix, Breton insists that it lies in the nature of countries like Mexico "repeatedly to come back to life and blossom on the ruins of this very civilization" (24). As we saw with Artaud, and as is often the case with the surrealists abroad, Mexico serves Breton as a blank screen on which to project certain preconceived ideals.

The essay's middle portion leaves aside historical and political scenarios to return to the vision of Mexico as a land of living myth. The message of the tombs now being excavated by archeologists, says Breton, "charges the air with electricity" (24). Rather than a savvy political entity with lessons to teach other countries, he now sees a land just emerging from a primitive state, still under the sway of its ancient deities: "Mexico, having barely awakened from its mythological past, keeps evolving under the protection of Xochipilli, the god of flowers and lyrical poetry, and of Coatlicue, the goddess of the earth and of violent death, whose effigies, more impressive, more intense than any of the others, exchange winged words and raucous calls from one end of the national museum to the other, above the heads of the Indian peasants who are the more numerous and more reverent of its visitors" (*Free Rein* 24). Breton is a poet (and a surrealist one at that), and it would be unjust to apply to his rhetoric the strictures that one might otherwise apply to an anthropological essay. In this I concur with the cultural historian James Clifford who suggests that "it is best to suspend disbelief in considering the practices—and the excesses—of surrealist 'ethnographers'" (121). This caveat aside, in exploring the European image of Mexico as it was filtered through the surrealist sensibility, it is important to note that while authenticating the pre-Columbian deities Xochipilli and Coatlicue as active presences in modern-day Mexico, Breton still represents the past as a state of sleep or unconsciousness from which the country needs to emerge. He seems torn here between valuing progress (Mexico "awakens"; it "keeps evolving") and valuing a past steeped in myth. The terms of this debate become even more complicated when we consider that in the above-quoted passage, the site of his vision is not an inhabited quotidian space, but a museum, the Museo Nacional de Antropología. At a far remove from Artaud as a participant-observer in the circle of peyote dancers, Breton is situated here as an outside observer of indigenous people who are in turn observing their own past—one that has been recovered, ordered, and represented to them by archeologists and museum curators.

Breton cites Xochipilli and Coatlicue among the pantheon of Aztec deities because they embody the forces of life and death. The life-death juxtaposition was one that fascinated virtually all European visitors to Mexico in this period: Breton in fact calls it "the principle lure of Mexico" (*Free Rein* 24). Within the surrealist ideal of the reconciliation of opposites, it would be difficult to find more enticing examples than Mexico's Day of the Dead ceremonies, José Guadalupe Posada's etchings of cartoonish skeletons dancing in a cantina, or Manuel Ávarez Bravo's photographs of a factory where caskets for children are made. (At this point, in a sober nod to reality, Breton cites the infant mortality rate for Mexico at 75 percent.) In another stunning image of death-in-life, Breton describes a tumbledown nineteenth-century mansion in the heart of Guadalajara, in which a sealed room holds the embalmed body of the former mistress of the house (26). This mansion becomes for him an oneiric space of still-to-be revealed meanings: "Naturally, the presence of that great lady, all the more oppressive for being invisible, seems to account for the dreamlike atmosphere of the house" (26).

Everywhere he looks, Breton sees the marvelous within scenes of ordinary life in Mexico. In perhaps the best example of this, he recalls his final visit to the Guadalajara mansion, when he entered a darkened living room in the early morning. "There, all alone, stood a magnificent creature, sixteen or seventeen years old, her hair disarranged in an ideal way. She had answered the door and, having laid down her broom, was smiling like the dawn of the world without showing the least sign of confusion" (28). The girl, he realizes, is naked beneath an old evening gown. Breton is so spellbound by this young woman that he fails to inquire who she is, and is left wondering whether she is "the daughter or sister of one of the individuals who had haunted that place in the days of their splendor, or was she of the race of those who invaded it?" (28). Significantly, he concludes that he does not need to know, since her mere existence is enough: "*Such is beauty*" (28). The entire sweep of Breton's "Memories of Mexico" is encapsulated in the image of this woman: she is young and yet ancient, clothed and yet naked, smiling and yet tragic. We might also conclude that Breton represents *himself* with precision in this final image. Enraptured by what he beholds, he chooses not to ask the questions that might turn this marvelous vision into a prosaic reality. Convulsive beauty does not bear up under too much knowledge.

The objects that Breton had gathered during his sojourn in Mexico, including pre-Columbian ceramic figures, *retablos* (ex-votos), masks, candy skulls, toys, photographs by Álvarez Bravo, and paintings by Posada and Kahlo, were exhibited in 1939 at the Renou et Colle gallery in Paris under the simple title "México." This exhibit constituted the latest in a series of representations of European interest in Latin America as a site of the "primitive" or the surreal, dating back to the early 1920s. In the evolution of this interest, pre-Columbian artifacts reflected the new wave of avant-garde fascination with the "other," following on the sustained attention to the African, Oceanic, and Pacific Northwest cultures. Articles on pre-Columbian art by Tristan Tzara and others had appeared in important journals in the 1920s and 1930s. Avant-garde writers and artists were frequent visitors at Paris's famous Musée d'Ethnographie du Trocadéro, where a major exhibit called Les Arts Anciens de L'Amérique opened in 1928. Toward the end of the 1930s, interest had begun to shift from pre-Columbian cultures to those of modern-day Mexico. A 1937 issue of *Minotaure*, for example, featured reproductions of woodblock prints by Posada. The eclectic mix of Breton's 1939 exhibit attests to the growing attention paid to the modern face of Mexico—albeit still as a site of *l'exotique*.

One of the important outcomes of Breton's visit to Mexico was the 1940 Exposición Internacional de Surrealismo at the Galería de Arte Mexicano, organized in France by Breton and in Mexico City by César Moro and the Austrian artist Wolfgang Paalen. The exhibition catalogue was printed in Spanish and English (a French version is notably absent), with a cover photograph by Álvarez Bravo. Moro's introduction to the catalogue evinces a true excitement about the first "official" appearance of international surrealism on Mexican soil. Surrealism, he claims, is the "magical word of the new century" (Moro, "Presentación" 474). He goes on to locate the event of the exhibition in his adopted land, Mexico, where a "heavenly combustion" is taking place in "the brilliant pre-Columbian night." Moro not only reflects the attitude of ethnographic surrealism that posits Latin America as a land of intriguing primitivism; he calls for these cultures to align themselves with the international movement represented by the exhibit:

> La Noche purísima del Nuevo Continente en que grandiosas fuerzas de sueño entrechocaban las formidables mandíbulas de la civilización en México y de la civilización en el Perú. Países que guardan, a pesar de la invasión de los bárbaros

españoles y de las secuelas que aún persisten, millares de puntos luminosos que deben sumarse bien pronto a la línea de fuego del surrealismo internacional. (475)

[The purest night of the New Continent in which great forces of the dream collide with the formidable jaws of civilization in Mexico and in Peru. Countries that hold, in spite of the invasion of the barbaric Spaniards and the consequences that persist to this day, thousands of luminous points that must soon join the line of fire of international surrealism.]

The exhibition featured many of the luminaries of the European avant-garde as well as Mexican painters such as Agustín Lazo, Guillermo Meza, and Antonio Ruiz, on whom Breton had turned a favorable eye. Several photographs by Álvarez Bravo were displayed, as well as a handful of pre-Columbian objects from Diego Rivera's private collection. The grouping of artists is curious: Rivera and Kahlo were included in the European portion of the exhibition, while non-Mexican painters such as the Guatemalan Carlos Mérida and the Peruvian César Moro were included with the Mexicans. Although the opening of the exhibit on January 17, 1940 attracted many of Mexico's cultural and social elite, including the muralists Diego Rivera and José Clemente Orozco, Xavier Villaurrutia and a number of the Contemporáneos writers, and the painters Miguel Covarrubias and María Izquierdo, the response to the exhibition in the Mexico City press was generally dismissive.[8]

Earlier in this chapter I examined Villaurrutia's flirtation with surrealism as emblematic of the Contemporáneos group's ambivalent embrace of avant-garde attitudes and techniques. Among the poets and writers that Breton lists in "Memory of Mexico" as "mes amis"—Carlos Pellicer, Xavier Villaurrutia, Rodolfo Usigli, Agustín Lazo, and César Moro—it was Moro alone, the only non-Mexican in his list, who truly took surrealism to heart in this era. As we saw in Chapter 5, Moro resided in Mexico from 1938 to 1948, and there wrote his only collection of poems in Spanish, *La tortuga ecuestre*. During the decade after Breton's visit, Moro was the only writer living in Mexico to continue seriously exploring surrealism. To cite only a few of his many contributions to the literary life of the moment, apart from his codirection of the 1940 Surrealist Exposition, Moro published in May of 1938 a brief anthology called *Los surrealistas franceses* in the journal *Poesía*. He contributed poems and translations to several issues of the surrealist-influenced journal *El Hijo Pródigo* (1944–46) and elsewhere published Spanish translations of Leonora Carrington's stories. Finally, in collaboration with Wolfgang Paalen he edited the journal *Dyn*. Prior to the return of Octavio Paz from Europe in 1953, no other Latin American figure would loom as large as Moro in Mexico's shadowy surrealist landscape.

The War Exiles in Mexico

The intensified avant-garde interest in Mexico, piqued by the search for "primitive" and "authentic" civilizations and more concretely by the journeys of Artaud and Breton, set the stage for an influx of Europeans during the early years of the Second World War. The reasons for this influx were cultural but also political: during the Lázaro Cárdenas regime (1934–40), Mexico relaxed the visa requirements for émigrés from many European countries and granted automatic citizenship to immigrants from Spain, many of whom were fleeing the civil war and the subsequent Franco regime. By the end of the period, the list of surrealist-affiliated artists who spent months or even years in Mexico would include Wolfgang Paalen and Alice Rahon, Benjamin Péret and Remedios Varo, Leonora Carrington, Kurt Seligmann, Gordon Onslow Ford, Roberto Matta, Kati and José Horna, and Esteban Francés, as well as César Moro. In the following pages, I examine a few of the most striking texts produced by these émigrés, in which Mexico's shape as a "found object" becomes increasingly convoluted.

Wolfgang Paalen

The Austrian Paalen (1905–59) and his wife Alice Rahon, a French poet and painter, settled in Mexico City in 1939 and did not return to Europe until 1952. (Paalen would later journey back to Mexico in 1954 with his second wife, Isabel Marín, and would end his own life five years later in the village of Taxco.) The Paalen-Rahon home in the colonial San Ángel district of the city was a veritable museum of artifacts from various world cultures, both ancient and modern (Sawin 250–53). Paalen made numerous trips to the Mexican provinces in search of artifacts and developed an expertise in pre-Columbian art. One of Paalen's most important contributions to international art was the journal *Dyn* (whose title was taken from the Greek word *dynaton*, meaning "the possible"), which he published in Mexico City between 1942 and 1944. By 1942, Paalen was attempting to move beyond surrealism in an effort to restore a greater balance between the imagination and the rational faculties. *Dyn* was widely distributed and is considered to be one of the most important surrealist-influenced journals of the period, though it is clearly eclectic in its approach. A double issue (4/5) that appeared in 1943 features art from North and South American native cultures, with articles contributed by Paalen as well as by the Mexican archeologist Alfonso Caso and the anthropologist Miguel Covarrubias. Though it originated in Mexico, *Dyn* was published not in Spanish but in English and French. This was probably because Paalen was primarily interested in reaching a North American audience; in fact, as Martica Sawin convincingly argues, Paalen served as a crucial link between surrealism and the movement that would become American abstract expressionism (267, 272). With the exception of his collaboration with Caso and Covarrubias on questions of Mexico's pre-Columbian history, the considerable role Paalen played in bringing Mexico into the European imaginary did not involve a significant dialogue with contemporary Mexicans on aesthetic issues. Once again we observe Mexico's place as object rather than subject in the avant-garde dialogue of the day.

A brief essay called "The Volcano-Pyramid: A Mythological Hypothesis Suggested by the Appearance of a New Volcano" brilliantly illustrates both Paalen's acumen and his ambivalent attitude toward contemporary Mexico. Written in 1943, the piece refers to the sudden emergence of the Paricutín volcano in a farmer's field in the central state of Michoacán. The appearance of this volcano occurred in February of that same year and captured the imagination of Mexican citizens and foreigners alike. "This event," comments Sawin, "entered into the mythology of the Surrealists in Mexico and became part of the litany of the marvelous in its expanded New World version. The violent eruption of the earth into flame was the perfect exemplification of Breton's dictum on convulsive beauty" (287). What is striking about Paalen's essay is the first paragraph, in which he locates his immediate concern in present-day rural Mexico:

> The birth of a volcano no longer gives rise to a myth. To conjure away the dangers of their new volcano, the villagers of Paricutín dance before the Christian fetish, the "miraculous" crucifix. They dance badly, their steps as out of rhythm as their beliefs—a confused mixture of decapitated paganism and decayed Catholicism. The creative image no longer emerges where the magic conception has degenerated into petty superstition; it is only in the debris of the great past of these Indians that we find the vestiges of one of the most monumental cosmogonies that man has ever conceived. (323)

Artaud had observed the Tarahumaras in their own territory and had participated, to some degree at least, in one of their most significant rituals. Breton had observed, from a kind of neutral distance, an undifferentiated group of "Indian peasants" in an urban museum, respectfully noting their reverential attitude toward the relics of their past. In contrast, Paalen observes the Purépechas in their own land, but he writes from the marked distance that separates the traditional scientist from his object of study. He makes little attempt to hide his disdain for the culture he observes, noting that they dance "badly" and that both their feet and their beliefs are "out of rhythm." Like the great anthropologists of his day, Paalen is interested in the shared symbolic substratum of cultures, but he is convinced that in the rite he witnesses among the Purépecha in 1943, such symbolism has been lost. Like Artaud, he makes pronouncements about a contemporary tribal belief system without having had direct access to their language. To be sure, Paalen lays the blame for the supposed cultural inferiority on a colonial past that "decapitated" the once-whole pagan beliefs. But rather than seeing the possibility for creative syncretism in a village dance around a crucifix, he sees only "petty superstition." In short, this essay reveals one common form of response among the 1940s émigrés to the country they inhabited, in which astute observations concerning pre-Hispanic cultures and their place in "the great cosmic symbolizations" are presented alongside an openly disparaging view of contemporary (in this case indigenous) culture.

Benjamin Péret

After Breton, the most important surrealist literary figure to arrive in Mexico from Europe was Benjamin Péret, who lived there from 1941 to 1947 with his second wife, the Spanish painter Remedios Varo. (Prior to this extended stay in Mexico, Péret had lived in Brazil from 1929 to 1931 in the company of his first wife, the Brazilian singer Elsie Houston.) Péret was one of the original founders of the surrealist movement and the only figure of note, apart from Breton, to remain faithful to its tenets throughout the course of his lifetime. The influence of Mexico on Péret is apparent in both his poetry and his essays. In 1942, he states in a letter to the artist Kurt Seligmann, "I have begun to occupy myself with an anthology of myths, legends, and folktales from America, from both the present and the pre-Columbian period. Naturally I am writing from the point of view of the marvelous and I am sure there is material for a magnificent collection" (qtd. in Sawin 265). This is orthodox surrealism at its best: energized by the new material made available in Mexico, Péret is fascinated with the country's present as well as its past, and he is prepared to see the "marvelous" in either direction. Péret's research on Latin American folklore and mythology was collected posthumously in 1960 under the title *Anthologie des mythes, légendes et contes populaires d'Amérique*. His interest in the connection between magic and poetry, a line of thinking informed by his familiarity with Latin American folklore and myth—and which would later influence the thinking of Octavio Paz—can be seen in his essays *La Parole est à Péret* [*Magic: The Flesh and Blood of Poetry*] (1943) and *Le Déshonneur des poètes* [*The Dishonor of Poets*] (1945), both considered important surrealist tracts. Finally, it is worth noting that Péret published a translation into French of the sacred Mayan text *The Book of Chilam Balam* (1955), a publication that helped further French interest in pre-Columbian cultures.

Péret's book-length poem *Air mexicain*, written in Paris shortly after his return in 1947, comprises a long meditation on Mexico's mythology and history.[9] It is written in a dynamic combination of short, dense verses and much longer verses that read as lyrical prose. The critic and translator Elizabeth R. Jackson sees this piece as Péret's "ultimate creation, a fine fresco that melds the judgment and sophistication of a modern man's insights with an empathized primitive imagination—in his own view, the most valuable and the purest expression of the human spirit" (97). The work's title connotes both the physical atmosphere of Mexico and a melody sung in its honor. *Mexican Air* reads for the most part as an automatic text in which images follow one another in breathtaking rapidity, bombarding the reader with both concrete cultural allusions and flights of lyricism. But out of this often confusing mélange emerges a rather clear portrait of a pre-Columbian civilization that eventually succumbs to the brutality of the Spanish conquest and, later, to the imperialist forces of the "black North" (67).

The opening salvo of the poem alludes to Mexico's volcanic landscape and quite possibly to the birth of the Paricutín volcano in 1943: "Fire in mourning spurts from every pore / Dust of sperm and blood covers his face tattooed with lava / His cry echoes in the night like the sign of the end of time / The shudder in haste on his thorny skin has been running since the corn has been preening in the wind / His heartfelt gesture brandished at arm's length ends after fifty-two years in a blazing mass of joy" (67). In this passage, geography is intertwined with human physiognomy, as the face of the volcano is covered not only with lava but also with sperm and blood. The first of the poem's numerous references to corn—Mexico's staple crop since pre-Hispanic times—likewise connects geography to life. The apocalyptic end of a world "after fifty-two years" reflects the division of the Aztec calendar into a succession of 52-year periods, each ending in a natural disaster that would give rise to a new *sol* or epoch.

Early in the poem, images of a mythic time-space evoke a world that anteceded even Aztec deities such as the rain god Tlaloc: "No one could say where the sea began since the rivers were running back into the egg that rosy Tlaloc himself still undisclosed was not yet hiding in his tiger's gullet" (69). From that point forward, numerous references to the Aztec world create a picture that neither idealizes nor condemns it. Péret recalls the motif of human sacrifice—always a commonplace in Western discussions of Aztec culture—in fiercely lyrical terms: "The rain tiger demanded its feast of hosts enchanted by a glorious end the grandfather of fire his gift of flowers smelling like beating hearts" (75). Here Péret alludes to the fundamental Aztec metaphor of the human heart as a flower, associated with the so-called flowery wars or ritual battles in which prisoners were destined to become sacrificial victims; this was the human destiny that signaled a "glorious end."

Enter Cortés: "From the eye that awakens the better to put to sleep had come down the bearded white plumed serpent on top of the hills of adoration making offerings as of old to lights and shadows waltzing lifelong" (77). The poem here makes clear allusion to Quetzalcoatl or the "Plumed Serpent," the Aztec god of the arts, of writing, and of knowledge. According to Aztec legend, Quetzalcoatl (a semidivine, semihistorical figure) had in the remote past sailed off to the east, promising to return one day from that direction. Early in the Spanish conquest of Tenochtitlan, the Aztecs began to associate Cortés with Quetzalcoatl, a misconception that undoubtedly facilitated the conquistador's access to and eventual destruction of the Aztec capital. Thus Péret's poem paradoxically marks the arrival of the "bearded white plumed serpent" as a moment of awakening that would eventually "put to sleep" the indigenous civilization. (It is pertinent to recall here Breton's use of the metaphors of waking and sleeping to characterize what he saw as Mexico's relative engagement in the "civilized" world.)

The long verse that follows evokes the deity Tezcatlipoca, whose name in Nahuatl, "Smoking Mirror," alludes to obsidian, a sacred stone associated with divination, discord, and war: "But the smoking mirror rolling on hearts that were gifts to its family arrives with a leap from cities made too sacred by oblivion for men to inhabit where two seas hold the horn of plenty in their hands wishing to clasp together so as to pray the flayed man to return at the promised time" (77). In this allusively dense passage, Péret conflates motifs from Aztec mythology and Spanish-Christian rule. The horn of plenty is a common visual trope for Mexico, given its inverted triangle shape that is "held" by two seas (i.e., the Gulf of Mexico and the Pacific). In this poem these two seas clasp their hands together in a Christian gesture of prayer. But the object of their prayer is the promised return of the "flayed man," the embodiment of the Aztec deity Xipe Totec, a god of life, death, and rebirth. Xipe Totec's appearance in this poem may serve to mark the Spanish conquest as a simultaneous destruction and new birth for Mexico, much in the same way that a volcano both destroys and prepares the ground for new life. This would explain the passage that immediately follows: "and the vapor of feverish blood leading with the breath of volcanoes creates a dizziness as exhilarating as the fulfillment of a predicted destiny" (77).

Lest the reader infer from Péret's poem that the Spanish conquest was simply a foretold, even "exhilarating" destiny that was finally fulfilled, *Air Mexicain* subsequently presents a searing indictment of that historical event. It is interesting to note that at this point the poem loses much of its hermetic character. Though still propelled by complex images, its lyricism is more rhetorically direct:

> No doubt that the great plumed serpent weary from hopeless migration will return to its people crater-eyed hands full of crystal song-flowers plucked from the night full of fruits gilding their lives . . .
> Oh no the abject cross that kills casts torture fires and the host marked by smallpox decays all it touches

> They go on casting men far off their ancestors' home without a single red dog in front to guide them over deserts devoid of night and day through chill winds that fracture the soul and insulting untamed floods
> Led by men with sinful words dressed in robes of thick mud *sweeping dishes with their noses* all demand gold valueless when weighed against the feathers of morning or night and commit tortures in the name of a king kneeling before two crossed rods (81)

The reader cannot miss the message of these lines: the Spanish conquest was a brutal event that destroyed one civilization in order to impose another on it. Surrealist free association gives way, at this point in the poem, to the implacable logic of history.

Yet even with this increased clarity of message, the poem retains its surrealist character in the theme of human liberty that underlies the entire breadth of the history it evokes, from the Aztecs to the Spaniards to Benito Juárez to Emiliano Zapata. This is why the indictment of the conquest is followed by a future-tense vision of "a song of liberty hotter than that of the deserts baked by the tyrant of summer" (83). This segment of the poem reads as a prophetic litany of life in Mexico when freedom will finally be achieved: "A song that breaks the shackles of slaves amazed that they now breathe light bears off the galley like a drowned ox and driving out of the dark mob of crucifix-lickers kindles the heat of the fire that claims its own creatures / The air will be clearer filled only with voices void of spies or constraints / The water will be more limpid reflecting only faces free from suffering and sin" (83). These lines need no explication: they speak of an ideal of freedom that will never be realized, but one that has reinvented itself several times in Mexican history.

In sum, Benjamin Péret displays a considerable knowledge of Mexican folklore and pre-Columbian cosmology, as did Wolfgang Paalen, and he places this knowledge in the service of a text whose techniques are fundamentally surrealist. Unlike Paalen's "The Volcano-Pyramid," however, Péret's text tends to exalt Mexican culture (both ancient and modern) and to lament its destruction at the hands of "barbaric" invaders and imperialists. To be sure, *Mexican Air* retains a lyric distance from contemporary Mexican life (the *campesino* here falls into the vague category of "the disinherited"), whereas for Paalen the contemporary indigenous Mexican was a concrete, although spiritually diminished, human being. Finally, we note that Péret's presentation of Mexican culture as a product of cultural syncretism prefigures the important later developments of this theme by writers such as Octavio Paz and Carlos Fuentes.

Leonora Carrington

The final wartime émigré I consider here is Leonora Carrington (1917–2011), a fiery young British painter and fiction writer who arrived in Mexico in 1943. Carrington and Remedios Varo were in fact the only artists from this group to make Mexico their permanent home: Varo died in Mexico City in 1963, and Carrington continued living there until her death in 2011. Arguably, Carrington is the member of the émigré group who most fruitfully absorbed Mexican culture into both aspects of her art. As her biographer Susan Aberth observes, the move to Mexico liberated Carrington from the constraints of her wealthy and possessive English family, from a difficult relationship with the German surrealist artist Max Ernst, and from the growing anxiety produced by the onset of war in Europe.[10] Thus "immersed in a new country rich with dynamic cultural and religious hybrids, she was now positioned to develop her creative visions in a manner that would ultimately lead to artistic recognition and success" (57).

The decade of the 1940s was a tremendously productive one for Carrington, in part due to her close friendship with Varo, who provided the social and creative energy behind the group that formed around her husband, Benjamin Péret. Says Aberth of this group, "Their social gatherings continued in spirit the sense of play and fun of those they had left behind in Europe and New York. There were costume parties, provocative all-night story-tellings, Surrealist games, practical jokes, and on occasion a fantastical meal prepared by Carrington and Varo" (60). Food, in fact, became a focal point for Carrington's experimental genius and, in its mythical and symbolic applications, for her painting. While many of the other émigrés kept a certain distance from their immediate surroundings, Carrington was fascinated by everyday life in Mexico City—particularly the open air markets and the indigenous medicinal healers or *curanderos*. The surrealist spirit in Carrington was drawn to the "paradoxical intermingling of the colonial Spanish with the surviving pre-Hispanic Indian culture," a combination that would inspire Carrington to experiment with unexpected cultural mixes in her painting (Aberth 62). Concretely, Mexican imagery appears in her work in traditional culinary objects such as the *comal* and the *metate*, in pyramidal structures, and in the famous *calavera* or human skull first popularized in the engravings of José Guadalupe Posada.

Many surrealist visual artists also experimented with writing, but in Carrington's case, writing was a true vocation. (Varo filled entire notebooks with automatic writing rich in surrealist imagery, but chose never to publish her written work.) Carrington published two novels and numerous short stories, several of which saw the light in international surrealist venues such as *Le Surréalisme, même* (Paris), *View* and *VVV* (New York), and *Las Moradas* (Lima), as well as in Breton's *Antologie de l'humour noir*.[11] Like many of her paintings, the stories are best described as a mix of myth, folklore, fairy tale, and occult symbolism. Always true to her hermetic belief system, Carrington fashions her fiction around archetypal motifs (often with a particularly alchemical character) such as the quest and the marriage of opposites. Her symbolic system is both universal and extremely personal or idiosyncratic, and it often has a particularly feminist bent.

Although most of Carrington's fiction reveals an essentially European imagination, two stories in particular stand out for their grounding in Mexican folklore. The first, "A Mexican Fairy-Tale," features a young pig-herder, Juan, who one day hears a voice crying out from a ruin. There are elements of straightforward social realism here: Juan is afraid of a wealthy villager named Don Pedro, who in turn is afraid of his boss, "somebody called Licenciado Gómez, who wore neckties and dark glasses and lived in the town and owned a black motor-car" (152). But as the tale develops, magical or fantastical elements appear and eventually dominate the plot: there are talking birds, pigs that cut themselves into tiny fragments of roasted meat, ants who wear jade bracelets on each ankle, and human tears that turn to stone. The particularly surrealist character of the prose is apparent in such images as a talking bird that is heard "laughing like a drainpipe" (153). Juan is forced to undertake a mythic journey of disintegration and rebirth, together with his companion María, who is Don Pedro's daughter. The tale ends with the immolation of the two children, who are then fused into a single entity, Juan-Mari. Here, as elsewhere in the story, the archetypal plot bears particularly Mexican markers, with the narrator prophesying that "they will return again to earth, one being called Quezalcoatl" (158).

Another prose tale by Carrington, a brief drama called "The Invention of Mole," has a much more ludic character. The *mole* of the title refers to the spicy chile and cacao sauce that accompanies many traditional Mexican dishes. The cast of characters, which includes Montezuma, the Archbishop of Canterbury, "The Great Witch Tlzxcluhuichiloquitle," and native fauna such as ocelots and quetzals, reflects the play's eclectic mix of cultures. Humor is created by the ironic juxtaposition of values, as for instance when Montezuma, speaking in Nahuatl, questions the "relatively passive role" played by common people in Christian rites, wondering if they get "mortally bored" (169). Upon the protestations of the archbishop, Montezuma replies, "So, then, the people watch the same ceremony over and over again, without miracles, magic, sacrifices, or dances! Such a religion is bound to stagnate completely in a few centuries!" (170). Here Carrington both pokes fun at her own Northern European Catholic heritage and places the Aztec practice of human sacrifice in a new light. In contrast to the archbishop, who expresses himself in inflated, cliché-ridden rhetoric ("The Holy Church is founded on the Rock of Eternity and the very gates of Hell shall not prevail against her"), Montezuma reveals himself to be a true philosopher-theologian. Compared to what he observes in Christian thought and practice, he says, "our own anguish is something more vital, our desires, our passions, our deep thirst for marvels must be satiated. Otherwise we'd all turn into phantoms, or into something worse, empty ideas" (170). The reader of "The Invention of Mole" is thus prepared by this darkly humorous contrast for the outcome of the play, in which the archbishop is carried off, shrieking, to be sacrificed and stewed "in the most exquisite sauces" (173).

Unlike the majority of her fellow surrealist émigrés, Carrington managed—in the more than six decades of her life spent primarily in Mexico—to garner the respect and admiration of the Mexican intelligentsia and artistic community. In fact, says Aberth, "Carrington has long been considered part of the artistic heritage of Mexico" (8). This is due in great part to her willingness to appreciate Mexico as a living community of people and not simply as the site of pre-Hispanic artifacts or the impenetrable indigenous "other" and by her efforts not only to mine Mexican culture for her own artistic purposes but also to hold that culture up as a critical mirror to her own.

Conclusion

Martica Sawin pointed out near the end of the twentieth century that "A debate over the impact of Surrealism on Mexican art continues without much prospect of resolution" (286). As was generally the case with Artaud and Breton, the presence in Mexico of the dynamic group of surrealist-affiliated émigrés went virtually unnoticed or was openly rejected by the Mexican artistic community.[12] The overall lack of communication and appreciation was mutual: even apart from the language barrier, there was certainly an attitude of insularity on the part of the émigrés, who often shared a common background and a nostalgia for Europe or New York and who did not actively seek the company of their Mexican colleagues. Many, like Paalen, felt alienated from the everyday life of Mexico City even while they found themselves inspired by the Mexican landscape, its myths, or its turbulent history.[13] Others, like Carrington and Péret, absorbed a wealth of Mexican folklore, mythology, and even contemporary imagery into their work, even while retaining their essential identities as Europeans.

If the debate over the impact of surrealism on the Mexican visual arts remains unresolved, such a debate scarcely exists in the realm of literature, since the impact on writers in this early phase was negligible. In this chapter I have examined some extraordinary literary texts produced by European surrealists for whom Mexico was an object of fascination, provocation, or consternation—all of which contributed to the problematic myth of Mexico as the quintessential surrealist locale. Chafing at this imposed vision, constrained by a culture of nationalistic fervor, and in some cases too introspective to appreciate surrealism's spirit of collective revelation, Mexico's writers in the 1930s and 1940s resisted the magnetic pull of surrealism. In the early 1950s, however, a new generation of surrealist writing would arrive on Mexican soil in the person of Octavio Paz, the young poet and essayist who was destined to become Mexico's most important cultural figure in the second half of the twentieth century. Paz's story—and thus the story of an arguably "authentic" (though always controversial) Mexican surrealism—will be told in Chapter 10.

PART III

*A Surrealism of One's Own,
1950–1980*

CHAPTER 7

The Argentine Surrealist Journals

> El surrealismo atraviesa como un relámpago magnífico el campo de la conciencia contemporánea.
> —*A Partir de Cero*, No. 1

Introduction

The European surrealist movement, as we saw in Chapter 1, experienced a gradual demise after World War II. The experimental, irrational, and often playful character of surrealism did not square well with the realities of a war-devastated continent, which perhaps explains why many intellectuals and artists felt themselves pulled in the direction of Sartrean existentialism, with its emphasis on personal responsibility and historical groundedness. Latin Americans in this period were also in many cases drawn to existentialism as a philosophy, but not as an exclusive ethic. On the whole, the varied social, political, and cultural conditions in this region left ample space for overlapping or even contradictory modes of thought. One crucial historical event during this period, particularly for Mexico and Argentina, was the arrival of European exiles fleeing both the Spanish Civil War and the Second World War—artists and writers who brought new blood to the intellectual organism.

As the midpoint of the twentieth century neared, many Latin American countries were facing demons of their own: the lengthening shadow of the military (or militant populism) over civilian life, North American cultural, economic, and political imperialism, debt crises, widespread poverty, and social unrest in numerous forms. At the same time, a kind of cultural stagnation gripped the middle-class elements of cities like Buenos Aires, Lima, Montevideo, and Mexico City. As the Argentine pioneer surrealist Aldo Pellegrini wrote of this period, "Even the more comfortable classes are adrift in an anguished uncertainty, in a palpable disintegration" ("Introduction" 8). For some writers, surrealism in this period appeared as a form of new humanism that suggested creative ways of facing these demons. This and other factors led to a significant second wave of surrealist production in some parts of Latin America in the 1950s and 1960s (and in some cases even later). In this and the following three chapters, I will examine the reemergence of Latin American surrealism in forms that far exceeded the early movements in originality and literary quality.

In an essay called "Surrealism—The Sacred Disease of Our Time: Observations on its Impact on Spanish American Literature,"[1] Jaime Alazraki contends that there is a fundamental difference between surrealism as style and surrealism as philosophy or world view. When Octavio Paz states succinctly that "surrealism is an attitude of the human spirit," he is voicing a belief shared by numerous Latin Americans writers (*Obras* 2: 204). Of particular interest to Alazraki are those writers who cannot be identified as surrealists *per se* but whose writings "nevertheless show clear and deep imprints of surrealism" (22). From about 1950 onward, surrealism in Latin American literature almost always takes an unorthodox approach with regard to the French model. A very limited number of authors in this period identify their work explicitly as surrealist; in fact, they are typically eager to eschew any direct relationship, particularly with regard to automatic writing or other issues of technique or "style." But in spite of these writers' self-conscious distancing from surrealism, the "deep imprints" are undeniably there. José Miguel Oviedo, referring in 1980 to the revolution in Latin American fiction known as the "Boom," observed that "poetry has undergone a series of changes which are no less revolutionary. A group of poets, somewhat younger than Neruda, infected by the spirit of the vanguard and principally by that of surrealism, are the founders of that poetry which prevails today and which, in some way, is orienting the experiences of the new poets of the present: they are Octavio Paz, Enrique Molina, and Nicanor Parra" ("A Permanent Discussion" 313). It is significant that each of these poets—whose work I will examine in the following chapters—has at least one foot on the threshold of surrealism.

As I have argued previously, the ability of surrealist thought to reinvent itself on other continents several decades after its inception in Europe can be viewed as a result of its inherently contradictory or protean nature. Because surrealism was both an aesthetic and an attitude toward life, because its insistence on *looking* embraced both the visible and the hidden, because it spoke in both universal and vernacular terms, because it plumbed both the individual and the collective consciousness—in short, because surrealism was an amorphous beast with a single, penetrating stare, it managed to adapt itself surprisingly well in certain new habitats. In Part III of *Breton's Ghost*, I work from the premise that Latin American surrealism, far from being a mere echo of the European movement, develops a strong voice of its own. Given their distance from the original movement, many writers of the 1950s and 1960s were able to judge it critically and to consciously appropriate some, but not all, of its substance. The following chapters will explore various ways in which this creative appropriation occurred in the "second wave" of Latin American surrealism, first in a number of small literary magazines in Argentina, and then in individual authors in Argentina, Chile, and Mexico.

The Surrealist Journals of Buenos Aires

There is no better introduction to the story of surrealism's reemergence in Argentina than the following passage from Julio Llinás's autobiographical novel *Fiat Lux* (1994), in which he describes his discovery of surrealism as a young man living in Paris in the 1950s:

> Levanté el brazo, lo estiré y aprisioné al surrealismo entre mis dedos. En una de mis peregrinaciones por las librerías, había tropezado con esta inscripción: "Maurice Nadeau—*Histoire du Surréalisme*". Saqué el volumen del anaquel y me puse a hojearlo febrilmente. Lo compré y comencé a leerlo por la calle, mientras caminaba. Seguí leyéndolo en el tren, por las veredas, mientras subía las escaleras hacia mi cuarto, mientras me desvestía, mientras orinaba, durante toda la noche y buena parte de la mañana. En ese libro estaba contenida la historia secreta de mi pensamiento, latía un humor feroz, trágico y vital. Los nombres de Tristán Tzara, de André Breton, de Benjamín Péret, de Paul Éluard, de Louis Aragon, desconocidos para mí hasta ese momento, iban marcando mi cerebro como hierros candentes. (99)

> [I raised my arm, I reached out and grasped surrealism. In one of my wanderings through bookstores, I stumbled upon this title: "Maurice Nadeau—*Histoire du surréalisme*." I took the book off the shelf and began leafing through it feverishly. I bought it and began to read it on the street while I walked. I kept reading on the train, on the sidewalks, walking up the stairs toward my room, getting undressed, going to the bathroom, all through the night and a good part of the morning. That book held the secret history of my thought; in it beat a fierce humor, tragic and alive. The names of Tristan Tzara, André Breton, Benjamin Péret, Paul Éluard, Louis Aragon, unknown to me before then, began marking my brain like firebrands.]

Llinás's words serve as a testimonial to the power that the surrealist movement still exercised over young writers half a world away from France, and almost three decades after its birth. But Llinás is also clear about the limited paths that were open to the belated adepts of the movement. He observes that "el surrealismo francés institucionalizó el escándalo . . . Veinticinco años después, el surrealismo argentino persistía en el escándalo, aunque, claro está, bajo su forma más doméstica: la literaria. Todo se hacía en la penumbra y el susurro, sobre el papel, con una máquina de escribir y, en el mejor de los casos, con una tirada de quinientos ejemplares" [French surrealism institutionalized scandal . . . Twenty-five years later, Argentine surrealism kept that scandal alive, although, to be sure, in its tamest form: literature. Everything was done in shadows and whispers, on paper, with a typewriter and, in the best case of cases, with a print-run of five hundred copies] (112).

Chapter 3 followed the earliest traces of surrealist literature in Latin America with the short-lived but fervent experiments of the group that formed around Aldo Pellegrini and the little magazine *Que* in the late 1920s. For reasons undoubtedly connected to the politically and socially repressive atmosphere of the post-1930 era, it would take more than twenty years to overcome what Horacio Armani calls the "timidity" of that initial movement in Argentina (23). But by 1950, there was change in the air over Buenos Aires. As the contemporary novelist and critic César Aira observes, after the initial explosion of surrealism had taken place the movement was declared defunct—yet oddly enough, it would be found alive over and over again (*Alejandra Pizarnik* 13).

Building on Aira's metaphor—which repeats the commonplace of the cadaver so prevalent in commentaries on surrealism, including César Vallejo's "Autopsia"—we can affirm that Argentine surrealism did not die in the early 1930s but instead went into a state of dormancy. In terms of literary discourse, the voice of surrealism in this period continued to be heard in the sporadic texts by European writers published in Argentina's most widely circulated cultural journal, *Sur*. During this time certain writers, most notably Roberto Arlt, Adolfo Bioy Casares, and Jorge Luis Borges, wrote experimental prose that explored the absurd or the fantastical, thus exercising the free play of the imagination that was the avant-garde's strongest legacy. But poetry for the most part followed rather conservative neohumanist or neoromantic currents. It was the latter, with its roots in German romanticism, that would open the way for surrealism. The 1950s would see a proliferation of journals, collections of poetry, and art exhibitions in which surrealism was the primary if not the exclusive aesthetic current.[2]

The case of the "Generación del 1940" in Argentine poetry affords a fascinating instance of adaptation and amalgamation with respect to surrealism. In literary terms, this generation inherited the short-lived and generally conservative formal experiments of *el ultraísmo*, which had been championed by Borges in the early 1920s, as well as the sui generis but highly influential poetics of Macedonio Fernández and Oliverio Girondo. But the Generation of 1940 can be considered more as an interruption than a continuation of the vanguardist current. In sociopolitical terms, writers coming of age in the 1940s had to absorb not only the tragic European wars but also the increasing economic and civic tensions in their own national sphere. The patently anti-intellectual Peronist regime (1946–55) added to the growing sense of repression. The response to all this was, as César Fernández Moreno succinctly states, a retreat to solitude and silence (305). The members of the Generation of 1940 produced poetry that was philosophical in conception, elegiac in tone, and nostalgic in its evocation of a mythic golden age or an unreachable object of desire. In her book *Gender, Politics, and Poetry in Twentieth-Century Argentina* (1996), Jill Kuhnheim concludes that, paradoxically, the distancing of lyric poetry from historical events or social realities can be read historically: "For the 'lost generation' of the forties it is an elementary mode of survival, of perpetuating a role for the poet in an increasingly hostile society, and a way of disguising certain 'transgressive' differences in the positions and demands imposed upon particular poets" (2–3).

Onto this scene of repression and sadness bursts surrealism like an inexplicably cheerful madman.[3] Culturally rooted in Aldo Pellegrini's early promotions, what we might call "neo" or "second-wave" surrealism was grafted onto the body of a lyrically conservative neoromanticism. In poets like Enrique Molina and Olga Orozco, the "melancólica soledad ante lo telúrico" [melancholy solitude in the presence of the earth] is transformed into the exuberant recreation of an imaginative landscape, as oneiric as it is real (Giordano 788). Neither pure psychic automatism nor total social-artistic revolt, this rejuvenated Argentine surrealism nevertheless represents a freedom of the poetic imagination new to the literature of that period.

One significant marker of the renewed interest was a pair of public lectures on surrealism given by Aldo Pellegrini in Buenos Aires in 1950, both of which attracted a fair degree of attention (Poblete Araya 120–21). Even more important, several literary journals edited by well-known figures (including Pellegrini) emerged in this period as the primary vehicles for the dissemination of a reinvented aesthetic. An enthusiastic younger group of poets formed around the older Pellegrini, who retained his role as promoter and mentor. This new group included, among others, Enrique Molina, Francisco Madariaga, Carlos Latorre, Juan Antonio Vasco, Julio Llinás, and Juan José Ceselli. Mario Pellegrini, Aldo's son and the person responsible for archiving and reediting his father's work, declares that in this period "the surrealist adventure begins again in Argentina in its richest and most memorable stage" ("Nota" 6).

The story of surrealist or surrealist-leaning journals in this period in Argentina is a rich subject for study in and of itself, one that has been explored extensively by Graciela de Sola and Kyra Poblete Araya. Although these journals had a limited circulation, they exercised a certain authority within the literary milieu of Buenos Aires, and thus they provide an effective tool for gauging the cultural currents of the period. (Along with Mexico City, Buenos Aires constituted the publishing hub of Spanish America in those decades, as it continues to do today.) In the remainder of this chapter, I consider these journals and their primary contributors, highlighting a number of engaging texts that appeared in their pages. As we will see, this second iteration of Argentine surrealism alternates between a reverence for and a critique of the European movement. Furthermore, it attempts to define itself not only through literature but also through the visual arts and cultural criticism. Whereas Pellegrini's early group had been almost secretive in its endeavors and local in its reach, the next generation of surrealists inserts itself vociferously into the intellectual discourse in Argentina and abroad.

Ciclo

The public face of the new surrealism first appears with the journal *Ciclo: Arte, literatura y pensamientos modernos*, published in Buenos Aires in December of 1948 and April of 1949. Spearheaded by Aldo Pellegrini, *Ciclo* was codirected by Elías Piterbarg, a member of the original 1920s surrealist group, and by the psychoanalyst and writer Enrique Pichón Riviére.[4] In his introduction to the anthology *Siete surrealistas argentinos* (1999), Javier Cófreces comments that *Ciclo* maintained strong ties to surrealism but also introduced new perspectives related to other aesthetic currents, reaffirming in all cases "a sustained and uncompromisingly ethical spirit concerning art and expression" (11). More dedicated to criticism than to creative endeavors, the first issue of *Ciclo* presented excerpts of Henry Miller's *Tropic of Capricorn*, a commentary on Miller's works by Georges Bataille, a note by Breton on the surrealist painter Jacques Hérold, and Pellegrini's commentary on the work of Wolfgang Paalen, including reproductions of Paalen's paintings. *Ciclo*'s second issue includes, among other pieces, several essays on contemporary painting, a biographical sketch of Lautréamont, an essay by Pellegrini called "The Conquest of the Marvelous," and work by the Argentine poet Mario Trejo.

The longest text in the first issue of *Ciclo* is an essay by Piterbarg called "Surrealismo y surrealistas en 1948," which is of interest to the present study precisely because it carries out a sustained criticism of European surrealism. Piterbarg had spent time in Paris that same year and had attended the meetings of the postwar surrealist group, which included the Chilean *Mandrágora* poet Jorge Cáceres. Piterbarg's essay, based on interviews he conducted with Breton, Tristan Tzara, and the Yugoslav surrealist Marko Ristich, reveals a certain negative bias. He asks, for instance, if Breton is aware that the surrealist myth is truly a myth and if the surrealists can remain "indifferent" to the struggle of the masses (qtd. in Poblete Araya 106–7). In his commentary on the respondent's answers, Piterbarg accuses them of practicing both "facile Marxist loves" and an aggression toward the poets of the French Resistance (Poblete Araya 107). The premise of this essay is that the dialectic between poetic and political action has not been resolved by the surrealists. In the face of this failure, he asks, "How can one passively accept a perhaps degrading impotence?" (Poblete Araya 107).

Piterbarg concludes his reflections with these words: "In Paris I was struck by the impression that, whether they admit it or not, the surrealists . . . are limited to expressing their surrealism in the only way possible for them today: artistic or literary expression" (Poblete Araya 108–9). There is in this comment, as in Piterbarg's entire essay, a tone of disillusion, a supreme frustration that surrealism had failed to deliver on the promise of total revolution. As a "mere" mode of literary or artistic expression, surrealism becomes a pale shadow of what it once was, and those like Piterbarg who were initially impassioned by the movement's ideals can only lament its present state. The fact that this essay, which reads as a kind of epitaph, was included in a journal otherwise open to surrealist thought and expression reflects the more nuanced critical consciousness around surrealism that had developed in Argentina since the 1920s.

A Partir de Cero

Following closely on *Ciclo*, a journal called *A Partir de Cero: Revista de Poesía y Antipoesía* appeared in Buenos Aires (1952–56) under the direction of Enrique Molina. Molina would become the leading Argentine poet of the second generation of surrealism, as well as a painter and collage artist. (His poetic work will be discussed in Chapter 8.) The journal's title "signals a type of trajectory where the reader is led back to zero, or to the starting point of Latin American surrealism, and to the path it has taken since its birth in the Buenos Aires Circle of the late 1920s" (Ward 44). Aldo Pellegrini provides another possible interpretation of the phrase "starting from zero." Pointing to the "true aesthetic revolution" initiated by Dada and carried to fruition by the surrealists, he comments, "In these new aesthetic experiences, they were starting practically from zero: the only norm accepted was that of total freedom. It was the beginning of an art without canons" ("La poesía surrealista" 16). The Argentine contributors (of poems, stories, and even a one-act play) included Pellegrini, Julio Llinás, Carlos Latorre, Olga Orozco, Juan Antonio Vasco, Francisco Madariaga, and Antonio Porchia. *A Partir de Cero* also featured work by some of the principle names in international surrealism, including Artaud, Breton, Éluard, Moro, Péret, Leonora Carrington, Giselle Prassinos, and the Lebanese writer Georges Schehadé. Although it was limited to three issues, this journal represents in many ways the high point of surrealist reviews in Latin America. In terms of the essays, poems, and visual imagery included, *A Partir de Cero* adopts an unabashedly surrealist editorial stance. In fact, the direct inclusion of a series of texts espousing French surrealist principles (collected under the subheading "Línea de fuego") signals the desire to expose the Argentine reading public to the original principles of surrealism. Employing once again the metaphor of the corpse, Stefan Baciu remarks that the publication of this review at a time when the death of surrealism was being declared both in Argentina and abroad proves that the movement was "un 'difunto' bastante vivo" [a rather lively dead man] ("Introducción" 78).

A Partir de Cero stands apart from other primarily literary journals for its visual contents, many of which reveal an ironically humorous editorial eye. Indeed, the journal was conceived as a marriage of the verbal and the visual, in keeping with the surrealist ideal of dissolving the genre distinctions. Numerous drawings throughout the three issues evoke nineteenth-century magazine or catalogue illustrations. One striking drawing shows a man and two young girls in Victorian dress, standing in what appears to be a museum or gallery and viewing the decapitated head of a man displayed on a small table. In another image, three side-by-side drawings of a laughing boy carry a caption from Lautréamont's *Maldoror*: "But know that poetry is to be found everywhere where the stupidly mocking smile of duck-faced man does not exist" (261). Apart from these images with a distinctly antiquated flavor—which may have taken their cue from Max Ernst's collages—the journal presents artwork by contemporary artists. Examples include a surrealist object by the French artist Claude Cahun ("Object," 1936) and collages by the Argentine artists Álvaro Rodríguez, Marta Peluffo, Juan Esteban Fassio, and Enrique Molina.

Numerous images in *A Partir de Cero* suggest the theme of vision. One small drawing shows an antiquated textbook illustration of an eye and carries the caption "Inner Workings of the Eye"; another presents a schematic drawing of a camera obscura, illustrating the photographic principle of image reversal. This drawing creates a metacommentary on vision by including the figure of a man looking at the reversed image. Finally, both Cahun's "Object" and another small, crudely rendered drawing just above it both represent an eyeball turned on a vertical axis and embellished with pubic hair, images that link sight to sexuality. Taken together, these images serve to remind the reader to *look* beyond the words on the page, reflecting the surrealist insistence on seeking revelation beyond or behind the phenomenal world.

Molina's extensive introductory essay "Vía libre," which covers three of the eight pages of the first issue (May 1952), establishes the journal's aesthetic orientation and thus serves as a manifesto for the renewed surrealist impulse in Argentina. The title echoes the traditional mystical pathways (*via contemplativa*, *via activa*, and so forth) and simultaneously suggests the archetypal symbol of the open road, evoking surrealism's overarching goal: total human liberty. Molina begins by expounding on the surrealist ideal of living life as poetry: "Si identificamos la poesía y la vida, aquella planteará al hombre un compromiso esencial que desborda ampliamente el campo de lo literario para presentarse como una conducta fundamental" [If we identify poetry with life, poetry will set forth an essential commitment that extends well beyond the field of literature, to present itself as a fundamental mode of conduct] (n.pag.). This line of reasoning reiterates the identification of poetry with life, signaling the "rehumanization" of art that was one of the key features of the Latin American *vanguardia* (Unruh 21).

After this introduction, Molina's essay goes "back to zero" by naming some of those who had previously articulated the link between poetry and lived experience: Lautréamont, Rimbaud, and Breton. Only poetry can assume the "mission" of changing life, Molina declares, since it is "únicamente concebida como la fusión ardiente del sueño y de la acción, sosteniendo con una voluntad encarnizada una empresa de liberación total del espíritu" [uniquely conceived as the ardent fusion of dream and action, holding on with a savage will to the enterprise of the total liberation of the spirit] (n.pag.). Those who approach poetry from this angle, says Molina, face a terrible dilemma. They can accept the present order, whose value system leads to a repression of the forces of the imagination and of desire, or they can reject these rigid values and embrace "la recuperación de la vida en sus movimientos más espontáneos, arrancándola al pesado mecanismo de prejuicios racionalistas, de prohibiciones de toda índole, de terrores, de ideas recibidas y convencionalismos sólo fundados en el carácter puramente utilitario de la vida social" [the recuperation of life in its most spontaneous movements, tearing it from the heavy mechanism of rationalist prejudices, from every kind of prohibition, from fears, from received ideas and conventions founded only on the purely utilitarian character of social existence] (n.pag.).

From this point forward, "Vía libre" explores in greater depth the principle of poetry as lived experience—critical, revolutionary, and profoundly uncomfortable. Molina finds it inconceivable that, despite the evidence that humans everywhere live in desperation, there is still a need to insist on the "indissoluble unity" of poetry, love, and liberty (n.pag.). Much more than a "beautiful exercise," poetry as part of this essential triangle is

> una actividad dirigida hacia el descrédito permanente de todos los mitos, sociales, éticos y religiosos, en nombre de los cuales el hombre contemporáneo es dividido en una serie de compartimientos estancos desde cuyo interior sólo alcanza una visión fragmentaria, totalmente mezquina, de la realidad, también dividida en planos irreconciliables: oposición de lo irracional y lo racional, de la vigilia y el sueño, de lo objetivo y lo subjetivo, del sueño y la acción, etc. (n.pag.)
>
> [an activity directed toward the permanent discrediting of all myths—social, ethical, and religious—in the name of which contemporary man is divided into

a series of watertight compartments from whose interior he glimpses only a fragmentary and paltry vision of reality, a reality in turn divided into irreconcilable planes: opposition of the irrational and the rational, of waking and sleeping states, of objective and subjective, of dream and action, etc.]

Molina goes on to insist that the authentic poetic attitude must face "the gloomy conditions of our existence" and refuse any reconciliation with them, even to the point of completely rejecting them.

All of the above will be familiar to the reader of Breton's manifestoes; in fact, Molina's rhetoric in this piece reflects a rather direct appropriation of French surrealist theoretical writing. Although he speaks of poetry as lived experience, the essentializing nature of his terms ("contemporary man," "society," "the essential purity of life") leaves little room for a historical contextualization of this experience. There is one significant point in "Vía libre," however, at which Molina makes explicit reference to his particular moment in history. The subject is contemporary Argentine poetry, which he accuses of an almost total lack of a "spirit of rupture." He claims that this poetry is still weighed down by "orthopedic gimmicks" and is irremediably tied to Spanish poetic traditions that turn it into a "domesticated beast" (n.pag.) Molina develops this criticism further in the second issue of *A Partir de Cero* (December 1952), in a piece called "Un golpe de su dedo sobre el tambor" [His Finger Beating on the Drum], a phrase taken from Rimbaud. Here he enumerates the various routes taken by the poets of his day: either they craft themselves as "poets of preciosity" ("great dignity of expression" he quips, mocking the critics) or, alternatively, they carry "versified vulgarity" to its ultimate (i.e., pedestrian, folkloric) consequences. Molina concludes, "Queda entonces a cargo de los jóvenes abrir el camino de una poesía viva, de espaldas al repugnante juego de conformismos y adulaciones de todo género que exige de ellos" [It falls then to the young writers to open the way toward a living poetry, turning their backs on the disgusting game of conformity and flattery in endless guises that is demanded of them] (n.pag.). It is clear that in this moment Molina is responding to the real situation of poetry as he has experienced it in the Buenos Aires literary circles of the early 1950s. Notably, his rhetoric in these two brief sections comes across as more immediate, raw, and passionate than in other parts of the essays that contain them. This is not simply French surrealism repackaged; it is surrealism's call to revolt reasserted in Molina's own milieu.

Enrique Molina's adherence to surrealist principles stands in stark contrast to the critique by Piterbarg examined above, but it is in fact shared by the other contributors to *A Partir de Cero*. An essay by Aldo Pellegrini in the second issue called "El huevo filosófico" [The Philosophical Egg] expounds on surrealist notions of epistemology:

A la idea del hombre común de admitir como real solamente las apariencias sensibles, se opone la idea surrealista de la existencia de aspectos, o mejor, de planos múltiples y variados de la realidad. A la idea de la percepción sensorial como fuente única del saber, se opone la concepción surrealista del conocimiento, que proclama la existencia de infinitos contactos entre el hombre y el mundo escalonados desde lo sensible a lo suprasensible . . . El surrealista no se resigna, es esencialmente disconformista, y partiendo del principio de que la fuente de todo conocimiento está en el interior del hombre, se sumerge en el propio espíritu, atravesando el plano racional, y allí, en lo más hondo de su *yo*, encuentra el mundo. (n.pag.)

[In contrast to the understanding of the common man, who admits as real only what is revealed to the senses, stands the surrealist idea of the existence of aspects, that is, of multiple and various planes of reality. In opposition to the idea of sensorial perception as the only source of knowledge stands the surrealist conception of knowledge, which proclaims the existence of infinite points of contact between man and the world, on a scale from the sensory to the supersensory . . . The surrealist does not resign himself; he is essentially a nonconformist, and departing from the principle that the source of all knowledge is in the interior of man, he delves into his own spirit, crossing the rational plane, and there, in his most profound self, he finds the world.]

In this essay, Pellegrini sets the surrealist apart from the "hombre común," evoking a spiritual or intellectual elitism reminiscent of José Enrique Rodó's classic essay *Ariel* (1900). Pellegrini contends that whereas the common man learns primarily through sense perception, the more fully realized surrealist learns from the full range of his faculties, particularly those associated with the inner life. The surrealist's insistence on accessing "total thought" (whose primary vehicle, claims Pellegrini, is the language of poetry) places him at odds with the society he inhabits; he is the perpetual nonconformist.

I noted in Chapter 3 that in the texts of the 1920s journal *Que* there was an almost poignant discrepancy between the nonconformism asserted in Pellegrini's language of revolt and his actual social role—alongside Piterbarg and the other early surrealists—as a medical student and overall "good citizen." The discrepancy is even more marked in "El huevo filosófico," as Pellegrini, now a practicing physician and respected editor, assumes the role of trusted mentor to a group of younger writers. The nonconformism he envisions clearly lies in another realm than that of social roles: it is a desire to *think* in new ways, to achieve levels of consciousness not accessible through ordinary (rational) routes. But this noble ideal was not without its ironies, and thus not without its critics. César Aira remembers the visits of the younger writers to Pellegrini's bookstore, where the elder poet would share with them his "revolutionary secret": "Good citizens and proper heads of household on the outside, destroyers of the established order when they sat down to write" (*Pizarnik* 24). Aira has put his finger in the wound: the Argentine surrealists, perhaps even more than their European predecessors, found that true revolt was virtually impossible to carry out. As Llinás observed in the passage from *Fiat Lux* cited in the introduction to this chapter, the act of changing life remained a solitary operation, one carried out on the page or the canvas, with little reverberation within the poet's or the artist's larger milieu.

The third issue of *A Partir de Cero* (September 1956), printed in a smaller format than the previous two issues and including two inserts, contains numerous texts with a surrealist orientation: the story "The Sand Camel" by Leonora Carrington (translated by Olga Orozco); poems by Artaud, Ingemar Gustafson, Latorre, and Vasco; a one-act play written as a "collage of languages" by Llinás; and a humorous surrealist lexicon called "An Experimental Attempt at the Rectification of Language" by Llinás and Molina. This lexicon, a variant of the technique of the surrealist dialogue, pairs words with definitions that have no logical connection to them, obliging the reader to reconsider conventional assumptions about the communicative function of language. The term *poet*, for example, is given a triple (and triply absurd) definition: "Instrumento óptico con dos tubos provisto de cristales graduables para ver a distancia. / Monstruo marino de que habla el libro de Job y que los Santos Padres consideran en sentido moral como enemigo de las almas. / *Zool*. Dícese de los ungulados que tienen trompa prensil" [Optical instrument with two tubes containing adjustable lenses for viewing at a distance. / Sea monster mentioned in the *Book of Job* and which the Holy Fathers consider in moral terms to be the enemy of souls. / *Zool*. Said of ungulates with a prehensile trunk] (n.pag.). These "definitions" embody surrealist humor at its best—provoking laughter at the incongruous combinations but also provoking new ways of seeing the world. The fact that one of the definitions identifies the poet with an optical instrument reminds the reader that sight—linked to the unveiling of the marvelous—is crucial to the surrealist zeitgeist.

Letra y Línea

In the three-year interim between the second and third issues of *A Partir de Cero*, another review with ties to surrealism appeared in Buenos Aires. *Letra y Línea* (whose full subtitle reads *Revista de Cultura Contemporánea: Artes Plásticas, Literatura, Teatro, Cine, Crítica Literaria*) was published in four issues in 1953 and 1954 and was also directed by the indefatigable Aldo Pellegrini. Although the focus was again on poetry, this journal broadened its scope to include several forms of artistic expression. In contrast to the previous surrealist journals, *Letra y Línea* was formed around a heterogeneous group of writers, and thus its editorial stance is more diffuse. (Of the nine editor-contributors, only three were self-declared surrealists.) In the unsigned "Justificación" that opens the first issue, *Letra y Línea* declares that its pages are open to new writers (young or old), even when this means a confrontation with the literary establishment. In the spirit of avant-garde revolt, the editors place their faith "en la remoción de lo falso, en la eliminación de los prejuicios, en el derrumbamiento de la rutina" [in the removal of falsehood, in the elimination of prejudice, in the collapse of routine] (qtd. in Poblete Araya 156).

In comparison with its predecessors, this journal also opened itself more directly to polemical matters, giving rise to discussions that suggest that the Argentine surrealists were an intellectual thorn in the side of some of their contemporaries. The most notable polemic began in the third issue of *Letra y Línea*, in which the Italian-Argentine journalist Osiris Troiani directs his "Epistle to the Surrealists" mainly at Aldo Pellegrini. Troiani accuses the surrealists of constituting a mere literary salon (*tertulia de café*), one that is incapable of joining its own historical community (20). After leveling other charges relating to the surrealists' "anachronism" and "exoticism," Troiani flings an arrow that goes to the heart of the question of Latin American cultural identity: "To make matters worse, Argentine surrealism pays homage to the greats from other countries, but here it is only unruly; it toes the party line in Europe, but here only raises opposition" (23). In his "Response to Osiris Troiani," Pellegrini answers Troiani's diatribe point by point, vindicating the surrealist platform and providing counterevidence for each charge. His final clarification, aimed against the charge of lockstep orthodoxy leveled by Troiani, is that "el surrealismo no impone más dogma que el de la libertad integral. En este sentido no he dejado de chocar con las opiniones de algunos surrealistas amigos" [the only dogma that surrealism imposes is that of total freedom. In this regard I have clashed continually with some of my surrealist friends] (15).

This polemic sheds light on the intellectual environment of Buenos Aires in the 1950s and the place of surrealism in it. If we take into account many of the texts printed in the surrealist-affiliated journals, as well as the Troiani-Pellegrini debate, it becomes clear that a rupture from cultural conformity was the most commonly expressed desire, and that arguments arose over the *means* by which that break should be effected. For Enrique Molina in particular, but for the contributors to *Ciclo*, *A Partir de Cero*, and *Letra y Línea* in general, the most infuriating kind of conformity occurred in the sphere of literary expression. Here they saw a blind adherence to Spanish literary traditions, nepotistic practices, the coveting of prizes, and the adulation of mediocre talents. Moving the gaze outward, the conventionalism they attacked involved religion, politics, and social structures of all sorts. In their protest against this rigidity and shallowness, Pellegrini, Molina, and their cohort looked unabashedly to Europe: there they found both "new" literary models and a language with which to structure and communicate their aspirations. They remained for the most part unapologetic in their appropriation of this model.

Boa

The arts journal as a platform for public discourse around surrealism materialized one last time in Argentina with *Boa: Cuadernos Internacionales de Documentación sobre la Poesía y el Arte de Vanguardia*, directed by Julio Llinás. Llinás was the youngest member of the group that had convened in the early 1950s around Aldo Pellegrini and Enrique Molina. Shortly after his participation in the first issues of *A Partir de Cero* in 1952, Llinás traveled to Paris and remained there for two years. One of his closest associates in Paris was the Cuban painter Wilfredo Lam, who was part of a movement in the visual arts "striving to renew the unifying force of surrealism" (Giunta 74). Llinás, initially disappointed with the remnants of the original surrealist movement that he observed in the French capital, eventually found a way to reignite his enthusiasm by participating in the neosurrealist group "Phases," headed by Édouard Jaguer. He returned to Buenos Aires in 1954 hoping to establish a journal there, a goal that was finally reached in 1958.

Carefully designed and beautifully crafted, *Boa* was without doubt the most ambitious and the most international in scope of the surrealist-affiliated journals published in Latin America. By adopting the name of an indigenous South American snake, *Boa* simultaneously acknowledges the European journal *Cobra* (1948–51) and declares its own separate and autochthonous character.[5] *Boa*'s three issues presented original texts in Spanish by Pellegrini, Latorre, Llinás, Madariaga, Porchia, Rodolfo Alonso, and other Argentine writers, as well as translations of poets such as Jaguer (France) and Gherasim Luca (Romania), both younger members of the Parisian surrealist group. Leaning more toward contemporary visual arts than toward literature, *Boa* featured work by painters from Argentina but also from Belgium, Canada, Denmark, Germany, Egypt, France, Italy, Mexico, Poland, and Portugal. With the appearance of *Boa*, the art historian Andrea Giunta claims that "the Argentines now appeared as the exponents of a discourse that could be heard in its multiple voices, in many cities, simultaneously. *Boa* proved, in a certain sense, that the great hope of integrating the artistic centers of the world was becoming a reality" (78).

One of the goals of *Boa* was to actualize surrealism in Latin America by featuring certain transformations taking place in art and literature across the Western world. (The release of the second issue in June of 1958 was timed to coincide with an exhibition of surrealist-influenced art in Buenos Aires, titled *Phases* in a nod to Jaguer's French movement.) In the editorial essay that introduces the first issue, Llinás refers to quantum physics as proof that "nunca, como hoy, ha sido tan precario el concepto humano de la *realidad*" [never has the concept of *reality* been as precarious as it is today] (Llinás, *Boa* 1:1). Echoing the latter-day Breton, he cites the twentieth-century discoveries in physics as strong evidence of "una realidad *ulterior*, profundamente oculta" [an ulterior, profoundly hidden reality], a concept he uses to explain the artist's role in contemporary society. Although he repeats the familiar call for art to "change life," he is careful to delineate the type of change he is advocating, which has nothing to do with the salvation promised by social or political praxis. Llinás articulates a clearly anti-Marxist stance here: "La pintura, como la poesía, rechaza la unificación del plano del conocimiento con las condiciones materiales de la existencia y se lanza a las aventuras prohibidas, arrasando con todo, desentrañanado los signos de una nueva vida, en un terrreno en el que toda materialización es magia" [Painting, like poetry, rejects any attempt to merge the plane of knowledge with the material conditions of existence, and embarks upon forbidden adventures, demolishing everything, unearthing the signs of a new life in a terrain in which all materialization is magic] (Llinás, *Boa* 1:1). Here again we witness the surrealist conflation of poetry with knowledge, as well as its insistence on divorcing art from any immediate or practical social value.

I would argue that the contribution of Llinás's thought to the discourse surrounding surrealism in late-1950s Buenos Aires lies in his insistence on the international scope of the movement in its late phases, as well as on the inclusiveness of the category of art. From this perspective, his editorial work is important in that it documents certain changes taking place in the international neosurrealist movements and brings the Spanish American reading public up to date on such developments. But from another perspective, I would also argue that Llinás fails to signal a viable way forward for his contemporaries. While he calls attention to new discoveries in science, he restricts the artistic or philosophical value of those discoveries to the sense of occult realms of existence. Terms such as "magic," "forbidden adventures," "profoundly hidden reality," and "unexpected revelation" point to an esoteric current of thought that was one of the primary sources of surrealism. Whether through surrealist channels or not, esoterism enjoyed a revival in Buenos Aires in the mid-twentieth century, profoundly marking the work of such figures as the painter, poet, and linguist Xul Solar and the poets Olga Orozco and Alejandra Pizarnik, among others.[6] Even Borges's fascination with the Cabala can be connected, though more obliquely, to this strain of thought. In France, Breton himself was in these same years abandoning his revolutionary message and exploring the esoteric traditions.[7] Clearly Llinás was not alone in his leaning toward a sacred or revelatory explanation of the origins and the ends of art. But such an orientation may well have undermined his goal of renovating and globalizing the surrealist agenda from an Argentine perspective.

As a capstone to the decade of surrealist-affiliated journals, Aldo Pellegrini published in 1961 his *Antología de la poesía surrealista de lengua francesa*, which includes his own translations of the work of nearly seventy poets.[8] Pellegrini's long preliminary study, "La poesía surrealista," is an invaluable work of literary history in which he traces the development of the surrealist movement and explains the structure of its thought. In a personal letter to Pellegrini, Breton declared the anthology to be the most important contribution to the diffusion of surrealist poetry in any language (qtd. in Cófreces 21). According to Mario Pellegrini, the book had an appreciable impact in Spanish America: for many years, readers continued to write to the elder Pellegrini, recounting their discovery of the *Antología* and calling it "deslumbrante" [dazzling] (personal interview). It is reasonable to assume that this collection of international poetry gave added impetus to the diffusion of a surrealist aesthetic in Latin America in this period.

In sum, from *Ciclo* in 1948 to *Boa* in 1958–60, small literary-artistic journals in Buenos Aires put the surrealist coin back into circulation during an important decade of consolidation and critical consciousness; to this we add the appearance of Pellegrini's important anthology in 1961. After a long period of dormancy in the 1930s and 1940s, surrealism had reawakened in Argentina. The terms of surrealist discourse were again taken up and debated, the band of adherents grew broader, and attempts were made to connect surrealist practice in Argentina to that of numerous other countries. Literature was linked to the visual arts in more direct ways, and surrealist thought—particularly in its esoteric aspect—was used to theorize about the place of art in the modern world. If nothing else, the journals served as a nucleus of activity around which poets and painters gathered and exchanged ideas. And out of this exchange grew surrealism's strongest legacy in Argentina: the presence of a surrealist aesthetic in a number of important poets of the latter twentieth century. In the following chapter I will examine the work of three particularly accomplished Argentine writers in the period between 1950 and 1970: Enrique Molina, Olga Orozco, and Alejandra Pizarnik.

CHAPTER 8

"Another Ship Must Be Launched"
Surrealism in Argentine Poetry, 1950–1970

Introduction

In Chapter 7 we followed four surrealist-influenced literary and arts journals in Argentina from the late 1940s through the 1950s. These journals—*Ciclo*, *A Partir de Cero*, *Letra y Línea*, and *Boa*—constituted the public face of the second wave of Argentine surrealism. The more private face of surrealism in the fertile period that encompasses the decades of the 1950s and 1960s is reflected in the work of several individual writers. The complete list of writers—principally lyric poets—who self-identify as surrealists or whom critics have included in the second surrealist *promoción* includes Juan José Ceselli, Carlos Latorre, Julio Llinás, Francisco Madariaga, Enrique Molina, Olga Orozco, Aldo Pellegrini, Alejandra Pizarnik, and Juan Antonio Vasco. A thorough study of this moment in Argentine literary history can be found in Graciela de Sola's *Proyecciones del surrealismo en la literatura argentina* (1967), and a more recent collection of poetry within this line is presented in *Siete surrealistas argentinos*, edited by Javier Cófreces in 1999. The present chapter focuses on the three writers whose work best represents, in my view, the mature configurations of a "neosurrealist" poetics: Enrique Molina, Olga Orozco, and Alejandra Pizarnik.

Enrique Molina: The Nomad and the Dreamer

¡Todo el vasto mundo que cabe
Bajo el ala libre de un pájaro!

—E. Molina, "La gran vida"

We have already seen the significant role played by Enrique Molina (1910–96) in promoting surrealism in Argentina as the principal editor of the journal *A Partir de Cero*. A close friend and associate of Aldo Pellegrini until the latter's death in 1973, Molina eventually became the new hub around which surrealist activity in Buenos Aires circulated. But most important for our purposes, he gained a reputation as one of the most accomplished poets of his generation and the poet most definitively allied with surrealism. In the words of César Aira, Molina incarnates, "with a constancy and a vigor that few have maintained, the optimistic orthodoxy of surrealism in its facet of the marvelous and the adventurous" ("Molina" 371). To this I would add that, in contrast to the rhetorical orthodoxy of the essays published in *A Partir de Cero*, Molina's poetry reveals a highly individualized style that begins in surrealism but moves from there into uncharted Latin American territory.

Although he was born in Buenos Aires, Molina spent most of his childhood and adolescence in provincial towns, in proximity to the *pampa* or to the sea. He rebelled from an early age—with an imagination fueled by reading—against what he considered to be stifling social conventions. After completing a law degree that was never put into practice, he joined the Merchant Marine and thus was able to travel widely and live for brief periods of time in several Latin American countries (particularly in the Caribbean). As a consequence of the geography of his childhood and his extensive travels, Molina's poetry became one of vast and mutating landscapes reflecting both exterior and interior worlds.

Though primarily a poet, Molina is also the author of a widely read surrealist novel, *Una sombra donde sueña Camila O'Gorman* (1973). This novel, in which oneiric imagery blends seamlessly into historical fact, recounts the story of the daughter of an aristocratic Buenos Aires family who falls in love with a young priest and escapes with him to the Argentine countryside. Camila's own father, a businessman closely associated with the dictatorial government of Juan Manuel de Rosas, colludes with Rosas in ordering the capture of the couple. Camila and her lover are both summarily executed, even though authorities are aware that she is expecting a child. According to Molina's own account, this historical narrative impressed him as a particularly powerful illustration of the restrictive, even deadly nature of rigid patriarchal systems. Although *Camila* takes place in the nineteenth century, Molina saw parallels in the socially restrictive society of his own day. In concert with surrealist ideals, he was also drawn by Camila and the priest's "poetic" response to the limitations placed on their love ("Poesía, amor y libertad" n. pag.).

In terms of the surrealist aesthetic—that which best defines Molina's poetic sensibility overall—the reader can discern two intertwining modes. The first derives from Molina's spatial imagination and manifests as a kind of surrealist geography. To the extent to which this geography is identifiably American, Molina develops an effective way of "cannibalizing" European surrealism through this mode. In a 1994 interview with Jacobo Sefamí, Molina alludes to André Breton's famous comment about Mexico's surrealistic character and then references Alejo Carpentier's discussion of the "marvelous real" in Latin America. Building on this conceptualization of Latin America as a magical space, Molina states, "In America the landscapes are not good citizens: they are an exuberance, an exaggeration in every sense, the desert areas as much as the jungle. I feel myself to be profoundly American. And in America there is a profound way of feeling that is animistic, and that still exists in everything, even in the official religions" ("Itinerario" 144). Molina's comment takes us one step closer to understanding the persistence of the motif of Latin America's surrealistic or marvelous character. For Molina, as for Artaud, Breton, Carpentier, and others, the landscape is represented as prodigious, outsized, exuberant, or exaggerated. Inhabiting this landscape is a human race inexorably connected to it through a consciousness that is "animistic," sharing a spirit with all animate and inanimate beings. Insofar as this type of consciousness invites an aesthetic response that highlights the unusual, the irrational, or the fantastic, surrealism—along with *lo real maravilloso* and, later, magical realism—has thus been associated by both foreign and native-born writers with what is most "authentically" Latin American.

The second surrealist mode in Molina's poetics is the erotic—a mode that often overlaps with the sense of the marvelous in the natural world. Jason Wilson observes that Neruda's pervasive influence over other Latin American poets is evident in the "sensual materialism" that marks Molina's first three volumes of poetry (*Companion* 97). Although Neruda's influence is undeniable, I would argue that the sensual materialism so evident in Molina's work is more often imbued with a sense of *mystery* that transcends the objective "thingness" of the exterior world so central to Neruda's poetics. In this context, it is important to note the influence of Rainer Maria Rilke and the poets of Spain's Generation of 1927 (in particular, Luis Cernuda).

As in Breton, Éluard, and other surrealist poets, the erotic is often represented in Molina with relation to an essentialized female presence. Cristina Piña asserts that Molina's representation of the erotic is the point at which all his poetic concerns converge, and moreover, that his construction of the female figure takes on particularly "tropical" qualities: "If, as in the case of the French surrealists, one of the axes of his poetry is the woman and the erotic relationship, in this case she is a primordial and opulent woman, whose sexuality, admirably summoned by the poems, signals the primitive and the tropical within a natural environment also marked by excess and by the dazzling sense of origins. But this is an origin that is arrived at through transgression and the rejection of all formal convention, whether in life or in writing" ("Estudio" 17). Notably, Piña's critical language here—including terms such as "primordial," "excess," "dazzling," and so forth—also reflects the vision of an inherently marvelous Latin American environment.

Moving beyond his poetic initiation in Argentina's neoromantic Generación del 40, Molina develops his surrealist affinities in three principal collections: *Costumbres errantes o la redondez de la tierra* (1951), *Amantes antípodas* (1961), and *Las bellas furias* (1966). Out of his rich and extensive oeuvre, I have chosen to examine one long poem from *Las bellas furias* that reflects the intertwining modes of surrealist geography and sensual materialism. Like many of Molina's poems, "Rito acuático" [Aquatic Rite] lyrically narrates a recollected experience. Also in typical Molinesque fashion, the speaker of this poem is a traveler, one whose sense of exile opens him to the experience of being grounded in the wider world.

Rito acuático

Bañándome en el río Túmbez un cholo me enseñó a lavar la ropa
Más viva que un lagarto su camisa saltaba entre inasibles labios
    susurrantes
y las veloces mujeres de lo líquido
fluyendo por las piernas
con sus inagotables cabelleras bajo las hojas de los plátanos
minuciosamente copiados por el sueño
de esa agua cocinada al sol
a través del salvaje corazón de un lugar impregnado
por el espíritu de un río de América—extraña
ceremonia acuática—desnudos el cholo y yo
entre las valvas ardientes del mediodía ¡oh lavanderos
nómades! purificados por el cauterio
de unas olas
por la implacable luz del mundo

Lavaba mis vínculos con los pájaros con las estaciones
con los acontecimientos fortuitos de mi existencia
y los ofrecimientos de la locura
                Lavaba mi lengua
la sanguijuela de embustes que anida en mi garganta
—espumas indemnes exorcizando un instante todas las inmundas
    alegorías del poder y del oro—
en aquel delirante paraíso del insomnio
Lavaba mis uñas y mi rostro
y el errante ataúd de la memoria
lleno de fantasías y fracasos y furias amordazadas
                         aguas aguas aguas
tantas dichas perdidas centelleando de nuevo
desde gestos antiguos o soñados
mi vientre y el musgo de mis ingles

>   lavaba cada sitio de destierro ennegrecido por mi aliento cada
>   instante de pasión dejado caer como una lámpara
>   y mis sentidos amenazadores como una navaja asestada en la aorta
>   pero por eso mismo más exaltantes a cada latido que los disuelve
>   en el viento
>   por eso mismo más abrasadores a cada pulsación tendida como
>   una súplica de anzuelos.
>
>   Lavaba mi amor y mi desgracia
>   tanta avidez sin límites por toda forma y ser
>   por cada cosa brillando en la sangre inaferrable
>   por cada cuerpo con el olor de los besos y del verano
>   ¡Dioses! ¡Dioses!
>   ¡Amor de la corriente con sexos a la deriva entre costas que se
>   desplazan!
>   Dioses feroces e inocentes dioses míos sin más poder que su fuga
>   pájaros en incendio cada vez más remotos
>   mientras retorcía mi camisa
>   en el gran desvarío de vivir
>   —¡oh lavador!—tal vez nunca acaso ni siquiera
>   jamás un instante en el agua del Túmbez (*Antología poética* 145–46)

[When I was bathing in the Tumbes River, a *cholo*[1] taught me how to wash my clothes / Livelier than a lizard, his shirt leapt among the ungraspable murmuring mouths /and the swift women of the liquid world / slipping through the legs / with their boundless flowing hair under the leaves of banana trees / minutely copied by the dream /of that water baked in the sun / through the wild heart of a place impregnated with the spirit / of a river of America—strange aquatic rite—/ both naked, the *cholo* and I /among the radiant valves of midday, oh nomad / washermen! purified / by the cauterizing waves / by the relentless light of the world // I washed my bonds with birds with seasons / with the chance happenings of my existence / and the offerings of madness / I washed my tongue the leech of fraud that nests in my throat /—untouched foam instantly exorcizing all the filthy allegories of power and gold—/ in that raving paradise of insomnia I washed my fingernails and my face / and the wandering coffin of memory / brimming with fantasies and failures and muzzled furies / waters waters waters / so many lost joys sparkling again / out of used-up gestures or gestures dreamed / my belly and the moss of my groin / I washed every site of exile blackened by my breath / every instant of passion dropped like a lamp / and my senses threatening like a knife at the aorta / but for that very reason excited with every beat that dissolves them in the wind / for that very reason burning more with every pulse held out like a plea of fishhooks. // I washed my love and my misfortune / such boundless eagerness for every form and being / for each thing that shines in the ungraspable blood / for each body with its odor of kisses and summer / Gods! Gods! / Love of the current with genitals adrift between the shifting banks / Gods fierce and innocent, gods of mine with no power but their flight / birds on fire, farther and farther, / while I wrung my shirt / in the great raving of life /oh washerman!—maybe never perhaps not even / ever an instant in the waters of the Tumbes]

Considered within surrealist parameters, it is clear that "Aquatic Rite" is by no means a hermetic poem driven by a purely automatic process. Much of its language points directly to the perceptible world ("a river of America," "my belly," "I wrung my shirt"). From the first line forward the poem situates itself in a recognizable—if, for most readers, exotic—place, the Tumbes River. The speaker and his Peruvian companion are clearly identifiable figures engaged in what, for the *cholo* at least, is a quotidian activity, bathing and washing clothes in a river. Apart from these elements, however, "Aquatic Rite" reveals itself to be a poem with all the marks of a surrealist imagination.

To begin with, there is a productive tension here between dream and reality, the rational and the irrational, producing the sur-reality of which Breton spoke. In the clearest example of this, the banana trees along the riverbank—a concrete, real-world image—are "minutely copied by the dream / of that water baked in the sun." The speaker is simply referring here to trees reflected in water. But by introducing the word "dream," he invites the reader to see this landscape as simultaneously real and not real. The heat and bright sunlight intensify the sense of mirage. Adding to the play of dream and reality are four direct allusions to irrational states of mind: "the offerings of madness," "that raving paradise of insomnia," "the wandering coffin of memory / brimming with fantasies," and, most significant, "the great raving [*desvarío*] of life." Molina wants his reader to balance precariously on that *point sublime* between the real and the unreal.

The imagery of the poem, though grounded in an ordinary scene in a real place, develops more associatively than discursively, a technique clearly observable in the paratactic line "I washed my bonds with birds with seasons." Immediately after the prosaic phrase "a *cholo* taught me how to wash my clothes," the language takes a surprisingly metaphorical turn, with the shirt leaping "livelier than a lizard" and the bubbling river waters becoming so many mouths that no human hand can catch. Drawing on the ancient motif of the long-haired water nymph or the siren (with her "murmuring mouth"), the speaker attributes erotic feminine qualities to the flowing water that caresses the men's legs. Thus the scene of washing turns unexpectedly into a scene of intensified sensuality and desire, in which the totality of the natural world erotically connects the "washermen" (*lavaderos*) to each other and to their liquid milieu.

In true surrealist fashion, the eroticism of this poem presents a positive, celebratory valence, linking sexuality to a total experience of freedom. It veers from orthodox surrealism, however, in that the scene is implicitly auto- and even homoerotic: the arousal experienced by the speaker is a response to the sensuous delights of his own body in the river and also to the simple, joyful companionship of the *cholo*. Whereas female sexuality appears only as a mythicized presence, male sexuality is concrete and yet transcendent: "both naked, the *cholo* and I / among the radiant valves of midday, oh nomad / washermen . . ." In this passage the term "nomad" reminds the reader that the traditionally female domestic act of washing in the river is being performed here by men who are free to roam, who join each other in their itinerant existence.

Also crucial to the poem's eroticism is the fact that the sensuality experienced by the speaker erases the body-spirit duality. The ordinary task of washing the body becomes a sacred act of purification, a baptism into a new life. In addition to the word *rito* in the title, which is reiterated in the phrase "strange aquatic rite," the speaker applies the adjective "purified" to himself and his companion, and he even tells the reader that the purification is necessary to exorcize "all the filthy allegories of power and gold," to cleanse "every site of exile blackened by my breath"—in other words, to undo the effects of living in an abject world. The very structure of the poem reinforces the transcendent nature of the act of bathing in the river. The second stanza begins with the words "I washed," which are then repeated anaphorically four more times in the second and third stanzas, allowing the poem to be read as a litany. Finally, the repeated allusions to light and radiance, as well as the very direct reference to the sacred in the phrase "Gods! Gods!" (linked by its placement at the right margin of the page with the earlier phrase "waters waters waters"), reinforce the poem's enactment of an encounter with the marvelous in the everyday world.

In sum, Enrique Molina's "Aquatic Rite" illustrates one possible route toward the Latin Americanization of the surrealist aesthetic. As we have seen, this poem is conventionally surrealist in its dynamic play between reality and the dream, in its associative language and unexpected metaphors, and in its theme of celebratory (even sacred) eroticism. The poem *re*appropriates these surrealist principles, however, by situating itself in a real and autochthonous natural landscape, a mode not generally seen in European surrealism. The dream of the sunbaked water evoked in the poem's first lines moves "through the wild heart of a place impregnated with the spirit / of a river of America"—lines that recall Molina's claim that there is a profound and animistic feeling in Latin America, a sensibility that the poet tries consciously to capture, as well as what Piña calls "a dazzling sense of origins" in Molina's work. The autoerotic nature of this poem and the controlled use of imagery are further markers of difference from orthodox surrealism.

Cófreces attributes the convergence of remarkable talent around the surrealist nucleus in the 1950s to the exceptional organizing and theorizing efforts of Aldo Pellegrini and simultaneously to Enrique Molina's poetic imagination, which extended Latin American surrealism beyond its previous frontiers: "It was no longer the images of French poets translated into Spanish, in versions by César Moro or Pellegrini himself: Molina invigorated the surrealist trend out of his own startling poetics."[2] The force of his personality; his unwavering dedication to the surrealist ideals of liberty, love, and poetry; and the strength of his lyric voice made of Molina a prodigious force in Argentine poetry during the second half of the twentieth century.

Olga Orozco: The Poetics of Danger and Refuge

Ten years younger than Enrique Molina, and his close friend and protégée, Olga Orozco (1920–98) would become one of the Argentina's most respected writers, author of nine volumes of poetry and two collections of short stories. In her early work at least, she shares the elegiac tone and the neoromantic preoccupations of the Generation of 1940. As with many members of that generation, Orozco lists her primary literary influences as certain romantic poets, particularly Giacomo Leopardi and Friedrich Hölderlin, and those she deems "the antecedents of surrealism itself"—Nerval and Novalis, Baudelaire, Lautréamont, and Rimbaud (Sefamí, *Imaginación* 125). When questioned about the influence of surrealism in her work, Orozco responded, "Although I may not be an orthodox surrealist, I believe there are elements in common: the prevalence of the imaginary, delvings into the unconscious, the flow of images, the immersion in dream and in the depths of oneself as a source of wisdom, the belief in a limitless reality, beyond all appearances and beneath all surfaces, and the zeal for capturing that reality entirely, in all of its facets" (*Páginas* 277).

In the early 1950s, Orozco was a contributor to the neosurrealist journal *A Partir de Cero* (examined in Chapter 7), and although she counts the Argentine surrealists from Pellegrini to Molina to Madariaga and Llinás as "old friends," her direct affiliation with this group was limited (*Páginas* 277). Orozco's poems resemble those of Molina in formal terms: they are constructed of long-breathed lines in which images accumulate in complex associative strings. As they unfold across the page (or pages), these poems move between lyric narrativity and metaphysical reflection, employing language that that is highly figurative and often hermetic. But in contrast to Molina, Orozco's poetic voice tends toward oracular discourse and heavily rhythmic, repetitive structures that suggest liturgy, ritual, or even magical incantation. Orozco's work also differs from Molina's in its loose ties to the material world and, correspondingly, its sustained attention to *el otro lado* [the other side]—the fiercely desired but unreachable absolute.

Orozco was born in a small town on the Argentine *pampa*, where she spent the first eight years of her life. As in the case of Molina and Francisco Madariaga, this childhood landscape of vast plains and shifting dunes is imaginatively recreated in both her poetry and her fiction. Like the majority of Argentines, she was a descendent of European immigrants (Basque, Irish, and Sicilian) and thus inherited a perspective in which Old World stories and superstitions were overlaid on a New World culture and geography. Orozco insists that this background is crucial to understanding her writing: "This is important, especially considering my maternal grandmother's side of the family, because she maintained a rather magical, animistic view of the world, which undoubtedly was inherited from her Celtic ancestors. For her, the entire world was made up of things in movement. Objects were always lying in ambush, waiting to aid you or to condemn you, to protect you or to take you into the abyss. Everything was a danger or a refuge" (Sefamí, *Imaginación* 96). There are clear echoes here of Molina's assertion that Latin American culture is built on a substratum of animistic beliefs. But furthermore, Orozco's assertions parallel a surrealist view of the world as the site of potentially marvelous encounters, moments in which the plane of the invisible reveals itself to the perceptive eye.

Orozco's representation of these encounters is unique in the way it gives preeminence to the dynamic of "danger and refuge" mentioned above. The poetic subject in her work is not the leisurely *flâneur* of the Parisian surrealists or even Molina's sensuous and melancholic nomad. Orozco's adult subject never strays far from her childhood double—"la criatura que fui" [the child that I was]—and thus retains an intense awareness of her own precarious place in a universe full of potentially threatening objects or forces (*También la luz* 14). Again, geography informs poetics: Orozco describes her native province as an extremely arid land of "fantastic" proportions, with winds so powerful that entire sand dunes would shift places from one day to the next: "Besides, since there are wide reaches of desert, with no vegetation, each little object—a bone, a rock—takes on a striking relief, it appears huge, as in a surrealist painting. Any isolated presence assumes the characteristics of a revelation, of an apparition" (qtd. in Sefamí, *Imaginación* 97). One can easily imagine the paintings of Yves Tanguy—with their desolate landscapes and strange objects placed in high relief against ground, water, or sky—as the backdrop for Orozco's poems and stories.

Orozco stands out from many of her contemporaries in that her work "moves beyond surrealism in its metaphysical searching" (Crow 7). The desire for revelation, for a glimpse into the unknown, is certainly a drive shared by the surrealists and by countless other poets. But as I have argued elsewhere,[3] in Orozco's poetry the language of desire and revelation is uniquely organized around a set of tropes associated with the occult or esoteric traditions, a tendency that took definitive shape beginning with her 1962 volume *Los juegos peligrosos* [The Dangerous Games]. Here surrealism as a poetic language is evident in the unusual images and metaphors, but this language emerges not out of "pure psychic automatism" but rather out of a systematic construction of metaphors, symbols, and allegories that is solidly grounded in neo-Platonic belief systems such as Gnosticism and hermeticism.

Central to this thought is the doctrine of cosmic unity and its corollary, the interrelationship by analogy of all things. Thus occult practices such as alchemy, divination, and witchcraft have at their core the desire to reestablish a fractured unity. Orozco's work as a poet was a repeated attempt to regain that unity through the power of the word: this is why she insists that "magic and poetry are profoundly joined at their roots: both attempt an analogical conversion of the universe, a linking that is not that of normal cause and effect. Through them, everything is possible, by virtue of a mysterious alchemy" (*Páginas* 279). In this vein, Orozco takes the practice of black magic as the organizing trope of her poem "Para hacer un talisman" [To Make a Talisman], which represents a ritual for turning the heart into a powerful charm. I quote the poem here in its entirety:

> Se necesita sólo tu corazón
> hecho a la viva imagen de tu demonio o de tu dios.
> Un corazón apenas, como un crisol de brasas para la idolatría.
> Nada más que un indefenso corazón enamorado.
> Déjalo a la intemperie,
> donde la hierba aúlle sus endechas de nodriza loca
> y no pueda dormir,
> donde el viento y la lluvia dejen caer su látigo en un golpe de azul
>   escalofrío
> sin convertirlo en mármol y sin partirlo en dos,
> donde la oscuridad abra sus madrigueras a todas las jaurías
> y no logre olvidar.
> Arrójalo después desde lo alto de su amor al hervidero de la
>   bruma.
> Ponlo a secar en el sordo regazo de la piedra,
> y escarba, escarba en él con una aguja fría hasta arrancar el último
>   grano de esperanza.
> Deja que lo sofoquen las fiebres y la ortiga,
> que lo sacuda el trote ritual de la alimaña,
> que lo envuelva la injuria hecha con los jirones de sus antiguas
>   glorias.
> Y cuando un día un año lo aprisione con la garra de un siglo,
> antes que sea tarde,
> antes que se convierta en momia deslumbrante,
> abre de par en par y una por una todas sus heridas:
> que las exhiba al sol de la piedad, lo mismo que el mendigo,
> que plaña su delirio en el desierto,

hasta que sólo el eco de un nombre crezca en él con la furia del
   hambre:
un incesante golpe de cuchara contra el plato vacío.

Si sobrevive aún,
si ha llegado hasta aquí hecho a la viva imagen de tu demonio o
   de tu dios;
he ahí un talismán más inflexible que la ley,
más fuerte que las armas y el mal del enemigo.
Guárdalo en la vigilia de tu pecho igual que a un centinela.
Pero vela con él.
Puede crecer en ti como la mordedura de la lepra;
puede ser tu verdugo.
¡El inocente monstruo, el insaciable comensal de tu muerte!
(*Eclipses y fulgores* 41–42)

[Your heart is all you need, / made in the living image of your demon or your god. / Just a heart, like a crucible full of live coals for idolatry. / Simply a helpless, enamored heart. / Leave it in the wild, / where grass howls its dirges like a mad wet nurse / and it cannot sleep / where wind and rain whip it with the lash of a blue chill / without turning it to marble or splitting it in two, / where darkness opens its dens to every wandering pack / and it cannot forget. / Hurl it, then, from the heights of its love into the roiling mist. / Then spread it to dry in the deaf lap of stone, / and dig, with a cold needle dig until you extract the last grain of hope. / Let fevers and nettle suffocate it, / let beasts of prey shuffle it in their ritual trot, / let it be wrapped in insult made from the tatters of former glories. / And when one day a year imprisons it with a century's talons, / before it grows too late, / before it becomes a dazzling mummy, / open its wounds wide and exhibit them one by one, / beggarly, before the sun of pity; / in the desert let it whimper its delirium / until only the echo of a name grows within it, summoning all the fury of hunger: / the spoon's incessant banging against an empty plate. // If the heart still survives, / if it has come this far as the living image of your daemon or your god, / behold a talisman more inflexible than the law, / stronger than the weapons or the evil of the enemy. / Guard it in the vigil of your chest like a sentinel. / But keep watch with it. / It can grow within you like the bite of leprosy, / it can be your executioner. / The innocent monster, insatiable guest at the table of your death!]

Orozco's semantic field in "To Make a Talisman" is drawn from the occult tradition of protective magic: the poem enacts a set of instructions for creating an object meant to protect its bearer from harm. (The inherently verbal nature of this creation is apparent in the Greek origin of the word *talisman*: *telesma* means "incantation.") In Orozco's poem, the ritual acts required for creating this magical object are extreme or transgressive in that they are associated with violence, bestial aggression, pain of every sort, fury, and even madness. The speaker acknowledges the transgressive nature of these acts by claiming, in language that subverts the biblical allusion, that the object is made in the image of a god *or a demon*; in fact, it represents a space of "idolatry." Notably, all these magical deeds are performed on an object located in the ordinary (and not the magical) side of existence: the lovesick human heart.

The disturbing image of a heart left exposed to the elements (*a la intemperie*) recalls the desert landscapes of Orozco's childhood, in which a small object can acquire sharp relief and thus appear as *desmesurado*, disproportionate to its surroundings. It also creates a powerful symbol for the dynamic of danger and refuge that becomes a distinguishing feature of Orozco's poetics. At work in the scene being enacted here is the principle of analogy, which operates along these lines: if the talisman in general functions as a form of protection, then the magically transformed heart-talisman should function as protection from psychic or emotional dangers. In order to be properly prepared for this function, the heart must undergo an initiatory rite so brutal that it may not survive. But if it does survive, it will become a talisman with the power to ward off all evil. Read allegorically (a type of reading to which many of Orozco's poems offer themselves), the suffering induced by emotionally difficult situations can strengthen us, becoming in effect our protection from further pain.

And here is the twist, the poem's true revelation. A mere four lines from the end, the poem turns suddenly on the word *but*, and here the speaker unexpectedly warns her interlocutor that this powerful object may turn into "your executioner." The heart-talisman that has been subjected to extreme suffering may become an oxymoronic "innocent monster," literally feeding on the death of the one it was meant to shield from harm. The structure of this poem, in which a long series of instructions for a rite of magical protection suddenly turns into a warning of mortal danger, points directly to the title of the volume from which this poem is taken—*The Dangerous Games*. This unexpected turn reminds the reader that in the realm of human emotions, there are no magical spells or practices that can ultimately protect us from our condition of vulnerability. The poem's structure and the allegorical reading it invites also enact the surrealist conviction that poetry is a path to knowledge: only by following the poem step by step to its surprising conclusion can we experience the revelation that "magic" (even verbal magic) is a powerful force, but one whose ends we may not foresee.

Alejandra Pizarnik: The Disarticulation of the Self

Susan Rubin Suleiman has observed that as the French surrealist movement "grew weaker and more embattled, it became more welcoming to women, especially young women from other countries" (170). Alejandra Pizarnik (1936–72) was one of those young women, a latecomer to the European surrealist feast and also the last major figure in the line of the Argentine second-wave surrealists. Pizarnik is also arguably the Argentine poet who most successfully applied surrealist techniques to her own creative vision. She spoke once in an interview of her desire to write "terribly exact poems" as a drive that contradicted her "innate surrealism" ("Algunas claves" 249). This innate surrealism surfaces in Pizarnik's literary essays, including "Relectura de *Nadja*, de André Breton" and her "Prólogo a *Textos de Antonin Artaud*" (both from 1967).

In a characterization applicable to many Latin America poets of the period in question, César Aira declares that Pizarnik "lived and read and wrote in the wake of surrealism" (*Pizarnik* 11). Critics such as Francisco Lasarte and Suzanne Chávez-Silverman have rightly disputed Pizarnik's surrealist affinities, insisting that her work lacks the surrealists' characteristic optimism and faith in the "magical" potentiality of language. These critics also insist on the vigilance that Pizarnik maintained over her poetic practice, an approach that distances her from the automatic, free-associative techniques of orthodox surrealist writers. David William Foster questions whether Pizarnik's work can best be characterized as part of a "retarded" surrealistic movement, "a matter of an Argentine neosurrealism," or a sui generis response to "something like an already permanently established surrealistic option in Western culture" (326)—all of which, in my view, are acceptable terms for describing Pizarnik's poetics.

Rather than revisiting these debates or explicating the surrealist nature of Pizarnik's imagery, in the following pages I will focus on one significant poetic trope in her work that reveals unexpected ties to surrealism. Concretely, I will examine her use of the doll or mannequin motif in its implicit relationship to the work of the German surrealist artist Hans Bellmer. I will argue that Pizarnik, in work ranging from her early dense lyrics to the expansive and sometimes obscene prose of her last years, constructs a poetic self that bears a remarkable resemblance to Bellmer's constructed and photographed dolls or *poupées*.[4] To track such resemblances is perhaps to set foot on a slippery slope: one must take into account significant differences in the modes of representation (sculpture and photography on the one hand, poetry on the other), in the artists' culture of origin, and in their respective biographical and historical contexts. Nevertheless, a comparative look at Pizarnik's doll imagery and Bellmer's *poupée* can deepen our understanding of Pizarnik's poetic representation of the self, in particular her allusions to loss of selfhood through the tropes of doubling, deformation, and fragmentation. Additionally, such a comparison will allow us to consider certain questions regarding the representation of women in surrealist and neosurrealist art and literature.

The connection I wish to draw between Bellmer's dolls and Pizarnik's poetic self takes a particularly problematic turn when we consider the question of gender. Feminist criticism has attested to the male surrealists' view of the female as child muse, angel, erotic object, essentialized Woman—anything but creative individual. What happens, then, when the female artist adopts surrealist attitudes or methods? The crucial question, as Gwen Raaberg formulates it, is, "How have the women Surrealists been able to position themselves as creative subjects within this discourse? In what ways and to what extent have they accepted the male surrealist discourse, and how have they significantly changed—subverted, inverted, and extended that discourse?" (4). Such questions are particularly applicable to a critique of writers like Pizarnik, who as latecomers had the potential to establish a greater distance from certain features of the historical surrealist iconography and discourse. The comparison with Bellmer can provide new insights into Pizarnik's work when we consider that, while acting as a writer highly conscious of her own artistic agency, she obsessively constructs female figures that lack agency—that is, figures manipulated by forces that disarticulate, reduce, or even destroy them. While positioning herself as a creative subject (to borrow Raaberg's terms), Pizarnik creates objects that suffer passively. This dynamic speaks to Pizarnik's lifelong struggle with mental illness, a struggle she engaged in primarily with the weapon of the written word.[5] Thus articulation in a linguistic sense continually plays itself out against disarticulation—disjointedness, disassemblage, dismemberment—in her representation of the female body and psyche.

Hans Bellmer (1902–75) crafted his first doll in 1933, initiating what would become an obsessive process that Rosalind Krauss has called the "construction of dismemberment" (86). Like Pizarnik's "little statue of terror," the first doll was approximately four-and-a-half feet tall, made of papier-mâché and plaster over a skeleton of wood and metal. Breton and the other surrealists immediately embraced Bellmer's work, publishing several of the photographs in the December 1934 volume of *Minotaure* under the title "Doll. Variations on the Assemblage of an Articulated Minor." By the time he constructed his second doll in 1935, he had made an important technical discovery: the ball joint. While the second doll's surface uncannily recalls human flesh, the obsessive recombinations of limbs and appendages around the central ball joint leave very little that resembles a human body. In the more than one hundred photographs that Bellmer made of this doll, she is placed in settings that "present a clandestine, malevolent world in which the doll is variously bound, beaten, tied to a tree, hanged on a hook, or taken apart and strewn on a stairway" (Taylor 76). Significantly, the second doll often wears white bobby socks and Mary Jane shoes, a detail that reminds the viewer that, no matter how misshapen, mutilated, or unnatural, this is the representation of an adolescent girl. The psychological power evinced by these photographs "derives from the juxtaposition of shocking victim poses and innocent flirtatiousness . . . The dolls' dramatic poses in many of the photographs appear to be melancholic acquiescence: resignation in the face of their violated condition" (Lichtenstein 16).

The gender issue in the case of Hans Bellmer is complicated by the fact that, among his surrealist contemporaries, he strikes many critics as a particularly distressing example of the surrealist objectification of women. Mary Ann Caws's description of the surrealist image of women places Bellmer in the role of prime transgressor: "Headless. And also footless. Often armless too; and always unarmed, except with poetry and passion. There they are, the surrealist women so shot and painted, so stressed and dismembered, punctured and severed: is it any wonder she has (we have) gone to pieces? It is not just the dolls of Hans Bellmer, lying about, it is more" ("Seeing the Surrealist Woman" 11). To be fair, we must acknowledge Bellmer's work as complex and enigmatic (therein lies its peculiar force) and resist the assumption of misogynist *intentions*. Viewing Bellmer's work historically, critics such as Hal Foster and Therese Lichtenstein have suggested that the *poupée* may have represented a protest against the Nazi attitudes toward the body and toward the degenerate Other—a category that included women, homosexuals, Jews, communists, and the mentally ill. Nevertheless, as Foster acknowledges at the end of his essay, "there are problems with this work that cannot be resolved away. The *poupées* produce misogynistic effects that may overwhelm any liberatory intentions" (122). For the purposes of a comparison with Pizarnik's work, it is the powerlessness of Bellmer's dolls, their averted gaze or empty stare, their dismemberment and the unmistakable marks of suffering that are of interest, regardless of the artist's intended message.

Although there is no direct evidence that Pizarnik knew the works of Hans Bellmer, it is reasonable to postulate some familiarity on her part. Pizarnik lived in Paris for two intervals during the 1960s; there she came into contact with the "old guard" of surrealism, including Georges Bataille, Max Ernst, and Jean Arp, all of whom she held in high regard (Bordelois 288). Given her affinity with surrealism and her residence in Paris during the years Bellmer was also living there, it is probable that Pizarnik was aware of the *poupée*. In any case, the significant presence of the doll figure in both Bellmer and Pizarnik is not an odd coincidence but a common appropriation of a centuries-old motif that was the object of renewed avant-garde interest. The surrealists in particular, initially influenced by Giorgio de Chirico, were fascinated with mannequins and automata, as evidenced by the 1938 *Exposition Internationale du Surrréalisme* in Paris, which featured an entire street of mannequins variously dressed and manipulated by artists such as Ernst, Kurt Seligmann, and André Masson.[6] Bellmer's work, in its turn, stimulated further interest in this figure: his biographer Peter Webb calls his *poupée* the prototype of the surrealist mannequin (46).

In contrast to Bellmer's dolls, Pizarnik's *muñecas* (which appear with increasing frequency in her later work) are not depicted in sensuous detail but are evoked somewhat abstractly in epithets such as "the little dead girl," "the open-eyed one," "the little forgotten one," "beautiful automaton," "the sleeping one," "little blind princess," "the celestial silent one," "little paper doll," "tiny pink marionette," and so forth.[7] Despite differences, certain undeniable similarities obtain in these reiterated figures: they are all female, they tend to be diminutive, and they are often trapped in somnolent or semiconscious states. Mechanical, passive, or silent, they lack agency and sometimes are not even alive. They exist in isolation, without meaningful links to any larger human context. If they have a material substance at all, that material is almost always paper or cardboard, signaling both artificiality and fragility. Although the dolls, mannequins, and other diminutive figures in Pizarnik's poetry are grammatically gendered as female, there is very little direct reference—as there is in Bellmer's work—to sexual anatomy. Yet in both cases adolescent female sexuality is evoked, with its double charge of innocence and seductiveness. Though in a distinct mode of representation, the "coexistence and confusion of the perverse and the banal, of evil and guilelessness" that critics observe in Bellmer's dolls apply to Pizarnik's doll imagery as well (Taylor 79).

Alienation, sexual anxiety, and a sense of vulnerability are traits that mark Pizarnik's lyric "I" and that also reverberate in the visual impressions created by Bellmer's work. The first fragment from a series entitled "Los pequeños cantos" [Little Songs] directly connects articulation to alienation: "nadie me conoce yo hablo la noche / nadie me conoce yo hablo mi cuerpo" [no one knows me I speak the night / no one knows me I speak my body] (*Obras* 234). The suppressed connector between the clauses creates a fundamental ambiguity: does the lyric self speak the night and her body because no one knows her or in spite of the fact that no one knows her—or is there yet another other possibility? Should the parallel construction beginning with "I speak" lead the reader to conflate "the night" with "my body"? The construction of these lines adds to the shadowy figuration of the poetic self. In the fourth fragment of the "Little Songs," the doll figure appears as part of a metaphor for language:

> una muñeca de huesos de pájaro
> conduce los perros perfumados
> de mis propias palabras que me vuelven (*Obras* 234)

[a bird-boned doll / leads the perfumed dogs / of my own words that return to me].

The image of the fragile bird-boned doll eerily echoes a photograph of the first Bellmer *poupée*, which shows the doll's head carefully placed next to the head of a bird-like creature. Both heads are wrapped in black gauze and cradled on a bed of lace.[8] Pizarnik's doll in the above passage is an active figure, leading the "perfumed dogs," but by the third verse we realize that this action is circular and therefore without consequence. It is significant that the "dogs" being led are metaphors for words, which invariably turn back on the speaker. Such an image hints at Pizarnik's complicated relationship to poetry as a creative act that continually fails to shift the subject out of her enclosed subjective space.

In many poems, the female subject's vulnerability is linked to her condition of semiconsciousness, emblematized by the act of sleepwalking: "una niña de seda / sonámbula ahora en la cornisa de niebla" [a silk girl / sleepwalking on the cornice of fog] (*Obras* 74). This image creates a breathtaking sense of imminent danger, a premortem that contrasts with the postmortem impression given by many of Bellmer's photographs. In some cases, Pizarnik's speaker signals vulnerability in a female third person, an "other" with whom she immediately identifies: "A solas danza la misteriosa autónoma. Comparto su miedo de animal muy joven en la primera noche de las cacerías" [The mysterious automaton dances alone. I share her fear of being a very young animal on the first night of the hunt] (*Obras* 120). Again, danger or even death is imminent, and the female figure lacks agency in her trancelike state.

An even more deliberate shift from third to first person occurs in another image of vulnerability and ruin: "Maniquí desnudo entre escombros" [Mannequin naked among the rubble] with the speaker concluding several lines later, "Hablo de mí, naturalmente" [I speak of myself, naturally] (*Obras* 193). This self-reflexive rhetoric points to a significant difference between Pizarnik and Bellmer. Although psychoanalytical arguments have been made for Bellmer's masochistic identification with the fragile and abused dolls he fabricated,[9] his created images remain resolutely "other," outside himself as creator. For Pizarnik, in contrast, the distance between the poetic voice and the doll is minimal or nonexistent. Pizarnik constantly reminds the reader that the figures she creates are not objects of an external gaze but embodiments of her own alienated self: "Figuras de cera los otros y sobre todo yo, que soy más otra que ellos" [Wax figures the others and above all I, who am more other than they] (*Obras* 138).

The images I have discussed thus far involve a whole-bodied doll, but in fact Pizarnik's poetry often represents the female figure as disarticulated or dismembered. The motif is an ancient one, and it remains open to numerous interpretations. In his essay on "The Uncanny" (1919), Freud remarks that "dismembered limbs, a severed head, a hand cut off at the wrist, feet which dance by themselves—all these have something particularly uncanny about them" (151). Freud's essay revolves around a discussion of E. T. A. Hoffmann's story "The Sandman," first published in 1817, whose female protagonist Olympia is revealed to be a doll. In Offenbach's opera adaptation of the story, which Bellmer saw shortly after it opened in 1933, Olympia is torn limb from limb at the end of the first act. The opera no doubt suggested certain visual and plastic possibilities within the interconnected motifs of the double, the uncanny, and the disarticulated doll. Bellmer in fact speaks of the process of sculpting the *poupée* as one of "creating beauty and also distributing the salt of deformation a bit vengefully" ("Memories of the Doll Theme" 174).

By contrast, the "salt of deformation" in Pizarnik is a source not of objectivized aesthetic pleasure but of subjective angst. Pizarnik's female figure is often represented as headless or as completely dismembered: "el cuerpo desatado y los huesos desparramados" [the body unfastened and the bones scattered] (*Obras* 144). Who or what are the causes of this violence? In the case of Bellmer's dolls, the artist himself is on the most concrete level the force behind the doll's disintegration. One 1934 photograph features Bellmer's own semitransparent image superimposed on an image of the first doll. He bends over to stand head-to-head with the doll, which consists of the torso with its exposed mechanized interior, the head (with disheveled hair and beret), one plaster-cast leg, and one skeletal, broomstick leg. She looks away, while he stares fixedly at the camera. Though shadowy, the artist is complete, in control, in touch, while the doll is none of these.

Pizarnik's agents of corporeal disintegration are never concrete or fully externalized. David William Foster shows that the integrity of Pizarnik's poetic subject, both physical and psychic, is violated by personified abstract forces (such as night or death) or by hypostasized entities (such as articles of clothing or body parts); the *yo poético* often appears as a passive victim of these destructive forces: "El viento me había comido / parte de la cara y las manos. / Me llamaban ángel harapiento. / Yo esperaba" [The wind had eaten / part of my face and my hands. / They called me ragged angel. I waited] (*Obras* 111). Even more pertinent to the doll characterization—often related to the motif of doubling—is the suggestion of self-duplication in which the subject is both agent and victim: "Las muñecas desventradas por mis antiguas manos de muñeca, la desilusión al encontrar pura estopa" [The dolls disemboweled by my old doll hands, the disappointment of finding pure stuffing] (*Obras* 153).

An important passage from the quintessentially surrealist prose poem "Extracción de la piedra de locura" [Extraction of the Stone of Folly] takes place in a ruined garden, where the subject disarticulates herself:

> Visión enlutada, desgarrada, de un jardín con estatuas rotas. Al filo de la madrugada los huesos te dolían. Tú te desgarras. Te lo prevengo y te lo previne. Tú te desarmas. Te lo digo, te lo dije. Tú te desnudas. Te desposees. Te desunes. Te lo predije. De pronto se deshizo: ningún nacimiento ... Ahora tus despojos, recogerlos uno a uno, gran hastío, en dónde dejarlos. (*Obras* 139)

[Vision in mourning, torn apart, of a garden with broken statues. At the edge of dawn your bones ached. You tear yourself apart. I am warning you and I warned you of this. You dismantle yourself. I tell you this, I told you this. You undress yourself. You dispossess yourself. You detach yourself. I foretold this for you. Suddenly it's come apart: no birth . . . Now for your scraps: to pick them up one by one—such ennui—where to leave them?]

The physical disarticulation described in this "vision in mourning"—the figure literally tearing herself apart—is reinforced by the verbal disarticulation implicit in the slippage between the "you" and the "I." The rhetorical force of this passage in Spanish is achieved by the obsessive repetition of verbs of undoing, all marked by the prefix *des*—*desgarrar, desarmar, desnudar, desposeer, desunir,* and *deshacer*—all gathered together in the final crucial noun *despojos*: the spoils, scraps, or waste left after an act of plunder or destruction. The outcome is death, or at least the failure of birth ("ningún nacimiento"). Although the speaker addresses a second person *tú*, the very reflexive and interior nature of these verbs suggests a doubling rather than a true relationship between separate beings. If this reading is accurate, the poetic subject is relating the story of her own dismemberment and her sense of bewilderment at the task of gathering the dispersed parts. The fact that this scene is presided over by "broken statues" is yet another clue to the uncanny forces at work.

The statue, the mannequin, and the doll are all externalized images of the psychic notion of doubling, a theme that has been amply explored in literature, art, and psychoanalysis, and one that was particularly dear to the romantics and the surrealists. Otto Rank, a contemporary of Freud, argues in broad terms that the double "personifies narcissistic self-love," and that the notion of the immortal soul may have been the original double of the body (86). Rank claims that for the primitive mind, the double (including shadows and reflections) was conceived as a means of ensuring the survival of the ego, but that it later developed a second character as a harbinger of death. Citing Rank, Freud notes that themes of uncanniness "are all concerned with the idea of a 'double' in every shape and degree" (140). Freud concludes that "the 'uncanny' is that class of the terrifying which leads back to something long known to us, once very familiar"—that is, the return of the repressed (123–24). Like Rank, Freud appeals to an atavistic sense, a recurrence in the modern consciousness of "primitive" animistic thought that attributed a material existence (and magical powers) to the dead. Thus the doll is uncanny because it "reminds" us of death-in-life, a perception exacerbated by the involuntary, repetitive mechanical processes at work in such a figure.

Bellmer's fascination with images of the double is evident in both his theoretical writings and his artistic production. His essay "Notes on the Subject of the Ball Joint" explains the power of desire to displace, replace, or double parts of the body. The repression of sexuality in puberty, Bellmer argues, leads to the imaginative multiplication of body parts and the projection of sexual images onto nonsexual spaces. In keeping with this view of sexual repression, the photographs of the second doll evoke a two-tiered notion of the double: First, the doll itself, in its uncanny likeness to an adolescent female body, is obviously a simulacrum of a living being. Second, the doll corporeally manifests the doubling or multiplying of body parts with her numerous limbs and appendages.

Pizarnik's most striking use of the doll figure to explore themes of doubling and loss of selfhood occurs in the poetic prose she produced in the years immediately preceding her death. One recurrent scene-motif, recalling Lewis Carroll's *Through the Looking Glass*, features a surrealist version of the tea party: "Debajo de un árbol, frente a la casa, veíase una mesa y sentadas a ella, la muerte y la niña tomaban el té. Una muñeca estaba entre ellas, indeciblemente hermosa, y la muerte y la niña la miraban más que al crepúsculo, a la vez que hablaban por encima de ella" [Under a tree, facing the house, there was a table, and seated at it were death and the girl, drinking tea. A doll, indescribably beautiful, was seated between them, and death and the girl looked at her more than at the twilight, simultaneously talking over her head] (*Obras* 198). The contrast here between the childish innocence of the tea party and the literal communion with death recalls the bobby socks, lace, and hair-bows of Bellmer's dolls, whose expressions always suggest the lurking presence of death. In the tea party scene, the doubling becomes a triangulation, with the beautiful and clueless doll and savvy Death representing opposite but simultaneous projections of the girl's psyche. A single uncanny image ends this brief prose poem: "La muñeca abrió los ojos" [The doll opened her eyes] (198). The doll, initially an inert figure capable only of attracting the gaze of others who speak "over her head," suddenly performs a minute but significant act of self-awareness. Pizarnik ends the piece with this image, leaving the doll's agency as an enigmatic possibility.

Given that in the work of both Bellmer and Pizarnik the doll functions as a reiterated trope, a figure on whom sometimes sordid dramas of selfhood and otherness are played out, what can we conclude about the relationship of this figure to its creator? How does the gender dynamic with respect to the doll function differentially in the male artist and the female poet? It seems clear that Pizarnik insists on an ambivalent relationship of subject to object—as does Bellmer, but for strikingly different reasons. There are concrete instances in Pizarnik's poetry of a female subject who expresses dismay at being—in the tradition of Pygmalion's ivory statue—the object not only of his gaze but of his act of creation. The speaker of "Extracción de la piedra de locura" recounts such an act: "Sonríe y yo soy una minúscula marioneta rosa con un paraguas celeste yo entro por su sonrisa yo hago mi casita en su lengua yo habito en la palma de su mano cierra sus dedos un polvo dorado un poco de sangre adiós oh adiós" [He smiles and I am a tiny pink marionette with a sky-blue umbrella I enter through his smile I make my little house on his tongue I live in the palm of his hand he closes his fingers a golden dust a little blood good-bye oh good-bye][10] (*Obras* 137). The paratactic structure of this passage, with its suppressed connectors and insistent rhythm, reinforces the girl-marionette's breathless registry of her loss of agency. She exists—diminutively and decoratively—only as the product of "his" smile. She builds her house on his tongue, giving precedence to his voice. His power over her is, in short, total: an insignificant gesture on his part reduces her to dust. In this scenario Pizarnik's doll-subject mourns her dissolution at the hands of the one who created her—an emotive stance reminiscent of the doll that Bellmer imagines in her "limitless submissiveness," who "understood that she was reserved for despair" ("Memories of the Doll Theme" 174).

If the doll/mannequin—or more broadly, the representation of the immobilized, sometimes dismembered female body—served for the male surrealists as a site for the projection of desire, for Pizarnik it served as a site for the obsessive representation of damaged selfhood. In mapping out a new territory for those women artists who followed the initial surrealist project, Susan Suleiman claims that "a woman Surrealist . . . cannot simply assume a subject position and take over a stock of images elaborated by the male imaginary; in order to innovate, she has to invent her own position as subject and elaborate her own set of images—different from, yet as empowering as the image of the exposed female body, with its endless potential for manipulation, disarticulation and rearticulation, fantasizing and projection, is for her male colleagues" (164). In contrast to certain women artists associated with the historical surrealist movement such as Remedios Varo or Leonora Carrington, or to more contemporary artists such as the American photographer Cindy Sherman, whose work directly parodies Bellmer's, Pizarnik does not develop images of self-representation that significantly realign patriarchal views of the feminine. In the end, Pizarnik's use of the doll image is more straightforwardly tragic than it is ironic or subversive.

We can conclude that Pizarnik's own surrealist project responds more to the overwhelming needs of the self in pain than to the broader social or political agenda suggested by Suleiman. Rather than engendering a new set of "empowering" images arising from the figure of the doll, Pizarnik for the most part reiterates and exploits the conventional iconography associated with it. Yet in doing so, she creates a body of lyrical work that is haunting and incisive and that speaks powerfully to the reader. As we have seen in numerous images, the diminutive female figures she constructs in a ritual of self-representation lack agency. But Pizarnik as a writer does not: she is, after all, the dollmaker and not the doll. Like Frida Kahlo—another artist for whom the hazy boundaries of the self were a source of unremitting anxiety—Pizarnik uses her medium, language, to challenge the forces of silence and dissolution that she perceived as a constant threat. Until the moment of her suicide, Pizarnik avows that the writer's blank page is the only possible habitat for the fragile doll: "allí ha de poder vivir la muñequita de papel verde, celeste y rojo; allí se ha de poder erguir y tal vez andar en su casita dibujada sobre una página en blanco" [there she must be able to live, the little doll made of green, blue, and red paper; there she must be able to rise up and perhaps walk in her little house drawn on a blank page] (*Obras* 144).

Conclusion

In 1952, the young Argentine poet Julio Llinás made his long-awaited trip to Paris, capital of the dreams that had been nourished by the writings of Breton, Péret, Aragon, and others. There he paid a visit to the Dada icon Tristan Tzara, but he found the experience disconcertingly anachronistic: "He walked with me through the large rooms, like a modest guide of the museum of himself, of the museum of the man he had been or maybe of the man he would have liked to be, who knows" (*Fiat Lux* 235). A later visit to André Breton in his famous apartment at 42 Rue La Fontaine left an even stronger impression of disillusion. In a letter to Aldo Pellegrini in Buenos Aires, Llinás expressed his shock of disappointment at the state of surrealism he observed around him in Paris, but he also articulated a new hope: "Shit, violinistic shit. I'm breathing an air of oppression, of terror and misery . . . In America you find naiveté. Here, naiveté is a delicacy one eats cold. In America you find imbecility in its pure form. Here you find imbecility packaged and decorated with a bow, which is its most dangerous form . . . You speak to me of the surrealists over there as 'the remains of a shipwreck.' All right, but they are the fallout, the ruins of one and the same shipwreck: the one here. ANOTHER SHIP MUST BE LAUNCHED" (qtd. in Giunta 73). As Andrea Guinta notes, Llinás's diatribe against the weakening myth of surrealism in Europe and of a weakened Europe itself "was not free of arrogance and irreverence" (312), attitudes perhaps reflecting the sense of cultural superiority propounded by Rodó and echoed by Mariátegui, Paz, Molina, and numerous others in twentieth-century Latin America. In this case, a subjective sense of disaffection is projected onto another facet of the myth, that of America as the site of cultural rejuvenation: "I believe ferociously in America," says Llinás, "in America that breathes with its two lungs . . . Breton must be shown that surrealism is not him. Surrealism is life . . . When I return, we will truly do something" (qtd. in Giunta 73).

In the decades of the 1950s, 1960s, and 1970s, several noted Argentina writers did in fact "do something" in the spirit of renewal, "launching a new ship" in the form of literary-artistic journals and incorporating surrealist imagery into their own poetics in ways that no longer mimicked the French surrealists. Like the Cuban painter and sculptor Wilfredo Lam, poets such as Enrique Molina and Francisco Madariaga transformed the inherited aesthetic by introducing a particularly American landscape into the surrealist imaginary. In other cases, like that of Llinás (in *Boa*) and Orozco, they experimented with the revival of the ancient traditions of esoteric thought. In general, they embraced the notion of an international surrealism and encouraged the dissolution of literary and artistic genre boundaries. In poets like Alejandra Pizarnik, they applied surrealist tropes to a highly subjective experience, and in doing so they created powerful new modes of poetic diction.

Surrealism as a literary aesthetic continued to inform the work of important poets in Argentina such as Juan Gelman, Carlos Barbarito, and Dolores Etchecopar (who is also an accomplished painter) well into the decade of the 1980s.[11] More surprising, perhaps, is the fact that surrealism as a revolutionary path, both political and aesthetic, surfaced once again in Buenos Aires in the late 1970s, with a collective of writers, artists, and activists that called themselves "Grupo Surrealista Argentino." In one of the paradoxes of cultural history, this group adopted a critical posture with regard to the 1950s surrealist venture, considering it a diluted version of surrealism's revolutionary ideals. They published two issues of the journal *Podemma* (1979–80), followed by three issues of *Signo Axcendente* in 1980–82. The group's prime movers were Alberto Arias and Silvia Grénier; other members included Luis Yara, Julio del Mar, Josefina Quesada, Juan Andralis, and Carmen Bruna. A manifesto published in the second issue of *Signo Ascendente* testifies to the radical posture of the group, whose activities were carried out in the midst of Argentina's infamous "Dirty War":

> En este país, donde algunos ya se han mostrado tan propensos a censurar lo que no pueden asimilar . . . y en cuya historia hay signos inequívocos de barbarie tal como el imborrable hecho de miles y miles de desaparecidos, en este país, afirmamos, son a nuestro juicio no menos que una crítica y una denuncia inapelables las que deben caracterizar la actitud que salvaguarde en su integridad moral al verdadero poeta. (1)[12]

> [In this country, where some have appeared so prone to censure what they cannot assimilate . . . and in whose history there are unmistakeable signs of barbarism such as the indelible fact of thousands and thousands of the disappeared—in this country, we affirm, nothing less than an irremediable critique and condemnation should characterize the attitude that safeguards the true poet in his or her moral integrity.]

The publication of such an open denouncement of Argentina's military dictatorship in those years of fear and silence was in itself a remarkable act of courage. Apart from this publication, the group's members participated in various human rights initiatives and subversive political activities. Yet what sets this group apart from other perhaps equally vocal and courageous groups in that historical moment is its combination of political engagement with literary and artistic activity, all firmly grounded in the postulates of French surrealism. In its gatherings, the Grupo Surrealista Argentino practiced automatic writing and other orthodox surrealist methods of tapping into the unconscious. This integration of the aesthetic and the political spheres is evoked in the same manifesto in *Signo Ascendente*, which proclaims, "Hacer nuestra la tradición surrealista, contruibuir en todo y por todo a la prosecución de la aventura surrealista, he aquí los ejes esenciales sobre los cuales se fundan nuestros objetivos" [To make our own the surrealist tradition, to contribute in everything and by every means to the pursuit of the surrealist adventure: these are the essential axes on which our objectives are founded] (1). Although the group's revolutionary activity diminished in the postdictatorship era, many of its participants went on to publish notable volumes of poetry with a distinctly surrealist imprint. The group continued to function into the 1990s, maintaining an active correspondence with surrealist groups in the United States, France, Spain, Sweden, and the Czech Republic. In retrospect, the emergence of the Grupo Surrealista Argentino in the late twentieth century within the context of a repressive Latin American military regime reaffirms surrealism's ability to adapt itself to far-ranging historical and cultural conditions.

CHAPTER 9

Chile
The Avatars and the Antagonists of *La Mandrágora*

Introduction

The decade of Chilean surrealist group activity under the sign of the journal *Mandrágora* (which was examined in Chapter 4) came to a close in 1948 with the international art exposition held at the Dédalo Gallery in Santiago. From that point forward, the presence of surrealism would be felt not in galleries, group manifestoes, or magazines but in the work of individual poets. In Stefan Baciu's assessment in 1974, "the surrealizing air in Chile is stronger and more stimulating today than in any other country on the continent" ("Introduction" 97). After tracing certain later developments in the work of Braulio Arenas and Enrique Gómez-Correa, the founders of the Mandrágora movement, this chapter will explore two important manifestations of that "surrealizing air" in the poetry of Gonzalo Rojas and the "antipoetry" of Nicanor Parra. Other important Chilean poets whose work deserves further analysis in light of their links to surrealism, but who fall outside the purview of the present study, include Rosamel del Valle (1901–65), Humberto Díaz Casanueva (1906–92), Carlos de Rokha (1920–62), and Ludwig Zeller (b. 1927).

In the 1940s, Chile saw an immediate reaction to the hermetic nature of the surrealist-influenced Mandrágora aesthetic in the form of "Poesía de la Claridad," which stressed communicability and transparency of expression. Subsequent to the Claridad movement, and roughly paralleling the Argentine literary experience, a rich new strain of poetry arose in the 1950s and 1960s— conversational and often ironic in tone, quotidian in subject matter, and sometimes politically or socially oriented. A particularly innovative form of this new poetry, called *antipoesía* and popularized by Chile's Nicanor Parra (b. 1914), was destined to become one of the prevailing voices in Latin American literature in the second half of the twentieth century. We saw in Chapter 8 how Argentine surrealist poetry in this period formed part of a

Figure 9.1 Ludwig Zeller, "Cuando el animal de fondo sube la cabeza estalla" *(1971)*

neoromantic, esoteric, or metaphysical strain that diverged markedly from the more popular current of conversational poetry. Chile's case is different: there, surrealism was in fact one of the great tributaries flowing into the antipoetical river.

The Crooked Path Forward: Braulio Arenas and Enrique Gómez-Correa

In Argentina, the birth and rebirth of surrealist activities can be credited primarily to Aldo Pellegrini; in Chile, the progression from the Mandrágora group to the later surrealist-oriented literature is largely due to the efforts of two men: Braulio Arenas and Enrique Gómez-Correa. The first step in this progression was the 1957 anthology *El A G C de la Mandrágora*, whose title signals the initiators of the Mandrágora movement (Arenas, Gómez-Correa, and Jorge Cáceres). The anthology opens with a "Vocabulario Mandrágora," an inventive lexicon that includes several entries for each letter of the alphabet, each initialed with A, G, C, or a combination of the three. I cite here a few engaging examples:

> ABEJA: La abeja sigue sin murmurar al algodón en rama que atraviesa el puente (A).
> CENICERO: Descendiente de la paloma mensajera, el cenicero cae al fondo del mar (C).
> ERROR: Amo mis errores como los disparos a quemarropa (G).
> FLOR: De modo que las flores están con la soga al cuello (G).
> KIMONO: El kimono es el diamante que raya el vidrio del kiosko (A).
> KIOSKO: El kiosko es la piedra que quiebra el vidrio del kimono (G).
> PAN: Migas de pan con todos sus guantes vivos, con todos sus gorriones (A). Como el pan en el bolsillo de un viejo guardapolvos (C).
> QUELONIO: Hablar umbela, hablar quelonio (G).
> VIDRIO: El carruaje que transportaba a gritos el vidrio de tu cuerpo (A).
> (11–21)

[BEE: The bee goes on its way without whispering to the cotton on the branch that crosses the bridge. / ASHTRAY: Descendent of the homing pigeon, the ashtray falls to the bottom of the sea. / ERROR: I love my errors as I love gunshots at point-blank. / FLOWER: So the flowers have a rope around their neck. / KIMONO: The kimono is the diamond that cuts the glass of the kiosk. / KIOSK: The kiosk is the stone that breaks the glass of the kimono. / BREAD: Bread crumbs with all their living gloves, with all their sparrows. / QUELONIO: To speak Umbela, to speak Quelonio. / GLASS: The carriage that transported, shouting, the glass of your body.]

These highly imaginative entries serve alternately as definitions, illustrations, analogies, or simply free associations, displaying the ludic qualities and the sense of semantic absurdity that the surrealists admired. They underscore the free play of the linguistic imagination that is one of surrealism's most enduring legacies in Latin American literature.

In commemoration of the fiftieth anniversary of André Breton's first manifesto, Arenas published in 1974 a text called *Actas surrealistas* [Surrealist Proceedings]. Like *El A G C de la Mandrágora*, it is primarily an anthology, but with a much broader scope. In fact, *Actas surrealistas* should be acknowledged—along with Pellegrini's 1961 *Antología de la poesía surrealista*—as a major contribution to the dissemination of international surrealism among a Spanish-speaking readership in the post-1950 period. It contains texts by the writers of the original Mandrágora group, as well as translations of Breton, Éluard, Desnos, Tzara, Aragon, Queneau, Paalen, Dalí, and numerous others. In the prologue, which is "full of renewed surrealist faith" (Goic 24 n. 55), Arenas recalls the cultural context in which French surrealism was born: "Los graznidos de mal agüero de los dadaístas anunciaban, entre carcajadas apolcalípticas y suicidios que pasaban por accidentes, el advenimiento de un amenazante mundo moderno, la llegada del siglo veinte, en fin" [The ill-omened croaking of the Dadaists announced, among apocalyptic laughter and suicides passed off as accidents, the coming of a threatening modern world, in a word, the arrival of the twentieth century] (7). The subsequent passage portrays the absurdity of that new world in a truly surrealist (and hilarious) enumeration:

> Era moderno el traje corto de las mujeres, la melena a lo garzón, los cigarrillos turcos, las boquillas de treinta centímetros, la práctica de los deportes, las quirománticas, el cemento, el salto alto, los empresarios, los ejecutivos, la teoría de la relatividad, los cowboys, los rascacielos, el psicoanálisis, la montaña mágica, las reinas norteamericanas de las salchichas, los príncipes arruinados, los grandes ventanales a lo Mondrian, los fetiches africanos, los rayos X, el ballet ruso, los gangsters de Chicago, los automóviles de carrera, los trust, los divorcios . . . (7)
>
> [*Modern* meant short skirts for women, bobbed hair, Turkish cigarettes, foot-long cigarette holders, the practice of sports, palmistry, cement, high jumping, entrepreneurs, executives, the theory of relativity, cowboys, skyscrapers, psychoanalysis, the magic mountain, North American pork queens, ruined princes, shop windows à la Mondrian, African fetishes, X-rays, the Russian Ballet, Chicago gangsters, race cars, trusts, divorces . . .]

Born amid the effort to forget the horror of war, all these cultural commonplaces simultaneously announced the new century's "specters": hunger, widespread pollution, the population explosion, the atomic bomb, and genocide (7).

Dada, Arenas contends, was incapable of responding to that new world except by trying to destroy it. But in 1924, "nacía el surrealismo, relampagueante como la imaginación, alucinante como la vida, y nacía con la creencia de que la poesía debía conducer al hombre a alguna parte" [surrealism was born, electrifying as the imagination, beguiling as life, and it was born with the belief that poetry should lead man in some direction] (8). Fifty years after its birth, and eight years after Breton's death, Arenas testifies to surrealism's continuing presence. After tracing a rather sui generis lineage that passes through the novels of chivalry, Santa Teresa, Luis de Góngora, Novalis, and even Kafka, he muses, "Si así se pudiera admitir esta línea genealógica de la imaginación, entonces podríamos asegurar que el surrealismo ha estado en todo momento mostrándonos el poder de su irradiación, el perenne manantial de su pensamiento" [If we could admit this genealogy of the imagination, we could be certain that surrealism has continued to show us the power of its irradiation, the perennial fountain of its thought] (9). Finally, Arenas asks if the recent death of Breton will mark the end of surrealism. In answer to this question, he acknowledges that the surrealist movement in all probability has ceased to exist, but he insists that this marks only one phase of the manifestation of the human imagination (13). Arenas then asks what remains of that "magical light," of Breton's fascination, of the white rabbits of Leonora Carrington, of the Andalusian dog of Buñuel and Dalí. Closer to home—he continues—will we not be haunted by the marvelous texts of César Moro, Octavio Paz, Aldo Pellegrini, Aimé Césaire, or Emilio Adolfo Westphalen? All these writers, Arenas declares in answer to his own question, are "magically present," and he offers the anthology as an affirmation of that presence (14).

Arenas outlived all of his Mandrágora contemporaries (with the exception of Gonzalo Rojas) and in his longevity evolved in directions that were decidedly antisurrealist. Shortly after Arenas's death in 1988, the poet Enrique Lihn published a piece in which he reflects on the fact that the Chilean National Prize for Literature was awarded to Arenas "mal y tarde" [late and badly] (*El circo en llamas* 232). Lihn comments acerbically that in the moment of the 1973 coup that toppled Salvador Allende, "Arenas exiled himself in a pathetic, hysterical, and bloodless collusion" (233). But the purpose of Lihn's article is not to further accuse the man, but rather to rescue his works from the ignominy in which this political turnabout had left them. The writer who had once in Bretonian fashion championed total liberty had "disappeared," in the eyes of many, as he supported the Pinochet dictatorship. However, Lihn asserts, "the writer who must survive . . . did not disappear, because he is real and is even of a certain *surreality*" (233). Lihn's play on the word *real*, which means both "real" and "royal" in Spanish, highlights Arenas's surrealist origins while it vindicates him as a writer worthy of honor in Chilean literature. Of his sizeable literary production, most appreciable in Lihn's view are several short prose pieces and certain poems written within a style of a "revisionist surrealism" (233). Perhaps the ultimate sad irony here is that Arenas himself called his surrealist poems "poorly made copies" (qtd. in Lihn 234). Like Aldo Pellegrini, Arenas struggled to find an original voice as a writer, even as he served as an indispensable conduit in his country for a new aesthetic of pure imaginative freedom.

Gonzalo Rojas, Mandrágora's Prodigal Son

Among the youngest members to be affiliated with the Mandrágora group in the early 1940s, Gonzalo Rojas (1917–2011) went on to become the most highly acclaimed writer of the group and one of Spanish America's most respected twentieth-century poets. As I observed in the introduction to this chapter, critics have identified two general currents in post-avant-garde Chilean poetry: Nicanor Parra's *antipoesía* and Rojas's "sacralization" of poetry as a means of changing the world. Marcelo Coddou, for example, claims that the Chilean "Generación de 1960"—including Gonzalo Millán, Omar Lara, Jaime Quezada, Federico Schopf, Floridor Pérez, Óscar Hahn, Manuel Silva Acevedo, and Waldo Rojas—owes a double allegiance to Rojas and Parra, the former tending to hold up the poetic speaker as a sacralized subject within an "exalted" discourse, and the latter presenting a demythified and ironic speaker (xvii).

Rojas was born in the southern seaport town of Lebu, the seventh son of a coal miner who died when Rojas was a young child. These working-class and provincial beginnings approximate Rojas's background to Neruda's, and indeed the palpable, material world of Chile—particularly its mountains, rivers, oceans, and underground mines—was as fundamental to his worldview as it was to that of his famous compatriot. Rojas became a teacher and eventually a university professor; in 1947, he founded an institute of higher learning that eventually was incorporated into the Universidad de Chile in Valparaiso. Rojas spoke of this form of work as *poesía activa*—a term that directly references the surrealist call to merge poetry with life. In a 1985 interview, Rojas elaborated on this attitude: "I have not only tried to make poetry, but to live poetically. That has been my attachment to active poetry, assuming poetry as conduct" (qtd. in Earle, "Breton y Rojas" 126).

In 1953, Rojas traveled to Europe for the first time and there met Breton and Péret. A decade earlier he had participated in Chile's nascent surrealist movement, publishing poems in *Mandrágora* and *Leitmotiv*. Though he no longer considered himself a part of the Mandrágora group, his enthusiasm for certain aspects of surrealism had not waned, and the meeting with the Parisian surrealists provided Rojas with a new impetus. In 1958 and 1959, under the auspices of UNESCO, Rojas spent a full year in Paris, coming into contact not only with the European intellectuals of the day but also with Octavio Paz and Julio Cortázar (both of whom professed significant ties to surrealism), as well as other Latin American writers and artists. Chile's 1973 coup d'etat occurred as he was about to assume the post of cultural attaché in Cuba; Rojas's passport was immediately revoked by the Pinochet government, and he remained in exile until 1979. During this period and subsequently, Rojas lived and taught in Germany, Spain, Mexico, Venezuela, and the United States. Rojas's work is widely read in Latin America and Spain, and he was the recipient of numerous literary prizes, including the prestigious Cervantes Prize in 2003.

Rojas was a circular and revisionist poet; that is, he made a practice of reworking previous poems and including them in his most recent collections. Among his prolific inventory of titles, beginning with *La miseria del hombre* in 1948, two volumes have garnered particular critical acclaim: *Oscuro* (1977) and *Del relámpago* (1981).[1] Jacobo Sefamí voices a common critical opinion when he states that "Rojas's finest poetry emerges with *Oscuro*. It is at this point that Rojas attained a unique voice within Latin American poetics, tightly linked to surrealist notions" ("Gonzalo Rojas" 495). Peter Earle echoes this observation when he claims that in spite of certain clear differences, "Rojas is in the current of Breton's discoveries and visions" ("Breton y Rojas" 125).[2] Rojas's work is complex and emerges from multiple discourses, and it is not my purpose here to apply a reductivist scheme to this complexity. Rather, my hope is to explore these "tight links" and in doing so to provide another striking example of the living presence of Breton's ghost in Latin American poetry.

Rojas himself spoke on several occasions of his earlier participation in the Mandrágora movement, and from there he explores his convergences with and divergences from the original principles of surrealism. He readily acknowledges, "Fui surrealista" [I was a surrealist], but clarifies that it was precisely the orthodox nature of the Mandrágora brand of surrealism that he eventually found too repetitive and stifling for his poetic impulses (Sefamí, *Imaginación* 50). Against what he calls the "hyperadhesion to Bretonion surrealism," he sought a truly liberating relationship with language. In this spirit, Rojas claims of his Mandrágora days that "el surrealista, en el sentido más estricto, del grupo aquel fui yo" [in the strictest sense of the word, the surrealist of that group was me] (Sefamí, *Imaginación* 60).

Like Braulio Arenas (and in contrast to many other Latin American writers), Rojas professes a faith in the practice of automatism: "Me encanta la asociación libre y esto de la escritura automática me parece maravilloso" [I love free association, and automatic writing seems marvelous to me] (Sefamí, *Imaginación* 62). In the majority of his poetry, however, this admiration does not lead to hermetic texts but rather to the "controlled automatism" we have seen in Molina, Pizarnik, and other Latin American poets of this later period, in which techniques that free the imagination are placed in the service of an ultimate coherence and a desire to communicate with the reader. While true oneiric imagery is uncommon in Rojas's work, there is a loosening of syntax (sometimes reminiscent of Vallejo) that can suggest reverie or obsessive thought. Structurally, the poems tend to build on associative leaps that create a sense of the unexpected—leaps that often have more to do with the ear than the eye.

In thematic terms, critics have observed that Rojas's work revolves around the surrealist triad of liberty, love or eroticism, and poetry, preoccupations that are intricately interwoven.[3] The theme of freedom in its many facets is ubiquitous, but it is grounded in the fundamental surrealist rebellion against complacently rational existence. In the poem "La vaca racional" [The Rational Cow] from the early collection *Fábula moderna*, Rojas creates an extended metaphor for conventional thought: "La vaca racional tiene los ojos de la envidia, / el cuerpo de una bella mujer, y por su baba / se expresa la miseria de los hombres" [The rational cow has the eyes of envy, / the body of a beautiful woman, and in its spittle / is expressed the misery of men] (*Antología del aire* 44). In opposition to the rational cow, this modern fable presents a magical tree, "el Árbol que viene al mundo libre, / distinto de los árboles que lloran su esclavitud en el paisaje" [the Tree that comes to the world free, / different from those trees that weep their slavery in the landscape] (44). The tree represents salvation in the world ruled by the rational cow. It is capable of dying to save other trees from death, and furthermore, "Por darle aire a los muertos, es capaz de vestirse de locura" [To allow the dead to breathe, it is capable of dressing in madness] (44). At the end of the fable, the cow succeeds in convincing others that the root of the presumably threatening tree is only "una amarra en el vacío" [a mooring in the void] (45).

Although not a partisan poet in any way, Rojas wrote poems of protest against the suppression of liberty under totalitarian regimes, not the least of which was Pinochet's Chile. Linking this preoccupation in his work directly to surrealism, Rojas commented in a 1985 interview, "I believe that my adherence to surrealism was fundamentally for this reason, for the defense of the project of freedom, but of a utopic freedom if you will, not of a freedom that turned towards sectarian political parties" (Busto Odgen 678). One striking example of Rojas's concern for freedom in a political context is the poem "Sebastián Acevedo," written for a man whose son was "disappeared" by the Chilean army. In an ultimate act of protest against the government's silence regarding the *desaparecidos*, Acevedo immolated himself in a public plaza in the city of Concepción. Rojas structures the poem as a litany based on the phrase "Sólo veo" [I only see]. The second stanza reads as follows:

> Sólo veo ahí llamear a Acevedo
> por nosotros con decisión de varón, estricto

> y justiciero, pino y
> adobe, alumbrando el vuelo
> de los desaparecidos a todo lo
> aullante de la costa: sólo veo al inmolado. (*Antología* 208)
>
> [I only see Acevedo burning / for us, with the will of a man, strict / and righteous, pine and / adobe, illuminating the flight / of the disappeared all along the howling / of the coast: I only see the immolated man.]

Although Rojas has said of himself "soy profano,"[4] like Vallejo he draws from a deep well of Christian imagery. In this poem, Sebastián Acevedo is erected in a Christlike pose, with the material metaphors of pine and adobe reminding the reader of his status as a common, flesh-and-blood man. As Christian dogma stresses that Jesus was crucified *for* his followers, the speaker of this poem assumes the first person plural to state straightforwardly that Acevedo died "por nosotros," that is, for all Chileans (if not for all repressed peoples). In an unexplained but powerful associative leap, the poem marks Acevedo's death as an act that frees Chile's *desaparecidos*, who are able to take flight along the coast, mystically illuminated by the flames of Acevedo's body.

The repetition of the phrase "Sólo veo" at the beginning and end of each stanza reinforces the role of the poet as *vidente*: the one who sees and perhaps prophesies. This conception of the poet is a prominent feature of the romantic tradition, but the surrealists shifted its meaning by insisting that every human being has the capacity to see beyond surface appearances, to witness the revelation of the marvelous in ordinary life. It follows, then, that in "Sebastián Acevedo" the authority traditionally associated with the seer's role is undermined by the adverb "sólo," which suggests that the poet sees only what others in the plaza in Concepción saw that day. Although the last stanza carries an affirmative tone—"Sólo la mancha veo del amor que / nadie nunca podrá arrancar del cemento" [I see only the stain of love that / no one will ever wrest from the cement]—the final phrase closes the circle by repeating "Sólo veo al inmolado" (209). The poet's obsessive vision is thus focused not on illuminated flight or the visible evidence of the power of love—though these images do arise—but simply on the sacrificed body of a man. Thus the poem demonstrates Rojas's sense of civic responsibility as a poet (to expose repression, to acknowledge common acts of courage) but also his sober reckoning of the limits of poetic vision. In this sense, Rojas's work challenges the surrealist ideal of knowledge or understanding gained through the flashes of illumination available to the seer-poet.

Human liberty in the shape of love or erotic desire is arguably the most persistent theme in Rojas's poetry and thus provides another crucial link to surrealism in his work. Although many poems are frankly sensual in the manner of Neruda's *Veinte poemas de amor*, they remind the reader constantly of the numinous or sacred character of erotic love. The title of the poem "Das heilige," for example, means "the sacred" in German, and accordingly the poem celebrates the erotic encounter as a rite in which the speaker pays homage to the "vagina sagrada" (*Diálogo con Ovidio* 66). Certain poems also tie erotic expression directly to the function of poetry, as in the late poem "Río Turbio," whose third section begins, "No con semen de eyacular sino con semen de escribir / le digo a la paloma:—ábrete, paloma, y / se abre;—recíbeme, y me recibe, erecto / y pertinaz; ahí mismo volamos / inacabables hasta más allá del Génesis" [Not with the semen of ejaculation but with the semen of writing / I say to the dove: "Open yourself, Dove," and / she opens; "receive me," and she receives me, erect / and obstinate; then and there we fly / endless, farther than Genesis] (*Antología* 290). As an analog to the act of writing, the erotic encounter in "Río Turbio" is represented in its double aspect of sacred ideal and carnal celebration.

To conjure the latter, Rojas directly adopts both the concept and the language of Breton's *amour fou* or "mad love" in the poem "Oriana":

> A elegir, madame: o el frenesí
> y el éxtasis del *amour*
> *fou* que es el único amor
> que habrá habido sobre la tierra, o
> la raja seca de la higuera
> maldita. (*Diálogo con Ovidio* 18)

> [Let's choose, Madam: either the frenzy / and ecstasy of *mad / love*, which is the only love / there has been on the earth, or / the dry splinter of the accursed / fig tree.]

There is an obvious irony in the speaker's invitation to the woman to make a choice between two types of love, since his immediate characterization of each type leaves no doubt in the mind of the reader—and presumably in that of the female interlocutor as well—that *amour fou* is the "only love" worth pursuing. The "accursed" fig tree that marks the alternative choice points to the biblical emblem of the leaf that covers the sexual organs—that is, to the civilizing act that diminishes the naked primordial being.

As is common in the surrealist conception of heterosexual desire, *la mujer* is often represented in Rojas's work as an essence or quality, a transcendent energy that attracts the male speaker with almost unspeakable force. Breaking with surrealist orthodoxy, however, Rojas represents the female figure with equal frequency as a real woman, ranging from the *novia* [girlfriend/bride] to the *puta* [whore]. She is a transcendent but simultaneously elemental, material being: "Mujer de fuego. Visible mujer" [Woman of fire. Visible woman]

(*Antología* 36). The tension between abstract (or collective) and concrete (or individual) objects of desire is reconstructed poetically in the final stanza of the well-known poem "¿Qué se ama cuando se ama?" [What Does One Love When One Loves?], which opens with a trope borrowed from Spanish mystic poetry: "Me muero en esto, oh Dios, en esta guerra / de ir y venir entre ellas por las calles, de no poder amar / trescientas a la vez, porque estoy condenado siempre a una, / a esa una, a esa única que me diste en el viejo paradiso" [I am consumed in this, oh Lord, in this war / of coming and going among them on the streets, of not being able to love / three hundred at once, because I'm forever condemned to one / to that one, to that only one that you gave to me in the ancient paradise] (*Antología* 73). In implicitly opting for the figure associated with Eve, the primordial and singular female companion, Rojas follows both Éluard and Breton, for whom the ideal of *amour fou* was not incompatible with monogamy—although this stance would open them to criticism from those who perceived in it a betrayal of the ideal of true erotic freedom.

It seems fitting to conclude this discussion of Rojas's poetry with a long poem called "A la salud de André Breton" [To André Breton's Health], written on the occasion of Breton's death in 1966. As an elegy, this poem joins numerous others in Rojas's repertoire in which the poet pays homage to those who have died in his lifetime—his own father and mother, the avant-garde poet Pablo de Rokha, his Mandrágora companion Jorge Cáceres, César Vallejo, Julio Cortázar, Paul Celan, John Lennon, and others. Written in traditional elegiac mode, these poems are also meditations on time and mortality; their tonal range stretches from reverence to bitter irony. "A la salud de André Breton" is a long poem divided into three sections, in which the speaker alternately refers to Breton in the third person, apostrophizes him in the second person, or allows him a direct first person voice. The poem begins with the lines:

> Y la Mosca decía, qué decía la Mosca: no es para tanto, nunca es
>   para tanto, la nariz
> no es para oler y todos reventamos:
> *tel qu'en Lui-même enfin l'éternité le change.*
> Hasta el siglo veintiuno, si vuelves. La comedia
> se acabó, y el océano, y el pescado perdido. (*Obra selecta* 15)

[And the Fly said, what did the Fly say: it's not so bad, it's never so bad, the nose / is not for smelling and every one of us bursts: / *tel qu'en Lui-même enfin l'éternité le change.* / Until the twenty-first century, if you come back. The play's / over, and the ocean, and the lost fish.]

The key to this hermetic stanza, and indeed to the entire poem, is the line written in French: *tel qu'en Lui-même* . . . This phrase is the first verse of a well-known sonnet by Stéphane Mallarmé called "Le Tombeau d'Edgar Poe," which was written in 1877 to commemorate the erection of a monument to the North American writer.

Rojas's appropriation of this line signals a fascinating reversal, in that it is now a South American writer who is using these words to commemorate a French poet. The first line of Mallarmé's sonnet translates approximately "Eternity changes him at last into Himself." The capital letter of the pronoun *Lui-même* (Himself) highlights the sense of a transcendent or true self that the artist becomes, not in his lifetime but within the collective memory that follows his death.

By placing Mallarmé's line in the middle of the initial stanza of "A la salud de André Breton," Rojas embeds the allusion to a transcendent eternity within numerous signifiers of the finality of death and the graceless mortality of the flesh: "the Fly," "we all burst," "the comedy is over," and so forth. The final image of the "pescado perdido" [lost fish] may be a play on the common phrase *pescado podrido* or rotten fish, linking it to the morbid portrayal of death in the first two lines. Alternatively (or simultaneously), it may allude to Breton's first collection of automatic texts, *Poisson soluble* [*Soluble Fish*]. All this—the man and his work—has been lost, the poem suggests, except that it will remain in the eternity of a vast cultural memory in which Breton becomes finally "Himself." This conception of immortality allows Rojas to present the poem as a *brindis*, a toast to a writer who begins to live only at the moment of death.

Even as Poe led a sometimes dissolute life, Breton is also depicted in this poem as a fallible, corruptible man. The second stanza adopts the rhetoric of an auction in which the writer's remains are put up for sale: how much, the speaker asks, for his "Etruscan arrogance," how much for his "errors." From there, the poem shifts into more traditional elegiac mode, evoking the image of Breton's funeral procession in "this dirty September":

> Las lilas de la lluvia para decirte adiós.
> Y allí mismo Nadja llorando, y el enigma. (*Obra selecta* 16)

[The lilacs of rain for saying good-bye. /And Nadja there weeping, and the enigma.]

Like Breton himself, Nadja is resurrected in this poem, raised from her real-life status as an anonymous Parisian mental patient to the immortality granted to her by literature—specifically, by Breton's own novelization of her. Accompanying Nadja is "the enigma," the mystery that death remains.

In the second part of the poem, Breton is brought to life as a speaker. This relatively brief section is marked as direct speech, and in it Rojas "quotes" Breton's work in an astonishingly complex play of intertextualities:

> —Nunca fui de La Charca, la belleza será convulsiva, denuncio a los adeptos,
> o no será. Salud, salud en el relámpago.
> Correr, correr corriendo escala arriba. Corto lo más alto en la arteria de la asfixia,
> y el espejo trizado, soy el vidrio esta sangre que yo mismo en el suelo: va a gotear.
> Vine a decir que nada que nunca, que nacemos. (*Obra selecta* 16)

["I never left La Charca, beauty will be convulsive, I denounce the initiates, / or it will not be. To your health, to your health in the lightning. / To run, run running up the stairs. I cut highest up in the artery of asphyxiation, / and the shattered mirror, I am the glass this blood that I myself on the floor: it's going to drip. / I came to say that nothing that never, that we are born."]

Apart from the famous phrase "Beauty will be convulsive, or it will not be," which is the last line of *Nadja*, the majority of the textual references in this section correspond to Breton's poem "Pleine Marge" [Full Margin]. The initial phrase, "I never left La Charca," is taken almost directly from the second line of Breton's poem, which reads, "Je n'ai jamáis habité au lieu dit La Grenouillère" [I've never lived in the place called La Grenouillère]. There is a significant twist here, however, in that Rojas has Breton claim that he never *left* the place, in contrast to his never having lived there.

La Grenouillère was a working-class bathing resort on the outskirts of Paris (and the subject of a famous 1869 painting by Monet); the name literally means "The Frog Pond," and Breton may simply have been referring to this locale. But the place name also points back to Poe, who referred to Boston as "the frog pond" in his indictment of Emerson, Thoreau, and the New England Transcendentalists (qtd. in Quinn 487). Poe's argument with these writers was based on what he saw as their pretentions to mysticism.[5] This is why Breton's poem opens with the phrase "Je ne suis pas pour les adeptes" [I am not one for followers], which Rojas quotes as "denuncio a los adeptos." Historically speaking, there is a profound irony here (of which Rojas was no doubt aware), given that Breton himself, while denouncing the "adepts" of bourgeois society, was accused in turn of converting the surrealist movement into a cabalistic sect of devotees. By inserting this phrase between the two halves of Breton's pronouncement about convulsive beauty, Rojas invites the reader to conflate the two sentiments—that is, to consider that denouncing false or facile mysticism may lead to a new kind of beauty, one that may be unsettling, violent, or tumultuous.

Within the already free-associative structure of these lines, Rojas employs another avant-garde technique by unsettling the syntax of the phrases immediately following the image of the shattered mirror. He represents the broken pieces of glass textually as a word collage, shifting the grammatical utterance "I myself am this blood that is going to drip on the floor" into the syntactically convoluted "I am the glass this blood that I myself on the floor: it's going to drip." After this line of true convulsive beauty, Rojas brings Breton's enunciation to an end with the redoubled negative "I came to say that nothing that never," which subsequently slides into the affirmative phrase "that we are born." Rojas portrays Breton as intending to prophesy absence and impossibility (*nada* and *nunca*) but pronouncing instead words of presence and hope: *que nacemos*. Lost in translation is the heavily rhythmical alliteration of the n (*nada/nunca/nacemos*), which in Spanish phonically emphasizes the final semantic shift toward (re)birth: *nacemos*.

The third and final section of "A la salud de André Breton" takes the motif of birth or rebirth as the starting point for a relatively straightforward homage to the founder of surrealism, articulated from a first-person plural point of view:

> Lo que te debe toda la escritura del mundo y el oxígeno,
>   lo que
> te debe la locura de la razón y el mar de las tormentas,
> lo que el ojo y la mano te deben, lo que el vidrio de las
>   cosas, lo que la libertad,
> la preñez, la niñez, lo que las nueve larvas
> del caos, y de golpe estamos vivos. (*Obra selecta* 16)

[What all the world's writing and its oxygen owe to you, what / the madness of reason owes to you, and the sea of torments, / what the eye and the hand owe you what the glass of things, what liberty, / pregnancy, childhood, what the nine larvae / of chaos, and suddenly we are alive.]

These lines need little glossing. Their hyperbolic diction can perhaps be attributed to the nature of eulogy, or perhaps to the larger-than-life reach of Breton's own ambitions, which were none other than to free humanity of all forms of bondage. The second stanza of the final section focuses on the motif of *l'amour fou*—"el loco, loco amor"—which as we have seen was fundamental to Rojas's poetics and the cornerstone of Breton's call to freedom.

In the poem's final stanza Rojas uses prophetic diction to claim for Breton the mantle of the prophet, "[el] último vidente que anduvo entre nosotros" [the last seer who walked among us]. This figure is a poet-prophet, one who is called to write "el otro lado / del vaivén de las cosas" [the other side of the to-and-fro of things]. The last epithet given to Breton in the poem is simultaneously South American and universal: he is a "motherless condor" who is "nadie, pero todos y todo" [no one, but everyone and everything]. With this phrase Rojas closes the circle of the poem, obliquely reminding the reader of Mallarmé's suggestion that the flawed and limited mortal being can become transformed after death into "Himself," a Self that is vast and timeless. It is in this sense that the poem constitutes a toast to the "health" of André Breton on the occasion of his death.

Nicanor Parra and the Carnivalization of Surrealism[6]

The elegiac and prophetic tone of Gonzalo Rojas's "A la salud de André Breton" is the hallmark of one strain of poetry—generally metaphysical, universal in theme, and grounded in the tradition of high lyricism—that persisted and renewed itself across Latin America in the second half of the twentieth century. Poets associated with the other principal strain, which took the form of *poesía de la claridad* or "poetry of clarity" in Chile, threw off the mantle of the prophet and returned poetic language to the domestic sphere or the street.[7] The role of surrealism in this bifurcation of poetic modes is more complicated than it would appear. On the one hand, surrealism was most naturally associated with the metaphysical or high-lyrical strain: its themes were universalizing, its tone was serious, and its language was self-consciously poetic and often obscure. These qualities apply particularly to the work of the Mandrágora poets and to a great portion of Rojas's work (although Rojas employs a wide range of poetic diction). But surrealism was avant-garde in spirit and thus promoted innovative modes of expression, which meant that simple or conversational diction was also within its reach. Most importantly, surrealist expression—at least in theory—embraced the dialectic of high and low, which left it open to the incorporation of nontraditional poetic language.

The poet who understood this high-low dynamic most fully was Nicanor Parra. In the following pages I will argue that, complicating the perception of Parra as a highly unconventional poet, he in fact draws from certain elements of orthodox surrealism. By appropriating and then effectively transforming these elements, he creates a viable path forward for Latin American poetry in the second half of the twentieth century. As Federico Schopf observed in 2006, "More than fifty years after the appearance of *Poemas y antipoemas* (1954), it is now clear that antipoetry has inaugurated a new beginning in the arena of Spanish American poetry in the twentieth century" (*Desorden* 172). Gonzalo

Rojas also readapts, personalizes, and rejuvenates the surrealist aesthetic, as we have seen, but in Parra's hands the transformation is more radical. This is due to Parra's deeply felt ambivalence toward surrealism, including an open rejection of the Mandrágora group, which led him to carry the surrealist project to extremes that its more orthodox adherents had been unwilling or unable to reach.

Goic observes that "freedom is the great impulse that characterizes Parra's antipoetry and its most sustained surrealist trait" (25). As history has amply shown, the earlier surrealists—in particular, the Parisian group and the early Spanish American groups of Aldo Pellegrini and Braulio Arenas—struggled with the actual practice of political liberty or full-fledged revolt against the societies they inhabited. Even more conspicuous is the difficulty these poets experience in enacting the principle of total freedom within the language of their texts. "Undirected thought"—that is, the unfettered expression of the unconscious that Breton proclaimed as the goal of automatic methods—remained an elusive ideal. The awareness of this relative failure had become so evident by the time Parra's generation had matured that he feels compelled to quip "absolute freedom of expression" as an ironic allusion, one that exposes the very impossibility of that ideal (149). Parra's antipoetry, more than the work of any surrealist before him, textually *performs* the surrealist desire for freedom. It does so by presenting a speaker who exists in a constant state of revolt against the world and also by placing a full range of expressive possibilities in his repertoire. This means that the language of the unconscious is admissible but is not privileged as it is in orthodox surrealism; more privileged in fact are everyday turns of phrase, clichés, slogans, and jokes. I will investigate two poetic "zones" in which Parra executes this performance: first, the representation on the very surface of the text of the speaker's unconscious mental processes (which constitute the implicit *sub*text of most surrealist poems), and second, the extensive enactment of surrealist *humour noir*.

Nicanor Parra was born in 1914 near the town of Chillán, in the central valley of Chile, and spent his childhood and adolescence between that rural locale and a working-class neighborhood in Santiago. In contrast to Rojas, Arenas, and other writers of his generation, Parra was not officially a student of literature; rather, his formal schooling and professional training were in math and physics. His love of poetry grew quickly alongside his passion for the sciences, however, and he published his first collection of poems in 1937. From 1943 to 1945, Parra studied physics at Brown University in Rhode Island, but he had no significant contact with the North American literary world during that period (Morales 194). In 1949, he traveled to England, where he continued his studies of physics at Oxford. It was at this point, he claims, that he began neglecting his studies in order to read poetry; he discovered in particular the

English metaphysical poets and William Blake, readings that awoke in him a true consciousness of his own poetic craft (Morales 198). Upon his return to Chile in 1951, Parra became a professor of mathematics and physics at the Universidad de Chile, a profession he continued to exercise for many decades. It is important to note that Parra remained on the edges of the literary encampment in Chile during his formative years as a poet: while those of his generation were attending readings, staging public demonstrations, publishing small magazines, and engaging in café debates, Parra was absorbed in his studies of theoretical physics. His literary education, though it eventually covered a prodigious territory, proceeded at its own pace and was guided by highly subjective tastes. It is this aspect of Parra's biography, in my view, that accounts for the freshness of his voice and for the ease with which he integrates nonliterary discourses into his poetry.

In spite of this marginal existence with respect to formal literary training, Parra experienced an early and sustained contact with surrealism, both through *Mandrágora* and through his reading of the French and Spanish surrealists, particularly Breton, Éluard, and Federico García Lorca. Parra's first collection of poems, *Cancionero sin nombre* (1937), is clearly modeled after Lorca's *Romancero gitano* (1928) in its recreation of popular poetic ballads interlaced with oneiric imagery. This particular approach to surrealism, however, eventually appeared to Parra to be a creative dead end. It was only in 1954, after a 17-year silence, that his masterwork *Poemas y antipoemas* was published. According to the poet, the third section of this volume, in which his most radical experiments begin to occur, constitutes "a genre that owes practically everything to Kafka and to surrealism" (Morales 199).

Parra comments in an interview with Leónidas Morales that his early interest in surrealism was intensified and transformed after his return to Chile from the United States in 1945 (203). It was at this point that he found himself surrounded by a group of younger poets (including Alejandro Jodorowsky, who would later become a renowned filmmaker, Enrique Lihn, and Jorge Teillier) who encouraged him to continue experimenting along nonconformist, ironic, and ludic lines he had begun to develop. In addition to practicing automatic writing on his own, with this group Parra began practicing surrealist games such as the *cadavre exquis*—later transformed by Parra into the "*cadáver vulgar*"—as well as an invention they called the *Quebrantahuesos*, which consisted of grouping large newspaper headlines and illustrations at random in a Santiago shop window.[8] Parra is explicit about his attraction to surrealism—"I would say that surrealism has been a lifelong love" (Morales 201)—and yet he is conscious of his belated condition with respect to the original movement. Thus Parra distinguishes the *Quebrantahuesos* activity from that of the surrealist collage: "But they were seeking poetic, unexpected effects, and we were not. I, for one, was seeking effects that could be called coarse or crude" (202).

Parra is careful to note that his renewed interest in surrealism at this point (in the late 1940s and early 1950s) was not aligned with the Mandrágora movement, a disclaimer also made repeatedly by Rojas. Comparing the work of Braulio Arenas to his own experiments with language, Parra claims that Arenas "never carried his games to such an extreme as this . . . His surrealism was a poetical, minor one, purely decorative" (Morales 204). Rather than acknowledging any debt to Mandrágora, Parra states that his surrealist influences at that point were straightforwardly Bretonian: "I knew the surrealist manifestoes inside and out" (194). His rejection of the Chilean brand of surrealism, along with the neoromantic aesthetic that preceded it, is later made explicit in the poem "Manifiesto," which serves as a manifesto of sorts for antipoetry. Certain poets, the speaker of this poem claims, should be tried and sentenced "por construir castillos en el aire / por malgastar el espacio y el tiempo / redactando sonetos a la luna / por agrupar palabras al azar / a la última moda de París" [for building castles in the air / for wasting space and time / penning sonnets to the moon / for grouping words together at random / in the latest Paris fashion] (*Poemas para combatir la calvicie* 148).[9]

It is clear that the impulses that led to Parra's development of a radically new form of expression—the *antipoemas*—were in large part reactions to the literary world he inherited. The iconic figure of that world was of course Pablo Neruda. Though Parra at one time formed part of the circle of younger poets that surrounded Neruda, and the two maintained a lifelong friendship and mutual admiration, Parra felt constricted (as had the Mandrágora poets) by the very authority that Neruda's poetry came to represent. But Parra was reacting not only to the stentorian voice of Pablo Neruda but to the overall situation of Chilean literature at mid-century, which he viewed as being largely imported or derivative. In sum, Parra saw the need to reject a poetics that depended on *codified* language of any sort, and thus he searched for a more homegrown and authentic form of expression. In the words of the critic José Ibáñez-Langlois, "It was a question of cleansing European surrealism of its artifice, its pointless obscurity, its decadent uprooting of life, by means of a local answer—and for that reason alone a universal one—bound to an everyday language and a real experience of man *in situ*" (13). Thus was born the "antipoem," Chilean in origin but surprisingly universal in its reach.

Definitions and explanations of *antipoesía* abound in the critical literature on Parra's work. My goal here is not to simply reiterate those explanations but to organize them so as to show the complex relationship of antipoetry to surrealism. (It should be noted that Parra's work has evolved beyond *Poemas y antipoemas*, but his poetic project has retained most of the characteristics that gave that volume its power.) Parra himself explored the origins of antipoetry on several occasions. In a typical demythologizing gesture, he states that the antipoem "is after all nothing other than the traditional poem enriched with surrealist sap—'creole surrealism' or what you will" ("Poetas de la claridad" 46). This statement may surprise Parra's readers, given that at first glance the antipoems seem entirely nontraditional and appear to differ profoundly from surrealist expression. Goic voices a common assumption when he states, after acknowledging the surrealist impulse toward freedom inherent in antipoetry, that "in other aspects it shows no relationship to this tendency" (25). The antipoem, for instance, tends not to employ oneiric imagery or surprising metaphors, two of the basic techniques of surrealism. In fact, antipoetry employs little figurative language of any sort. Quite to the contrary, says the speaker of the poem "Manifiesto," "Nosotros conversamos / en el lenguaje de todos los días . . . no creemos en signos cabalísticos" [We converse / in everyday language . . . we don't believe in cabbalistic signs] (147).

Another obvious difference lies in the narrative and dramatic elements common to antipoetry but generally absent from surrealist texts. Parra creates a *personaje* or fictitious character who is the antipoet himself, speaking in a voice that dramatizes his strained relationships within an alienated social milieu. Yet another significant contrast is that surrealist poetry often carries a mythic charge, while in antipoetry all myths are debunked, including those relating to surrealism. Thus the speaker of "Los vicios del mundo moderno," in his long diatribe against what he perceives as modern vices, includes "la exaltación de lo onírico y del subconsciente en desmedro del sentido común" [the exaltation of oneiric states and the unconscious to the detriment of common sense] (64). Toward the end of this poem, the demythified character of poetry itself is made patent: "y la poesía reside en las cosas o es simplemente un espejismo del espíritu" [and poetry resides in things, or else it is a mere mirage of the spirit] (65).

If poetry is drained of its mythic content, by extension the poetic speaker (i.e., the antipoet whose voice he embodies) is relieved of his prophetic duties. In this spirit, Parra decried Huidobro's famous dictum "the poet is a little god"[10] and called the surrealist poets "so many hermetic priests" (Yamal 10). The antipoet, in contrast, is an ordinary man, one of the *dramatis personae* in the tragicomedy of everyday life. He doubts the possibility of arriving at any *point sublime*; indeed, he often finds himself "al borde del abismo" [at the edge of the abyss] (103), or in "un desastroso estado mental" [a disastrous mental state] (49). Given the self-imposed limitations of the antipoet, the romantic-surrealist proposition to change life through the subversion inherent in poetry is severely constricted. The antipoet is at best capable of observing the life around him in all its absurdity; he is fully immersed in that life but has no pretentions of bettering it. Finally, it should be noted that one of the original surrealists' goals had been to democratize poetic creation: they made a mantra of Lautréamont's aphorism, "Poetry should be made by all. Not by one" (333). In practice, however, the surrealist speaker often adopted an oracular stance that set him apart from others. Parra set out to alter that stance, insisting that the antipoet "doesn't try to pass for a seer or any kind of superior being" (J. Piña 32). To reaffirm this position, in "Manifiesto" the antipoet states pointedly— and reiterates at the close of the poem—"Los poetas bajaron del Olimpo" [The poets came down from Olympus] (147, 150).

Beyond these straightforward differences between a surrealist poetics and that of antipoetry, the genealogy becomes more tangled. To begin with, in spite of their declarative and colloquial language, Parra's poems at times employ a technique that mimics automatic writing. Parra himself has stated that important poems such as "El individuo" were largely the product of an automatic method (Morales 198). That is, the poetic structure is built on fragment and contradiction, unexpected combinations and incongruencies, creating what Ricardo Yamal calls a "collage of superimposed realities" (18). As he explains his methodology, Parra draws on the surrealist concept of syntax: "It is impossible to put one word next to another without having this immediately signify something. Why the effort, then, to impose a meaning upon them from the outside? It seems to me that this must be the central mechanism of antipoetry: to allow words to gather together of their own accord" (Urondo 8). Parra's language here—which, as we will see, will be echoed by Octavio Paz—closely parallels Breton's notion of the spark of illumination that is ignited when two unlike entities are juxtaposed, a form of psychic and linguistic energy largely outside of the poet's conscious control (*Manifestoes* 37).

However, Parra also notes the limits of automatism for his poetic purposes: "Surrealist poems in general were ultra-fragmentary; they did not even sustain a given state of mind, and it was hard to know what they were about. Free associations generally occurred on a purely rhetorical rather than a psychological plane, in spite of the fact that they were filled with lightning bolts" (Morales 199). From these commentaries we can gather that automatic techniques were important to Parra, but only as a method of generating poems that ultimately cohered around a particular existential situation or mental state. He recognizes the imaginative power of the "flashes of lightning" generated by automatic techniques (here we recall Gonzalo Rojas's motif of the *relámpago*) but wishes to put them in the service of a recognizable meaning.

To be sure, many of Parra's antipoems fit this paradigm of conscious control of automatism, but it is important to note that others fit more closely Parra's very description of the hermetic surrealist text. One prime example of this is the brief poem "Paisaje" [Landscape]:

> ¡Veis esa pierna humana que cuelga de la luna
> como un árbol que crece para abajo,
> esa pierna temible que flota en el vacío
> iluminada apenas por el rayo
> de la luna y el aire del olvido! (44)

[Do you see that human leg that hangs from the moon / like a tree growing downward, / that dreadful leg floating in the void / barely illuminated by a ray of light / from the moon and the air of forgetfulness!]

This is not an immediately accessible poem: its "meaning" can only be deduced partially from the suggestiveness of the images. The dismembered human body—which will become a primary motif in the late surrealism of the Argentine poet Juan Gelman[11]—in combination with terms such as "dreadful" and "floating in the void," point to a certain abject state of mind, but that psychic situation remains unconnected to any particular being or circumstance. The image of the leg hanging from the moon recalls Neruda's "Walking Around," which is often cited as a text typical of his surrealist-influenced period. In that poem, the speaker wanders disconsolately through a modern urban wasteland, seeing, among other things, "hospitales donde los huesos salen por la ventana" [hospitals with bones coming out of the windows] (*Obras completas* 1: 216). In Parra's poem, the simile created by the image of the leg hanging from the moon "like a tree growing downward" can be considered purely hermetic, in that neither term of the comparison (leg/tree) serves to illuminate the other. In sum, the language of "Paisaje" demonstrates that the distinction between purely automatic texts and texts that employ automatic techniques in the service of coherent compositions is not always as simple as either poets or readers might wish to believe.

The techniques of automatism were intended to allow the poet access to the otherwise hidden reaches of the unconscious. Irrational imagery, whether in written texts or the visual arts, was the result of these excavations of the psychic subsoil. But practitioners of automatic techniques generally avoid direct allusions to these psychic processes in their art, since to do so would be to acknowledge some level of artifice. Here we find another instance in which Nicanor Parra productively reconfigures the practice of surrealism. If the surrealists wanted to reveal the workings of the unconscious, Parra does so as well, but always from an exteriorized, highly self-conscious, and ironic point of view. Certain tropes drawn from romanticism but central to surrealism are reiterated throughout Parra's poetry: madness or delirium, dreams or hallucinations—in brief, irrational states of mind. But rather than using these tropes as vehicles for arriving at a poetic revelation, Parra names them directly, surgically exposing the unconscious to the viewing audience. In Freudian terms, there is no "latent structure" here, and thus no repressed truth to be uncovered. This technique allows the antipoet to speak ironically of "mi célèbre método onírico" [my famous oneiric method] (60), inviting the reader to chuckle with him at this method and to dismiss any supposed wisdom resulting from it.

Although there are numerous allusions to irrational mental states in the *antipoemas*, perhaps the clearest example of Parra's demythifying approach to such states occurs in the poem "Notas de viaje" [Travel Journal], in which the speaker tells us that he left his job for several years in order to travel and to sleep (60). In the various contexts in which he finds himself, odd thoughts intrude on his consciousness: "Durante el baile yo pensaba en cosas absurdas: / pensaba en unas lechugas vistas el día anterior / al pasar delante de la cocina, / pensaba en un sinnúmero de cosas fantásticas relacionadas con mi familia" [During the dance I thought about absurd things: / I thought about some heads of lettuce glimpsed the day before / when I walked by the kitchen, / I thought endless weird things related to my family] (46). As opposed to the romantic or surrealist poetic voice who actively pursues these irrational drifts of mind, and who revels in their potential for illumination, the antipoet merely informs us that his intrusive thoughts disturb him and cause him to isolate himself from others. The last lines of this enigmatic poem read

> Aquellas escenas fotográficas afectaban mi espíritu,
> me obligaban a encerrarme en mi camarote;
> comía a la fuerza, me rebelaba contra mí mismo,
> constituía un peligro permanente a bordo
> puesto que en cualquier momento podía salir con un contrasentido. (46)

> [Those photographic scenes affected my spirit, compelling me to shut myself up in my cabin; / I had to force myself to eat, I rebelled against myself, / on the ship I was a constant danger / since at any moment something ridiculous could slip out of my mouth.]

On the one hand, the speaker here seems to be describing a rather normal state of consciousness: every human being experiences sudden flashes of odd thoughts, often at inopportune moments. Neither is the content of these intrusive mental pictures—lettuce glimpsed in the kitchen or thoughts about the family—particularly unusual. What *is* unusual here are the speaker's own reactions to these mental meanderings. He is so frightened by them that he locks himself away, loses his appetite, and perceives himself as a danger to others. The fact that this perceived danger is linked not to potential acts of violence but to *language* is significant: here the poem invites us to relate the antipoet's experiences to those of poets in general. Rimbaud spoke in his famous "Lettre du voyant" of the poet's need to make himself a seer "by a long, gigantic and rational *derangement of all the senses*" (307). Parra's antipoet, by referring overtly to his supposedly irrational mental states, by reducing them to trivialities, and then by showing that it is the poet himself who creates or exacerbates his situation of subjective anguish and social isolation, subverts the entire romantic-surrealist configuration of poetic revelation through delirium.

Apart from the Rimbaudian "derangement of the senses," which is represented in Parra's antipoetry as an ordinary yet disturbing phenomenon, one of the primary means by which the surrealists hoped to tap into the unconscious was through humor, especially what they called "black humor." (Breton's influential *Anthologie de l'humour noir,* published in 1940, was widely read among Latin American intellectuals.) In terms of method, surrealist humor was often generated by absurdities, incongruities, and non sequiturs. Here again, Parra transforms his inherited materials, practicing radical dislocations of meaning but carrying the joke farther than did most orthodox surrealists. Parra's humor is also more sustained and more evidently directed toward social satire than is the humor found in earlier surrealist texts. Everyone and everything can be the object of an antipoetical joke—even the antipoet himself, even his attempts at being funny. Following in the tradition of Cervantes and Quevedo, Parra refuses to construct this speaker-protagonist as the privileged outsider who can criticize from a safe distance: the antipoet is infected by the chaos and alienation that pervades his society. As the butt of his own dark jokes, he invites us not to take him as a person seriously. But his suffering is another matter.

The poem that enacts most extensively what Parra calls his "metaphysical humor" (qtd. in J. Piña 22) is "Lo que el difunto dijo de sí mismo" [What the Deceased Said about Himself], a long poem first published in *Versos de salón* [Salon Verses], the volume that followed *Poemas y antipoemas* in 1962. In this piece, the antipoet reviews his life from the vantage point of death. In typical Parrian fashion, the speaker begins by parodying the language of public discourse: "Aprovecho con gran satisfacción / esta oportunidad maravillosa / que me brinda la ciencia de la muerte / para decir algunas claridades / sobre mis aventuras en la tierra / más adelante, cuando tenga tiempo, / hablaré de la vida de ultratumba" [It is with great satisfaction that I avail myself / of this marvelous opportunity / afforded me by the knowledge of death / to pronounce a few certainties / regarding my adventures on earth; / later on, when I have time, / I shall speak of life beyond the grave] (111). The language is formal, but the situation, of course, is fantastical; in this way a tonal disparity is created that provides the first hint of seriously playful irony. Taken as a whole, the poem is a tour-de-force of acerbic humor in which one cultural icon after another—religion, the academy, bourgeois conventions of work and marriage, even maternity—is dismantled.

As we saw with the antipoet's transparent references to irrational states of mind, near the outset of this poem he brings his ludic intent to the surface: "Quiero reírme un poco / como lo hice cuando estaba vivo: / el saber y la risa se confunden" [I want to laugh a little / as I did when I was alive: / knowledge and laughter are one and the same] (111). There is a hint of the medieval *exemplum* here, as the antipoet suggests that through laughter wisdom can be attained. But lest the reader take the promise of wisdom too seriously, the antipoet reveals his own unstable (and possibly unethical) nature: "Estuve a punto de volverme loco" [I was about to go crazy], he comments as he relates the story of a lawyer who accuses him of having abandoned his first wife (112); later he mentions that he was labeled as "enfermo de los nervios" [suffering from a nervous affliction]; and finally he characterizes himself as "Desesperado, loco de remate" [Desperate, totally crazy] (114). Like Don Quixote, the antipoet is a walking comic tragedian.

Many of the jokes woven into this text parody the literary world. Pablo Neruda's harrowing journey across the Andes in 1949 as he fled from political persecution (a story Neruda narrates with eloquence in his 1971 Nobel Prize acceptance speech) is the likely subtext of this stanza:

> ¿Mis relaciones con la religión?
> Atravesé la cordillera a pie
> disfrazado de fraile capuchino
> transformando ratones en palomas. (112)

[My relationship to religion? / I crossed the sierra on foot / disguised as a Capuchin monk, / turning mice into doves.]

Here Parra pokes fun at Neruda's priestly or monkish aura, as well as the characteristic Nerudian practice of exalting the ordinary.

The Gallicized literature practiced by many of Parra's Latin American predecessors and contemporaries is also ridiculed in these verses: "Escribí en araucano y en latín / los demás escribían en francés / versos que hacían dar diente con diente" [I wrote in Araucanian and in Latin / the others were writing verses in French / that made my teeth chatter] (112). The antipoet seems at first to claim for himself a more local and authentic idiom, given that he writes in the language of Chile's native Araucanians, but he immediately subverts this claim by adding that he also writes in Latin, the "high" language of the conquerors and of the church. Conspicuous by its absence is *castellano* or Spanish, the idiom of the average Chilean that the antipoet purports to represent.

In numerous other instances in the poem, the deceased antipoet treats his own literary activity in a farcical tone. "Ya no recuerdo cómo ni por qué / 'abracé la carrera de las letras'" [I don't remember how or why / "I embraced the profession of *belles lettres*"] (112). By placing the second verse in quotes, Parra points to this language as trite and self-important, thereby calling his own literary values into question. This line of irony continues later in the poem: "Para no molestarme con el público / simulaba tener ideas claras / me expresaba con gran autoridad / pero la situación era difícil / confundía a Platón con Aristóteles" [In order to avoid trouble with the public / I pretended to have clear ideas / I expressed myself with great authority / but it was a tough situation / I confused Plato with Aristotle] (14). The object of this sustained joke is obviously the humanist academy in general, made up of pretenders who lack even the fundamentals of traditional Western knowledge (Plato and Aristotle) but who nevertheless carry on with great pomp, careful above all to avoid confrontations with the public they are charged with educating.

Finally, in a confessional and metapoetical flourish, the defunct antipoet laughs at himself by admitting that in life he tried unsuccessfully to be comical: "Intenté deslumbrar a mis lectores / a través del sentido del humor / pero causé una pésima impresión" [I attempted to dazzle my readers / with my sense of humor / but I created a terrible impression] (112). Staging his humorous approach to poetry through the soliloquy of a dead poet who admits his own shortcomings (along with those of his critics), Parra invites us to laugh at the fact that we may not be laughing. This dialectic of the ludic and the serious is inverted once again in the poem's final stanza, which features the cartoonish figure of the poet threatening his readers: "¡No se rían delante de mi tumba / porque puedo romper el ataúd / y salir disparado por el cielo!" [Don't laugh at my graveside / since I might break through this coffin / and go shooting across the sky!] (114). The imagined farcical scene at the poet's tomb, coupled with the changeable and ultimately irreverent attitude of the speaker toward both poetry and death, provides a striking contrast to Gonzalo Rojas's sober approach to these themes in his elegy for Breton. This contrast illustrates clearly how two poets from the same country and the same period can draw on surrealist strategies to craft a vastly different poetics.

We can conclude from these examples that Nicanor Parra's antipoetry could not have developed as it did without surrealism, but that in practice it moves far beyond surrealism, appearing in many ways to be its "photographic negative." Federico Schopf calls Parra's poetics "the most radical legacy of the avant-garde" ("El surrealismo" 179). I have illustrated this dynamic legacy by focusing on Parra's self-conscious allusions to irrational states of mind and his use of black humor. Parra's surrealist (anti)genealogy could also be traced through the themes of eroticism and personal liberty, both instances of profound nonconformity and alienation for the speaker. But perhaps Parra's greatest debt to surrealism—as well as his own greatest legacy—concerns language itself. The prosaic, conversational, or ironic character of Parra's diction leads the reader to assume there is a wide breach between antipoetical and surrealist language. But if we consider that antipoetry is an attempt to encompass metonymically the *totality* of human language, we come face to face with the surrealist dream of capturing the totality of human experience.[12] The surrealists believed this ideal could be achieved through channeling directly the language of dream, reverie, and delirium. Parra scoffed at those methods and suggested that advertising slogans, popular rhymes, and everyday mental meanderings could also reveal the profundities of human nature. This is an approach to language and art that Breton and his followers discovered and too soon forgot.

Few today dispute the importance of Parra's poetics for the evolution of Spanish American poetry in the second half of the twentieth century. The lesson of liberty in poetic language, which Parra took from the surrealists but carried to extremes they had not envisioned, is arguably the most significant one of all. As Morales asserts, after 1954 poets no longer had to fight over their rights to words, to pit a poetics of the spoken against a poetics of the written text, to favor learned diction over "el garabato" [scribbling] (131). Parra's unique combination of wide-ranging diction, ironic tone, and dramatic characterization of the antipoet is certainly inimitable. But antipoetry remains a dynamic model, one that asks to be carried forward in new guises. In the words of the Chilean writer and critic Fernando Alegría, a contemporary of both Rojas and Parra: "From the surrealist sunset, antipoetry has been pulling out tools and the components of a time bomb. Meanwhile, the period of Molotov cocktails goes by. The antipoets no longer negate themselves. They make signs from one country to another, they take the crossbar off the door, they give their cudgel blow. They distribute health and agitation" (198).

As in Argentina, a small-scale surrealist revival has taken place in Chile in the late twentieth and early twenty-first centuries, particularly in the form of collectives in which poetry and the visual arts are both practiced. One key figure in this activity is the artist Jorge Leal Labrín, who lived from 1978 to 1994 in France and Italy, where he collaborated with the neosurrealist movement *Phases*. A frank defender of automatism in painting, Leal Labrín has staged surrealist expositions and "happenings" worldwide and has lectured on surrealism in the Southern Cone, including the role of the Mandrágora movement. In the 1980s, he coedited the arts journal *Ojo de Aguijón: Revista Surrealista Bilingüe*, published in French and Spanish. As a final testimony to the tendency of surrealism to reinvent itself in Latin America, in 1996 a group of young Chilean writers that has been dubbed "Los nietos de la Mandrágora" [The grandchildren of Mandrágora] (Ortega Parada 205) gathered around the literary magazine *Derrame*, which has worked to develop an international online presence for surrealist poetry. The poets in this group (many of whom are also visual artists) include Aldo Alcota, Magdalena Benavente, Carlos Delgado Páez, Milán Bodis-Suckel,

Miguel Angel Huerta, Emilio Padilla, Enrique de Santiago, Carlos Sedille, Jorge Solís, Rodrigo Verdugo, and Roberto Yáñez. In an online essay called "Surrealismo en Chile: Una nota sobre su actualidad," Verdugo speaks to surrealism's renewed energy in that country: "Surrealism, beyond its particular historical framework, maintains itself in a constant state of verification, demonstrating an ongoing relevance." In the face of criticism that would dismiss surrealism on various fronts, says Verdugo, contemporary surrealist groups across the globe "organize expositions, edit journals, and maintain their adhesion to surrealist principles, continuing to develop many of the resources introduced by that timeless movement." It would appear that Enrique Gómez-Correa's *entusiasmo* has found a new voice.

CHAPTER 10

Octavio Paz
Surrealism's Favorite Son

Introduction

In a speech given at a memorial for Octavio Paz in 1999, the Chilean poet Gonzalo Rojas recalls that he first became acquainted with Paz "reading him on my feet, like my entire generation, and rereading him in *The Bow and the Lyre* and *The Labyrinth of Solitude*" ("Octavio aquí y ahora" 193). At the end of this homage, Rojas concludes, "What I mean is that genuine surrealism was a 'sacred disease' of the century—a healthy disease, moreover, in the period between the wars—*imagination, mad love, and liberty*—and that the only surrealists among us were Roberto Matta and Octavio Paz" (198). Rojas's comments stand as yet another testimony to the vital force that surrealism represented for many writers of his generation. They also point directly to Octavio Paz (1914–98) as the iconic figure associated with surrealism in Latin American literature. As Rojas intimates, in Paz and in the Chilean painter Roberto Matta, European surrealism was absorbed and then powerfully reconfigured, even coming to exert a "reverse influence" over European painting and poetry. Within the context of Latin American literature, Paz represents the culminating point of surrealist thought and expression, and he thus serves as a fitting subject for the final chapter of this study.[1]

Over the past decades, numerous critics have examined the role surrealism plays in the development of Paz's thought and his creative work. In *The Poetic Modes of Octavio Paz* (1972), Rachel Phillips explores surrealism as one of three key approaches to reading Paz's work. In *Octavio Paz: A Study of His Poetics* (1979), the British critic Jason Wilson makes a particularly strong and sustained argument for the centrality of surrealism to Paz's poetry and prose. In 1997, Evodio Escalante responds to and deepens Wilson's perspective in his essay "La vanguardia requisada." More recently, Olivia Maciel Edelmen (2008) studies surrealism in the work of Paz, Xavier Villaurrutia, and Luis Cernuda, and Víctor Manuel Mendiola (2011) reads one of Paz's most important poems, "Piedra de sol" [Sun Stone], in the light of surrealism. I refer the reader to these studies for a comprehensive look at this intricate relationship. In the pages that follow, after considering Paz's development as a writer and thinker through his ongoing engagement with surrealism, I will concentrate on one strain of thought—the belief in the "magical" powers of poetry—that reveals a crucial but less examined link between Paz and the principles of surrealism.

Paz's stature as a writer of poetry, poetic prose, cultural criticism, and literary theory and criticism, and also as an intellectual ambassador, is difficult to overestimate. Long before he was awarded the Nobel Prize for Literature in 1990, he was broadly recognized as Latin America's leading intellectual. Within his own country, however, Paz was a controversial and often embattled figure. As was the case with Neruda in Chile, the very authority of his literary voice caused a reaction among writers of his own and subsequent generations: since the early 1980s, states Rubén Medina, "Paz has managed to raise himself to the status of the absolute *caudillo* of Mexican culture" (12). Ambitious, outspoken, and armed with a formidable erudition, Paz became the touchstone for much of Mexico's cultural discourse and debate in the second half of the twentieth century. Surrealism at first occupied a rather shadowy corner of this discourse. Through both his poetry and his essays, Paz illuminated that corner, although this act often exposed it to the harsh light of further criticism.

Octavio Paz was born during the Mexican Revolution, but he grew up relatively protected from the immediate turmoil. The decades following the revolution witnessed ongoing social and political upheavals within the overall context of a stable but rigid and often corrupt one-party system. As Wilson observes, Paz's works must be considered in the light of his need to create an idealistic order out of the confusion of his times; as a religiously educated but agnostic young man, Paz "turned elsewhere for models in a climate hostile to anything that was not zenophobically Mexican" (*Octavio Paz* 2). This early predisposition for a liberal and broadly constructed view of the world, coupled with his extensive travels and time spent living abroad, fashioned in Paz a truly global consciousness that remained nevertheless firmly rooted in its *mexicanidad*. Stated otherwise, it is impossible to approach Paz's work without acknowledging the "in-betweenness" of his position as a writer and thinker, which includes his position "between the European avant-garde and his provenance from a marginal and ex-centric literature" (Aguilar Camín 233).

The triumph in 1917 of what had been a largely populist revolution awoke in the Mexican people a passion for reconstructing their identity as a nation—politically, historically, socially, racially, and aesthetically. Within this reconstruction, the story of Mexico's pre-Columbian past gained a new prestige through major archeological finds and through the translation and study of indigenous texts. Following the prescriptions of socialist realism, Mexican muralism presented the modern industrial worker and the *campesino* alongside the pre-Hispanic indigenous prince or slave: all were exalted as the face of modern Mexico. As we saw in Chapter 6, this intensified cultural nationalism was one factor that led in the 1930s and 1940s to a kind of willed ignorance or an outright rejection of surrealism, which was viewed as "a greenhouse flower"—an exotic import having little or nothing to do with Mexican realities (qtd. in Bradu 221). André Breton's four-month stay in Mexico in 1938 had aroused some strong opinions on either side of the intellectual divide, but in the end, surrealism traveled back to France in the suitcases of its founder.

The question of national identity was one that had preoccupied Paz from an early point in his career as a writer, but his exposure to surrealism had come early as well. In his homage to Breton in 1966, Paz recalls how as an adolescent he had come across *L'Amour fou*, a text that "opened the doors of modern poetry to me" ("André Breton" 53). As an aspiring poet in his early twenties he had frequented the gatherings of the Contemporáneos group; there he learned from poets such as Xavier Villaurrutia, Gilberto Owen, and Jaime Torres Bodet, who experimented with dream imagery and automatic writing but who tended to approach surrealism from a purely aesthetic angle and thus to distance themselves from its ideas. (As we saw in Chapter 6, Ortiz de Montellano is the one exception to this rule.)

Paz's own generation of poets in Mexico City took shape around the journal *Taller*, which was published between 1938 and 1941. *Taller* brought to prominence such writers as Rafael Solana, Efraín Huerta, Alberto Quintero Álvarez, and Neftalí Beltrán. The *Taller* poets were interested in the social and political role of poetry and aligned themselves with the leftist (and generally pro-Stalin) ideologies of the Lázaro Cárdenas regime (1934–40). In an essay called "Poesía mexicana moderna," Paz acknowledges the affinities of this group with the Spanish mystic poets, the German and English romantics, and the surrealists. He goes on to clarify: "Pero no nos interesaba el lenguaje del surrealismo, ni sus teorías sobre la 'escritura automática': nos seducía su afirmación intransigente de ciertos valores que considerábamos—y considero—preciosos entre todos: la imaginación, el amor y la libertad, únicas fuerzas capaces de consagrar al mundo y volverlo de veras 'otro' " [But we weren't interested in the language of surrealism, nor in its theories about "automatic writing": we were seduced by its uncompromising affirmation of certain values that we considered—and that I still consider—the most beautiful of all: imagination, love, and liberty, the only forces capable of consecrating the world and transforming it into something truly "other"] (*Obras completas* 4: 66). In sharp contrast to *Contemporáneos*, *Taller* published no texts by the French surrealists. The magazine made no mention of Breton's visit to Mexico (although its first issue appeared only four months after his departure) and in fact published a long diatribe against surrealism by the Guatemalan poet Luis Cardoza y Aragón. In sum, Paz's ambivalence toward or outright rejection of surrealism in the late 1930s and early 1940s points once again to the overall hostile environment that surrealist ideas initially faced in Mexico.[2]

In 1937 (immediately prior to Breton's trip to Mexico), the 23-year-old Paz traveled to Valencia, Spain, to participate in the Second International Congress of Antifascist Writers, working in behind-the-lines support of the Republican cause in the Spanish Civil War. The vision of a free and egalitarian society that he experienced in Republican Spain contributed to Paz's lifelong commitment to political and social liberty, which in turn led to a disparaging view of his own nation's relative rigidity. Crucial to Paz's poetic development in this period were his encounters in Spain with other intellectual militants in the antifascist cause, including his fellow Spanish Americans Vicente Huidobro, Pablo Neruda, and César Vallejo, the Spanish filmmaker Luis Buñuel, and the Spanish poets Miguel Hernández, Antonio Machado, and Luis Cernuda. Cernuda was a poet with surrealist leanings who was later exiled in Mexico, and whose work was to exert a long-lasting influence over Paz.[3] Paz returned to Mexico in 1938 via Paris, where he had a brief introduction to the French surrealist group.

During a five-year sojourn in his native land, Paz experienced the bitter reality of the fall of Republican Spain, a growing disenchantment with leftist ideologies in Mexico and abroad, and a struggle with his own sense of solitude and alienation. Crucial to his formation in this period were the friendships he established with many of the European exiles who moved temporarily or permanently to Mexico, including Leonora Carrington, Remedios Varo, Wolfgang Paalen, and Benjamin Péret (whose work was examined in Chapter 6). Of these encounters, he comments,

> Me sentí inmediatamente atraído. Muchas de sus opiniones me deslumbraban, otras me intrigaban y algunas me dejaban perplejo. Ellos y ellas me parecían adeptos de una comunidad de iniciados, dispersos por el mundo y empeñados en una búsqueda antiquísima: encontrar el perdido camino que une al microcosmos con el macrocosmos. Eran los herederos del romanticismo pero también de los gnósticos del siglo IV. (*Obras* 2: 19–20)

> [I felt immediately attracted. Many of their opinions dazzled me, others intrigued me, and still others left me perplexed. All of them seemed to me to belong to a community of adepts, scattered throughout the world and engaged in an ancient search: finding the lost path that unites microcosm with macrocosm. They were the inheritors of romanticism but also of the fourth-century Gnostics.]

This testimony is significant in that it demonstrates that from early in his career Paz was attracted to currents of thought—particularly the monistic world view and the notion of true knowledge as an esoteric search—that his later contact with surrealism would allow him to develop more fully.

Paz lived and wrote in the United States in 1944 and 1945 under the auspices of a Guggenheim Fellowship: there he was exposed to surrealist painting, finding himself particularly intrigued by the works of Max Ernst. In 1945, Paz moved to Paris, where he served as a Mexican cultural attaché. In the French capital he renewed his friendship with Péret, who in turn introduced him to Breton. In the years between 1945 and 1951, and again between 1959 and 1962, Paz lived in Paris and maintained a steady though somewhat tangential relationship to the postwar surrealist group. Wilson surmises that Paz's relationship with Breton was "probably the most absorbing and influential friendship in Paz's life as a poet" (*Octavio Paz* 33). Apart from his attendance at café discussions and readings, Paz occasionally participated in protests, signed manifestoes, and contributed writings to key surrealist venues such as *Le Surréalisme, même*.

This sustained encounter was crucial to Paz's poetic development not in matters of style or technique (following in the path of the Contemporáneos, he had already experimented with automatic writing and oneiric imagery in earlier work) but as a world view—that is, as a plausible response to the ethical dilemmas that he faced in this moment in history. Wilson frames the dilemma and its resolution in these terms: "Could Paz find a substitute to his political activity that had tried to fuse the individual into a collectivity, without falling back into the romantic error of the marginalized solitary lyric poet? Over these years Paz had insisted on a communal solution to individual alienation. It is at this level of quest that the brotherhood of surrealists, governed by André Breton's intransigent ethical stance, became a viable alternative that bound the poet to social change" (*Octavio Paz* 27). In the context of the present study, it is crucial to recall that Paz forged this vital relationship with the Parisian surrealist group precisely at the moment of Breton's return from exile in New York, when many began to dismiss the movement as irrelevant to European cultural life. The timing of Paz's years in Paris and his subsequent return to Mexico in 1953 as a sort of apostle of surrealism points to the "afterlife" that was possible for the surrealist movement as it spread beyond Europe in the postwar period.

In contrast to several of the Latin American writers examined earlier in this study, and in contrast to his *Taller*-era skepticism, Paz's appreciation for surrealism from the late 1940s onward is straightforward and unapologetic: as late as 1973, he calls it the most important movement of the twentieth century (*Obras* 6: 303). As several studies have shown, surrealist techniques are clearly discernible in his poetry from this middle period, most notably in the collections *¿Águila o sol?* [Eagle or Sun?, 1951], *Semillas para un himno* [Seeds for a Hymn, 1954], *La estación violenta* [The Violent Season, 1958] (which contains the important long poem *Piedra de sol* [Sun Stone]), and *Salamandra*

(1962). In these works, surrealist techniques are used to explore the relationship between poetry and history, with a particular concern for the meanings of pre-Columbian history for modern Mexico. In Maciel Edelman's words, these works reflect "the transformative power of myth, the possibility of conciliating opposites," both ideas gleaned from surrealism (113). At the end of ¿Águila o sol?, which is a collection of prose poems, the speaker posits, "Cuando la historia duerme, habla en sueños . . . cuando la historia despierta, la imagen se hace acto, acontece el poema: la poesía entra en acción" [When history sleeps, it speaks in dreams . . . when history awakens, the image becomes an act, and the poem happens: poetry enters into action] (*Obras* 11: 194). This statement employs the surrealist notion of dream-speech (implying that history can speak to us through the imagination) and furthermore equates poetry with action, that is, with a praxis that can change the world. This is the configuration of ideas that I will examine later in this chapter under the rubric of "poetry as magic."

But in addition to his poetic works in this period, Paz also championed surrealism from the vantage point of a public intellectual. In 1954, he participated in a series of lectures on "The Great Themes of Our Time" at Mexico's National University. His presentation, called "Estrella de tres puntas: El surrealismo" [Three-pointed Star: Surrealism], was published in *Universidad de México* in 1956 and reprinted in his widely read 1957 volume of essays *Las peras del olmo*.[4] He also expounds directly on surrealism in numerous other short texts, most of which were reedited in a volume published in 1996 under the title *Estrella de tres puntas: André Breton y el surrealismo*. The essay "André Breton or the Quest of the Beginning" stresses the archetypal or mythical value of language that Breton sought to restore, particularly in the postwar period.[5]

Another intriguing piece concerned with surrealism, "Un catálogo descabalado," was originally written as an open letter published in the journal *Plural*, which was founded and edited by Paz. The letter was directed to Fernando Gamboa, the principle organizer of an exposition called *El arte del surrealismo* in Mexico City in 1973. In it, Paz finds himself in the unlikely position of defending surrealism against its purported advocates in Mexico. His argument is not with the exposition itself—which featured works by Wilfredo Lam, Roberto Matta, and numerous others, and which Paz praised for allowing a bit of "fresh air" into the closed atmosphere of Mexican art—but with the exhibition catalogue. He points out several factual errors in the catalogue, some of them egregious, and accuses its writers of "deforming the meaning of surrealism" (*Obras* 6: 304). He lays the blame for this deformity on the originators of the exposition, the International Council of the Museum of Modern Art in New York, but also on their Mexican counterparts, whose perspective suffers from "cultural nationalism."

Paz expresses shock that this catalogue "fuese una tentativa por amputar al surrealismo de su dimensión crítica y subversiva lo mismo frente a las ignominias del Occidente capitalista y cristiano que ante las monstruosas perversiones del socialismo en Europa Oriental y en otras partes del mundo" [was an attempt to excise surrealism from its critical and subversive dimension, in the face of both the ignominies of Western and Christian capitalism and of the monstrous perversions of socialism in Eastern Europe and elsewhere in the world] (*Obras* 6: 304). Paz's language here gives the reader a clear sense of the depth of his political and ethical views and especially of his conviction that surrealist thought provided a legitimate response to the failed world systems that still held sway in the late twentieth century. That conviction is stated outright as a final challenge to the perspective of Gamboa and his colleagues: "El surrealismo es un movimiento de subversión de la sensibilidad y la imaginación que abarca lo mismo a los dominios del arte que a los del amor, la moral y la política" [Surrealism is a movement that subverts sensibility and the imagination, embracing the reign of art but equally those of love, ethics, and politics] (*Obras* 6: 304). In spite of his vehement response to the catalogue, Paz produced a long poem called "Poema circulatorio: Para la desorientación general," whose circular form was reproduced on a spiral staircase within the Mexican exhibition. The poem invokes the figures of Artaud, Buñuel, Carrington, Kahlo, Moro, Péret, and others in Mexico in order to assert that

>   el surrealismo
>   NO ESTÁ AQUÍ
>   allá afuera
>   al aire libre
>   al teatro de los ojos libres (*Obras* 12: 55)

[surrealism / IS NOT HERE / it is there outside / in the open air / in the theater of unfettered eyes]

Finally, Paz published a hybrid text in 1974 called "Sobre el surrealismo hispanoamericano: El fin de las habladurías." Part litany, part poem, part essay, this piece first appeared in *Plural* as a review of Stefan Baciu's *Antología de la poesía surrealista latinoamericana*.[6] It is crucial to the present study because it is one of the few texts by a Latin American writer to address directly the question of surrealism on native ground. Here, as in the previously cited letter to Gamboa, Paz defends surrealism from its detractors and attempts to clarify its purposes for those who have misunderstood it. The essay opens with a series of metaphors for surrealism, anaphorically constructed on the reiterated phrase "Surrealism has been":

> El surrealismo ha sido la manzana de fuego en el árbol de la sintaxis
> El surrealismo ha sido la camelia de ceniza entre los pechos de la adolescente poseída por el espectro de Orestes
> ....
> El surrealismo ha sido el bálsamo de Fierabrás que borra las señas del pecado original en el ombligo del lenguaje
> El surrealismo ha sido el escupitajo en la hostia y el clavel de dinamita en el confesionario y el sésamo ábrete de las cajas de seguridad y las rejas de los manicomios
> ....
> El surrealismo ha sido el clavo ardiente en la frente del geómetra y el viento fuerte que a media noche levanta las sábanas de las vírgenes
> ....
> El surrealismo ha sido el puñado de sal que disuelve los tlaconetes del realismo socialista ("Sobre el surrealismo hispanoamericano" 153)

[Surrealism has been the apple of fire in the tree of syntax / Surrealism has been the camellia of ash between the breasts of the adolescent possessed by the specter of Orestes / Surrealism has been the balm of Fierabras that erases the marks of original sin in the navel of language / Surrealism has been the spitting on the host and the dynamite carnation in the confessional and the open sesame of lockboxes and bars on asylum windows / Surrealism has been the burning nail in the forehead of the geometrician and the strong wind that lifts the sheets of virgins at midnight / Surrealism has been the fistful of salt that dissolves the tumors of socialist realism]

It is important to note Paz's choice of verb tense in this litany: the present perfect *ha sido* recognizes surrealism as a movement that began in the past but that still has validity for the present. In the brief series cited above, the reader will recognize the familiar tenets of surrealism: greater imaginative possibilities for language (a language whose original innocence is acknowledged), the rejection of petrified religious and political systems and of "geometric" or rigidly rational thought, and the exaltation of eroticism and of liberty in its various incarnations, even that of madness.

The long enumeration of these surrealist metaphors for surrealism ends abruptly with the phrase "El surrealismo ha sido esto y esto y esto y esto" [Surrealism has been this and this and this and this], at which point Paz breaks off the poetic litany and shifts into a more conventional mode of discourse for a book review. He laments that Baciu's anthology (published by the respected publisher Joaquín Mortiz) has received little attention from Mexican critics, and he praises the book as the first serious and well-documented study of a topic that is "at once secret and public" (154). Surrealism is secret, he claims, because few truly know it; it is public because everyone speaks of it as if it were a key for opening every door (154). Paz speaks broadly of surrealism as an international phenomenon, reiterating its importance as "una actitud vital, total—ética y estética—que se expresó en la acción y la participación" [an attitude toward life that was total—ethical and aesthetic—and that expressed itself in action and participation] (156). He then discusses in detail the contents and structure of Baciu's anthology (which opens with a 116-page introduction), concluding that this book is the first important contribution to the history of Spanish-American surrealism (160).

Paz uses this review as a platform from which to summarize for the reader the major figures associated with surrealism in this region—from the members of the Mandrágora group, whom he praises for their courage in a politically decisive moment in Chile, to Peru's César Moro and Argentina's Enrique Molina. He even mentions "Mexico's Octavio Paz" in this context, although he provides the disclaimer that his surrealist activities were mainly carried out in Paris (158). He corroborates Baciu's decision to separate those writers directly involved with the surrealist movement (*los surrealistas*) from those who merely absorbed its influence (*los para-surrealistas* and *los surrealizantes*). Finally, Paz cites the need for an updated anthology of Spanish American poetry that would show those influences in "la poesía *viva* de nuestra lengua" [the *living* poetry of our language] (160). He also calls for critical studies that would demonstrate the contribution of Spanish American poets to international surrealism and the influence of Spanish American surrealists on poetry written in their own tongue (160). In sum, this review stands as an important document in the gradual awakening of readers in the Spanish-speaking world to the relationship between the surrealist movement and literary production in Spanish.

In all the previously cited essays, as well as in his important works of literary history and theory—*El arco y la lira* [The Bow and the Lyre] (1956) and *Los hijos del limo: La poesía moderna del romanticismo a la vanguardia* [Children of the Mire: Modern Poetry from Romanticism to the Avant-Garde] (1974)[7]— Paz argues vigorously for the integration of surrealism into twentieth-century thought. In these essays we witness again the belated position of Latin American writers with regard to the historical surrealist movement (Peru's César Moro being the one notable exception), a position that allows for a certain critical distance and for greater creative flexibility. For Wilson, Paz's success in transforming surrealism was due to his ability to abstract the movement from its historically concrete position and thus to create a "transhistorical poetics" (*Study* 23). Evodio Escalante goes further, claiming that what Paz adopts is no longer surrealism as such—the movement that in his *Taller* years had been the target of his criticism—but rather "a looser, modified, broad-spectrum surrealism, free of bothersome particularities" (3). By erasing the traces of the present in surrealist thought, Escalante claims, Paz not only places surrealism in an atemporal context; he responds productively to its protean nature: "Paz approaches surrealism from a *multiple perspective*, which at times can seem contradictory, and which in fact is so, but which for that very reason displays an admirable richness (of hues, of values) that cannot be reduced to a single phrase" (4).

Octavio Paz, Surrealism, and the Magic of the Word

> The oldest of the old follows behind us in our thinking and yet it comes to meet us.
> —Martin Heidegger

In his eulogizing essay "André Breton or the Quest of the Beginning," Paz observes that "there is a strong magical element in Breton's view of language. He not only made no distinction between magic and poetry; he also was convinced all his life that poetry was a force, a substance, an energy truly capable of changing reality" (50). Like Breton, Paz maintained a lifelong fascination with the connection between poetry and magic, and in his view surrealism represented the modern current of thought that clarified and resurrected this connection. Paz claims that with the advent of surrealism, "La actividad poética vuelve a ser una operación mágica" [Poetic activity becomes once again a magical operation] (*Obras* 2: 205). Like the French surrealists, Paz grounds his thought in the ancient belief in the *logos* as a power capable of transforming the world: "The poet speaks, and as he speaks, he *makes*. This making is above all a making of himself: poetry is not only self-knowledge but self-creation. The reader repeats the poet's experience of self-creation, and poetry becomes incarnate in history. Behind this idea lives the old belief in the power of words: poetry thought and lived as a magical operation destined to transmute reality . . . The conception of poetry as magic implies an aesthetic of action. Art ceases to be exclusively representation and contemplation; it becomes also an intervention in reality" (*Children of the Mire* 60). Questioning the Saussurian premise that language is an arbitrary convention linking signifier and signified, Paz returns to the archaic notion of the direct correspondence between words and things, a correspondence that allowed words to effect real changes in the material world.

In the history of Western thought, belief in a direct or unmediated relationship between words and the things they designated prevailed well into the Renaissance. Michel Foucault explains this belief in these terms: "In its original form, when it was given to men by God himself, language was an absolutely certain and transparent sign for things, because it resembled them. The names of things were lodged in the things they designated" (36). Since the seventeenth century, a more rational (and limiting) view of language has prevailed over the notion of a direct, unmediated power. The one notable exception to this rule (significant particularly in relation to surrealism) is Freud, who revived the notion of "word magic" within the framework of psychoanalysis: in his *Introductory Lectures*, Freud asserts that "words were originally magic and to this day words have retained much of their ancient magical power" (17). Taking these historical precedents into account, we can ask what Paz and the surrealists—following in a long line from the German Romantics through Baudelaire and Rimbaud—mean when they refer to poetic language as "the magical art." How should we understand the fact that the direct correspondence between word and thing is a belief that still gives meaning to modern poetics, having long ago been discredited by science?

In the following pages I will argue that Paz reformulates surrealist ideas, together with ideas gleaned from the Spanish-American *modernistas*, in order to craft them into a poetics in which verbal magic—ostensibly an irrational idea—is presented in ordered and logical terms. This reformulation is one of many attempts by Paz to conflate the otherwise distinct roles of poet and thinker. That is, he develops a sustained argument meant to convince the reader of the validity of its conclusion (that poetry can effectively "intervene in reality"), but he does so by recasting the rules of logical argument in mythopoetic terms. Paz bends the rules of logical discourse in two ways. First, he builds his argument on premises drawn from the same esoteric world view that he wishes to confirm: that of the world as a unified whole, from which he derives particular definitions of the key concepts *rhythm* and *analogy*. Second, he employs a rhetorical language that often reflects poetic values rather than those of discursive reason.

The obvious risk for the writer in this approach is that of confusing or failing to convince the reader. The reader confronts a risk as well: falling under the "spell" of the rhetoric and thus being falsely convinced. This is why Enrico Mario Santí speaks of *El arco y la lira* as "a dazzling text whose rhetoric—that powerful epigrammatic style so his own—blinds us to his argument" (112).[8] One could argue that much of Paz's essayistic prose succumbs to these risks and that its value as intellectual discourse is therefore diminished. But I would posit, to the contrary, that Paz's approach intentionally disorients (or rather, *re*-orients) the reader, initiating him or her not into the illogical but into a different form of logic. In this view, the argument of an essay works not by placing logic in an antithetical relationship to verbal magic but by enacting a synthesis of the two. The reader is then allowed to participate in the development of thought on both reflective and intuitive-affective levels.

Paz's strategy of crafting his essayistic prose simultaneously as nonmechanistic logic and as poetry, and thus of involving his reader in varied modes of apprehension, can be traced to two of his literary-philosophical masters. The first is Breton, for whom the very antirational stance of surrealism dictates such an approach. Breton does not eschew rational thought but rather describes its limitations for the modern age. "Under the pretense of civilization and progress," he claims, "we have managed to banish from the mind everything that may rightly or wrongly be termed superstition or fancy; forbidden is any kind of search for the truth which is not in conformance with accepted practices" (*Manifestoes* 10). Paz's second master in this context is Martin Heidegger, whose ideal philosopher was the *poet-thinker*. Heidegger's hybrid text "The Thinker as Poet" enacts this double role by philosophically exploring the theme of human thought in the form of lyric poetry. The fifth segment of this poem speaks of the "dangers [that] threaten thinking," that is, the obstacles that arise against the fullest use of the mind. In a seeming paradox, the poem tells us that "The good and thus wholesome / danger is the nighness of the singing / poet" (8). Heidegger suggests here that poetry—that is, song as opposed to discursive speech—does indeed present a danger for the cultivation of rational thought, but that this is a *healthy* danger. In other words, while poetry is not identical with the systematic construction of arguments that constitutes philosophy, when it is brought "nigh" to philosophy it can exert a positive influence over those arguments. Within this paradigm of the poet-thinker, the philosopher who also employs figurative language and the rhythms of song, Paz builds his argument about poetic magic.

The centerpiece of the theory of poetry in question is Paz's claim that the essence of magic is change—metamorphosis—and that in the modern world this change can be brought about by the subject's experience of a work of art: "Le pedimos al arte el secreto del cambio y buscamos en toda obra, cualesquiera que sean su época y su estilo, ese poder de metamorfosis que constituye la esencia del acto mágico" [We ask from art the secret of change, and we seek in any work, no matter what its period or its style, that power of metamorphosis that constitutes the essence of the magical act] (*Obras* 6: 253). It is important to note here that for Paz, change is fundamentally a communal act: the poem is the catalyst for transformation in both poet and reader, and from there it opens possibilities for change within the larger society. Poetry effects this change, Paz asserts, through two interrelated forces: analogy and rhythm, which I will discuss subsequently.

In 1955, André Breton sent a five-question survey to a number of contemporary artists and intellectuals on the theme of the relationship between art and magic. (Questionnaires of this sort were a common surrealist tactic for exploring cultural themes.) Breton published his findings from this inquiry in a book called *L'Art magique* in 1957: included are responses by Heidegger, Bataille, Lévi-Strauss, Carrington, Paalen, Caillois, Moro, and Péret, among numerous others. Paz's own answers to the questions, initially reproduced in Spanish under the title "Arte mágico" in the collection *Las peras del olmo* in that same year, constitute a remarkable text that serves to elucidate his aesthetic theories and their implicit or explicit ties to surrealism. I will discuss several of these answers in an attempt to organize Paz's ideas about "magical" language before considering the respective roles of analogy and rhythm in his poetics.

Breton's first question initially establishes a relationship between the ancient *mage*—wizard, shaman, or magician—and the modern artist, both of whom are concerned with "casting a spell over the universe"; he then asks his respondents to comment on the presence of such a relationship in their own work. Paz begins his answer by claiming that magical beliefs have been a part of human activity from the most remote origins of civilization to the modern age: "Secreta o abiertamente, la magia circula por el arte de todas las épocas" [Secretly or openly, magic circulates through the art of all eras] (*Obras* 6: 251). At this point, Paz introduces the all-important notion of *metamorphosis*—the capacity to cause real change in the world—which has always been the goal of magic and which applies particularly to the aesthetic experience: "Entre magia y arte hay un flujo y reflujo continuo: la poesía descubre correspondencias y analogías que no son extrañas a la magia, para producir una suerte de hechizo verbal; al mismo tiempo, poeta y lector se sirven del poema como de un talismán mágico, literalmente capaz de metamorfosearlos" [Between magic and art there is a continual ebb and flow: poetry discovers correspondences and analogies that are not alien to magic, in order to produce a kind of verbal enchantment; the poet and the reader simultaneously make use of the poem as they would a magic talisman that is literally capable of transforming them] (*Obras* 6: 251).[9] It is pertinent to recall at this juncture Rimbaud's belief in *l'alchemie du verbe*, as well as his insistence that *Il faut changer la vie*. Taken together, these ideas constitute the surrealist belief that language can bring about an actual shift in material reality. Paz's use of the adverb *literally* is significant in this context. He adopts this ancient belief in literal change but goes beyond (and even against) the surrealists to seek out rational causes for its validity.

Breton's second question contextualizes magic within the modern world. It asks whether magic—defined as the attempt to reconcile the powers of nature with those of human desire—can be "rehabilitated," and if so, whether such a rehabilitation could be dangerous. Given the potential for danger, Breton questions whether magic is even desirable (*Obras* 6: 252). Paz's response to this query evokes a monistic and animistic conception of the cosmos as "un todo en el que las partes están unidas por una corriente de secreta simpatía. El todo está animado y cada parte está en comunicación viviente con ese todo" [a whole in which all the parts are united by a current of secret sympathy. The whole is alive, and each part exists in living communication with that whole] (*Obras* 6: 252). He refers here to the fundamental premise of all esoteric or neo-Platonic thought, according to which the fragmented nature of the universe gives rise to beliefs and practices meant to recover a sense of wholeness. The "current of sympathy" that Paz refers to here is *secret* precisely because it is hidden from view for the uninitiated—and poetry is one fundamental way in which the hidden can be revealed.

It is in the nature of reality, Paz goes on to say, that all objects desire to transform themselves, to become *other*. The magical object brings this desire to the surface of consciousness: "*Nos invita a cambiar y a ser otros sin dejar de ser nosotros mismos*" [It invites us to change and to become "other" while still remaining ourselves] (*Obras* 6: 253). Paz intimates here that by recognizing the essential unity of the cosmos, we can dissolve at least temporarily the boundaries between subject and object, thus achieving the desired wholeness. This preoccupation with wholeness-through-otherness—and thus with the dissolution of the ego-bound self—becomes a touchstone of Paz's thought, linking twentieth-century structuralism to the esoteric worldview of the German and English romantics, and even to Buddhism.[10]

Paz's thought thus far appears to be operating on a highly abstract, suprahistorical level. But read differently, his responses can be seen as fully grounded in a concrete historical moment. When Paz speaks of a primordial sense of wholeness or belonging, he places it on a continuum between two extremes: solitude and community. Writing at the mid-point of the twentieth century, as a Mexican largely alienated from his own society and inhabiting a larger Western "wasteland," Paz sees solitude as the primary mode of modern existence: "En nuestro tiempo la nota predominante es la soledad. El hombre se siente cortado del fluir de la vida; y para compensar esta sensación de orfandad y mutilación acude a toda clase de sucedáneos: religiones políticas, embrutecedoras diversiones colectivas, promiscuidad sexual, guerra total, suicidio en masa, etcétera" [In our time the predominant note is solitude. Man feels cut off from the flow of life, and to compensate that feeling of orphanhood and mutilation, he turns to all sorts of substitutes: political religions, numbing collective amusements, sexual promiscuity, all-out war, mass suicide, and so forth] (*Obras* 6: 253). This is where Paz's claim for poetry as verbal magic descends from the plane of abstraction to that of action: his insistence on magical thinking is not only part of his defense of poetry but also a cry for a certain type of response to the lived realities of the Western world in the 1950s.

In answer to Breton's fourth question, Paz's conception of magic is channeled unequivocally into his aesthetic theory. Asked to explain his methods of examining or comprehending "a work of magical art," Paz upholds the value of the spectator's immediate response to a work of art, which he calls "la experiencia directa, desnuda y sin intermediarios" [the direct, naked experience, without intermediaries] (*Obras* 6: 255). This is because only in this presumably unmediated fashion can the listener or viewer experience the sense of *lo otro* that invites him to step outside of himself—though he may feel repulsed—and merge with that quality of otherness inherent in any work of art. The compressed syntax, the repetitiveness, and the affective rhetoric of the following description of that encounter brilliantly enact the synthesis of poet and thinker:

> Vértigo, extrañeza, reconocimiento. Horror y, simultáneamente, deseo de penetrar en aquello que de tal modo ataca y disgrega nuestra certidumbre de ser conciencia personal y autónoma. Los dos movimientos contrarios se reconcilian en el deseo de dar el "salto mortal" y alcanzar la "otra orilla." En suma, la gama de sensaciones—asombro, horror, vértigo, fascinación, caída en el objeto—evoca siempre la vieja imagen de la metamorfosis. (*Obras* 6: 255)
>
> [Vertigo, amazement, recognition. Horror and, simultaneously, the desire to penetrate into whatever so attacks and disintegrates our certainty of being a personal and autonomous consciousness. The two contrary movements are reconciled in the desire to make that "mortal leap" and to reach the "other shore." In sum, the range of sensations—awe, horror, vertigo, fascination, a collapse into the object—always evokes the ancient image of metamorphosis.]

In this response, Paz employs the surrealist notion that inspiration, like magic, is a metamorphosis that takes place within the individual: it is the leap beyond the ego-self that occurs precisely at the moment of contact with another object or being. In the realm of poetry, Paz argues that this magical encounter is triggered by two particular means: analogy and rhythm.

Poetry as Analogy and Rhythm

Foucault argues that until the end of the sixteenth century, human knowledge was based on the fundamental concept of *resemblance*: the universe was to be explained principally by means of tracing similarities between things. Of the four primary types of resemblance that he documents, Foucault gives preeminence to analogy: "Its power is immense, for the similitudes of which it treats are not the visible, substantial ones between things themselves; they need only be the more subtle resemblances of relations. Disencumbered thus, it can extend, from a single given point, to an endless number of relationships" (21). Ancient analogical thought—like magical thought more generally—is thus grounded in a monistic world view in which all things are linked to all other things, whether or not those links are perceptible through the ordinary senses. Within the modern Western literary tradition, the German and English romantics were responsible for a revival of this mode of thought, which was subsequently filtered through Baudelaire and the French symbolists, reaching the twentieth century via surrealism. Breton attempts to show the modern tenor of surrealism's approach by distinguishing between poetic and mystical analogy: "Poetic analogy has this in common with mystical analogy: it transgresses the rules of deduction to let the mind apprehend the interdependence of two objects of thought located on different planes. Logical thinking is incapable of establishing such a connection, which it deems a priori impossible. Poetic analogy is fundamentally different from mystical analogy in that it in no way presupposes the existence of an invisible universe that, from beyond the veil of the visible world, is trying to reveal itself" (*Free Rein* 105). Breton retains the basic function of analogy—to connect two seemingly disparate objects of thought—but insists that modern (poetic) analogy reveals connections between objects located in empirical reality. This explanation distances the surrealist use of analogy from the neo-Platonic dictum of "As above, so below," which presupposed a world beyond human perception.

In the context of the present study, it is important to recognize that Octavio Paz arrived at his conceptions of analogy (and of verbal magic in general) through these channels, but also through his reading and systematic study of the early twentieth-century Spanish-American *modernistas*, especially Rubén Darío. The search of the romantic and symbolist writers, says Cathy Jrade, "led them to discover the analogical vision of esoteric doctrine. Modernism is heir to these movements" (9). For Darío, "If the universe is one harmonious extension of God and both individuals and the universe are made in God's image, all the elements of creation are analogous and correspond to each other; they are signs to be 'read' and deciphered" (Jrade 18). In the history of modernist criticism, it was Paz himself who first clearly identified Darío's debt to the esoteric traditions; in turn, Darío's poetic theories heavily influenced Paz's own.[11] In his discussion of Darío's *Prosas profanas*, Paz cites a fundamental tenet of analogical thought: "Language is a magic double of the cosmos" (*Siren* 37). "Language" in this context is not ordinary discursive speech but poetry, since "through poetry, language recovers its original being, becomes music again" (*Siren* 37). In short, Paz found in Darío both a theorist who reformulated certain conceptions that fascinated the younger writer (particularly that of analogical thought) and a poet who put a particularly Hispanic lyrical stamp on that thought.

Paz goes so far as to call analogy "the true religion of modern poetry, from Romanticism to Surrealism" (*Children of the Mire* 55). In the introduction to *The Bow and the Lyre*, he uses overtly poetic language to convey his definition of analogy: "Analogy: the poem is a shell that echoes the music of the world, and meters and rhymes are merely correspondences, echoes, of the universal harmony" (4). The lexicon Paz uses here could have been borrowed directly from Swedenborg, Novalis, Baudelaire, or Darío: *analogy, the music of the world, rhymes, correspondences, universal harmony*; taken together, these terms point unerringly to a neo-Platonic world view. What concerns Paz in this set of tropes is poetry, and he calls our attention to it not by talking about poetry but by creating it. The metaphor *poem = shell* (*caracol* in the original) conjures up for the reader the image of a small, closed-yet-open space whose spiral shape creates tonal resonances when breath or wind is blown into it. The conch shell can literally produce music; its emptiness provides a space to be filled; its location suggests the primordial, infinite, living space of the sea, and so forth: in "defining" analogy, Paz has chosen a rich poetic image that sets the reader's imagination to work. Reading Paz's definition, we come to understand analogy by experiencing it.

What is the relationship between analogy and rhythm, Paz's other key concept for understanding verbal magic? Paz claims in a double aphorism that "Analogy is the poet's language. Analogy is rhythm" (*Bow* 69). The equation *analogy = rhythm* leads the reader to consider rhythm not in its ordinary sense, as the regular recurrence of verbal or musical beats, but as an actual means of conceiving reality. Paz in fact straightforwardly discounts the conventional acceptance of the word *rhythm*, claiming that "rhythm is not measure: it is a vision of the world" (*Bow* 47). The explanation for this lies within a broad conception of language in which words, phrases, and verbal associations engage in a kind of magnetic attraction and repulsion, converging and dispersing according to certain rhythmic principles (*Bow* 42). In fact, Paz defines "the poem" metaphorically as "a magnetic object, a secret meeting place of many opposing forces" (*Bow* 14). For the ordinary user of language, the dynamic of attraction and repulsion among words occurs beyond conscious control, occasioning sometimes surprising results. The poet, however, is the conscious manipulator of language who—like the magician—aims *deliberately* to reproduce the "secret" rhythm that will give him power over words. To a marked degree, poetic creation consists "in this voluntary utilization of rhythm as an agent of seduction" (*Bow* 42). Notably, this conception of the poet's work as conscious, voluntary, and deliberate strays from the original surrealist ideal of "pure psychic automatism." Paz is exploring a middle ground between irrational, hidden, unconscious linguistic forces and the writer's conscious discovery and manipulation of them. In doing so, he is signaling a direction taken by virtually all post-1950 Latin American writers associated with surrealism.

The "seduction" made possible by rhythmic forces may end with the listener or reader, but it begins with the words themselves. Through this line of thinking Paz arrives at a pseudomagical definition of the poem: "Although the poem is not an enchantment or conjuration, in the manner of spells and sortileges the poet awakens the secret powers of language. The poet bewitches the language by means of rhythm. One image sprouts from another. Thus, the predominant function of rhythm distinguishes the poem from all other literary forms. The poem is a mass of phases, a verbal order, founded on rhythm" (*Bow* 45). What is surprising here is the notion that "the poet bewitches language," an assertion related to the earlier claim that the poet "seduces" words (*Bow* 42). In marked contrast to the notion of poetry as craft, as a conscious making or *poiēsis*, this conception speaks to the poet's ability to harness irrational powers. Poetry is thus freed from any sort of formal or structural constraint: even prose or so-called ordinary speech can be poetry if it works primarily as rhythm.

An excellent example of the "seductive" or magical properties of Paz's prose can be found in his 1954 lecture-essay "El surrealismo," in which he responds to the common charge that surrealism had become a corpse: "Pero el cadáver estaba vivo. Tan vivo, que ha saltado de su fosa y se ha presentado de nuevo ante nosotros, con su misma cara terrible de inocente, cara de tormenta súbita, cara de incendio, cara y figura de hada en medio del bosque encantado" [But the corpse was alive. So alive that it has leapt from its grave and has appeared again among us, with the same terrible face of innocence, face of sudden storms, face of fire, face and form of a fairy in the middle of the enchanted forest] (*Obras* 2: 203). Paz's prose here is highly lyrical and evocative both in its use of the central trope of the cadaver—an effective visual, even dramatic analogy—and in its anaphoristic structure. The passage thus works rhythmically in the most immediate sense of pulsating syllables linked by assonance: *cara/cara/cara/hada/encantado*. But it also works in the broader sense of "one image sprouting from another," with the face of the cadaver suggesting first storms, then fire, and then unexpectedly, a fairy in a forest.

In the cosmic sense in which Paz conceives of rhythm, the most fundamental and archetypal rhythm involves a movement between opposites: opening-closing, inhaling-exhaling, emptiness-fullness, yin-yang, self-other, and so forth. Jrade calls this movement a "cosmic pulse" and underscores its importance to the Spanish-American *modernistas*, suggesting that its origins may lie in the Plotinist image of emanation that enjoyed wide circulation among the romantics (19). Here Paz's thinking aligns him directly not only with the *modernistas* but with the surrealists. In "El surrealismo" he ties ancient beliefs, esoteric thought, and poetry together in a formulation based on the rhythmic reconciliation of opposites: "Como lo creían los antiguos, y lo han sostenido siempre los poetas y la tradición oculta, el universo está compuesto por contrarios que se unen y separan conforme a cierto ritmo secreto. El conocimiento poético—la imaginación, la facultad productora de imágenes en cuyo seno los contrarios se reconcilian—nos deja vislumbrar la analogía cósmica" [As the ancients believed, and as poets and the occult tradition have always maintained, the universe is composed of contraries that merge and separate according to a certain secret rhythm. Poetic knowledge—the imagination, the faculty that produces images in whose heart opposites are reconciled—allows us to glimpse the cosmic analogy] (*Obras* 2: 212–13). The Bretonian ideal of finding the point in the mind at which all perceived contradictions are reconciled becomes for Paz a matter of engaging fundamental rhythms.

Paz's explanation of verbal magic by way of rhythm and analogy returns us to the question at the center of his aesthetic explorations: How can poetry truly change reality? As we have seen, Paz's answers to Breton's questionnaire led him to the conclusion that the "direct" experience of a work of art allows the spectator to unfold outward from an enclosed subjectivity toward contact with *lo otro*, which Paz sees as a fundamental desire of the self. This movement cannot occur, he insists, within quotidian time; rather, a shift into what he calls archetypal or mythical time must occur, since this is a realm that allows both the past and the present to be "charged with possibilities" (*Bow* 51). Stated more simply, when one creates, reads, or listens to a poem, its rhythm produces a necessary change in the subject's perception of time. Poetic practice liberates consciousness by returning it to primordial time: "To set thought free, to wander, is to return to rhythm; reasons are transformed into correspondences, syllogisms into analogies, and the intellectual march into a flow of images" (*Bow* 57). Paz draws directly from surrealism as he reiterates the call to "set thought free" in order to reach a deeper level of consciousness, which for him is a return to rhythm. In order to complete this portrait of the poet-as-thinker, I will briefly trace certain ways in which "reasons are transformed into correspondences" in Paz's own lyrical work.

The Poet-Thinker at Work

>. . . cada palabra palpita
>
>—Paz, "Viento entero"

If Paz directly enacts the concepts of analogy and rhythm in the language of his essays, such enactments are intensified in his poetry. "Poetry is one of the manifestations of analogy," he claims in *The Children of the Mire*; "rhymes and alliterations, metaphors and metonymies are modes of operation in analogical thought" (56). Paz put these modes into play in every poem he wrote, but in certain poems he also thematized the concepts of analogy and rhythm, allowing the reader to experience these forces on multiple levels. The most striking example of a poem built around the idea of analogy is "Noche en claro," a poem that Paz dedicated to Breton and Péret. The title of the poem has been translated by Eliot Weinberger as "Sleepless Night," but it also evokes the image of a clear, starry night, as well as the phrase "pasado en claro," meaning "clean copy." The poem recalls, in a mixture of anecdote and lyrical meditation, an autumn night in 1959 in which the three poets met in a Paris café and then wandered together through the streets of the city. This long poem masterfully textualizes Paz's resurrection of the ancient analogy of the universe as text.

In the first lines of "Noche en claro," the sight of a prostitute disappearing into "a greenish wall that closed behind her" prompts the speaker to reflect:

Todo es puerta
basta la leve presión de un pensamiento
Algo se prepara (*Obras* 11: 299)

[Everything is a door / you only need the light push of a thought / Something is going to happen]

In three brief lines, Paz creates a scene that embodies the surrealist notion of objective chance: an opening door suggests an imminent encounter with the unexpected. (The presence of a prostitute suggests particularly erotic possibilities.) The insistent alliteration of the /p/ in these lines (puerta / presión / pensamiento / prepara) pushes the reader forward in anticipation of the "something" that is about to happen. The sense of charged anticipation is resolved in the following lines: "Se abrió el minuto en dos / leí signos en la frente de ese instante" [The minute opened out, becoming two / I read signs on the face of that instant] (*Obras* 11: 299). When the minute—the emblem of ordinary measured time—splits into two, it creates its other or double, suggesting a return to the mythical or archetypal time of which Paz speaks in *The Bow and The Lyre*. Within this mythical temporal dimension, the speaker finds that time itself becomes a text to be deciphered ("leí signos").

But "Noche en claro" is situated in postwar Paris, where archetypal time can exist only in constant tension with profane or historical time. The latter is time marked in the poem with human measure—tragically—as "este mismo año enfermo / fruto fantasma que resbala entre las manos del siglo / año de miedo tiempo de susurro y mutilación" [this same sick year / phantom fruit slipping between the hands of the century / year of fear time of whispering and mutilation] (*Obras* 11: 300). Instead of mythical time in which the eternal return can provide meaning, postwar Europe represents a time of sterile repetition: "El tiempo daba vueltas y vueltas y no pasaba / no pasaba nada sino el tiempo que pasa y regresa y no pasa" [Time turned and turned and did not move / nothing moved but time that moves and returns and does not move] (*Obras* 11: 300). Stagnation is represented textually in this passage by the reiteration of the words *tiempo, vueltas, pasaba,* and *pasa*—as if the poet's utterance keeps stumbling on these terms and is unable to move forward.

A significant shift occurs at this point in the poem: the speaker recalls seeing a girl whose jacket displayed the image of an open hand with the letters L-O-V-E written on the fingers. In response to this memory he repeats the phrase "Todo es puerta / todo es puente" [Everything is a door / everything is a bridge] (*Obras* 11: 301). The three poets, walking along the banks of the Seine, suddenly see the entire city transformed into a text to be read:

> La noche se abre
>   mano inmensa
> constelación de signos
> escritura silencio que canta
> siglos generaciones eras
> sílabas que alguien dice
> palabras que alguien oye
> pórticos de pilares transparentes
> ecos llamadas señas laberintos
> Parpadea el instante y dice algo
> escucha abre los ojos ciérralos
> la marea se levanta
>   Algo se prepara . . . (*Obras* 11: 301)

[The night opens / an immense hand / constellation of signs / written silence that sings / centuries generations epochs / syllables that someone speaks / words that someone hears / porticoes of transparent pillars / echoes calls signs labyrinths / The moment blinks and says something / listen open your eyes close them / the tide is rising / Something is going to happen . . .]

The speaker's ability to interpret the signs of the urban night allows him synesthetically to *hear* the cosmic writing, and what he hears is true communication: syllables that are spoken are actually words that someone hears. Communication is also suggested by the fact that time itself (the moment) "says something." At this point the poem reiterates the motif of imminence with which it opened: "Algo se prepara."

In its entirety, "Noche en claro" (of which I have cited only brief segments) stands as a poetic enactment of Paz's understanding of "the magic of the word." The poem revolves around the central analogy of the universe as text, allowing the speaker to meditate on the various signs that appear to the wakeful consciousness. As noted above, the title "Noche en claro" alludes literally to a *clear* night, a clean slate on which meanings can be revealed. These meanings operate on the level of metaphor, as the central analogy unwinds into a revolving constellation of signs (to borrow one of Paz's own key images): "La ciudad se abre como un corazón / como un higo la flor que es fruto" [The city opens like a heart / like a fig the flower that is fruit] (*Obras* 11: 299). Paz's conviction that the world is a set of interconnected signs is made manifest in these multi-tiered metaphors. Finally, rhythm is enacted in the poem through the insistent use of poetic devices such as alliteration, assonance, and rhyme, but also in the broader sense given by Paz, that of the pulsing of attraction and dispersion. This is why the poem insists on the act of opening, a persistent counteraction to the rigidities of time that "turned around and around and did not move." The poem narrates a metamorphosis that occurs in the speaker's consciousness as the reality of quotidian time in a city recently devastated by war—"pila de años muertos y escupidos" [pile of years, dead and spat out]—is transformed by the presence of the beloved into an awareness of mythic time. Both time as eternal recurrence and the regenerative energies of erotic union are encapsulated in the final lines of the poem:

> Ciudad Mujer Presencia
> aquí se acaba el tiempo
> aquí comienza (*Obras* 11: 303)

[City Woman Presence / here time ends / here it begins]

My intent in this chapter has been to show how Octavio Paz, drawing on certain strains of esoteric thought revived by surrealism in the twentieth century, appropriates the archaic notion that words can exist in an unmediated connection to things, and that this connection allows for words to bring about change in the material world, which is also the goal of magic. As he explores this notion in his critical prose, Paz defends the power of the poetic word. Rather than representing an unreflective, simplistic return to ideas of language that have been debunked by modern anthropology and linguistics, Paz's explanations of analogy and rhythm offer a reasoned account of the seemingly irrational claim that poetry can truly alter reality. Nevertheless, Paz builds his arguments on assumed premises that he does not invite his reader to question, such as the view of the cosmos as an whole whose parts seek reintegration or the "natural" desire of the subject to fuse with the object. Furthermore, he explicates the functions of poetry by employing rhetoric that is in some cases highly metaphorical and lyrical. Both these methods of reasoning may leave the reader enchanted by his style but perplexed or unconvinced by his ideas.

How then are we to read Paz? In his elegy for Breton, Paz states that "he was not a philosopher but a great poet" ("André Breton" 48). By making this distinction, Paz invites us to read all of Breton, including his numerous theoretical pieces, as poetry—that is, to approach them with a different set of expectations than those we normally bring to bear on theoretical prose. Conceiving of thought in this way was in fact one of the great projects of surrealism, which was intended to establish poetry as a new (or resurrected) path to knowledge. In adopting this belief, Paz positions himself as a writer somewhere on the continuum between poet and philosopher, and he thus asks of his readers a willingness to travel that continuum with him. To read in this way is, in Heidegger's words, to "lead thinking into a dialogue with poetry" or to "inquire poetically" (96). In sum, a sober and mindful approach to Paz's critical prose—in this case, to his development of the concept of poetry as magic—will take into account what he calls "the intellectual march transformed into a flow of images" (*Bow* 57). It will allow for an apprehension of ideas through discursive reason (the careful construction of plausible arguments) but also through the more immediate and affective responses we normally reserve for poetry.

Conclusion

The story of surrealism in Mexico, in sum, is one of great paradoxes. In the period of the 1930s and 1940s, Europeans found Mexico to be the quintessential surrealist country, while most Mexicans adopted an attitude of resistance. Octavio Paz embodies yet another paradox: widely recognized as surrealism's greatest advocate and practitioner in Spanish American literature, he did not succeed in opening new paths for surrealism in his own country. When Paz returned home in 1953, having found in surrealism an answer to his most profound ethical dilemmas and a channel for his creative energies, the "battle of surrealism" began again. In the words of José Emilio Pacheco, this facet of the accepted cultural narrative in the 1950s is that of "a great poet corrupted by European decadence who returns to his country and spreads the virus of surrealism to the new generation" (50). Literary historians agree that the grandeur of Paz's work in the 1950s and 1960s served to silence his critics.

But while the generation of writers growing up in Paz's shadow found in surrealism one of many possible modes of poetic expression, none would embrace it as fully as he had. The one possible exception to this rule is Marco Antonio Montes de Oca (1932–2009), whose work is known for its dynamic, fluid, and often surprising imagery and its unexpected metaphors. In the words of Evodio Escalante, "[Montes de Oca's] extravagant writing, overloaded with images, is the closest thing to surrealism that could have occurred in Mexico, where it was always held in a straightjacket" (personal correspondence). Looking beyond Mexico, however, it is possible to argue that Octavio Paz initiated a positive shift in surrealism from an international standpoint. As Michael Richardson observes, Paz's work "had considerable impact in the movement of surrealism away from the critique of Western culture towards a concern with locating new values, going beyond the West whilst seeking out essential qualities of human becoming in the experience of the West itself" (24). In the broad scope of his intellectual and creative work, Paz explains, defends, and poetically enacts the core values of surrealism—its emphasis on poetry as an epistemological and ethical approach to life and its insistence on human liberty—values that would constitute the more widespread and longstanding legacy of surrealism in Latin America and elsewhere.

Conclusion
"Like a River"

Late in life, Philippe Soupault was interviewed by a group of students who were curious to hear his memories of the surrealist movement in its early years. Part of his response was an assertion of surrealism's lasting significance: "Surrealism is after all not a literary school or a religion; it is the expression of an attitude, a state of mind and especially an open indication of freedom. All the formulas, definitions, and masks that people have tried to impose on it have not been able to diminish its power. Historically, we could claim that it has got lost in the sands; but, like a river, its subterranean bed continues to cut deep" (22). The values that Soupault points to in his commentary are reflected in the story of Latin American surrealism that I have recounted in *Breton's Ghost*. With few exceptions, the writers associated with the movement in this region—particularly those in its later incarnations—privilege the view of surrealism as an attitude toward life, an ethical orientation.

Given that there is no set formula for identifying a surrealist text, much less a certain *actitud vital* on the part of a writer, I have relied heavily on the testimonies of the writers themselves and of their traveling companions on "the road to the absolute" (to borrow Anna Balakian's title phrase). At the same time, I have attempted to follow certain traces in the texts produced by these writers as evidence of a complex surrealist poetics that may or may not corroborate the writers' own perceptions. I owe my most memorable moments in the process of writing this book to these poetic texts, which, in true surrealist fashion, revealed time and again something that I had not expected to find.

Discussions of surrealism that take place at any point subsequent to the Second World War invariably revert to the question of its endurance as a movement. In fact, the charge that surrealism had turned into a *cadavre* was initially leveled in 1929, a mere five years after the appearance of the first surrealist manifesto. Thereafter, both detractors and supporters of the movement often reiterated the metaphor of the corpse, which they found to be either existing in various states of decomposition or dancing happily on its grave. Soupault employs instead a geographical metaphor that I find apt for addressing the question of surrealism's status as it evolved over time. It is not difficult to affirm that as a historical movement—the basis for group activities, proclamations, and publications—surrealism was at the height of its powers between 1924 and 1941. After the end of World War II, with the return of André Breton to France, the movement gained new followers and found new ways to insert itself into the cultural life of France and other European countries. But it was no longer considered by most to reflect the historical realities of the day. In this sense, and in terms of surrealism's initial revolutionary impulses and the sociopolitical transformations they sought to bring about, the movement must be termed a relative failure. Breton eventually called for the "occultation" of surrealism: he seemed to understand that the movement must take on a different character, one less directed toward an open revolt against bourgeois existence and more concerned with myth, archetype, and "universal" human values. Thus Breton's term "occultation" coincides to a certain degree with Soupault's: after 1945, surrealism gradually sunk underground, became hidden, and "got lost in the sands," although this has not been viewed as a necessarily negative development.

The primary argument of *Breton's Ghost* is that the currents of surrealism continued to run "like a river"—above ground or in subterranean channels—long into the second half of the twentieth century, on a continent several thousand miles from Europe. I have suggested that this occurred, first, because of the dynamic and even contradictory nature of surrealism in its initial conception. In contrast to earlier avant-garde movements, surrealism defined itself from the beginning as a revolt of the spirit, an attitude toward life that valued human liberty above all, and an aesthetic practice (open to all) that sought nothing less than to reveal the hidden contents of the psyche. This broad orientation opened the movement to the charge that virtually any act of the imagination, any revolt against social norms, might be labeled surrealist. But the efforts of Breton and others to place certain defining limits on the movement were successful, overall. As a result, the surrealism to which Latin American writers were exposed was both a closed and an open system: sufficiently closed to allow for a set of shared principles, yet sufficiently open to allow for a creative reimagining and evolution.

This reimagined surrealism in Latin America acknowledges many obvious parallels to the European movement, but there are numerous tangential and divergent paths as well. In the period from 1928 to approximately 1950, Aldo Pellegrini's group in Argentina, the Mandrágora group in Chile, and the Peruvian poets Xavier Abril, Emilio Adolfo Westphalen, and César Moro proclaimed and practiced a more or less orthodox surrealism. Although their poetry carries a markedly individual stamp (particularly in the case of Moro), their manifestos often sound like translations into Spanish of texts by Breton, Soupault, or Aragon. These early movements, faced with indifference or hostility in the bourgeois societies of Buenos Aires, Santiago, or Lima (societies to which the surrealists themselves maintained complicated ties), exercised a limited impact on their immediate cultural milieu and faded rather quickly from view. As I have shown, however, these movements laid the groundwork for the more original and more fully realized developments that followed.

From 1950 forward a noticeable shift occurred: surrealism in Argentina and Chile became a force to be reckoned with, both in literary-artistic journals and in the work of individual writers. It is in this later unfolding that noticeable variances from European surrealism appeared, due in part to geographical differences but in greater part, I believe, to the question of temporal lag. Put simply, the "second-wave" surrealists came of age in the wake of the historical surrealist movement. With the possible exception of Enrique Molina in Argentina, whose approach in his editorial work at is still that of a defiant orthodoxy, the Latin American writers born around the time of surrealism's inception in Europe (or later) occupy a necessarily belated position. In this position they absorbed two or more decades of Continental responses to surrealism, to which they added their own critiques and their own forms of creative appropriation.

We have direct and indirect testimonies of this belatedness. Julio Llinás, who arrived in Paris from Buenos Aires in 1952, eyes wide with enthusiasm for surrealist ideas and a reverent attitude toward its founder, was met with disillusion. "I had definitely arrived late for everything," he states flatly in a letter to Aldo Pellegrini (qtd. in Giunta 71). Octavio Paz, speaking in 1991 of his attendance at surrealist gatherings in Paris cafés in late 1950s, recalls, "More than once I told myself that I had arrived there twenty years late" (*Estrella* 11). In a similar vein, César Aira claims that his compatriot Alejandra Pizarnik, nourished on a set of readings that culminated with the surrealists, "was of that class of writers who come after all the books have been written, and who know it" (80). There is clearly a tone of disappointment, of dispiritedness, in each of these statements.

To arrive belatedly, however, is not necessarily to be diminished in one's creative capacity. Paz, after recognizing that the surrealist Paris of the 1950s was no longer that of the 1920s and 1930s, still holds out an affirmation: "But the ember of the great bonfire that was surrealism still heated my bones and fired my imagination" (*Estrella* 11). Aira takes account of Pizarnik's belated position yet goes on to assert that surrealism in Argentina had never in fact constituted anything but an afterlife—and that in this very quality lay its strength. I cite at length from Aira because his observations speak directly to the arguments of my study:

> When Alejandra Pizarnik began to write in the 1950s, everyone had given surrealism up for dead (which was nothing new). It was natural that a poet shaped as she was in surrealist tastes would exploit the methods of the dead school, as someone would use a watch that had belonged to a dead relative. Once the

ideology of these methods has dissipated, its mechanisms can serve to make new creations; that is, automatic writing can be used to make good poetry—which was exactly the opposite of what the surrealists had proposed. But the surrealists had done the same: the opposite of what they proposed. It was because of this internal contradiction that surrealism was dead from the very start (it was its own myth of origins), and yet it assured itself a long—and always posthumous—life. (*Pizarnik* 14)

Drawing from Walter Benjamin's notion of the "afterlife" of a work of art, Aira ostensibly begins by placing himself in the camp of those who had declared surrealism's early death. And yet, belated critic that he is, Aira goes beyond that clichéd position to declare that surrealism always was in effect a ghost of the living being that it had imagined itself to be. He observes that the afterlife of surrealism (in Argentina, if not elsewhere) constituted a new and extended period of productivity. The value of Aira's argument lies, I believe, in the dialectic it implies: if at a given point surrealism is neither dead nor still alive, then it may exist in some third form that is the synthesis of the previous two. In brief, the shapes of second-wave or neosurrealism, especially those that arose in historical contexts different from those of early twentieth-century Europe, are formed in full consciousness of the diminished nature of the original French movement, and in that awareness they find new and evolving sources of creativity.

* * *

What forms did this afterlife take? To answer this question, let us begin by reconsidering the characteristics that Latin American writers adopted and carried forward virtually unchanged from early conceptualizations of surrealism. I would argue that the first of these is a purely affective quality: the initial excitement of the Parisian movement of the 1920s was relived in parts of Latin America decades after it had been all but extinguished in Europe. The Chilean poet Enrique Gómez-Correa wrote in 1943: "Yo me siento poseído por el entusiasmo" [I feel possessed by enthusiasm], and his statement is symptomatic of the fervor felt by many (de Mussy 209). Surrealism's call to revolt and the methods that promised new revelations spoke powerfully to certain writers caught in the dead zone into which much Latin American literature had fallen in the early twentieth century and from which the experiments of the earlier avant-garde had not been able to free it.

Apart from a spirit of enthusiasm, surrealism introduced to many Latin American writers what Aira calls a "system of readings" that began with the romantics, wound its way through Baudelaire, Rimbaud, Lautréamont, and Mallarmé, and culminated with Breton's group (*Pizarnik* 14). On the list of "required reading" in this tradition were not only the poets noted above but also important works of literary history and criticism such as Marcel Raymond's *From Baudelaire to Surrealism* (1933), Albert Béguin's *L'Âme romantique et le Rêve* (1939), Maurice Nadeau's *History of Surrealism* (1944), and later, Octavio Paz's *The Bow and the Lyre* (1956) and *The Children of the Mire* (1974).

Finally, I would argue that what Paz calls the "triple axis" of themes emerging from French surrealism—love, liberty, and poetry—reappeared in the work of many Latin American writers. It is the rallying cry of surrealist journals such as *Que*, *Mandrágora*, and *A Partir de Cero*, and it emerges virtually intact even in the later work of Gonzalo Rojas and Octavio Paz. The basic premise underlying this thematic triad is that poetry is an activity of spirit, and its corollary is the belief that life must be lived as poetry. This belief leads Aldo Pellegrini to speak of "el vivir maravilloso" [living marvelously] (qtd. in Poblete Araya 119), which for Alejandra Pizarnik meant life lived as literature, a conscious decision to dedicate oneself wholly to the enterprise of words. In the case of Gonzalo Rojas, it meant something entirely different: Rojas discovered the poetic life as he taught miners in northern Chile to read. No matter what the interpretation, we find countless instances of poets referring to poetry as a praxis of life. Love—particularly erotic union—and liberty in all its imaginable forms are thematically intertwined with the exaltation of poetry as lived experience.

* * *

The points enumerated above suggest that surrealism's "leap across the pond" reproduced many characteristics of the Parisian movement in rather orthodox ways. This was true in particular of the early groups in Argentina and Chile, although even in these cases certain points of divergence are perceptible. But with time, the consciousness of belatedness produced a growing need for new models in Latin America, ones that could respond to the particular tensions of life in those countries. As a result, a marked cultural dissonance developed between the surrealist groups of the 1920s and 1930s and the next generation of writers—a dissonance that nevertheless proved productive. Writers from the 1950s onward typically profess their distance both from the European movement and from the activities of the early groups in their countries of origin, even articulating a disdain for those groups' apparently facile reproduction of French surrealism. The result was a conscious search for originality that produced eclectic bodies of work such as that of Gonzalo Rojas or even the deliberately antilyrical poetry of Nicanor Parra, which displays significant points of contact with surrealism even as it professes a wholly different approach.

One notable development after mid-century was that collective activity dissolved almost entirely. With the exception of the groups loosely formed around the surrealist-affiliated journals in Buenos Aires in the 1950s, surrealism was transformed into a set of attitudes and practices adopted by individual writers. As a result, the revolutionary social or political ideals of the original movement were lost: surrealism was no longer seen as a way to shake the foundations of a rigid society or bring about a broad shift in consciousness.[1] The desire for social or political revolt was replaced by a desire for inner transformation. In 1973, Paz decries "the attempt to amputate from surrealism its critical and subversive dimension" (*Obras* 6: 304). But he also acknowledges the shift from exterior to interior spheres: "An operation capable of changing the world, poetic activity is revolutionary by nature; a spiritual exercise, it is a means of interior liberation" (*Bow* 3). Although there was a clear sense of drawback from the ideal of changing the world to the hope of transforming a single human spirit, this hope remained a powerful force for many writers.

French surrealism had been born out of a perception of cultural exhaustion in Europe, and one of its major targets had been literature itself. "Literature," says Breton in the first manifesto, "is one of the saddest roads that leads to everything" (*Manifestoes* 29). After the initial Dada-inspired revolts of the first years, however, surrealism experienced a gradual shift away from cultural subversion and toward aesthetic vision. This shift is widely discussed and debated: it is cited alternately as evidence of the failure of surrealist ideals and evidence of its enduring value. I suspect it to be some of both. But the important assertion to be made for our present purposes is that in the historically younger countries of Latin American, where a national literary corpus was still in the process of being formed and the sense of exhaustion had not taken hold, the enthusiasm for surrealism was channeled into the building of new roads in art and literature. In short, what had begun as a radical shift away from literature and art developed primarily into a new literary and artistic modality.

The fulcrum of that shift is creative automatism. In Chapter 1, I discussed the significance of techniques such as automatic writing, dream narratives, and games such as the "exquisite cadaver"—as well as the problems that arose with these techniques and the criticisms that were leveled against them. Here is yet another instance of the belated position of Latin American writers: they witnessed the initial fervor associated with automatism but were simultaneously exposed to its numerous critiques. As a result, pure automatic techniques have been generally rejected by these writers. In direct opposition to the original conception of automatism, which valued the process over the product, they have sought through modulated means to obtain the *results* of automatic writing. The "controlled automatism" practiced by many of the writers examined in this study is explained in incisive terms by Gonzalo Rojas, who claims that "the poetic word cannot arise from formlessness, but rather from that which has form, and the form . . . implies a reflective attitude, it implies clarity. As

Baudelaire stated, the intoxication of that impulse must be met with control, with rigor, that is, with lucidity" (Busto Ogden 679). Rojas captures the creative tension of controlled automatism by highlighting both the intoxication felt by the poet when language is allowed to flow freely and the clarity of mind necessary to create form—that is, art and literature—out of formlessness.

The practice of controlled automatism has led to the widespread use of the surrealist image in a variety of texts, even those produced by writers with no ostensible ties to surrealism. The oneiric image itself, I would argue, became surrealism's most substantive contribution to twentieth-century poetics in Latin America. As Stefan Baciu observes in the introduction to his anthology of Latin American poetry, "It becomes a matter of something broader and deeper: a certain surrealist language, images used by poets of that movement, frequent oneiric visions, poetic forms that appear unconnected but that in reality obey a certain almost secret technique: all of this can be found in Latin American poetry since 1950, and this occurrence represents a notable leap forward" (xxxviii). I underscore Baciu's assessment of surrealism's contribution to poetic language overall: in Latin America, surrealism built on the dynamism and sensory richness first introduced by the *modernistas* and then expanded on by the early *vanguardistas*. Unlocking the image from all need for rational locution proved vital in the development of a truly modern poetics.

In Chapter 2, I suggested the metaphor of the communicating vessels (a metaphor Breton uses to speak of the fluid exchange between dream and waking consciousness) as a way of addressing the question of Latin American surrealism's relationship to its European origins. In that chapter and others, I have considered the question of cultural imperialism with regard to surrealism, both in the way many Europeans branded Latin America as a quintessentially surrealist site and in the way Latin Americans appropriated or "cannibalized" the European-born movement. In the first instance, the evidence presented in Chapter 6 and elsewhere affirms the place of Latin America as a source of creative inspiration for many European surrealists. Such inspiration depended, however, on a projected imaginary that often, in spite of the surrealists' well-intentioned attempts at cultural relativism, resulted in a distorted, reductive, or mythified view of the "object" in question.

Regarding the reception of surrealism by Latin Americans, Valentín Ferdinán voices a concern shared by others when he concludes that this movement and its ideals were "fundamentally inadaptable" to Latin American social and political realities (73) and that in the literary sphere, surrealist influence produced only writers of lesser stature. In answer to this concern, the texts examined in *Breton's Ghost* reveal the multiple ways in which Latin American writers have practiced a creative reconfiguration of French surrealism. The work of César Moro, Enrique Molina, Olga Orozco, Alejandra Pizarnik, Gonzalo Rojas, Nicanor Parra, and

Octavio Paz, among numerous others, was profoundly and productively shaped by the techniques of surrealism and by its revolutionary spirit. One important point made by this study is that surrealism in Latin American literature is not a fixed entity but an evolutionary process: from Aldo Pellegrini to Octavio Paz, the road is long and the scenery ever changing. What may have begun as a cultural importation from Europe developed into a highly individual poetics that in its turn has influenced writers across the Americas and (in the case of Paz, at least) in Europe.

Since the 1970s, surrealism has become virtually impossible to identify as a discrete literary philosophy or aesthetic practice, having been absorbed, in Latin America as elsewhere, into the cultural mainstream. In 1992, the Mexican critic Sandro Cohen observed that the notion of distinct literary schools had lost all validity. "In a good poem written in 1990, a Renaissance form can coexist with a coloquial tone that employs surrealist images with an oriental touch, and no one is surprised" (22). Cohen's remark corroborates my earlier observation that the surrealist image constitutes the most enduring legacy of Breton's movement as it expanded beyond its temporal and geographical frontiers. Behind the widespread use of this type of image, I would add by way of conclusion, lies the surrealist sense of the marvelous contained in everyday reality, an alternative way of *seeing* that endures beyond any consideration of literary schools or artistic influences. The last word on this subject I leave to Octavio Paz, who in a conversation with Breton in 1966 conjectured, "I have no idea what the future of the surrealist group will be; I am certain, however, that the current that has flowed from German romanticism and Blake to surrealism will not disappear. It will live a life apart; it will be the *other* voice" ("André Breton" 55).

Notes

Introduction

1. The text of this exposition is found in Jennifer Mundy's *Surrealism: Desire Unbound* (2001).
2. In framing her book on Walter Benjamin, Margaret Cohen comments further that she wishes to "draw attention to the subterranean but vital presence of surrealism in subsequent key moments of twentieth-century French thought" (13). Although avant-garde French theory, as Clifford notes, has gravitated toward the "renegade" surrealism of Georges Bataille, Cohen vindicates the importance of Breton, particularly his thought regarding "modern materialism," for Benjamin and his successors.
3. An extensive study by Floriano Martins, to be called *Um novo continente: Poesia e Surrealismo na América*, is forthcoming from Edições Agulha Revista de Cultura (Fortaleza, Brazil) in 2012.
4. Unless otherwise noted, all translations from the Spanish are my own.

Chapter 1

1. For a lucid and wide-ranging discussion of the meanings of "authenticity" in modern art and literature, see Lionel Trilling's *Sincerity and Authenticity*, especially Chapters 5 and 6.
2. Anna Balakian argues forcefully for the constructive nature of surrealism when she claims that "their tone of determined optimism is not duplicated by any other contemporary philosophy or art" (47). Susan Sontag observes in a similar vein that "far from being subversive, the spirit of the Surrealists is ultimately constructive and falls well within the humanist tradition" (lvii). Many of those who in contrast see surrealist impulses as primarily negative or destructive cite its roots in Dada (which tended toward nihilism) and its early proclamations concerning the exhausted bourgeois culture it was determined to dismantle.
3. I refer the reader to the essay "On Ethnographic Surrealism" in James Clifford's *The Predicament of Culture* for a fuller account of the early surrealists' fascination with primitive cultures and their forays into ethnography. This topic will be considered in some detail in Chapter 6.
4. For a comprehensive treatment of the interartistic phenomenon known as the *livres d'artistes* (artists' books) in surrealism, see Renée Riese Hubert's *Surrealism and the Book* (1988).

5. It is a complicated matter to trace Freud's precise contribution to surrealist thought, particularly since his writings were not translated into French until the late 1920s—that is, after the formal start of the surrealist movement. Breton's indebtedness to Freudian psychoanalysis is evident in the first manifesto, where he credits Freud directly with "bringing back to light" a knowledge of the nonrational mind that had been buried "under a pretense of civilization and progress" (*Manifestoes* 10). In the second manifesto, Breton attempts to reconcile psychoanalytic thought and Marxism: "Surrealism, which as we have seen deliberately opted for the Marxist doctrine in the realm of social problems, has no intention of minimizing Freudian doctrine as it applies to the evaluation of ideas: on the contrary, Surrealism believes Freudian criticism to be the first and only one with a really solid basis" (*Manifestoes* 159–60).
6. In different guises, the question of political commitment would profoundly mark the consciousness of many of Latin America's most prominent twentieth-century writers as well. The names of César Vallejo, Pablo Neruda, Nicolás Guillén, Julio Cortázar, Ernesto Cardenal, Roque Dalton, Ernesto Sábato, Juan Gelman, Octavio Paz, Mario Vargas Llosa, Heberto Padilla, and Gabriel García Márquez head up a potentially much longer list.
7. Quite apart from philosophical differences, Sartre had personal-political reasons for this stance: whereas Breton had passed the war years in exile in America, Sartre had spent eight months as a German prisoner and had subsequently participated in the French Resistance.

Chapter 2

1. Though the Francophone Caribbean does not fall under the purview of the present study, it is crucial to acknowledge surrealism's debt to Aimé Césaire and Suzanne Roussi Césaire. In addition to their own poetic production, both contributed to the international surrealist movement by editing the influential journal *Tropiques* (1941–45).
2. Spengler's *The Decline of the West* was translated into Spanish in 1923. According to González Echevarría, "It was an immediate best-seller whose impact on Latin American was instantaneous and pervasive" (55). Spengler's premise, that discrete human civilizations arise, flourish, and die in a foreseeable pattern and that Europe's marked decline in the early twentieth century opened the path for the rise of other cultures, resonated deeply with Latin American thinkers.
3. Larrea's New World narrative, of course, follows in a long line of mythical constructions of Latin America as a site of cultural rebirth, beginning with many of the sixteenth-century Spanish chronicles of the conquest and taking a particularly Latin American shape with José Vasconcelos's influential essay *La raza cósmica*, first published in 1925.
4. As González Echevarría has demonstrated in *Alejo Carpentier: The Pilgrim at Home*, Carpentier's essay on *lo real maravilloso* enters into dialogue with several previous texts, particularly with regard to contemporary theories of magic. These texts include Franz Roh's "Nach-Expressionismus," which was published in the Cuban journal *Revista de Occidente* in 1927, Jorge Luis Borges's essay "El arte narrativo y la

magia," and the works of Frazer, Lévy-Bruhl, and Tylor. Carpentier was undoubtedly also familiar with Mabille's *The Mirror of the Marvelous* and with Juan Larrea's *El surrealismo entre Viejo y Nuevo Mundo*.
5. Carpentier's essay "De lo real maravilloso americano" was first published in *El Nacional* in Caracas in 1948; the following year it was published in Havana as the prologue to *El reino de este mundo*; since then it has been re-edited numerous times. I cite from a translation included in Lois Parkinson Zamora and Wendy B. Faris, *Magical Realism: Theory, History, Community*.

Chapter 3

1. For the discussion of Argentina surrealism in this chapter and in Chapters 7 and 8, I am indebted to Graciela de Sola and Javier Cófreces, who were generous with materials and with their time during my research in Buenos Aires in 2009.
2. The periodical *Ultra*, which the Chilean avant-garde poet Vicente Huidobro edited in Madrid in 1921–22, became the vehicle for *el ultraísmo*, a movement whose name signaled the intent to push beyond all previous forms of artistic expression. Although it began in Spain, the figure most directly associated with this movement is Jorge Luis Borges (1899–1986), who introduced it into the Buenos Aires literary scene in 1921. Borges was later to express regret over this experimental phase of his poetic career.
3. This "Justificación" was later identified as the work of Aldo Pellegrini. In 2001, Mario Pellegrini published a complete edition of Aldo Pellegrini's work under the title *La valija de fuego (Poesía completa)*. Pellegrini's texts in *Que* are taken from this edition.
4. As it stands, the unaccented *Que* reads either as "What?" or "That," an ambiguity that has often lead editors to add an orthographic accent [*Qué*] that the surrealists had explicitly eliminated.
5. The term *solenoglyph* refers to any snake with tubular fangs.
6. Unruh states that the discourse in Latin American *vanguardista* manifestoes typically "celebrated the continent's humanism, energy, 'ancestral' spirit, and radical newness as powerful antidotes to European cultural exhaustion" (130). In contrast, the *Que* manifesto is surprisingly negative in tone, lacking any sense of celebration.
7. For a fuller picture of the ideological and aesthetic positioning of the Latin American *vanguardia* vis-à-vis their European counterparts, I refer the reader to two excellent studies: Vicky Unruh's *Latin American Vanguards* (1994) and Beret E. Strong's *The Poetic Avant-Garde: The Groups of Borges, Auden, and Breton* (1997).

Chapter 4

1. While Enrique Anderson-Imbert directly labels Neruda "a surrealist" (452), Emir Rodríguez Monegal makes the more cautious observation that *Tentativa del hombre infinito* "seems to follow in the tracks of surrealist poetry" (54), and Gordon Brotherston limits the perceived affinity to "something of the uninhibitedness of the surrealists 'automatic writing'" (114).

2. René de Costa cites a 1924 text in which Neruda appears to embrace automatic methods for his own writing: "I write and write without being enchained by my thoughts, without bothering to free myself from chance associations." The poet then goes on, however, to explain a simultaneous act of revision of this raw material: "I build in my words a construct with free matter and while creating I eliminate what has no existence nor any palpable hold" (qtd. in *The Poetry of Pablo Neruda* 44).
3. All parenthetical page citations from *Mandrágora* refer to the facsimile edition of the journal included in Luis de Mussy's *Mandrágora: La raíz de la protesta o el refugio inconcluso*.
4. After their years of antibourgeois protest under the sign of La Mandrágora, Braulio Arenas and Enrique Gómez-Correa went on to lead lives as respectable Chilean citizens. In 1984, Arenas won the Chilean Premio Nacional de Literatura; Gómez-Correa studied law and became a career diplomat. Closer to the model of the *poète maudit*, Jorge Cáceres died under mysterious circumstances at the age of 26. Teófilo Cid worked for the Chilean government; he struggled, however, with alcoholism and led a generally dissolute life. For further biographical details of the Mandrágora poets, see de Mussy 63–68.

Chapter 5

1. The dates in parenthesis are Abril's own references to his previous collections of poetry.
2. The notation "Lima la horrible, 24 de julio o agosto de 1949" appears on a poem called "Viaje hacia la noche," collected in the volume *La tortuga ecuestre y otros textos* (66).
3. According to Ferrari, Moro's entire *oeuvre* consists of approximately 70 poems written in Spanish and 300 written in French (231).
4. Moro's *Antología del surrealismo* was first published as a supplement in the Mexican journal *Poesía* (No. 1) in 1938. I cite here from the expanded version of this anthology, titled *Versiones del surrealismo* (1974).
5. The phrase "Nero's emerald" is an allusion to the popular tradition according to which the Roman emperor Nero, who was short-sighted, used a large concave emerald as a lens to allow him to watch the gladiatorial contests.
6. Vallejo's articles on the topic of art and politics are collected in the section "El arte y la revolución" in *Ensayos y reportajes completes*, 365–473.
7. Vallejo's "Autopsia del superrealismo" was first published in Buenos Aires in *Nosotros* (no. 250, March 1930: 342–47). This was followed by publication in *Amauta* (no. 30, April–May 1930: 44–47), soon after the death of Mariátegui, who had done so much to champion the cause of surrealism, and finally in Santiago de Chile in the journal *Letras* (June 1930: 27–28). It has since been reproduced in numerous anthologies and histories of the Latin American avant-garde. I cite here from Jorge Schwartz's *Las vanguardias latinoamericanas*.

Chapter 6

1. The image of Mexico as a site of surrealist encounters had been prefigured in the famous "Surrealist Map of the World," published in 1929 in the journal *Variétés* in Brussels. On this map, "Mexique" takes up the entire space of North America below Canada, wholly eclipsing the United States.
2. In this chapter I rely heavily on Luis Mario Schneider's *México y el surrealismo* (1978) and Fabienne Bradu's *Breton en México* (1996).
3. Because I was unable to secure reproduction rights to the original Spanish version of Villaurrutia's "Nocturno de la estatua," I cite here only the translation published by Eliot Weinberger.
4. For a full recounting of the early reception of French surrealism in Mexico, see Schneider 1–33.
5. The influence of surrealism on Artaud's thought is particularly apparent in his essay "The Theater of Cruelty (Second Manifesto)." Artaud, in turn, exercised a profound influence over twentieth-century drama. Sontag claims that "upon that art, theater, he has had an impact so profound that the course of all recent serious theater in Western Europe and the Americas can be said to divide into two periods—before Artaud and after Artaud" (xxxviii).
6. The texts of Artaud's lectures in Mexico are included in Volume VIII of his *Oeuvres complètes* as follows: "Surréalisme et Révolution" (171–83), "L'homme contre le Destin" (184–95), and "Le Théatre et les Dieux" (196–206). I cite the second of these lectures, translated as "Man against Destiny," from Artaud's *Selected Writings*, edited by Susan Sontag (1988).
7. Subsequently (on June 21 and 25), Breton was able to give versions of these lectures, though to a much smaller and more exclusive audience, in Mexico City's Palacio de Bellas Artes.
8. For the full story of the Exposición Internacional del Surrealismo and the largely negative response to it by the Mexican press, see Schneider 171–83.
9. For my discussion of *Air mexicain* I draw from Elizabeth R. Jackson's translation in *A Marvelous World: Poems by Benjamin Péret* (67–87).
10. See Aberth's *Leonora Carrington: Surrealism, Alchemy, and Art* (2004) for a thorough and insightful account of the development of Carrington's art and its particular relationship to surrealism.
11. Carrington's stories have been gathered into various collections, the most recent and complete of which are *The Seventh Horse and Other Tales* (Dutton, 1988), *The House of Fear* (Dutton, 1988), and *The Hearing Trumpet* (Exact Change, 1996).
12. Exceptions to this rule—that is, Mexican painters in whose work the influence of surrealism can be observed—include Gunther Gerzso, José Chávez Morado, and Juan Soriano. María Izquierdo and Frida Kahlo have also been identified by art critics as painters influenced by surrealism. Breton claimed in 1938 that Frida Kahlo's work "blossomed forth . . . into pure surreality, despite the fact that it had been conceived without any prior knowledge whatsoever of the ideas motivating the activities of my friends and myself" (*Surrealism and Painting* 144). Both Kahlo and Izquierdo, for their part, resisted inclusion in the surrealist movement.

13. The one place in Mexico City where the surrealists found themselves welcomed was the Galería de Arte Mexicano, whose director, Inés Amor, hosted the 1940 Exhibición Internacional del Surrealismo and subsequently arranged individual shows for Carrington, Varo, and others.

Chapter 7

1. The phrase that Alazraki quotes, "the sacred disease of our time," is taken from Octavio Paz's essay "André Breton or the Quest of the Beginning."
2. Three noteworthy art exhibitions took place in Buenos Aires in these years: in 1962, "El surrealismo en la Argentina"; in 1967, a surrealist exhibition at the Instituto Di Tella; and in 1970, in the Galería Gradiva, an exposition entitled "Lautréamont 100 Años." Two decades later, the Biblioteca Nacional de Buenos Aires hosted an exhibit called "Surrealismo Nuevo Mundo."
3. In this highly reductionist history of Argentine poetry of the mid-twentieth century I have left aside an important poetic school that flourished alongside surrealism, *el invencionismo*. "Inventionism" was championed primarily by the poet Edgar Bayley and in many ways inherited the avant-garde poetics of Vicente Huidobro's *creacionismo*.
4. Enrique Pichón-Riviére (1907–77) was a Swiss-Argentine psychiatrist who is credited with being among the first to initiate the practice of psychoanalysis in Argentina.
5. In a letter to Éduoard Jaguer, Llinás declares, "I don't want to imitate *Phases* . . . *Boa* will be a South American magazine joined in spirit and by its relations, its director and, I admit, by a certain concept of honesty, to *Phases*. It borrows from *Phases* the epigraph 'International notebooks . . . ,' receives information from *Phases*, and would like to become her subtropical sister" (qtd. in Giunta 78).
6. For a full treatment of esoterism in the poetic work of Olga Orozco, Alejandra Pizarnik, and Jacobo Fijman, see my *Evil, Madness, and the Occult in Argentine Literature* (2002).
7. Breton's shift toward esoteric thought is apparent in the *Second Manifesto of Surrealism*, where he calls for "the profound, the veritable occultation of Surrealism" (*Manifestoes* 178). He goes on to say, "I think we would not be wasting our time by probing seriously into those sciences which for various reasons are today completely discredited," among which he gives special attention to astrology. In a 1953 radio interview, Breton insisted that this turn toward the occult in the postwar period, for which his critics attacked him on many fronts, was inherent in surrealist thought from its incipience (*Conversations* 218).
8. Pellegrini's *Antología de la poesía surrealista de lengua francesa* was reedited in Barcelona in 1981 and again in 2006, under the simplified title *Antología de la poesía surrealista*.

Chapter 8

1. The mouth of the Tumbes River is located on the northern coast of Peru. I have retained the word *cholo* in Spanish due to its untranslatability: it refers broadly to

a Spanish American person of mixed European and indigenous descent. In Peru, *cholo* means simply "Peruvian"; thus the *cholo* of this poem is a local inhabitant, whereas the speaker is an outsider.
2. I quote from an unpublished (and untitled) essay by Javier Cófreces, intended to serve as introduction to the proposed reedition of Graciela de Sola's *Proyecciones argentinas del surrealismo.*
3. For a more thorough discussion of Orozco's metaphysical concerns, as well as for an examination of the esoteric traditions in her work as well as that of Alejandra Pizarnik and Jacobo Fijman, see my *Evil, Madness, and the Occult in Argentine Poetry*, chapters 2 and 3.
4. I refer the reader to the images of Bellmer's *poupées* that can be found in Sue Taylor's *Hans Bellmer: The Anatomy of Anxiety* (2000) and Therese Lichtenstein's *Behind Closed Doors: The Art of Hans Bellmer* (2001). Taylor's online essay "Hans Bellmer in the Art Institute of Chicago: The Wandering Libido and The Hysterical Body" also contains images of the dolls.
5. In her biography of Pizarnik, Cristina Piña provides a thorough assessment of Alejandra's lifelong addiction to amphetamines and her intense mood fluctuations. We know, mostly through the testimony of her close friends such as Olga Orozco and Yvonne Bordelois, that Pizarnik made several attempts at suicide before finally succeeding in 1972, from an overdose of sleeping pills. When considered in relation to her poetry, the question of mental illness is complicated by Pizarnik's attempts to emulate the aesthetic, if not the lifestyle, of Rimbaud and other "decadent" poets, as well as her open admiration for the surrealists' conscious cultivation of madness as a means to open the doors of creativity.
6. Bellmer's interest in de Chirico's mannequins is discussed in Webb's *Hans Bellmer* (48). See also Chapter 5 of Hal Foster's *Convulsive Beauty*, in which the surrealist fascination with mannequins is discussed at length.
7. There are myriad references to diminutive female figures in Pizarnik's early poetry, beginning with *La última inocencia* in 1956. However, the term *muñeca* [doll] does not appear until the 1968 collection *Extracción de la piedra de locura*. From this point forward, references to dolls appear frequently.
8. It is pertinent to recall here another of Pizarnik's lyric fragments: "Mi niñez y su olor / a pájaro acariciado" [My childhood and its scent / of a caressed bird] (38). There is an almost explicit link between this passage and a photograph from Bellmer's first doll series, in which a male hand (the artist's?) caresses the head of the doll, whose gaze is averted and who appears to evade the contact.
9. Sue Taylor, for instance, claims that "if the photographs of the second doll, depicting untold violence against vulnerable female subjects, parallel conscious beating fantasies, their overt sadism represents only the manifest content of such fantasies. The latent content of these images is masochistic suffering, aggression turned in on the self" (91).
10. The verbs in this passage ("Sonríe" and "cierra") are marked as third-person singular with no identifying subject pronoun, and they thus could be translated using either "he" or "she" in English. The possessive adjective *su/sus* is likewise generically ambivalent. However, the last sentence of the previous paragraph of this text refers

to "un muchacho viviente" [a living boy], which I take to be the subject of the verbs in the passage I am analyzing.
11. See my "Surrealism Revisited: The Poetry of Dolores Etchecopar" in *Letras Femeninas* (2004) and "Juan Gelman and the Poetics of Surrealism" in *La Nueva Literatura Hispánica* (2006).
12. I am indebted to Alberto Arias, Silvia Grénier, and Javier Cófreces, who provided me with original materials and critical commentary on the Grupo Argentina Surrealista. Given that the original journal is no longer available, I take the citations from *Signo Ascendente* from an unpublished essay by Cófreces (see note 2 above).

Chapter 9

1. With the exception of the poem "A la salud de André Bretón," which is taken from Rojas's *Obra selecta* (1997), all poems cited in this section are from the collections *Antología del aire* (1995) and *Diálogo con Ovidio* (2000).
2. Additionally, Coddou identifies three important strains within surrealism that form the basis of Rojas's poetics: expression of the unconscious, the "unity of man" as an overarching ideal, and the negation of social orders in the search for a reality that turns necessarily toward political activity (*Poética de la poesía activa* 109).
3. José Olivio Jiménez was the first to observe the surrealist thematic triad (poetry-love-liberty) in Rojas's poetry, and he links this triad to a previous one belonging to Darío and the *modernista* poets: harmony or cosmic rhythm, an "intuition of Origin," and Unity ("Una moral del canto" 26–27).
4. Rojas's comment "soy profano" was made at a reading at the Residencia de Estudiantes in Madrid in 1996, by way of introducing a poem about the Spanish sixteenth-century mystic Santa Teresa de Jesús. The text of this reading is reproduced in *La voz de Gonzalo Rojas* (33).
5. In his essay called "A Chapter on Autography," published in 1841, Poe placed Emerson among "a class of gentleman with whom we have no patience whatever—the mystic for mysticism's sake" (qtd. in Quinn 328).
6. I owe this subtitle to Cedomil Goic, who spoke of Nicanor Parra's *antipoesía* as "la carnavalización de la literatura" (24).
7. The principle proponent of the "poetry of clarity" in Chile was the poet Tomás Lago, who presented the early work of Parra, along with that of Óscar Castro and Victoriano Vicario, in a 1942 collection called *Tres poetas chilenos*.
8. Two humorous examples of the *quebrantahuesos* are "Vaca perdida aclara actitud ante vaca encontrada" [Lost cow clarifies its attitude before found cow] and "Profesor universitario afirma que es absurdo pensar" [University professor affirms that it is absurd to think] (qtd. in J. Piña 34).
9. Unless otherwise noted, I cite in this section from Parra's anthology *Poemas para combatir la calvicie* [Poems for Combating Baldness], edited by Julio Ortega (1993).
10. The speaker of "Manifiesto" declares: "Nada más compañeros / nosotros condenamos / —y esto sí que lo digo con respecto— / la poesía de pequeño dios / la poesía de vaca sagrada / la poesía de toro furioso" [No more, Comrades / we condemn / —and this I do say with respect— / the poetry of the little god / the poetry of the sacred cow / the poetry of the furious bull] (*Poemas para combatir la calvicie* 150).

11. See my "Juan Gelman and the Poetics of Surrealism," 71–94.
12. Parra has stated, "In reality, poetry has to do with the human experience in its totality, with the totality of man" (Morales 207).

Chapter 10

1. Voicing an opinion widespread among writers and critics, Cedomil Goic declares that "surrealism's most outstanding figure in contemporary literature is, without a doubt, the Mexican Octavio Paz" (26). Notably, André Breton referred to Paz as "the Spanish-language poet who touches me most" (*Conversations* 242).
2. Evodio Escalante argues that Paz's later explanations of his *Taller* years amount to a sort of revisionist history. The pro-Stalin leanings of much the Mexican left (including Paz) in the late 1930s were a decisive factor in the general rejection of Breton, whose criticism of Stalin was severe. Given the authoritarian turn taken by the Stalinist regime, Paz later expressed regret for not recognizing Breton's foresight. In his later writings, claims Escalante, "it is obvious that Paz tries to 'erase' this grievous aspect of his intellectual history" (personal correspondence, November 10, 2011).
3. Paz claims that "Cernuda discovers the modern spirit through surrealism" (*Obras* 3: 24). Critics generally agree that Cernuda's collections *Un río, un amor* (1929) and *Los placeres prohibidos* (1931) are the works that show the clearest surrealist affinities. Later, Cernuda incorporates his experience in Mexico as an exile from the Spanish Civil War in his 1952 collection *Variaciones sobre un tema mexicano*, which also employs oneiric imagery.
4. Paz's lecture "Estrella de tres puntas: El surrealismo" only served to broaden the polemics between surrealism's few defenders and its many detractors in Mexico. See Wilson's *Octavio Paz: A Study of his Poetics* pages 18–20 for details.
5. I cite from Helen R. Lane's translation of the essay "André Breton o la búsqueda del comienzo," which is included in the essay collection *Alternating Current*.
6. "Sobre el surrealismo hispanoamericano" was later reprinted as a prologue to Baciu's *Surrealismo latinoamericano: Preguntas y respuestas*, and subsequently in a collection of essays by Paz called *In/Mediaciones*. I cite from the latter version.
7. I cite from Ruth Simms's translation of *The Bow and the Lyre* (1973) and Rachel Phillips's translation of *Children of the Mire* (1991).
8. Santí's essay "Octavio Paz: Crítica y poética" investigates the complex relationship between Paz's discursive modes, highlighting in particular the dangers inherent in using Paz's theoretical essays as a guide to reading his poetry.
9. In his essay "Charms and Riddles," Northrop Frye examines the precise ways in which verbal language can, in fact, produce concrete effects in the listener, by inducing a state of somnolence or by otherwise suppressing the conscious will.
10. Lloyd King explores at length Paz's appropriation of the concept of "lo otro" in his essay "Surrealism and the Sacred in the Aesthetic Credo of Octavio Paz."
11. In the essay "The Siren and the Seashell," Paz claims that there is a "current of occultism that pervades Darío's work . . . It is a question of a central current that constitutes a system of thought and also a system of poetic association. It is his idea of the world or, rather, his image of the world" (53). Jrade's book *Rubén Darío and*

the Romantic Search for Unity thoroughly explores this esoteric current, particularly with regard to Darío's interest in Pythagorean thought.

Conclusion

1. The one notable exception to this is the Grupo Surrealista Argentino, who used the surrealist call for revolt as a springboard for protest against the military dictatorship of the 1970s and 1980s.

Works Cited

Aberth, Susan L. *Leonora Carrington: Surrealism, Alchemy and Art.* Hampshire, England: Lund Humphries-Ashgate, 2004.
Abril, Xavier. *Hollywood: Relatos contemporáneos.* Madrid: Ediciones Ulises, 1931.
———. *Poesía soñada.* Ed. Marco Martos Carrera. Lima: Universidad San Martín de Porres, 2006.
Aguilar Camín, Héctor. *Saldos de la Revolución: Cultura y política de México, 1910–1980.* Mexico City: Nueva Imagen, 1982.
Aira, César. *Alejandra Pizarnik.* Rosario, Argentina: Beatriz Viterbo Editora, 1998.
———. "Enrique Molina." *Diccionario de autores latinoamericanos.* Buenos Aires: Emecé, 2001.
Alazraki, Jaime. "El surrealismo de *Tentativa de un hombre infinito* de Pablo Neruda." *Hispanic Review* 40.1 (1972): 31–39.
———. "Surrealism—The Sacred Disease of Our Time: Observations on Its Impact on Spanish American Literature." *Surrealismo/surrealismos: Latinoamérica y España.* Ed. Peter G. Earle and Germán Gullón. Philadelphia: Department of Romance Languages, U of Pennsylvania, 1975. 20–23.
Alegría, Fernando. "Antiliterature." *Latin America in Its Literature.* Ed. César Fernández Moreno et al. Trans. Mary G. Berg. New York: Holmes and Meier, 1980. 181–99.
Alquié, Ferdinand. *The Philosophy of Surrealism.* Trans. Bernard Waldrop. Ann Arbor: U of Michigan P, 1965 [1955].
Altuna, Elena. "César Moro: Escritura y exilio." *Revista de Crítica Literaria Latinoamericana* 20.39 (1994): 109–25.
Anderson Imbert, Enrique. *Spanish American Literature: A History.* Trans. John V. Falconieri. Detroit: Wayne State UP, 1963.
Andrade, Lourdes. *Para la desorientación general: Trece ensayos sobre México y el surrealismo.* Mexico: Editorial Aldus, 1996.
Andrade, Oswald. "Manifiesto Antropófago." *Las vanguardias latinoamericanas: Textos programáticos y críticos.* Ed. Jorge Schwartz. Mexico: Fondo de Cultura Económica, 2002. 173–80.
Anguita, Eduardo. "'Segundo prólogo' to the *Antología de poesía chilena nueva.*" *Las vanguardias latinoamericanas: Textos programáticos y críticos.* Ed. Jorge Schwartz. Mexico: Fondo de Cultura Económica, 2002. 393–97.
Apollinaire, Guillaume. *Les mamelles de Tirésias: Drame surréaliste en deux actes et un prologue.* Paris: Éditions Sic, 1918.

Aragon, Louis. *Le Paysan de Paris*. Paris: Gallimard, 1926–1961.
Arenas, Braulio. *Actas surrealistas*. Santiago: Nascimento, 1974.
———. "Letter from Chile." *VVV: Almanac for 1943* 2–3 (March 1943): 124–26.
———, Enrique Gómez-Correa, and Jorge Cáceres. *El A G C de la Mandrágora*. Santiago de Chile: Ediciones Mandrágora, 1957.
Armani, Horacio. *Antología esencial de la poesía argentina (1900–1980)*. Buenos Aires: Aguilar Argentina, 1981.
Artaud, Antonin. *Oeuvres Complètes*. Vol. 8. 26 vols. Paris: Gallimard, 1990.
———. *Selected Writings*. Ed. Susan Sontag. Trans. Helen Weaver. Berkeley: U of California P, 1988.
———. *The Theater and Its Double*. Trans. Mary Carolina Richards. New York: Grove Press, 1958.
Asturias, Miguel Ángel. *El Señor Presidente*. Buenos Aires: Losada, 1948.
Baciu, Stefan, ed. *Antologia de la poesía surrealista latinoamericana*. Mexico City: Joaquín Mortiz, 1974.
———. Introduction. Antología de la poesía surrealista latinoamericana. Ed. Baciu. Mexico City: Joaquín Mortiz, 1974. 7–119.
———. *Surrealismo latinoamericano: Preguntas y respuestas*. Valparaíso, Chile: Ediciones Universitarias de Valparaíso, 1979.
Balakian, Anna. *Surrealism: The Road to the Absolute*. Chicago: U of Chicago P, 1959.
Bary, Leslie. "El surrealismo en Hispanoamérica y el 'yo' de Westphalen." *Revista de Crítica Literaria Latinoamericana* 14.27 (1988): 97–110.
Bataille, Georges. *The Absence of Myth: Writings on Surrealism*. Ed. and trans. Michael Richardson. London: Verso, 2006.
Bédouin, Jean-Louis. *Vingt ans de surréalisme: 1939–1959*. Paris: Denoël, 1961.
Béguin, Albert. *El alma romántica y el sueño*. Trans. of *L'Âme romantique et le Rêve*. Mexico City: Fondo de Cultura Económica, 1981 [1939].
Bellmer, Hans. "Memories of the Doll Theme." *Behind Closed Doors: The Art of Hans Bellmer*. By Therese Lichtenstein. Berkeley: U of California P, 2001. 169–74.
———. "Notes on the Subject of the Ball Joint." *Hans Bellmer: The Anatomy of Anxiety*. By Sue Taylor. Cambridge: MIT Press, 2000. 212–18.
Benedikt, Michael. *The Poetry of Surrealism: An Anthology*. Boston: Little, Brown, 1974.
Benjamin, Walter. "Surrealism: The Last Snapshot of the European Intelligentsia." *Reflections: Essays, Aphorisms, Autobiographical Writing*. New York: Harcourt, 1978. 176–92.
Birkenmaier, Anke. *Alejo Carpentier y la cultura del surrealismo en América Latina*. Madrid: Iberoamericana, 2006.
Bolton, Robert. "Speaking with Forked Tongues: 'Male' Discourse in 'Female' Surrealism?" *Surrealism and Women*. Ed. Mary Ann Caws, Rudolf Kuenzli, and Gwen Raaberg. Cambridge: MIT Press, 1991. 50–62.
Bordelois, Ivonne. *Correspondencia Pizarnik*. Buenos Aires: Seix Barral-Planeta, 1998.
Bradu, Fabienne. *André Breton en México*. Mexico City: Vuelta, 1996.
Breton, André. *André Breton: Selections*. Ed. Mark Polizzotti. Berkeley: U of California P, 2003.

———, ed. *Anthologie d l'humour noir*. Paris: Editions du Sagittaire, 1945.
———. *L'Art magique*. Paris: Club Français de l'Art, 1957.
———. *Communicating Vessels*. Trans. Mary Ann Caws and Geoffrey T. Harris. Lincoln: U of Nebraska P, 1990 [1955].
———. *Conversations: The Autobiography of Surrealism*. Trans. Mark Polizzotti. New York: Marlowe and Company, 1993.
———. *Free Rein (La Clé des champs)*. Trans. Michel Parmentier and Jacqueline d'Amboise. Lincoln: U of Nebraska P, 1995.
———. *Manifestoes of Surrealism*. Trans. Richard Seaver and Helen R. Lane. Ann Arbor: U of Michigan P, 1969.
———. *Nadja*. Trans. Richard Howard. New York: Grove Press, 1960 [1928].
———. *Surrealism and Painting*. Trans. Simon Watson Taylor. Boston: MFA Publications, 2002 [1928].
Brotherston, Gordon. *Latin American Poetry: Origins and Presence*. Cambridge: Cambridge UP, 1975.
Bürger, Peter. *Theory of the Avant-Garde*. Trans. Michael Shaw. Minneapolis: U of Minnesota P, 1984.
Busto Odgen, Estrella. "Una entrevista con Gonzalo Rojas." *Revista Iberoamericana* 52.135–36 (1986): 677–85.
Calinescu, Matei. *Five Faces of Modernity: Modernism, Avant-Garde, Decadence, Kitsch, Postmodernism*. Durham: Duke UP, 1987.
Carpentier, Alejo. "En la extrema avanzada: Algunas actitudes del 'surrealismo.'" *Las vanguardias latinoamericanas: Textos programáticos y críticos*. Ed. Jorge Schwartz. Mexico: Fondo de Cultura Económica, 2002. 454–59.
———. "On the Marvelous Real in America." *Magical Realism: Theory, History, Community*. Ed. Lois Parkinson Zamora and Wendy B. Faris. Durham: Duke UP, 1995. 75–88.
Carrington, Leonora. *The Seventh Horse and Other Tales*. Trans. Kathrine Talbot and Anthony Kerrigan. New York: Dutton, 1988.
Castañón, José Manuel. *César Vallejo a Pablo Abril, en el drama de un epistolario*. Valencia, Spain: Ediciones Universidad de Carabobo, 1960.
Caws, Mary Ann. *The Poetry of Dada and Surrealism*. Princeton: Princeton UP, 1970.
———. "Seeing the Surrealist Woman: We Are a Problem." *Surrealism and Women*. Ed. Caws Rudolf E. Kuenzli and Gloria Gwen Raaberg. Cambridge: MIT Press, 1991. 11–16.
———, ed. *Surrealist Painters and Poets: An Anthology*. Cambridge: MIT Press, 2002.
Chadwick, Whitney. *Mirror Images: Women, Surrealism, and Self-Representation*. Cambridge: MIT Press, 1998.
Chanady, Amaryll. "The Territorialization of the Imaginary in Latin America: Self-Affirmation and Resistance to Metropolitan Paradigms." *Magical Realism: Theory, History, Community*. Ed. Lois Parkinson Zamora and Wendy B. Faris. Durham: Duke UP, 1995. 125–44.
Chávez Silverman, Suzanne. "The Discourse of Madness in the Poetry of Alejandra Pizarnik." *Monographic Review* 6 (1990): 274–81.

Clifford, James. *The Predicament of Culture: Twentieth-Century Ethnography, Literature, and Art.* Cambridge: Harvard UP, 1988.

Coddou, Marcelo. *Poética de la poesía activa.* Madrid: Ediciones Lar, 1984.

———. Prologue. *Obra selecta.* By Gonzalo Rojas. Caracas: Biblioteca Ayacucho and Santiago de Chile: Fondo de Cultura Económica, 1997. xiii–lxxx.

Cófreces, Javier. *Siete surrealistas argentinos.* Buenos Aires: Leviatán, 1999.

Cohen, Margaret. *Profane Illumination: Walter Benjamin and the Paris of Profane Illumination.* Berkeley: U of California P, 1993.

Cohen, Sandro. "Poesía mexicana, 1975–1990." *Perfiles: Ensayos sobre literatura mexicana reciente.* Ed. Federico Patán. Boulder: Society of Spanish and Spanish-American Studies, 1992. 1–25.

Cortázar, Julio. "Un cadáver viviente." *Realidad* 5.15 (1949): 349–50.

———. "Muerte de Antonin Artaud. *Sur* 163 (May 1948): 80.

Costa, René de. "Huidobro y el surrealismo." *Surrealismo/surrealismos: Latinoamérica y España.* Ed. Peter G. Earle and Germán Gullón. Philadelphia: Department of Romance Languages, U of Pennsylvania, 1975.

———. *The Poetry of Pablo Neruda.* Cambridge: Harvard UP, 1979.

Coyné, André. "El poeta y su bestiario." Epilogue. *La tortuga ecuestre y otros poemas en español.* By César Moro. Ed. Américo Ferrari. Madrid: Biblioteca Nueva, 2002. 85–93.

Crow, Mary. Introduction. *Engravings Torn from Insomnia.* By Olga Orozco. Trans. Mary Crow. Rochester, NY: Boa, 2002.

Durozoi, Gérard. *History of the Surrealist Movement.* Trans. Alison Anderson. Chicago: U of Chicago P, 2002.

Earle, Peter G. "Breton y Rojas, hacia la plenitud." *Poesía y poética de Gonzalo Rojas.* Ed. Enrique Giordano. Santiago de Chile: Monografías del Maiten, 1987. 125–30.

———. Introduction. *Surrealismo/surrealismos: Latinoamérica y España.* Ed. Earle and Germán Gullón. Philadelphia: Department of Romance Languages, U of Pennsylvania, 1975.

Escalante, Evodio. "La vanguardia requisada." *Fractal* 2.4 (January–March 1997): 67–87. http://www.mxfractal.org/F4escala.html.

Ferdinán, Valentín. "El fracaso del surrealismo en América Latina." *Revista de Crítica Literaria Latinoamericana* 28.55 (2002): 73–111.

Fernández Cozman, Camilo. *Las ínsulas extrañas de Emilio Adolfo Westphalen.* Lima: Naylamp Editores, 1990.

Fernández Moreno, César. *La realidad y los papeles: Panorama y muestra de la poesía contemporánea argentina.* Buenos Aires: Aguilar, 1961.

Ferrari, Américo. *La soledad sonora: Voces poéticas del Perú e Hispanoamérica.* Lima: Pontífica Universidad Católica del Perú, 2003.

Foote, Susan. "El surrealismo en Chile y la revista *Leitmotiv.*" *Acta literaria* 20 (1995): 37–44.

Forster, Merlin H. "Latin American *Vanguardismo*: Chronology and Terminology." *Tradition and Renewal: Essays on Twentieth-Century Latin American Literature and Culture.* Ed. M. H. Foster. Urbana: U of Illinois P, 1975. 12–50.

Foster, David William. "The Representation of the Body in the Poetry of Poetry of Alejandra Pizarnik." *Hispanic Review* 62.3 (1994): 319–47.
Foster, Hal. *Compulsive Beauty*. Cambridge: MIT Press, 1993.
Foucault, Michel. *The Order of Things: An Archeology of the Human Sciences*. Trans. of *Les mots et les choses*. New York: Random House-Vintage, 1973.
Fowlie, Wallace. *Age of Surrealism*. Bloomington: Indiana UP, 1960.
Freeman, Judi. *The Dada and Surrealist Word-Image*. Cambridge: MIT Press, 1989.
Freud, Sigmund. *Introductory Lectures on Psychoanalysis*. Trans. and ed. James Strachey. New York: Norton, 1966.
———. "The Uncanny." *On Creativity and the Unconscious: Papers on the Psychology of Art, Literature, Love, Religion*. Ed. Benjamin Nelson. New York: Harper, 1958. 122–61.
Frye, Northrop. "Charms and Riddles." *Spiritus Mundi: Essays on Literature, Myth, and Society*. Bloomington: Indiana UP, 1976. 123–47.
Giordano, Carlos. "Entre el 40 y el 50 en la poesía argentina." *Revista Iberoamericana* 125 (1983): 783–96.
Giunta, Andrea. *Avant-Garde, Internationalism, and Politics: Argentine Art in the Sixties*. Durham: Duke UP, 2007.
Goic, Cedomil. "El surrealismo y la literatura iberoamericana." *Revista Chilena de Literatura* 8 (Abril 1977): 5–34.
González Echevarría, Roberto. *Alejo Carpentier: The Pilgrim at Home*. Austin: U of Texas P, 1990.
Hayman, Ronald. *Artaud and After*. Oxford: Oxford UP, 1977.
Heidegger, Martin. *Poetry, Language, Thought*. Trans. Albert Hofstadter. New York: Harper, 1971.
Hopkins, David. *Dada and Surrealism: A Very Short Introduction*. Oxford: Oxford UP, 2004.
Hubert, Renée Riese. *Surrealism and the Book*. Berkeley: U of California P, 1988.
Huerta, Efrain. "Fiesta del surrealismo." *El Nacional* [Mexico City] 24 May 1938: 3.
Ibáñez-Langlois, José Miguel. "La poesía de Nicanor Parra." Introduction. *Antipoemas: Antología*. By Nicanor Parra. Barcelona: Seix Barral, 1981. 9–66.
Jackson, Elizabeth R. "Péret's Works: A Perspective." Appendix. *A Marvelous World*. By Benjamin Péret. Trans. Elizabeth R. Jackson. Baton Rouge: Louisiana State UP, 1985. 93–97.
Jiménez, José Olivio. "Una moral del canto: El pensamiento poético de Gonzalo Rojas." *Poesía y poética de Gonzalo Rojas*. Ed. Enrique Giordano. Santiago: Monografías del Maitén, 1987. 23–30.
Jimeno-Grendi, Orlando. "Mandrágora mántica." *Anales de Literatura Chilena* 6.6 (2005), 109–18.
Jrade, Cathy Login. *Rubén Darío and the Romantic Search for Unity: The Modernist Recourse to Esoteric Tradition*. Austin: U of Texas P, 1983.
King, Lloyd. "Surrealism and the Sacred in the Aesthetic Credo of Octavio Paz." *Hispanic Review* 37.3 (1969): 383–93.

Krauss, Rosalind E., and Jane Livingston. *L'Amour Fou: Photography and Surrealism.* Washington, DC: Corcoran Gallery of Art, 1985.
Kuhnheim, Jill. *Gender, Politics, and Poetry in Twentieth-Century Argentina.* Gainesville: UP of Florida, 1996.
Lago, Tomás. "Luz en la poesía." *Tres poetas chilenos.* Santiago de Chile: Cruz del Sur, 1942. 6–25.
Lama, Víctor de. Introduction. *César Vallejo: Antología poética.* Madrid: Edaf, 1999. 11–52.
Langowski, Gerald. *El surrealismo en la ficción hispanoamericana.* Madrid: Gredos, 1982.
Larrea, Juan. *Del surrealismo a Machu Picchu.* Mexico City: Joaquín Mortiz, 1967.
———. *El surrealismo entre Viejo y Nuevo Mundo.* Mexico City: Cuadernos Americanos, 1944.
Lasarte, Francisco. "Más allá del surrealismo: La poesía de Alejandra Pizarnik." *Revista Iberoamericana* 49.125 (1983): 867–77.
Lauer, Mirko. "La poesía vanguardista en el Perú." *Revista de la crítica literaria latinoamericana* 8.15 (1982): 77–85.
———, and Abelardo Oquendo, eds. *Vuelta a la otra margen.* Lima: Casa de la Cultura del Perú, 1970.
Lautréamont, Comte de [Isidore Ducasse]. *Maldoror: Les Chants de Maldoror.* Trans. Guy Wernham. New York: New Directions, 1965.
Lazo, Agustín. "Reseña sobre las actividades sobrerrealistas." *Universidad Nacional de Mexico: Cuadernos de Arte* 3 (March 1938): 1–18.
Lichtenstein, Therese. *Behind Closed Doors: The Art of Hans Bellmer.* Berkeley: U of California P, 2001.
Lihn, Enrique. *El circo en llamas: Una crítica de la vida.* Santiago de Chile: LOM, 1986.
———. "El surrealismo en Chile." *Nueva atenea* [Concepción de Chile] 423 (1970): 91–96.
Lima, Sérgio. *A aventura surrealista.* 2 vols. Petrópolis, Brazil: Vozes, 1995.
Llinás, Julio. *Boa: Cuadernos Internacionales de Documentación sobre la Poesía y el Arte de Vanguardia* [Buenos Aires]. Nos. 1 (May 1958), 2 (June 1958), and 3 (July 1960).
———. *Fiat Lux.* Buenos Aires: Atlántida, 1994.
———, and Enrique Molina. "Ensayo experimental de rectificación de lenguaje." *A Partir de Cero* 3 (1952): n. pag.
Mabille, Pierre. *Mirror of the Marvelous: The Classic Surrealist Work on Myth.* Trans. Jody Gladding. Rochester, Vermont: Inner Traditions, 1998.
Maciel Edelman, Olivia. *Surrealismo en la poesía de Xavier Villaurrutia, Octavio Paz, and Luis Cernuda. México (1926–1963).* Lewiston, NY: Edwin Mellen, 2008.
Malt, Johanna. *Obscure Objects of Desire: Surrealism, Fetishism, and Politics.* Oxford: Oxford UP, 2004.
Mariátegui, José Carlos. *El artista y la época.* Lima: Biblioteca Amauta, 1970.
———. "Presentación de *Amauta*." *Las vanguardias latinoamericanas: Textos programáticos y críticos.* Ed. Jorge Schwartz. Mexico: Fondo de Cultura Económica, 2002. 333–35.
———, and T. R. Martínez, eds. *Amauta.* Lima: n.p., 1926–30.

Martins, Floriano. *Um novo continente: Poesía e surrealismo na América*. Fortaleza, Brazil: Edições Agulha Revista de Cultura, 2012.

———. *Un nuevo continente: Antología del surrealismo en la poesía de Nuestra América*. Caracas: Monte Avila, 2008.

Masiello, Francine. *Lenguaje e ideología: Las escuelas argentinas de vanguardia*. Buenos Aires: Hachette, 1986.

Matthews, J. H. *An Introduction to Surrealism*. University Park: Pennsylvania State UP, 1965.

Medina, Rubén. *Autor, autoridad y autorización: Escritura y poética de Octavio Paz*. Mexico City: El Colegio de México, 1999.

Mendiola, Víctor Manuel. *El surrealismo de "Piedra de sol: Entre peras y manzanas*. Mexico City: Fondo de Cultura Económica, 2011.

Meyer-Minnemann, Klaus, and Sergio Vergara [Alarcón]. "La revista *Mandrágora*: Vanguardismo y contexto chileno en 1938." *Acta literaria* 15 (1990): 51–69.

Molina, Enrique. *Antología poética*. Ed. E. Espejo. Madrid: Visor, 1991.

———. "Itinerario de memorias: Entrevista con Enrique Molina." Interview with Jacobo Sefamí. *Revista Chilena de Literatura* 44 (April 1994): 141–48.

———. "Poesía, amor, y libertad." Interview with Lía Rosa Gálvez. November 1993. 27 July 2011. http://www.lanacion.com.ar/853434-poesia-amor-y-libertad.

———. *Una sombra donde sueña Camila O'Gorman*. Buenos Aires: Losada, 1973.

———. "Vía libre." *A Partir de Cero: Revista de Poesía y Antipoesía* 1 (1952): n.pag.

Morales, Leónidas. *La poesía de Nicanor Parra*. Santiago: Universidad Austral de Chile, Editorial Andrés Bello, 1972.

Moro, César. *Los anteojos de azufre*. Ed. Andrés Coyné. Lima: Editorial San Marcos, 1958.

———. *Obra poética*. Ed. Ricardo Silva-Santisteban. Lima: Instituto Nacional de Cultura, 1980.

———. "Presentación." Introduction to the catalogue of the Exposición Surrealista in Mexico, 1939. *Las vanguardias latinoamericanas: Textos programáticos y críticos*. Ed. Jorge Schwartz. Mexico: Fondo de Cultura Económica, 2002. 473–76.

———. *La tortuga ecuestre y otros textos*. Ed. Julio Ortega. Caracas: Monte Ávila, 1976.

———. *Versiones del surrealismo*. Ed. Julio Ortega. Barcelona: Tusquets, 1974.

Mundy, Jennifer. *Surrealism: Desire Unbound*. London: Tate, 2001.

Mussy, Luis G[ueneau] de. *Mandrágora: La raíz de la protesta o el refugio inconcluso*. Santiago de Chile: Universidad Finis Terrae (Escuela de Historia), 2001.

Nadeau, Maurice. *The History of Surrealism*. Trans. Richard Howard. Cambridge: Harvard UP, 1989 [1944].

Neruda, Pablo. *Obras completas*. 3 vols. Buenos Aires: Losada, 1957.

———. *Tentativa del hombre infinito*. Santigo: Nascimento, 1926.

Nicholson, Melanie. "Bellmer's Argentine Doll: Alejandra Pizarnik and the Disarticulation of the Self." *Studies in Twentieth and Twenty-First Century Literature* 32.1 (2008): 100–123.

———. *Evil, Madness, and the Occult in Argentine Poetry*. Gainesville: U of Florida P, 2002.

———. "Juan Gelman and the Poetics of Surrealism." *La Nueva Literatura Hispánica* 10 (2006): 71–94.

———. "Surrealism Revisited: The Poetry of Dolores Etchecopar." *Letras Femeninas* 30.2 (2004): 94–110.

Nougé, Paul. *Histoire de ne pas rire.* Lausanne: L'Age d'homme, 1980.

Núñez, Estuardo. *La literatura peruana en el siglo XX, 1900–1965.* Mexico: Pormaca, 1965.

———. "La recepción del surrealismo en el Perú." *Surrealismo/surrealismos: Latinoamérica y España.* Ed. Peter G. Earle and Germán Gullón. Philadelphia: Department of Romance Languages, U of Pennsylvania, 1975.

Orozco, Olga. *Eclipses y fulgores.* Barcelona: Lumen, 1998.

———. *Páginas de Olga Orozco seleccionadas por la autora.* Buenos Aires: Celtia, 1984.

———. *También la luz es un abismo.* Buenos Aires: Emecé, 1995.

Ortega, Julio. *La imaginación crítica: Ensayos sobre la modernidad en el Perú.* Lima: Ediciones Peisa, 1974.

Ortega Parada, Hernán. *Ludwig Zeller: Arquitectura del escritor.* Santiago de Chile: Editorial Cuarto Propio, 2009.

Otto, Rudolf. *The Idea of the Holy: An Inquiry into the Non-Rational Factor in the Idea of the Divine and its Relation to the Rational.* New York: Oxford UP, 1950 [1923].

Oviedo, José Miguel. "A Permanent Discussion." *Latin America in Its Literature.* Ed. César Fernández Moreno et. al. Trans. Mary G. Berg. New York: Holmes and Meier, 1980. 301–19.

———. "Sobre la poesía de César Moro." *Lexis* 1.1 (July 1977): 101–5.

Paalen, Wolfgang. "The Volcano-Pyramid: A Mythological Hypothesis Suggested by the Appearance of a New Volcano." *Surrealist Painters and Poets.* Ed. Mary Ann Caws. Cambridge: MIT Press, 2002 [1945]. 323–25.

Pacheco, José Emilio. "La batalla del surrealismo (Octavio Paz y la revista *Estaciones*)." *Surrealismo/surrealismos: Latinoamérica y España.* Ed. Peter G. Earle and Germán Gullón. Philadelphia: Department of Romance Languages, U of Pennsylvania, 1975.

Paoli, Robert. *Estudios sobre literatura peruana contemporánea.* Florence: Parenti, 1985.

Parra, Nicanor. *Cancionero sin nombre.* Santiago de Chile: Nascimento, 1937.

———. *Poemas para combatir la calvicie: Antología.* Ed. Julio Ortega. Mexico City: Fondo de Cultura Económica, 1995.

———. *Poemas y antipoemas.* Santiago de Chile: Nascimento, 1954.

———. "Poetas de la claridad." *Atenea* [Concepción, Chile] 131 (1958): 46–47.

———. *Versos de salón.* Santiago de Chile: Nascimiento, 1962.

Paz, Octavio. "André Breton and the Quest of the Beginning." *Alternating Current.* Trans. Helen R. Lane. New York: Viking, 1973. 47–59.

———. *The Bow and the Lyre: The Poem. Poetic Revelation. Poetry and History.* Trans. Ruth L.C. Simms. Austin: U of Texas P, 1973 [1956].

———. *Children of the Mire: Modern Poetry from Romanticism to the Avant-Garde.* Trans. Rachel Phillips. Cambridge: Harvard UP, 1991 [1974].

———. *Convergences: Essays on Art and Literature.* Trans. Helen R. Lane. London: Bloomsbury, 1987.

———. *Estrella de tres puntas: André Breton y el surrealismo*. Mexico City: Vuelta, 1996.

———. "Hieroglyphs of Desire: A Critical Study of Villaurrutia by Octavio Paz." Trans. Esther Allen. *Nostalgia for Death*. By Xavier Villaurrutia. Port Townsend, WA: Copper Canyon Press, 1993. 91–148.

———. *Obras completas de Octavio Paz*. 18 vols. Barcelona: Círculo de Lectores, 1994–2004.

———. *The Siren and the Seashell and Other Essays on Poets and Poetry*. Trans. Lysander Kemp and Margaret Sayers Peden. Austin: U of Texas P, 1976.

———. "Sobre el surrealismo hispanoamericano: El fin de las habladurías." *In/Mediaciones*. By Paz. Barcelona: Seix Barral, 1979. 153–61.

Pellegrini, Aldo. Introduction. *Antología de la poesía viva latinoamericana*. Barcelona: Seix Barral, 1966. 7–16.

———. "El huevo filosófico." *A Partir de Cero* 2 (1952): n. pag.

———. "La poesía surrealista." *Antología de la poesía surrealista de lengua francesa*. Buenos Aires: Argonauta, 2006. 15–43.

———. "Respuesta a Osiris Troiani." *Capricornio* 7 (September–October 1954): 9–15.

———. *La valija de fuego (Poesía completa)*. Buenos Aires: Argonauta, 2001.

Pellegrini, Mario. "Nota del Editor." *La valija de fuego*. By Aldo Pellegrini. Ed. Mario Pellegrini. Buenos Aires: Argonauta, 2001. 5–7.

———. Personal interview, 18 July 2009.

Péret, Benjamin. *Air mexicain*. Paris: Librairie Arcanes, 1952.

———. *Anthologie des Mythes, Légendes at Contes populaires d'Amérique*. Paris: Éditions Albin Michel, 1959.

———. *Le Livre de Chilám Balám Chumayel*. Paris: Denoël, 1955.

———. *A Marvelous World: Poems by Benjamin Péret*. Trans. Elizabeth R. Jackson. Baton Rouge: Louisiana State UP, 1985.

Peyre, Henri. "The Significance of Surrealism." *Yale French Studies* 31 (1969): 23–36.

Pezzoni, Enrique. *El texto y sus voces*. Buenos Aires: Sudamericana, 1986.

Phillips, Rachel. *The Poetic Modes of Octavio Paz*. London: Oxford UP, 1972.

Pina, Cristina. *Alejandra Pizarnik*. Buenos Aires: Planeta, 1991.

———. "Estudio preliminar." *Poesía argentina de fin de siglo*. Buenos Aires: Vinciguera, 1996. 8–47.

Piña, Juan Andrés. *Conversaciones con la poesía chilena: Nicanor Parra, Eduardo Anguita, Gonzalo Rojas, Enrique Lihn, Oscar Hahn, Raúl Zurita*. Santiago de Chile: Pehuén, 1990.

Pizarnik, Alejandra. "Algunas claves de Alejandra Pizarnik." Interview with Marta Moia. *El deseo de la palabra*. Barcelona: Ocnos, 1975. 246–51.

———. *Obras completas: Poesía completa y prosa selecta*. Ed. Cristina Piña. Buenos Aires: Corregidor, 1994.

Poblete Araya, Kira. *El surrealismo en la Argentina a través de sus revistas literarias*. San Juan: Editorial Fundación Universidad Nacional de San Juan, 2004.

Ponge, Roberto. "Notas sobre a recepção e presença du surrealismo no Brasil nos anos 1920–1950." *Alea: Estudos Neolatinos* 6.1 (2004): 53–65.

Quinn, Arthur Hobson. *Edgar Allan Poe: A Critical Biography*. Baltimore: Johns Hopkins UP, 1998.
Raaberg, Gwen. "The Problematics of Women and Surrealism." *Surrealism and Women*. Ed. Mary Ann Caws et al. Cambridge: MIT Press, 1991. 1–10.
Rank, Otto. *The Double: A Psychoanalytic Study*. Trans. Harry Tucker Jr. Chapel Hill: U of North Carolina P, 1971.
Raymond, Marcel. *From Baudelaire to Surrealism*. London: Methuen, 1970 [1933].
Richardson, Michael. Introduction. *Refusal of the Shadow: Surrealism and the Caribbean*. Ed. Michael Richardson. Trans. Krzysztof Fijalkowski and Michael Richardson. London: Verso, 1996.
Riffaterre, Michael. *Text Production*. Trans. Terese Lyons. New York: Columbia UP, 1983.
Rimbaud, Arthur. *Complete Works, Selected Letters*. Ed. Wallace Fowlie. Chicago: U of Chicago P, 1966.
Rodríguez Monegal, Emir. *El viajero inmóvil: Introducción a Pablo Neruda*. Buenos Aires: Losada, 1966.
Rojas, Gonzalo. *Antología del aire*. Santiago: Fondo de Cultura Económica, 19965.
———. *Diálogo con Ovidio*. Mexico City: Aldus, 2000.
———. *Obra selecta*. Ed. Marcelo Coddou. Caracas: Biblioteca Ayacucho and Santiago de Chile: Fondo de Cultura Económica, 1997.
———. "Octavio aquí y ahora." *Cuadernos hispanoamericanos* 589–90 (1999): 193–99.
———. *La voz de Gonzalo Rojas*. Madrid: Publicaciones de la Residencia de Estudiantes, 2004.
Sábato, Ernesto. "Trascendencia y limitación del surrealismo." *Hombres y engranajes*. Buenos Aires: Emecé, 1951.
Santí, Enrico Mario. *Escritura y tradición: Texto, crítica y poética en la literatura hispanoamericana*. Barcelona: Laia, 1988.
Sartre, Jean-Paul. *"What Is Literature?" and Other Essays*. Cambridge: Harvard UP, 1988.
Sawin, Martica. *Surrealism in Exile and the Beginning of the New York School*. Cambridge: MIT Press, 1997.
Schneider, Luis Mario. *México y el surrealismo (1925–1950)*. Mexico: Arte y libros, 1978.
Schopf, Federico. *El desorden de las imágenes: Vicente Huidobro, Pablo Neruda, Nicanor Parra*. Santiago: Editorial Universitaria, 2010. 173–221.
———. "El Surrealismo en Chile." *Adiós a la familia*. By Braulio Arenas. Santiago de Chile: Editorial Universitaria, 2000. 173–79.
———. *Del vanguardismo a la antipoesía: Ensayos sobre la poesía en Chile*. Santiago de Chile: Lom, 2000.
Schwartz, Jorge. Introduction. *Las vanguardias latinoamericanas: Textos programáticos y críticos*. Ed. Schwartz. Mexico: Fondo de Cultura Económica, 2002. 33–94.
———, ed. *Las vanguardias latinoamericanas: Textos programáticos y críticos*. Mexico: Fondo de Cultura Económica, 2002.
Sefamí, Jacobo. *De la imaginación poética: Conversaciones con Gonzalo Rojas, Olga Orozco, Álvaro Mutis y José Kozer*. Caracas: Monte Avila, 1996.

———. *El espejo trizado: La poesía de Gonzalo Rojas*. Mexico City: Universidad Nacional Autónoma de México, 1992.

———. "Gonzalo Rojas." *Latin American Writers, Supplement I*. Ed. Carlos A. Solé and Klaus Müller-Bergh. New York: Scribners-Gale, 2002. 493–507.

Shattuck, Roger. *The Banquet Years: The Arts in France 1885–1918*. New Cork: Anchor, 1961.

———. "Introduction." *The History of Surrealism*. By Maurice Nadeau. Cambridge, MA: Harvard-Belknap, 1989. 11–34.

Siebenmann, Gustav. "Cesar Vallejo y las vanguardias." *Hispania* 72.1 (March 1989): 3–41.

Silva-Santisteban, Ricardo. "André Breton en el Perú." *Avatares del surrealismo en el Perú y en América Latina*. Ed. Joseph Alonso, Daniel Lefort, and José A. Rodríguez Garrido. Lima: Institut Français d'Études Andines-Pontífica Universidad Católica, 1992. 79–108.

Sola [Maturo], Graciela de. *Proyecciones del surrealismo en la literatura argentina*. Buenos Aires: Ediciones Culturales Argentinas, 1967.

Sontag, Susan. "Artaud." Introduction. *Antonin Artaud: Selected Writings*. New York: Farrar, Straus and Giroux, 1976. xvii–lix.

Soupault, Philippe. "Traces which Last." *Yale French Studies* 31 (1969): 9–22.

Spengler, Oswald. *The Decline of the West*. Trans. and ed. Charles Francis Atkinson. New York: Knopf, 1926–1928.

Stich, Sidra. *Anxious Visions: Surrealist Art*. New York: Abbeville Press, 1990.

Strong, Beret E. *The Poetic Avant-Garde: The Groups of Borges, Auden, and Breton*. Evanston: Northwestern UP, 1997.

Sucre, Guillermo. *La máscara, la transparencia*. Mexico City: Fondo de Cultura Económica, 1985.

Suleiman, Susan Rubin. "A Double Margin: Reflections on Women Writers and the Avant-garde in France." *The Politics of Tradition: Placing Women in French Literature. Yale French Studies* 75 (1988): 148–72.

Taylor, Sue. *Hans Bellmer: The Anatomy of Anxiety*. Cambridge: MIT Press, 2000.

Teitelboim, Volodia. "Primer prólogo." *Las vanguardias latinoamericanas: Textos programáticos y críticos*. Ed. Jorge Schwartz. Mexico: Fondo de Cultura Económica, 2002. 388–93.

Torre, Guillermo de. *Literaturas europeas de vanguardia*. Madrid: Caro Raggio 1925. [Revised and expanded edition published as *Historia de las literaturas de vanguardia*. Madrid: Ediciones Guadarrama, 1965.]

Trilling, Lionel. *Sincerity and Authenticity*. The Charles Eliot Norton Lectures, 1969–1970. Cambridge: Harvard UP, 1971.

Troiani, Osiris. "Epístola a los surrealistas." *Capricornio* 5 (March–April 1954): 19–25.

Tythacott, Louise. *Surrealism and the Exotic*. London: Routledge, 2003.

Unruh, Vicky. *Latin American Vanguards: The Art of Contentious Encounters*. Berkeley: U of California P, 1994.

Urondo, Francisco. "Nicanor Parra: La guitarra desafinada." *La Opinión Cultural* [Buenos Aires] 9 July 1972: 8.

Vallejo, César. "Autopsia del superrealismo." *Las vanguardias latinoamericanas: Textos programáticos y críticos.* Ed. Jorge Schwartz. Mexico: Fondo de Cultura Económica, 2002. 465–70.
———. *Ensayos y reportajes completos.* Ed. Manuel Miguel de Priego. Lima: Pontificia Universidad Católica del Perú, 2002.
———. "Literatura proletaria." *Las vanguardias latinoamericanas: Textos programáticos y críticos.* Ed. Jorge Schwartz. Mexico: Fondo de Cultura Económica, 2002. 516–19.
———. *Obra poética completa.* Madrid: Alianza, 1999.
Vasconcelos, José. *La raza cósmica: Misión de la raza iberoamericana, Argentina y Brasil.* Mexico City: Espasa-Calpe, 1976 [1925].
Verani, Hugo J. *Las vanguardias literarias en Hispanoamérica.* Mexico City: Fondo de Cultura Económica, 1990.
Verdugo, Rodrigo. "Surrealismo en Chile: Una breve nota sobre su actualidad." 1 June 2012. http://www.festivaldepoesiademedellin.org/pub.php/es/Escuela/XIII/verdugo.html.
Vergara Alarcón, Sergio. *Vanguardia literaria: Ruptura y restauración en los años treinta.* Santiago de Chile: Ediciones Universidad de Concepción, 1994.
Villaurrutia, Xavier. "Introducción a la poesía mexicana." *Xavier Villaurrutia: Obras. Poesía, Teatro, Prosas varias, crítica.* Mexico City: Fondo de Cultura Económica, 1953. 764–72.
———. "Nocturno de la estatua." *Nostalgia for Death: Poetry by Xavier Villaurrutia and Hieroglyphs of Desire: A Critical Study of Villaurrutia by Octavio Paz.* Trans. Eliot Weinberger and Esther Allen. Port Townsend, WA: Copper Canyon Press, 1993.
Ward, Alexandra. "*A Partir de Cero*: A Study of Text and Image in Argentine Surrealist Journals of the 1950s." Senior Thesis, Bard College, 2008.
Webb, Peter. *Hans Bellmer.* London: Quartet, 1985.
Westphalen, Emilio Adolfo. *Abolición de la muerte.* Lima: Ediciones Perú Actual, 1935.
———. "Digresión sobre surrealismo y sobre César Moro entre los surrealistas." *Avatares del surrealismo en el Perú y en América Latina.* Ed. Joseph Alonso, Daniel Lefort, and José A. Rodríguez Garrido. Lima: Institut Français d'Études Andines-Pontificia Universidad Católica, 1992. 203–16.
———. *Las ínsulas extrañas.* Lima: Compañía de Impresiones y Publicidad, 1933.
———. *Otra imagen deleznable.* Mexico City: Fondo de Cultura Económica, 1980.
Wilson, Jason. "Coda: Spanish American Surrealist Poetry." *Companion to Spanish Surrealism.* Ed. Robert Havard. Suffolk, UK: Boydell and Brewer-Tamesis, 2004. 253–76.
———. *A Companion to Pablo Neruda: Evaluating Neruda's Poetry.* Woodbridge, UK: Tamesis-Boydell and Brewster, 2008.
———. *Octavio Paz.* Boston: Twayne, 1986.
———. *Octavio Paz: A Study of His Poetics.* London: Cambridge UP, 1979.
Yamal, Ricardo. *Sistema y visión de la poesía de Nicanor Parra.* Valencia, Spain: Albatros, 1985.
Zeller, Ludwig. Personal interviews. 19 and 26 February, 2012.

Index

Aberth, Susan, 129, 131, 239n10
Abril, Pablo, 82, 97
Abril, Xavier, 6, 28, 80, 81, 82–84, 84, 85, 92, 228, 238n1
Adán, Martín, 5, 78, 80
Adorno, Theodor, 32
Agar, Eileen, 25
Aira, César, 138, 145, 146, 152, 163, 229–30
Alazraki, Jaime, 60, 136, 240n1
Alegría, Fernando, 200
Alonso, Rodolfo, 148
Alquié, Ferdinand, 16–17
  See also surrealism: and philosophy
Álvarez Bravo, Manuel, 118, 121, 122
Amauta (journal), 6, 79–81, 82, 83, 85, 93, 98, 238n7
  See also Mariátegui, José Carlos
Amor, Inés, 240n13
amour fou. See Breton: *Mad Love*; surrealism: and the erotic
analogy, principle of, 162, 213, 214, 215, 217–25
Anderson Imbert, Enrique, 237n1
Andrade, Oswald de, 10
  See also Anthropophagist movement
Anguita, Eduardo, 61
Anthropophagist movement (*antropofagia*) 3, 10,
  See also Andrade, Oswald de
Apollinaire, Guillaume, 24, 104, 107
Aragon, Louis, 19, 24, 25, 26, 137, 172, 178, 228
Arenas, Braulio, 28, 33, 62–75, 77, 175, 177–80, 181, 190, 192, 238n4
  See also Mandrágora movement (Chile)

Argentina, ix, x, 4, 6, 7, 8, 34, 36, 47–57, 69, 74, 77, 103, 107, 117, 228, 229, 135–74, 230, 231, 240n2, 240n4, 242n12
  See also Arias, Alberto; Grénier, Silvia; Llinás, Julio; Madariaga, Francisco; Molina, Enrique; Orozco, Olga; Pellegrini, Aldo; Pizarnik, Alejandra
Arias, Alberto, 173, 242n12
Arlt, Roberto, 138
Armani, Horacio, 138
Arp, Hans [Jean], 64, 116, 165
Artaud, Antonin, 25, 40, 239n4, 141, 153, 163, 209
  "Conquest of Mexico, The," 108–9
  in Mexico, 38, 103, 107–15, 116, 118, 119, 120, 123, 124, 131, 239n5, 239n6
  "Voyage to the Land of the Tarahumaras, A," 110–13
Asturias, Miguel Ángel, 5, 36
automatic writing. *See* techniques (surrealist)
automatism (psychic), 17, 21, 24, 34–35, 59, 60–61, 65, 66, 68, 106, 139, 159, 181, 194, 195, 200, 219, 232–33
avant-garde, *passim*
  European, 10, 25, 36–38, 48, 55–57, 63, 68, 122, 204
  French theoretical (1960s and 1970s), 3, 235n2 (Introduction)
  Latin American (*la vanguardia* [*vanguardismo*]), 43, 47, 55–57, 59–61, 68–69, 77–80, 93, 99, 138, 143, 203, 211, 232–23, 238n7

avant-garde, *passim (continued)*
  Contemporáneos (Mexico) (movement and journal), 104–7, 122, 205, 207
  creacionismo (Chile), 61, 240n3 (*see also* Huidobro, Vicente)
  estridentismo (Mexico), 103–4
  indigenismo, 78
  invencionismo (Argentina), 240n3
  "Los Nuevos" (Colombia), 9
  manifestoes, 50–51, 55, 70, 83, 144, 175, 237n6
  nadaísmo (Columbia), 9
  Peruvian, 77–81, 82, 92–93 (*see also* Mariátegui, José Carlos)
  El Techo de la Ballena (Venezuela), 9
  Tzántzicos (Ecuador), 9
  ultraísmo (Argentina), 47–48, 103, 138, 237n2
  See also *Négritud* movement

Baciu, Stefan, 4, 31–33, 142, 175, 209–11, 243n6
Balakian, Anna, 3, 8, 18, 35, 107, 227, 235n2
Barbarito, Carlos, 173
Bary, Leslie, 95
Bataille, Georges, 19, 69, 140, 165, 214, 235n2
Baudelaire, Charles, 22, 69, 72, 91, 158, 213, 217, 218, 230, 231, 233
Bédouin, Jean-Louis, 4, 28
Béguin, Albert, 231
Bellmer, Hans, 163–71, 241n4, 241n6, 241n8
Benavente, Magdalena, 200
Benedikt, Michael, 1, 4, 16
Benjamin, Walter, 17, 32, 178, 230, 235n2
Bioy Casares, Aldolfo, 138
Birkenmaier, Anke, 41, 43
Blake, William, 67, 93, 191, 234
Boa (journal), 148–50, 151, 173, 240n5
Bolton, Robert, 2–3
Bopp, Raúl, 9
Borges, Jorge Luis, 47–48, 138, 149, 236–37n4, 237n2, 237n7

Bradu, Fabienne, 116, 239n2
Brazil, 3, 9, 10, 34, 55, 125, 235n3
  See also Andrade, Oswald de; Martins, Floriano
Breton, André, *passim*
  Anthology of Black Humor (*Antologie de l'humour noir*), 130
  Communicating Vessels (*Les Vases communicantes*), 26
  death of, 185, 186–87
  exile in New York, 27–28, 207
  as leader of French surrealist movement, 17, 117, 179, 188–89
  Mad Love (*L'Amour fou*), 63, 205
  Manifestoes of Surrealism, ix, 6, 15, 16, 17–88, 21, 22, 24–26, 41, 48, 80, 98, 100, 106, 144, 178, 192, 227, 232, 236n5, 240n7
  "Memory of Mexico" (*Souvenir du Mexique*), 118–21
  in Mexico, 27–28, 115–22, 123
  Nadja, 19, 23, 70, 107, 163, 186–88 (see also *femme enfant*)
Brotherston, Gordon, 237n1 (Chapter 4)
Bruna, Carmen, 173
Buñuel, Luis, 25, 83, 103, 117, 179, 206, 209
Bürger, Peter, 3, 23

Cáceres, Jorge, 28, 62, 63, 70–71, 72, 140, 177, 185, 238n4
Cahun, Claude, 142
Caillois, Roger, 4, 214
Calinescu, Matei, 3
Cárdenas, Lázaro, 109, 123, 205
Cardoza y Aragón, Luis, 206
Caribbean region, 18, 36, 38–39, 41, 67, 152, 236n1
  See also Césaire, Aimé; Richardson, Michael
Carpentier, Alejo, ix, 2, 36, 41–44, 52, 153, 236–37n4, 237n5
  "marvelous real," the (*lo real maravilloso*), 36, 41–44, 152, 153, 236–37n4, 237n5

Carrington, Leonora, 25, 85, 122, 123, 129–31, 141, 146, 171, 179, 206, 209, 214, 239n10, 239n11, 240n13
Carroll, Lewis, 170
Cassano, Mariano, 48
Caws, Mary Ann, 1, 4, 22, 24, 165
Cernuda, Luis, 153, 203, 206, 243n3
Cervantes, Miguel de, 197, 198
Césaire, Aimé, 2, 4, 27, 38–39, 179, 236n1
  Tropiques (journal), 236n1
  See also *Négritud* movement
Césaire, Suzanne Roussi, 38–39, 236n1
Ceselli, Juan José, 139, 151
Chadwick, Whitney, 1
Chanady, Amaryll, 43
Char, René, 25
Chávez Morado, José, 239n12
Chávez-Silverman, Suzanne, 163
Chile, ix, x, 4, 6, 7, 8, 28, 33, 35, 47, 59–75, 77, 86, 107, 137, 175–201, 204, 211, 228, 229, 231, 237n2, 238n4, 242n7
  See also Arenas, Braulio; Cáceres, Jorge; Gómez-Correa, Enrique; Mandrágora movement; Neruda, Pablo; Parra, Nicanor; Rojas, Gonzalo; Zeller, Ludwig
Chirico, Giorgio de, 57, 85, 104, 116, 165, 241n6
Churata, Gamaliel (Arturo Peralta), 5, 78
Ciclo (journal), 140–41, 147, 150, 151
Cid, Teófilo, 62, 72, 238n4
Clifford, James, 2, 25, 119, 235n3
  (Introduction), 235n3 (Chapter 1)
  See also surrealism: and ethnography
Coddou, Marcelo, 180, 242n2
Cófreces, Javier, 140, 151, 157, 232n1, 237n1, 241n2, 242n12
Cohen, Margaret, 3, 235n2
Cohen, Sandro, 234
Colombia, 9, 34
Cortázar, Julio, 5, 10, 181, 185, 236n6
Costa, René de, 2, 59, 60, 238n2
Covarrubias, Miguel, 122, 123, 124
Coyné, André, 90

Cuba, 2, 4, 9, 41–43
  See also Carpentier, Alejo; Lam, Wilfredo
Cuesta, Jorge, 104, 107

Dada, 3, 4, 9, 10, 23, 24–25, 32, 56, 108, 141, 172, 178–79, 232, 235n2
Dalí, Salvador, 25, 27, 83, 95, 104, 116, 117, 178, 179
Darío, Rubén, 69, 218, 242n3, 243–44n11
  See also *modernismo* (Latin American)
DeCollage (Brazilian movement), 10
Delgado Páez, Carlos, 200
Desnos, Edmond, 24, 25, 107, 178
Devéscovi, Juan, 82
Díaz Casanueva, Humberto, 61, 175
Domínguez, Óscar, 116
Dominican Republic, 10
dream. See surrealism: and dream consciousness (*lo onírico*)
Duchamp, Marcel, 27, 28
Durozoi, Gérard, 1
Dyn (journal), 122–23

Ecuador, 9, 34
Eguren, José María, 77, 93
Eielson, Jorge Eduardo, 100
Eliade, Mircea, 19
Eliot, T[homas] S[tearns], 7
Éluard, Paul, 24, 26, 28, 57, 63, 85, 92, 107, 137, 141, 153, 178, 185, 191
Ernst, Max, 25, 27, 28, 90, 129, 142, 165, 207
Escalante, Evodio, 203, 211, 225, 243n2
Etchecopar, Dolores, 173, 242n11

Faris, Wendy, 237n5
femme enfant, 23
Ferdinán, Valentín, 31–33, 40, 233
Fernández, Macedonio, 138
Fernández Cozman, Camilo, 93, 94
Fernández Moreno, César, 139
Ferrari, Américo, 79, 84, 238n3
Fini, Leonor, 25
Foote, Susan, 73

Forster, Merlin, 4
Foster, David William, 163, 168
Foster, Hal, 1, 165, 241n6
Foucault, Michel, 212–13, 217
Fowlie, Wallace, 2, 3
Francés, Esteban, 123
Franco, Jean, 31
Frazer, James, 19, 236–37n4
freedom. *See* surrealism: freedom or liberty, principle of
Freeman, Judi, 23
Freud, Sigmund, 25, 83, 167, 169, 212–13, 236n5
  See also surrealism: Freudian thought in; surrealism: and the unconscious
Frye, Northrop, 243n9
Fuentes, Carlos, 128

García Lorca, Federico, 25, 191
García Márquez, Gabriel, 236n6
Gelman, Juan, 173, 195, 236n6, 242n11, 243n11
Generation of 1927 (Spain), 7, 153
Gerbasi, Vicente, 9
Gerzso, Gunther, 239n12
Giacometti, Alberto, 25
Giorgio, Marosa de, 9
Girondo, Oliverio, 33, 47, 48, 138
Goic, Cedomil, 74, 100, 190, 193, 196, 242n6, 243n1
Gómez-Correa, Enrique, 28, 62–63, 67, 68–70, 72–73, 77, 175, 177, 201, 230, 238n4,
González Echevarría, Roberto, 31, 42, 236n2, 236n4
Gorki, Edmund, 64
Gorostiza, José, 104, 106
Gracq, Julien, 25
Grénier, Silvia, 173, 242n12
Grupo Surrealista Argentino, 173–74, 244n1
Grupo Surrealista São Paulo, 10
Grupo Viernes (Venezuela), 9
Guillén, Nicolás, 236n6
Guinta, Andrea, 172

Hahn, Óscar, 180
Haiti, 38–39, 42, 43
l'hasard objectif. See surrealism: "objective chance"
Heidegger, Martin, 212, 214, 224
Heliodoro Valle, Rafael, 118
Hernández, Miguel, 206
Hérold, Jacques, 37, 63, 140
Hidalgo, Alberto, 78
El Hijo Pródigo (journal), 122
Hoffmann, E. T. A., 167
Hölderlin, Friedrich, 158
  See also romanticism
Hopkins, David, 29, 39
Horna, José, 123
Horna, Kati, 123
Hubert, Renée Riese, 235n4
Huerta, Efraín, 117, 205
Huerta, Miguel Ángel, 201
Huidobro, Vicente, 59–60, 61, 63, 66, 67, 86, 193, 206, 237n2, 240n3
humour noir. See Breton: *Anthology of Black Humor*; surrealism: and humor

Ibáñez-Langlois, José, 192
imagery. *See* techniques
Izquierdo, María, 122, 239n12

Jackson, Elizabeth R., 125–26, 239n9
Jaguer, Édouard, 148, 240n5
Jarry, Alfred, 63, 82, 86–87
Jiménez, José Olivio, 242n3
Jimeno-Grendi, Orlando, 61–62
Jodorowsky, Alejandro, 191
Jrade, Cathy, 218, 220, 243–44n11
Jung, Karl, 19

Kafka, Franz, 7, 179, 191
Kahlo, Frida, 4, 116, 121–22, 171–72, 209, 239n12
King, Lloyd, 243n10
Krauss, Rosalind, 164
Kuhnheim, Jill, 139

Lacan, Jacques, 3, 32
Lago, Tomás, 242n7

Lam, Wilfredo, 4, 28, 42, 64, 148, 173, 208
Lama, Víctor de, 97
Lane, Helen R., 243n5
Langowski, Gerald, 4, 5
Larrea, Juan, 39–40, 236n, 236–37n4
Lasarte, Francisco, 163
Latin American avant-garde (*la vanguardia* [*vanguardismo*]). *See* avant-garde: Latin American
Latorre, Carlos, 139, 141, 146, 148, 151
Lauer, Mirko, 78, 93
Lautréamont, Comte de (Isidore Ducasse), 16, 22, 60, 69, 82, 86–87, 88, 91, 95, 140, 142, 143, 158, 194, 230, 240n2
Lazo, Agustín, 105, 116, 122
Leiris, Michel, 25
Leitmotiv: Boletín de hechos e ideas (journal), 73, 180
Letra y línea (journal), 146–48, 151
Lévi-Strauss, Claude, 19, 214
Lévy-Bruhl, Lucien, 19, 236–37n4
Lezama Lima, José, 9
Lichtenstein, Therese, 165, 241n4
Lihn, Enrique, 31, 74, 179–80, 191
Llinás, Julio, 33, 137–38, 139, 141, 146, 148–50, 151, 158, 172–73, 229, 240n5

Maar, Dora, 25
Mabille, Pierre, 18, 38, 113, 236–37n4
Machado, Antonio, 206
Maciel Edelman, Olivia, 203, 208
Madariaga, Francisco, 139, 141, 148, 151, 158, 173
magic, as property of language, 9, 22, 41, 125, 149, 158, 160, 163, 204, 208, 212–25
magical realism, 5, 36, 153, 237n5
Magritte, René, 63, 64
Mallarmé, Stéphane, 60, 186, 189, 230
Malt, Joanna, 1
Mandrágora movement (Chile); *La Mandrágora* (journal), 6, 7, 33, 41, 59, 61–75, 107, 175–76, 177–81, 189–90, 191–92, 200, 211, 228, 231, 238n3, 238n4
Manifestoes of Surrealism. See Breton, André
Mansour, Joyce, 28
Maples Arce, Manuel, 103
Mariátegui, José Carlos, 6, 34, 77–81, 82–83, 85, 97, 99, 172, 238n7
See also *Amauta* (journal)
Martin Fierro (journal), 61
Martinique, 2, 4, 27, 38
Martins, Floriano, 4, 235n3
"marvelous real," the (*lo real maravilloso*), *see* Carpentier, Alejo
Marx, Karl. *See* surrealism: Communism, Marxism, socialism, and Stalinism, relationship to
Masiello, Francine, 55
Masson, André, 25, 27, 64, 165
Matta Echaurren ("Matta"), Roberto, 4, 27, 28, 64, 73, 123, 203, 208
Matthews, J. H., 4
Mauss, Marcel, 19
Medina, Rubén, 204
Mendiola, Víctor Manuel, 203
Mérida, Carlos, 122, 239n12
metaphor. *See* techniques
Mexico, ix, 2, 4, 6–7, 8, 18, 27, 34, 36–40, 55, 80, 82, 84, 86, 92, 103–32, 135, 137, 139, 152, 203–25, 239n1
as "surrealist place *par excellence*," 6–7, 37, 117–18, 131, 225, 233, 239n1
See also Artaud: in Mexico; Breton: in Mexico; Cuesta, José; Ortiz de Montellano, Bernardo; Paz, Octavio; Torres Bodet, Jaime; Trotsky, Leon; Villaurrutia, Xavier
Meyer-Minnemann, Klaus, 31, 73, 74
Meza, Guillermo, 122
Miller, Henry, 140
Minotaure (journal), 118, 121, 164
Miró, Joan, 104, 116
modernismo (Latin American), 77–78, 93, 104, 242n3
See also Darío, Rubén

Molina, Enrique, 7, 33, 63, 136, 139, 141–48, 150, 151–58, 159, 172, 173, 181–82, 211, 229, 233–34
Mondrian, Piet, 27, 178
Montes de Oca, Marco Antonio, 225
Las Moradas (journal), 92, 95, 100, 129–30
Morales, Leónidas, 191
Moro, César, 6, 33, 63, 77, 80, 81, 84–92, 93, 94, 95, 96, 100, 116, 121, 122, 123, 141, 158, 179, 209, 211, 214, 228, 233, 238n3, 238n4
Antología del surrealismo, 86, 238n4
and French surrealist movement, 86, 92
in Mexico, 85, 90, 116, 121–23
La tortuga ecuestre, 85, 90, 122, 238n2
Mundy, Jennifer, 235n1
Mussy, Luis de, 62, 64, 238n3, 238n4
Mutis, Álvaro, 9

Nadeau, Maurice, 1, 26, 137, 231
Naville, Pierre, 24, 25
Négritud movement, 38–39, 67
See also Aimé, Césaire
Neruda, Pablo, 2, 6, 7, 33, 59–61, 64–65, 75, 96, 136, 153, 180, 184, 192, 195, 198, 204, 206, 236n6, 237n1 (Chapter 4), 238n2
Residencia en la tierra, 60
Tentativa del hombre infinito, 60, 237n1 (Chapter 4)
Nougé, Paul, 15
Novalis, 25, 158, 179, 218
Novo, Salvador, 104
Núñez, Estuardo, 80

Ocampo, Victoria, 57
Onslow Ford, Gordon, 123
Oppenheim, Meret, 25
Oquendo, Abelardo, 93
Oquendo de Amat, Carlos, 178
Orozco, Olga, 7, 22, 139, 141, 146, 149, 150, 151, 158–62, 173, 233, 240n6, 241n3, 241n5
Ortega, Julio, 31, 86, 242n9

Ortega y Gasset, José, 62
Ortiz de Montellano, Bernardo, 104–6, 114–15, 118, 205
Osorio, Nelson, 68
Otto, Rudolf, 19
Oviedo, José Miguel, 31, 86, 90, 136
Owen, Gilberto, 104, 205

Paalen, Wolfgang, 4, 85, 116, 121, 122, 123–25, 128, 131, 140, 178, 206
"Volcano-Pyramid, The," 124–25, 128
Pacheco, José Emilio, 225
Padilla, Emilio, 201
Paoli, Roberto, 94
Paraguay, 9, 34
Paris, 2, 7, 10, 19, 24, 27, 28, 29, 36, 38, 39, 40, 41, 42, 44, 47, 48, 59, 63, 82, 84, 85, 86, 92, 93, 97, 100, 107, 109, 121, 125, 137, 140, 141, 148, 159, 165, 172, 180, 186, 187, 190, 192, 206, 207, 211, 221, 222, 229, 230, 231
Parra, Nicanor, 7, 8, 35, 136, 175, 180, 189–200, 231, 233
Poemas y antipoemas, 189, 191, 192, 197
A Partir de Cero (journal), 135, 141–46, 147, 148, 151, 152, 158, 231
Paz, Octavio, ix, 2, 7, 8, 20, 22, 23, 24, 25, 31, 32, 33, 36, 63, 74, 75, 100, 101, 104, 105, 107, 122, 125, 128, 132, 136, 172, 179, 181, 194, 203–25, 229, 231, 232, 234, 236n6, 240n1, 243nn1–11
El arco y la lira (*The Bow and the Lyre*), 203, 211, 213, 218, 222, 231, 243n7
Los hijos del limo (*Children of the Mire*), 211, 212, 218, 222, 231, 243n7
Pellegrini, Aldo, 6, 7, 33, 48–57, 61, 62, 63, 65, 69, 77, 81, 107, 135, 138, 139, 140, 141, 144–48, 150, 151, 157, 158, 172, 177, 178, 179, 180, 190, 228, 229, 231, 234, 247n3, 240n8

Index • 263

"surrealist fraternity" (pioneer Argentine surrealist group), 47, 48–57, 74
See also *Ciclo* (journal), *Que* (journal); *A Partir de Cero* (journal)
Pellegrini, Mario, 48, 52, 139, 150, 237n3
Pellicer, Carlos, 122
Peralta, Alejandro, 78
Péret, Benjamin, 24, 63, 85, 123, 125–28, 129, 131, 137, 141, 172, 180, 206, 207, 209, 214, 221, 239n9
"Air mexicain," 125–28, 239n9
Peru, 5, 6, 8, 34, 36, 77–101, 121, 122, 156, 211, 228, 240–41n1 (Chapter 8)
See also Abril, Xavier; Mariátegui, José Carlos; Moro, César; Vallejo, César; Westphalen, Emilio Adolfo
Peyre, Henri, 28–29
Pezzoni, Enrique, 56
Phillips, Rachel, 203, 243n7
Picabia, Francis, 25
Picasso, Pablo, 25, 104
Pichón Riviére, Enrique, 140, 240n4
Pierre, José, 28
Pinochet, Augusto, 179, 181–82
Piña, Cristina, 153, 241n5
Piterbarg, Elías, 48, 47, 140–41, 144, 145
Piterbarg, Ismael, 48
Pizarnik, Alejandra, 7, 22, 33, 149, 150, 151, 162–72, 173, 181, 229, 231, 233, 240n6, 241n3, 241n5, 241n7, 241n8
Poblete Araya, Kira, 139
Podemma (journal), 173
Poe, Edgar Allan, 69, 107, 186, 187, 242n5
poetry, 106, 136, 144, 153, 158, 189, 218–25, 232–33
antipoesía (antipoetry), 8, 35, 175, 180, 189–200, 242n6
decadent poetry (*poètes maudits*), 69, 72, 238n4, 241n4

as knowledge, 8, 162, 183, 212, 220–21
and magic (*see* magic, as property of language)
as mode of surrealist expression, 2, 4, 5, 21, 23, 24, 31, 32, 35, 51–52, 54, 60, 66, 70, 72, 82, 86, 95, 136, 138, 145, 150, 151, 152, 174, 176–77, 193, 194, 200, 204, 205, 211, 225, 233
Poesía de la Claridad (Chile), 175, 189, 242n7
poesía negra ("black poetry") (*see* Mandrágora Group [Chile])
poetic devices (*see* techniques [surrealist])
poetry-life conflation in surrealism, 17–18, 67, 72, 142–43, 144, 180, 193, 208, 231
Porchia, Antonio, 141, 148
Posada, José Guadalupe, 118, 120, 121, 129
Pound, Ezra, 7
Prévert, Jacques, 25

Que (journal), 6, 47, 49–57, 237n3, 237n4
See also Pellegrini, Aldo

Raaberg, Gwen, 164
Rahon, Alice, 85, 123
Rank, Otto, 169
Ray, Man, 25
La Révolution surréaliste (journal), 48, 108
Richardson, Michael, 39, 225
Riffaterre, Michael, 21, 87
Rilke, Rainer Maria, 153
Rimbaud, Arthur, 26, 41, 42, 60, 69, 82, 86–87, 88, 143, 144, 158, 196, 197, 213, 215, 230, 241n4
Ristich, Marko, 140
Rivera, Diego, 27, 116, 118, 122
Rodó, José Enrique, 145, 172
Roh, Franz, 236n4

264 • Index

Rojas, Gonzalo, 7–8, 33, 63, 71, 72, 74, 175, 179, 180–89, 190, 192, 194, 199, 200, 203, 231, 232–33, 24n1, 242n2, 242n3, 242n4
"A la salud de André Breton," 284 89, 242n1
Rokha, Carlos de, 175
Rokha, Pablo de, 61,185
romanticism (the romantic tradition in literature), 6, 7, 9, 24, 25, 51, 60, 65, 67, 68, 69, 75, 77, 90, 104, 138, 139, 154, 158, 169, 177, 178, 183, 192, 193, 195, 196, 197, 205, 206, 207, 211, 213, 216, 217, 218, 220, 230, 234, 243–44n11

Sábato, Ernesto, 5, 16, 236n6
Sade, Marquis de, 69, 86–87, 88, 91
Sage, Kay, 25
Sánchez Peláez, José, 9
Santí, Enrico Mario, 213, 243n8
Santos Chocano, José, 78, 93
Sartre, Jean-Paul, 28, 135, 236n7
Sawin, Martica, 1, 123, 124, 131
Schneider, Luis Mario, 4, 107, 110, 239n2, 239n4, 239n8
Schopf, Federico, 180, 189, 199
Schuster, Jean, 28, 29
Schwartz, Jorge, 79, 238n7
Sedille, Carlos, 201
Sefamí, Jacobo, 152, 181
Seligmann, Kurt, 27, 123, 125, 165
Shattuck, Roger, 1, 16, 22
Sherman, Cindy, 171
Siebenmann, Gustav, 99
Signo Ascendente (journal), 173, 174, 242n12
Silva-Santisteban, Ricardo, 82
Simms, Ruth, 243n7
Sola, Graciela [Maturo] de, 4, 32, 48, 139, 151, 237n1, 241n2
Solar, Xul, 149
Solís, Jorge, 201
Sologuren, Javier, 100
Sontag, Susan, 108, 235n2, 239n5, 239n6
Soriano, Juan, 239n12

Soupault, Philippe, 24, 25, 227, 228
Southern Cone region, 44, 47, 63, 200
Spanish Civil War, 27, 39, 62, 135, 206, 243n3
Spengler, Oswald, 40, 62, 236n2
Stalin, Joseph, 26, 27, 75, 115, 117, 205, 243n2
See also surrealism: Communism, Marxism, socialism, and Stalinism, relationship to
Stich, Sidra, 1
Strong, Beret, 68, 237n7
Sucre, Guillermo, 88
Suleiman, Susan Rubin, 162, 171
Sur (journal), 138
Surrealism, *passim*
  adaptability of, 2, 3, 16, 32, 233
  "afterlife" of, ix, 3, 5, 15, 207, 229, 230
  as attitude toward life (*actitud vital*), ix, 17, 18, 81, 136, 144, 180, 211, 227, 228, 232 (*see also* poetry: poetry-life conflation in surrealism)
  and beauty, 1, 17, 68, 69, 120–21, 124, 168, 187–88, 241n6
  belatedness, concept of, 7, 33, 61, 137, 191, 211, 229–31, 232
  Communism, Marxism, socialism, and Stalinism, relationship to, 17, 26–27, 75, 82–83, 97–98, 100, 109, 114, 115, 140, 149, 204, 209, 210, 236n5, 243n2
  definition of (Breton), 17
  as dialectical process or resolution of opposites, 15–16, 23–24, 89, 120, 130, 140, 189, 199, 208, 220, 230
  and dream consciousness (*lo onírico*), ix, 9, 15, 17, 18, 20, 21, 22, 24, 26, 35, 36, 37, 60, 61, 65, 66, 69, 77, 83–84, 87, 91, 92, 94, 104–6, 108–9, 115, 120, 122, 139, 143–44, 152, 155–57, 158, 182, 191, 193, 195, 196, 200, 205, 207, 208, 232, 233, 243n3

and the erotic, ix, 2, 9, 23, 53, 71–72, 87, 88, 90–92, 104, 153, 156–57, 164, 182, 183–85, 199, 210, 222, 224, 231
esoteric or occult thought in, 18, 19, 67, 111, 113, 130, 149, 150, 159–61, 173, 177, 207, 213, 215, 216, 218, 220, 224, 228, 240n7, 241n3, 243–44n11
and ethnography, 2, 39, 40, 41, 109, 113, 119, 121, 235n3 (*see also* Clifford, James)
feminist critique of, 23, 162–65, 171
in fiction, 5, 21
freedom or liberty, principle of, 6, 17, 23–24, 26, 27, 35, 37, 50, 41, 54, 62, 65–66, 69, 74, 99, 100, 107, 128, 139, 141, 142, 143, 147, 156, 158, 179, 180, 182, 183, 185, 188, 190, 193, 199, 200, 203, 205, 206, 210, 225, 228, 231
Freudian thought in, 9, 25, 83, 195–96, 212–13, 236n5
historical French movement, 16, 23, 24–29, 34, 81, 100–101, 106, 115, 135, 137–38, 140–41, 178, 207, 227–32
and humor (*humour noir*) or the ludic, ix, 20, 25, 35, 53, 64, 78, 100, 106, 118, 130–31, 137, 142, 146, 178, 190, 191, 197–99, 242n8
influence on Latin American culture, 3–4, 43–44, 117–18, 131–32, 147–48, 228–34
and the irrational (critique of rationality), 15, 18, 43, 89, 106, 135, 143–44, 153, 156, 182, 195, 213, 219, 236n5
and madness, 17, 50–51, 53, 65, 69, 88–89, 155–56, 161, 182, 188, 195, 210, 241n5
mannequin or doll motif in, 162–72, 241n6

and the marvelous (*le merveilleux*), 18–19, 20, 22, 36, 37, 40, 42–44, 92, 120–21, 124, 125, 140, 146, 152–53, 157, 159, 181, 183, 231, 234, 236–37n4, 234n9 (*see also* Carpentier: "marvelous real" (*lo real maravilloso*)
neo-, second-generation, or second-wave, 7, 29, 57, 100, 132, 136, 137, 140, 141, 151, 163, 229, 230
"objective chance" (*l'hasard objectif*), 18, 19, 22, 35, 52, 67, 70, 222
and philosophy, ix, 16–17, 28, 32, 135, 136, 214, 234, 235n2 (*see also* Alquié, Ferdinand)
point sublime, concept of, 15, 23, 54, 89, 156, 193
and the "primitive" or exotic, 2, 19–20, 36–40, 43, 82, 109, 111, 113, 119, 121, 123, 126, 147, 153, 169, 235n3 (Chapter 1)
as revolt, rebellion, or revolution, 2, 8, 9, 17, 18, 23, 26–27, 32, 48, 50, 51, 53, 54–57, 65, 68, 70, 78, 82, 83, 86, 88, 93, 97–100, 108, 109, 115, 117, 136, 139, 141, 143, 144, 145–46, 147, 149, 173, 174, 182, 190, 228, 230, 232, 234, 244n1
and the sacred, 19, 22, 23, 136, 149, 157, 184, 203, 240n1, 243n10
sight or vision, motif of, 20, 23, 52, 54, 142, 146, 234
techniques of (*see* techniques)
themes in (*see* themes or motifs [surrealist])
and the unconscious, ix, 2, 5, 6, 9, 18, 19, 20, 22, 25, 35, 41, 49, 53, 59, 60, 61, 65, 66, 67, 83, 91, 104, 158, 174, 190, 193, 195, 197, 219, 242n2
Le Surréalisme, même (journal), 129, 207
Le Surréalisme au service de la Révolution (journal) 86

Sussman, David, 48
Swedenborg, Emmanuel, 218

Tablada, José Juan, 194
Taller (journal), 117, 205, 207, 211, 243n2
 See also Paz, Octavio
Tanguy, Ives, 25, 27, 87, 116, 159
Tanning, Dorotea, 25
Taylor, Sue, 241n4, 241n9
techniques (surrealist), ix, x, 5, 16, 21, 24, 34, 36, 60, 61, 66, 72, 81, 86, 94, 96, 105, 122, 128, 163, 181–82, 193–95, 207–8, 232, 234
 automatic writing, 20–21, 49, 52, 59, 60, 70, 98, 100, 129, 136, 174, 181, 191, 194, 205, 207, 229–30, 232, 237n1 (*see also* automatism [psychic])
 dialogue, 20, 146
 "exquisite cadáver" (*cadavre exquis*), 10, 20, 35, 191, 232
 "found object," 37, 123
 imagery, esp. oneiric or dream imagery, ix, 5, 6, 9, 11, 18, 19, 20–24, 27, 35–36, 44, 52–54, 59–60, 61, 77, 83, 87, 89, 91–92, 94, 95, 100, 104, 106, 107, 109, 126–27, 129–30, 141, 142, 152, 156–57, 158, 159, 163, 165, 167, 169–70, 171, 173, 182, 191, 193, 195, 205, 207, 208, 219, 220, 223, 225, 233, 234, 243n3
 juxtaposition (of unrelated entities), 3, 4, 8, 32–33, 63, 140, 161, 196, 298
 metaphor, 5, 19, 22–23, 35–36, 49, 52, 54, 84, 87, 94, 117, 156–57, 159–60, 166–67, 182, 193, 209–10, 218–19, 223, 225
 syntax, 21, 182, 188, 194, 210
Teillier, Jorge, 191
Teitelboim, Volodia, 61
themes or motifs (surrealist), 23–24, 50, 65, 72, 128, 142, 157, 169–70, 182, 183, 199, 214, 231

 love-liberty-poetry as thematic triad, 23, 35, 143, 158, 182, 231, 242n3
Torres Bodet, Jaime, 104, 107, 109, 205
Trotsky, Leon, 27, 115–17
 See also surrealism: Communism, Marxism, socialism, and Stalinism, relationship to
Tythacott, Louise, 20
Tzara, Tristan, 140, 172, 178, 121, 137

Unruh, Vicky, 50, 54, 68, 237n6, 237n7
Uruguay, 9, 35
Usigli, Rodolfo, 122
El Uso de la Palabra (journal), 85, 94

Valle, Rosamel del, 61, 172, 175
Vallejo, César, ix, 6, 7, 36, 39, 77, 78, 81, 82, 96–101, 138, 182, 183, 185, 206, 236n6, 238n6, 238n7
 "Autopsy on Surrealism," 96–101, 138, 238n7
la vanguardia (*vanguardismo*). *See* avant-garde: Latin American
Varela, Blanca, 100
Vargas Llosa, Mario, 236n6
Varo, Remedios, 25, 85, 123, 125, 129, 171, 206, 240n13
Vasco, Juan Antonio, 139, 141, 146, 151
Vasconcelos, José, 109, 236n3
Venezuela, 9
Verani, Hugo, 47, 60
Verdugo, Rodrigo, 201
Vergara, Sergio, 31, 73, 74
Vidales, Luis, 9
Villaurrutia, Xavier, 85, 104, 105–6, 122, 203, 205, 239n3
Vitale, Ida, 9
VVV (journal), 28, 63, 129

Webb, Peter, 165, 241n6
Weinberger, Eliot, 221, 239n3
Westphalen, Emilio Adolfo, 6, 33, 77, 81, 85, 92–96, 100, 179, 228

Wilson, Jason, 3, 31, 84, 153, 203, 204, 207, 211, 243n4
World War I, 18, 79, 25
World War II, ix, 5, 18, 25, 27, 37, 39, 72, 73, 84, 98, 123, 135
   post-war period, 14, 17, 37, 135, 227, 228

Yamal, Ricardo, 194
Yáñez, Roberto, 201

Zamora, Lois Parkinson, 237n5
Zapata, Emiliano, 119, 128
Zeller, Ludwig, 74, 175, 176

CPSIA information can be obtained at www.ICGtesting.com
Printed in the USA
LVOW072021260413

331192LV00004B/45/P